Which way Latin America?

The Centre for International
Governance Innovation
Centre pour l'innovation dans
la gouvernance internationale

The Centre for International Governance Innovation is an independent, non-partisan think-tank that addresses international governance challenges. Led by a group of experienced practitioners and distinguished academics, CIGI supports research, forms networks, advances policy debate, builds capacity and generates ideas for multilateral governance improvements. Conducting an active agenda of research, events and publications, CIGI's interdisciplinary work includes collaboration with policy, business and academic communities around the world.

CIGI was founded in 2002 by Jim Balsillie, co-CEO of RIM (Research In Motion). Its work is organized in six broad programme areas: shifting global order; environment and resources; health and social governance; international economic governance; international law, institutions and diplomacy; and global and human security.

For more information please visit: www.cigionline.org

Which way Latin America? Hemispheric politics meets globalization

Edited by Andrew F. Cooper and Jorge Heine

United Nations University Press

TOKYO · NEW YORK · PARIS

© United Nations University, 2009

The views expressed in this publication are those of the authors and do not necessarily reflect the views of the United Nations University.

United Nations University Press
United Nations University, 53-70, Jingumae 5-chome,
Shibuya-ku, Tokyo 150-8925, Japan
Tel: +81-3-5467-1212   Fax: +81-3-3406-7345
E-mail: sales@hq.unu.edu   general enquiries: press@hq.unu.edu
http://www.unu.edu

United Nations University Office at the United Nations, New York
2 United Nations Plaza, Room DC2-2062, New York, NY 10017, USA
Tel: +1-212-963-6387   Fax: +1-212-371-9454
E-mail: unuona@ony.unu.edu

United Nations University Press is the publishing division of the United Nations University.

Cover design by Maria Sese-Paul

Cover art by José Basso, *Tres casas con reflejo amarillo*, basso@josebasso.com, www.josebasso.com

Printed in Hong Kong

ISBN 978-92-808-1172-8

Library of Congress Cataloging-in-Publication Data

Which way Latin America? : hemispheric politics meets globalization / edited by Andrew F. Cooper and Jorge Heine.
    p.   cm.
Includes bibliographical references and index.
ISBN 978-9280811728 (pbk.)
1. Latin America—Politics and government—1980– 2. Globalization—Latin America. I. Cooper, Andrew Fenton, 1950– II. Heine, Jorge.
JL960.W45   2009
327.8—dc22   2009011635

Endorsements

"This is an ambitious and important volume. It brings together a group of the hemisphere's best analysts and thinkers to explain how profoundly Latin America has changed in recent years, and what those changes mean for the people and politics of the region and for its relations with the US and the rest of the world."

Peter Hakim, *President of Inter-American Dialogue*

"This excellent collection focuses on the dynamic interaction between Latin America and a fast-changing global system. Chapters expertly analyze crucial dimensions of this interaction, including democracy and the 'rise of the left', energy competition and resource nationalism, relations with China and India, the fraying of the Inter-American System, and such pivotal cases as Venezuela, Mexico, and Brazil. Contributors unpack both the impact of the world in and on the region, and the ever more complex and diversified relationship between the region and the world."

Andrew Hurrell, *Montague Burton Professor of International Relations, Balliol College, Oxford University*

"In a book that is timely, comprehensive, and insightful, Cooper, Heine, and their colleagues sharpen the 'big picture' of international relations in the Americas while examining key countries, large and small, in Latin America and the Caribbean. The authors present their thoughtful and informative analysis on salient topics, such as multilateral institutions, China and India, energy, Chávez, democracy and partisanship, and point the way to the future."

Jorge I. Domínguez, *Antonio Madero Professor of Mexican and Latin American Politics and Economics, Harvard University*

"Which Way Latin America? offers a fresh perspective on an old question that has yielded, up to now, tired answers. The authors survey the new landscape of more inclusive democracies and more independent foreign policies. The Obama Administration ought to read this to chart a new approach to the region."

Robert Pastor, *Professor of International Relations, American University and Former National Security Advisor for Latin America*

Contents

Tables and figures

Figures

Contributors

Dexter S. Boniface is associate professor in the Department of Political Science and director of the Latin American & Caribbean Studies Program at Rollins College in Winter Park, Florida, where he teaches courses in comparative politics and international relations, with a specialization in Latin American politics. He received his PhD in political science from the University of Illinois at Urbana-Champaign. His research interests include the political economy of contemporary Brazil and democracy-promotion efforts in Latin America.

His published work appears in journals such as *Comparative Politics*, *Global Governance* and *Latin American Politics and Society*. He is also co-editor (with Thomas Legler and Sharon F. Lean) of *Promoting Democracy in the Americas* (Johns Hopkins University Press, 2007).

Jorge G. Castañeda is Global Distinguished Professor of Politics and Latin American and Caribbean Studies at New York University and a fellow at the New America Foundation. He is a former foreign minister of Mexico and a renowned public intellectual, political scientist and prolific writer, with an interest in Latin American politics, comparative politics and US-Latin American relations. A member of the American Academy of Arts & Sciences, he has taught at Mexico's National Autonomous University (UNAM), Princeton and the University of California, Berkeley. Dr Castañeda has been a senior associate at the Carnegie Endowment for International Peace (1985–1987) and a John D. and Catherine T. MacArthur Foundation research and writing grant recipient (1989–1991).

Among his many books are *Leftovers: Tales of the Latin*

American Left, with Marco A. Morales (Routledge, 2008), *Ex Mex: From Migrants to Immigrants* (New Press, 2008), *Somos Muchos: Ideas para el Mañana* (New Press, 2004), *Perpetuating Power: How Mexican Presidents Were Chosen* (New Press, 2000), *Compañero: The Life and Death of Che Guevara* (Knopf, 1997) and *Utopia Unarmed: The Latin Amercan Left after the Cold War* (Random House, 1993). He is also a regular columnist for the Mexican daily *Reforma*, *The Los Angeles Times* and *Newsweek International* and writes frequently for *Foreign Affairs*.

Andrew F. Cooper is associate director and distinguished fellow at the Centre for International Governance Innovation (CIGI) and professor in the Department of Political Science at the University of Waterloo, where he teaches in the areas of international political economy, global governance and the practice of diplomacy. He has been a visiting professor at University of Southern California, Australian National University, Stellenbosch University and Harvard University. In a 2009 survey by the College of William and Mary he was ranked in the top five international relations scholars with the greatest influence on Canadian foreign policy in the last 20 years.

His recent books include *Emerging Powers in Global Governance: Lessons from the Heiligendamm Process*, edited with Agata Antkiewicz (Wilfrid Laurier University Press, 2008); *Global Governance and Diplomacy: Worlds Apart?*, edited with Brian Hocking and William Maley (Palgrave, 2008); *Celebrity Diplomacy* (Paradigm, 2008); *Regionalisation and Global Governance: The Taming of Globalisation?*, edited with Christopher W. Hughes and Philippe De Lombaerde (Routledge, 2007); and *Tests of Global Governance: Canadian Diplomacy and United Nations World Conferences* (United Nations University Press, 2004). His writing has appeared in journals such as *Foreign Policy*, the *Canadian Journal of Political Science* and *Third World Quarterly*, among many others.

Jorge Heine holds the chair in global governance at the Balsillie School of International Affairs, is a distinguished fellow at the Centre for International Governance Innovation and serves currently as vice-president of the International Political Science Association (IPSA). He was previously ambassador of Chile to India, Bangladesh and Sri Lanka (2003–2007) and South Africa (1994–1999). He has been a visiting fellow at St Antony's College, Oxford, and a research associate at the Wilson Center in Washington, DC. He is the author, co-author or editor of eight books, including *The Last Cacique: Leadership and Politics in a Puerto Rican City* (Pittsburgh University Press, *Choice Magazine* Outstanding Academic Book of 1994), *A Revolution Aborted: The Lessons of Grenada* (Pittsburgh University Press, 1991) and (with Leslie Manigat) *Cross Currents and Cleavages: International Relations of the Contemporary Caribbean* (Holmes & Meier, 1988), and some 70 articles in journals and symposium volumes. His opinion pieces have been published in *The*

New York Times, The Washington Post, The International Herald Tribune and *The Globe and Mail.* He was the first ambassador to present credentials to President Nelson Mandela, and for two years in a row Johannesburg's leading newspaper, *The Star*, included him among the 100 most influential personalities in South Africa.

Annette Hester is a senior fellow with the Centre for International Governance Innovation, a senior associate with the William E. Simon Chair in Political Economy at the Centre for Strategic and International Studies and an economist, writer and independent scholar. Previously, she was the founding director of the Latin American Research Centre at the University of Calgary.

Ms Hester is the author of numerous articles published in *Oil and Gas Journal, Estey Centre Journal* and the *Journal of Canadian Petroleum Technology*, as well as chapters in edited volumes, and is a frequent contributor to a variety of newspapers including *The Globe and Mail* and *The Calgary Herald.*

Sharon F. Lean is currently an assistant professor of political science at Wayne State University in Detroit, MI. She received her PhD in political science from the University of California-Irvine in 2004.

Dr Lean's research interests include Latin American politics, democratization and democratic consolidation, international organizations and international norms, civil society and the power of non-state actors in international and domestic politics. She is the co-editor of *Promoting Democracy in*

the Americas (2007) and has most recently authored "Democracy Assistance to Domestic Election Monitoring Organizations: Conditions for Success" in *Democratization* (April, 2007) and "The Presidential and Parliamental Elections in Nicaragua, November 2006" in *Electoral Studies* (2006).

Thomas Legler currently teaches at the Ibero-American University. He has previously held the position of assistant professor and coordinator of the International Relations Program at Mount Allison University, as well as holding posts at the University of Victoria and the University of Toronto. Dr Legler has an ongoing research interest in the international promotion and defence of democracy in the Americas, with a focus on the facilitation role of the Organization of American States during recent political crises in Peru (2000) and Venezuela (2002–present).

Dr Legler has published a number of works, including *Promoting Democracy in the Americas* (2007), which he co-edited, and *Intervention Without Intervening? The OAS Defense and Promotion of Democracy in the Americas* (2005*)*, which he co-authored with Dr Andrew F. Cooper. His publications have also appeared in *Journal of Democracy, Latin American Politics and Society, Canadian Foreign Policy* and *Hemisphere.*

Abraham F. Lowenthal is the Robert F. Erburu Professor of Ethics, Globalization & Development and professor of international relations at the University of Southern California, as well as senior fellow for Latin American & international affairs at the Pacific Council on International Policy. He is also a non-resident senior fellow at the Brookings Institution. Dr. Lowenthal was the Pacific Council's founding president and, before that, the founding director of the Latin American program at Woodrow Wilson International Center for Scholars and of the Inter-American Dialogue, the premier policy forum and think-tank on Western Hemiaffairs. He has also served as director of studies and later as a vice president at the Council on Foreign Relations in New York. He has authored, edited or co-edited a dozen books and published numerous articles on Latin America, including six in Foreign Affairs and five in Foreign Policy.

Marco A. Morales is currently working towards the completion of his PhD at New York University. Recently he has co-authored (with Jorge G. Castañeda) "Looking to the Future", which was published in the *Journal of Democracy* (2007), and co-edited (also with Jorge G. Castañeda) *Leftovers: Tales of the Two Latin American Lefts* (2008), which explores the resurgence of the left in Latin American and distinguishes the two paths it has followed.

Anthony J. Payne is currently the Pro-Vice-Chancellor (Social Sciences) Elect at the University of Sheffield and professor in the Department of Political Science, where has also served as the chairman of the department (1992–1995 and 1998–2001). He was also the director of the Political Economy Research Centre (PERC) from 1996 to 1999 and co-director from 2002 to 2004. Previously, he

has been the chairman of the International Advisory Council of the Institute of Commonwealth Studies at the University of London (2002–2006). His principal research interests are the politics of the Caribbean, international political economy and the politics of development.

His most recent books include *Key Debates in New Political Economy* (Routledge, 2006), *The Global Politics of Unequal Development* (Palgrave, 2005) and *The New Regional Politics of Development*, edited (Palgrave, 2004). He has also recently authored *Living in a Less Unequal World: The Making of Renewed Progressive Global Policy* (Institute for Public Policy Research, 2007) and *Repositioning the Caribbean within Globalization*, with P. K. Sutton (Centre for International Governance Innovation, 2007). He was managing editor of *New Political Economy* from 1995 to 2005, and remains one of the editors of the journal.

Luiz Pedone is a former chair of the Department of Political Science at the University de Brasília, where he taught for many years. Since 1995 Professor Pedone has researched the theme of mechanisms to combat corruption. He is the founder of Transparency, Consciousness and Citizenship – TCC-Brasil, and as member of the consultative board he was re-elected for the term 2006–2008. In 2003 Professor Pedone retired from UnB and moved to Rio de Janeiro, where he is currently a visiting researcher at the Program of European Studies at the Universidade Federal do Rio de Janeiro.

Nicola Phillips is professor of political economy and director of the Centre for the Study of Political Economy at the University of Manchester, United Kingdom. She is editor-in-chief of the journal *New Political Economy* and an associate fellow of Chatham House in London, and has held a variety of visiting posts across the United Kingdom, Europe and Latin America. Her research focuses on the political economy of development, with a particular emphasis on the Americas.

She is author of *The Southern Cone Model: The Political Economy of Regional Capitalist Development* (Routledge, 2004) and editor of *Globalizing International Political Economy* (Palgrave, 2005). Her recent work has also been published in the *Review of International Political Economy*, *The World Today* and *Latin American Politics and Society*. Her current work focuses on the emergence of China and India and its implications for global development, and on questions of migration and development.

Arturo Santa-Cruz is an associate professor at the Department of Pacific Studies, University Center for Social Sciences and Humanities, University of Guadalajara. He received his PhD in political science from Cornell University.

He is the author of *International Election Monitoring, Sovereignty, and the Western Hemisphere Idea: The Emergence of an International Norm* (Routledge, 2005) and *Un debate teórico empíricamente ilustrado: La construcción de la soberanía japonesa, 1853–1902* (Universidad de Guadalajara, 2000);

editor of *What's in a Name? Globalization, Regionalization and APEC* (Universidad de Guadalajara, 2003); and co-editor of *Globalization, Regionalization and Domestic Trajectories in the Pacific Rim: The Economic Impact* (University of Guadalajara-University of Technology, Sydney, 2004). He has also published several articles in specialized journals such as *International Organization* and the *Journal of Latin American Studies*, as well as book chapters.

Yasmine Shamsie is an associate professor in the Department of Political Science at Wilfrid Laurier University, where she teaches Latin American politics and international relations. She specializes in the political economy of democracy promotion, with a focus on the inter-American system. Her research has focused on OAS peacebuilding efforts in Haiti and its conflict-prevention work in Guatemala. She is a fellow at the Centre for Research on Latin America and the Caribbean (CERLAC) at York University. Dr Shamsie is co-editor of *Haiti: Hope for a Fragile State* (Wilfrid Laurier University Press, 2006).

Michael Shifter is vice-president for policy at the Inter-American Dialogue, a Washington-based forum on western hemisphere affairs. Since 1993 Mr Shifter has been adjunct professor at Georgetown University's School of Foreign Service, where he teaches Latin American politics. Mr Shifter writes and talks widely on US-Latin American relations and hemispheric affairs.

His recent articles have appeared in major US and Latin American publications, such as *The New York Times, Foreign Affairs, Foreign Policy, The Washington Post, The Financial Times, The Los Angeles Times, Journal of Democracy, Harvard International Review, Clarin, O Estado de S. Paulo* and *Cambio*, and he is co-editor, with Jorge Domínguez, of *Constructing Democratic Governance in Latin America* (Johns Hopkins University Press, 2008). He is also a contributing editor to *Current History*. Since 1996, he has frequently testified before Congress about US policy towards Latin America.

Sidney Weintraub holds the William E. Simon Chair in Political Economy at the Center for Strategic and International Studies. He is also professor emeritus at the Lyndon B. Johnson School of Public Affairs of the University of Texas at Austin. A former member of the US Foreign Service, Dr Weintraub held the post of deputy assistant secretary of state for international finance and development (1969–1974). He was also a senior fellow at the Brookings Institution.

Dr Weintraub is a prolific author who has written over 100 articles, books, monographs, chapters and commissioned papers. His numerous books include *Energy Cooperation in the Western Hemisphere: Benefits and Impediments* (CSIS, 2007), *Issues in International Political Economy: Constructive Irreverence* (CSIS, 2004), *Free Trade in the Americas: Economic and Political Issues for Governance and Firms* (Edward Elgar, 2004), *NAFTA's Impact on North America: The First Decade* (CSIS, 2004), *Financial Decision-Making in Mexico: To Bet a Nation* (Macmillan/University of Pittsburgh Press, 2000) and *Development and Democracy in the Southern Cone: Imperatives for US Policy Making in South America* (CSIS, 2000).

Laurence Whitehead is an official fellow in politics at Nuffield College, Oxford University, and senior fellow of the college. A past co-editor of the *Journal of Latin American Studies*, published by Cambridge University Press, he serves on the international advisory boards of a number of leading publications, including the *Journal of Democracy*. He is also the editor of the Democratization series published by Oxford University Press.

His latest book is *The Obama Administration and the Americas: Agenda for Change*, co-edited with Abraham F. Lowenthal and Theodore Piccone (Brookings Institution Press, 2009). His recent work also includes *State-crafting Monetary Authority: Brazil in Comparative Perspective*, edited with Lourdes Sola (Oxford Centre for Brazilian Studies, 2008), *Latin America: A New Interpretation* (Palgrave, 2005), *Democratization: Theory and Experience* (Oxford University Press, 2002) and *Emerging Market Democracies: East Asia/Latin America*, which he edited (Johns Hopkins University Press, 2002). He is also the co-editor of *Transitions from Authoritarian Rule*, with Guillermo O'Donnell and Philippe Schmitter (Johns Hopkins University Press, 1986).

Acknowledgements

Latin America is undergoing a process of accelerated change – a process that is little understood outside the region. These changes express themselves in the political, economic and social sphere, but all of them have been impacted and shaped by the different way the region is interacting with the international environment. In the first decade of the twenty-first century, Latin American countries are engaging the rest of the world in a much more proactive and dynamic manner than was the case in the past.

What is the effect of this "thickening" of ties with the global environment? In turn, what has been the impact of globalization on Latin America? What is the relationship of the newly emerging powers around the world with Latin America? How has the growing trend towards international political cooperation among Latin American nations changed their foreign policy? Do we see a convergence between the various regional and subregional integration schemes (such as Mercosur, the Andean Community, the Central American Common Market and CARICOM) and the foreign policy stance taken by their respective member states? What is the outlook of entities such as UNASUR, the South American Union of Nations, which has set for itself such ambitious undertakings as defence policy coordination through regular meetings of South American defence ministers, something unprecedented?

It was with the purpose of addressing these and similar questions that the Centre for International Governance Innovation (CIGI) convened the "Global Governance and the Contours of Domestic Politics in the Americas" workshop held in Waterloo and Elora, Canada, on 3–5

November 2006. It brought together specialists from three continents and 10 different countries to analyse the seismic changes affecting the hemisphere. They included Dexter S. Boniface, Megan Cain, Maxwell A. Cameron, Jorge Chabat, Claudia Curiel, Carlos Dade, Jean Daudelin, Eduardo del Buey, Edgar J. Dosman, Douglas Fraser, Annette Hester, James M. Lambert, Francisco López-Bermúdez, William Maley, Leslie Manigat, Luiz Pedone, Nicola Phillips, Ambassador Carlos Pujalte, Arturo Santa-Cruz, Yasmine Shamsie, Michael Shifter, Sidney Weintraub, Laurence Whitehead and Carol Wise. Andrew Hurrell, who presented a timely and informative talk during the conference, should also be thanked for his contribution to the endeavour.

At CIGI, Kelly Jackson and Erica Dybenko played a critical role in putting together the workshop and in the bulk of the work on the initial versions of this book manuscript. Andrew Schrumm, Thomas Agar and Ray Froklage provided research assistance and technical editing, while Max Brem, CIGI's head of publications, provided much sage advice as the manuscript was shepherded through its various stages. Joe Turcotte skilfully managed the latter stage of the manuscript development and provided a draft template for the cover design. Three anonymous readers for UNU Press provided some excellent editorial input.

As in other projects, John English, CIGI's founding executive director, and Daniel Schwanen, acting executive director during part of this period, created an environment superbly suited to the unfettered pursuit of academic research. CIGI was founded in 2002 by Jim Balsillie, co-CEO of RIM (Research In Motion), and collaborates with and gratefully acknowledges support from a number of strategic partners, in particular the Government of Canada and the Government of Ontario.

Special thanks need to be given to the high-quality work of Barry Norris, who delivered a comprehensive edited version of the manuscript. Cherry Ekins did an excellent job in copyediting, fact-checking, proofreading and otherwise guiding the book throughout the production process.

Chilean painter José Basso, based in Valparaíso and known for his luminous landscapes, was kind enough to authorize the use of his "*Tres casas con reflejo amarillo*" for the cover, thus providing a most suitable 'face' to this book.

The final thanks are for Robert Davis and his colleagues at United Nations University Press, whose enthusiastic support made it possible to bring our original vision into reality.

Andrew F. Cooper and Jorge Heine
Los Angeles, California, and Waterloo, Ontario, March 2009

Abbreviations

ACS	Association of Caribbean States
ALALC	Asociación Latinoamericana de Libre Comercio
ALBA	Bolivarian Alternative for the Americas
APEC	Asia-Pacific Economic Cooperation
ASEAN	Association of Southeast Asian Nations
bbl/d	barrels per day
bcm	billion cubic metres
BF	Bolsa Família (Family Scholarship), Brazil
BPC	Benefício de Prestação Continuada (Continuous Cash Benefits programme), Brazil
BPO	business process outsourcing
BRIC	Brazil, Russia, India, China
CAFTA	Central America-Dominican Republic-United States Free Trade Agreement
CAN	Comunidad Andina de Naciones (Andean Community of Nations)
CARICOM	Caribbean Community and Common Market
CEP	Conseil Electoral Provisoire (Provisional Electoral Council), Haiti
CEPAL	Comisión Economica para America Latina y el Caribe (UN Economic Commission for Latin America and the Caribbean)
CNE	Consejo Nacional Electoral (National Electoral Council), Venezuela
DPD	OAS Department for the Promotion of Democracy
ECLAC	UN Economic Commission for Latin America and the Caribbean
EPZ	export-processing zone

FARC	Revolutionary Armed Forces of Colombia
FDI	foreign direct investment
FTA	free trade agreement
FTAA	Free Trade Area of the Americas
GDP	gross domestic product
HDI	Human Development Index
HOPE	Haitian Hemispheric Opportunity through Partnership Encouragement Act, United States
IADC	Inter-American Democratic Charter
IBSA	India-Brazil-South Africa forum
ICT	information and communication technology
IFE	Instituto Federal Electoral (Federal Electoral Institute), Mexico
IFES	International Foundation for Electoral Systems
IMF	International Monetary Fund
IMMHE	International Mission for Monitoring Haitian Elections
IPE	international political economy
IRI	International Republican Institute, United States
IT	information technology
KPO	knowledge process outsourcing
LAC	Latin American and Caribbean
LAIA	Latin American Integration Association
LNG	liquefied natural gas
MAS	Movimiento al Socialismo, Bolivia
Mercosur	Southern Common Market
MFA	Multi-Fibre Arrangement
MINUSTAH	UN Stabilization Mission in Haiti
NAFTA	North American Free Trade Agreement
NDI	National Democratic Institute for International Affairs, United States
NED	National Endowment for Democracy, United States
NGO	non-governmental organization
NIC	newly industrializing country
OAS	Organization of American States
OECD	Organisation for Economic Co-operation and Development
OEM	original equipment manufacturing
OPEC	Organization of Petroleum Exporting Countries
PAN	Partido Acción Nacional (National Action Party), Mexico
PNPB	Programa Nacional de Produção e Uso de Biodiesel (National Programme for the Production and Use of Biodiesel), Brazil
PRD	Partido de la Revolución Democrática (Party of the Democratic Revolution), Mexico
PREP	Programa de Resultados Electorales Preliminares, Mexico
PRI	Partido Revolucionario Institucional (Institutional Revolutionary Party), Mexico
PSDB	Partido da Social Democracia Brasileira (Brazilian Social Democracy Party)
PT	Partido dos Trabalhadores (Workers' Party), Brazil

PWC	post–Washington Consensus
RNM	Caribbean Regional Negotiating Machinery
SGR	strategic global repositioning
TEPJF	Tribunal Electoral del Poder Judicial de la Federación (Electoral Tribunal of the Federal Judiciary), Mexico
UNASUR	Union of South American Nations
UNDP	UN Development Programme
UPD	OAS Unit for the Promotion of Democracy
UWI	University of the West Indies
WOLA	Washington Office on Latin America
WTO	World Trade Organization

Foreword

Abraham F. Lowenthal

Which Way Latin America? is a timely, insightful and informative volume that illuminates the winds of change as well as the structures that reinforce continuity in Latin America and the Caribbean today. It emphasizes the sources of both transformation and stability within the region, and the international forces that impinge upon and constrain its diverse countries.

The book deals with many of the Americas' major countries and subregions: Brazil, Mexico, Venezuela, the Commonwealth Caribbean and Haiti (though perhaps it short-changes the Hispanic Caribbean and Central America, countries that are more affected than many by global swings). In helpful detail, the volume takes up the growing roles of China, India and other new extra-hemispheric actors in Latin America and the Caribbean. It rightly stresses the central importance of competition for energy in the region. And it emphasizes issues of democratic governance and the emergence of competing movements of the left as increasingly influential in defining the direction of several countries. *Which Way Latin America?* covers a great deal, substantively and geographically, and I do not want to delay the reader long in reviewing it directly.

However, I am glad to provide a complementary perspective to the text, commenting on the new Barack Obama-led US administration and its first encounters with Latin America and the Caribbean.

Because the Obama administration entered office with the most daunting agenda faced by a US government in many decades, few observers predicted that it would devote much attention to Latin America and the Caribbean. None of the countries present an imminent threat to US national security or anything remotely comparable to the potential threats represented by Iran, Pakistan or North Korea. None is likely to be the source or target of significant international terrorism. And the various regional international trends reviewed in this volume have weakened inter-American cooperation over the past 20 years. Western hemisphere approaches to problem-solving have waned, and seemed unlikely to be reinvigorated in the trying circumstances of 2009.

Yet during its first months in office the Obama administration has taken an active interest in Latin America and the Caribbean. As president-elect, Obama met with only one foreign leader: Felipe Calderón of Mexico. His first foreign visitor to Camp David was Brazilian President Luiz Inácio (Lula) da Silva. As secretary of state, Hillary Clinton's first meeting with a foreign head of state was with Haiti's Prime Minister René Préval. Vice President Joseph Biden visited both Chile and Central America in March. Secretary Clinton, Joint Chiefs Chairman Michael Mullen, Attorney General Eric Holder and Homeland Security Secretary Janet Napolitano all visited Mexico during the new administration's first three months and made some important statements, preceding a visit to Mexico by President Obama himself in April. In the same month the Obama administration announced new initiatives toward Cuba, and followed up with exploratory conversations with Cuban officials to discuss the prospects for improving relations between the two countries. President Obama also participated in the Fifth Summit of the Americas in mid-April, winning praise throughout Latin America and the Caribbean for his adroit role there.

As this volume points out, the Americas is a region at a crossroads. It is not very surprising, then, that the new US administration has taken a strong initial interest in Latin America and the Caribbean. This book helps to shed light on this apparently surprising development through analysis of the recent trends in the region and their importance.

Why Latin America matters to the United States

Apart from the scheduling coincidence that the Fifth Summit of the Americas was already on the calendar, the main reason for the Obama administration's strong early engagement with Latin America, I believe, is the perception that though the countries of Latin America and the Caribbean pose no urgent issues for the United States, many of them are likely to be increasingly important to the country's future.

This is so not due to long-standing axioms about Western hemisphere security, extra-hemispheric threats and Pan-American solidarity. Instead, it is because of four much more contemporary reasons.

First is the perceived increase in importance of such transnational issues as energy security, global warming, pollution and other environmental concerns, crime, narcotics and public health. The Obama administration recognizes that these important issues cannot be solved or even managed without close and sustained cooperation from many of the countries of the Americas.

Second, there has been a blurring of the borders between the United States and some of its closest neighbours – especially in Mexico, Central America and the Caribbean – mainly because of massive and sustained migration and functional economic integration. This demographic and economic interdependence has given rise to complex and pervasive issues with both international and domestic facets – so-called "intermestic" questions – ranging from education to healthcare, immigrants' remittances to driving licences, youth gangs to portable retirement pensions, and narcotics trafficking to human and arms trafficking. The Obama administration knows that it cannot ignore these issues, which are high on the US public's priorities.

Third, Latin America has economic importance to the United States as a prime source of energy and other key resources, and a priority market for US goods and services. The United States obtains nearly half of its energy imports from countries of the Western hemisphere – more than half of that from Latin American and Caribbean suppliers – and the potential for expanded energy production in the Americas is high. In 2008 US firms exported goods and services to Latin America valued at US$273 billion, representing 20 per cent of all US exports and four times the value of US exports to China. US firms still have, but need to sustain, their competitive advantage in Latin American markets, which arises from proximity and familiarity plus cultural and demographic ties. This imperative is all the more important in a period of economic downturn.

Fourth, there are shared values in the Western hemisphere, as expressed in the Inter-American Democratic Charter. Not least is the commitment to fundamental human rights, including free political expression, effective democratic governance and consistent application of the rule of law. At a time when very difficult experiences in Afghanistan, Iraq and elsewhere have discouraged many in the United States about the prospects of expanding the international influence of US ideals, the new administration recognizes that shared commitment throughout the Americas to the norms of democratic governance and the rule of law is important and worth reinforcing. The Western hemisphere remains a largely congenial neighbourhood for the United States in an unattractive broader international environment.

The troubled state of inter-American relations

Despite Latin America's growing quotidian significance for the United States, however, the Obama administration understands that in recent years US policies towards the region have often been ineffective. Since the 11 September 2001 attacks, Washington has mainly viewed Latin America through the prism of international terrorism, mirroring a similar tendency during the Cold War to focus on anti-communism in the Americas rather than on the issues Latin Americans considered most important.

The administrations of both Bill Clinton and George W. Bush emphasized Western hemisphere summits as a means of showing attention to Latin America, but these meetings typically produced little beyond photo opportunities and largely rhetorical calls for cooperation. Both administrations continued to support a proposed Free Trade Area of the Americas (FTAA) long after this goal had become unfeasible. Instead of building better bridges towards its closest neighbours in the region, the United States did the opposite and began constructing a fence on the Mexican border in 2006. Whereas cooperation between the United States and the Western hemisphere had strengthened in the first post– Cold War years of the early 1990s, it waned in the late 1990s and continued to do so in the first years of the new century.

Perceived inattentiveness on the part of the United States, along with some of Washington's global policies during the Bush years, especially the invasion of Iraq, led to resentment in many Latin American countries. Venezuelan President Hugo Chávez took advantage of this antipathy with his aggressive anti-US public and chequebook diplomacy – subsidizing petroleum sales to Central American and Caribbean nations, providing other economic assistance to receptive neighbours, cooperating closely with Cuba to provide medical and other social services and promising to support major infrastructure projects in South America.

Meanwhile, as this volume emphasizes, many Latin American and Caribbean countries have deepened processes of subregional integration, in part through formal institutions, but even more through trade, investment, Latin America-based multinational corporations, professional and business networks and pragmatic cooperation. They have also been diversifying their international relationships, building cooperation with the countries of the European Union (EU), members of the Asia-Pacific

Economic Cooperation (APEC) forum and especially with China, India, Iran and Russia. Many Latin American countries no longer look to Washington for leadership or even for close cooperation. The Organization of American States (OAS) has been a disappointment, and the Inter-American Charter has not produced many meaningful results. Other hemisphere-wide institutions, including the Inter-American Development Bank, have weakened. As the international self-confidence and activity of many individual Latin American nations have increased, Western hemisphere approaches to problem-solving have waned.

Renewing inter-American cooperation: Key principles

As the Obama administration moves to reset the international relations of the United States more broadly, it is apparently positing that the emergence of a number of shared concerns in the Americas, strongly reinforced by the severe international economic crisis that began in the latter part of 2008, will make cooperative inter-American approaches more relevant and attractive once again, and that clear signals of a strong US interest in renewing cooperation to confront common challenges in the Americas could therefore yield immediate and important dividends. These premises, in my judgement, undergird the various steps in Latin America policy that the new administration announced during its opening months.

In striving to renew inter-American cooperation, the Obama administration has proceeded on the basis of three key principles.

First, the administration's initial priority is to gain the confidence of the American public and the international community as a whole in its commitment to slowing and then reversing the deterioration of the US economy, and restoring it to dynamism and growth. How well the new administration succeeds in meeting this urgent need will be highly relevant to the countries of Latin America, especially to those in the northern tier – Mexico, Central America and the Caribbean – that are so dependent on US investment, remittances, tourism and trade. By the same token, these same closest neighbours are relevant to the new administration's central economic challenge: they provide expanding and important markets for US goods and services. Latin America's capacity to respond effectively to the current economic downturn will thus affect the chances for a prompt and solid US recovery. The administration knows, therefore, that it needs to work closely with Latin American countries to avoid depression, restore economic dynamism and create jobs. Stabilizing the economies of Mexico, Central America and the Caribbean is particularly important in this context, both because of their direct commercial significance and because social and economic trends in these close neighbours will affect the United States through migration, crime and violence.

Second, instead of offering soaring rhetoric about partnership from Alaska to Tierra del Fuego, the new administration prefers to work with Latin American and Caribbean nations on a few select issues that can be addressed soon, if only partially, such as bolstering financial institutions, restoring credit and investment flows and tackling the problems of energy, the environment and citizen security. The administration aims to rebuild US credibility that has been damaged after years of unfulfilled pledges. Rather than scramble to counter Chávez and the "Bolivarian alternative" of anti-US movements, the Obama administration wants to concentrate on confronting the underlying issues that have created space for Chávez's inflammatory rhetoric and populist programmes, and for other radical populist movements.

Third, the new US authorities know that they must disaggregate Latin America and the Caribbean. During the past 20 years there has often been a tendency in Washington, in administrations of both parties, to emphasize convergence within the region: towards democratic governance, market-oriented economics, macroeconomic balance and regional integration. Although some of these convergent trends have indeed been important, if sometimes exaggerated, it is crucial to understand that key differences persist among the countries of Latin America and the Caribbean, and that some of these are growing, as this volume emphasizes. The most important differences lie primarily along five dimensions.

- Latin American countries vary in their degree of demographic and economic interdependence with the United States, which remains low in the southern part of Latin America, especially Argentina, Chile and Uruguay, while continuing to accelerate in Mexico, Central America and the Caribbean.
- They differ in the degree to which they have opened their economies to international competition. Brazil, Colombia, Mexico, Panama, Peru, the Dominican Republic and some Central American nations have liberalized their economies, but none has done so to the extent of Chile, and some other countries remain far behind or continue to resist globalization.
- Countries have advanced at different rates in achieving key aspects of effective democratic governance – such as checks and balances, accountability and the rule of law. These qualities have been historically strong in Costa Rica, Chile and Uruguay; they have been increasingly but unevenly robust in Brazil and have gained ground in Mexico, with

many ups and downs; but they have weakened in Argentina and Venezuela and are problematic in most of the Andean nations, much of
Central America and Haiti.

- The strength of civil and political institutions beyond the state – such as
non-governmental entities, the press, religious organizations and trade
unions – also varies enormously from place to place, with implications
for democratic accountability. They are strongest in Chile, Costa Rica,
the Dominican Republic, Uruguay and perhaps Argentina; they are
growing in Brazil and Mexico; they are regaining stature but continue
to be quite problematic in Colombia; they are weak in Bolivia, Ecuador, Paraguay, Peru, Venezuela and most of Central America; and
they are very weak in Haiti.

- Finally, Western hemispheric countries vary in the degree to which
they incorporate many traditionally excluded populations, including
more than 30 million marginalized, disadvantaged and increasingly politically mobilized indigenous people, especially in Bolivia, Ecuador,
Guatemala, the Peruvian highlands and southern Mexico; and in their
treatment of Afro-Latin Americans, who still face severe racial discrimination in a number of countries. Some of the toughest challenges
to US diplomacy arise from the countries that are struggling to incorporate large, previously excluded groups – in part by mobilizing anti-globalization, anti-capitalist and therefore anti-United States
sentiment.

Officials in the new administration are aware that only when all of
these important structural differences and their political consequences
are consistently understood – an aim to which this volume contributes –
can the countries of Latin America and the Caribbean come into clear
focus for US policy. Hemisphere-wide summit conferences or very broad
regional initiatives are much less likely to be effective, in this perspective,
than subregional efforts that bring together smaller clusters of countries
with comparable or complementary issues and concerns. Recognizing
this fundamental reality is a starting point for the Obama administration's reconsideration of US policies in the Americas.

Changing mindsets

It is much too early to be sure how the Obama administration's promising start towards renewing inter-American cooperation will fare. But
evidence from the administration's first 100 days suggests that it has
adjusted several important mindsets in ways that reflect the changes discussed in this volume.

Among the changes perceptible in the Obama administration's first 100 days are:

- a turn from obsessive concern with military security and the so-called "war on terrorism" to an emphasis on shared challenges involving economic growth, jobs, equity, citizen security, energy, migration, democratic governance and the rule of law
- a turn away from the so-called "war on drugs" to a more cooperative attempt to work together to reduce demand and mitigate harm – an attempt that starts with an honest appreciation of the role of the United States itself in fuelling and facilitating the drug trade and the associated traffic in small arms and bulk cash
- appreciation that some of the key issues affecting US-Latin American relations – particularly immigration, narcotics, trade and energy conservation and development – require new domestic initiatives that will have important repercussions in other countries of the Americas
- targeted priority on the special issues posed by relations with the closest neighbours in Mexico and the Caribbean Basin, and the prospects for strategic cooperation with Brazil on a number of key issues in the hemisphere and beyond; case-by-case, patient and nuanced management of relations with the nations of the Andean ridge; and a new approach to Cuba, turning away from denial, embargo and exclusion in favour of restoring communications, building trust and working towards cooperation on shared concerns
- both understanding and explaining to the people of the United States that the country would gain more stable neighbours, expanded markets, more attractive investment opportunities and more congenial tourist destinations and retirement havens if the countries of Latin America and the Caribbean could be helped to reduce extreme poverty, gross inequities, ethnic exclusion and rising unemployment.

One cannot be sure how far the Obama administration will go in reframing US approaches to Latin America and the Caribbean, how long these approaches will continue or what the impact of new policies will be. But it is precisely the changes that have occurred in the past two decades within Latin America and the Caribbean, in the international context and within the United States itself that make these new approaches both necessary and possible. This book provides an excellent introduction to these topics and acts as a reminder of the increasing importance of Latin America and the Caribbean.

Introduction

The effect of national and global forces on the Americas: Tsunami, tornado or just a mild breeze?

Andrew F. Cooper and Jorge Heine

On 20 April 2008 Fernando Lugo won the presidential elections in Paraguay, bringing to an end 61 years of Colorado Party rule and opening a new chapter in the history of one of the poorest and most backward nations in South America. A former clergyman, known as "the bishop of the poor" and closely associated with liberation theology, Lugo and his coalition, the Patriotic Alliance for Change, represent a radical change for a country that – even after the fall in February 1989 of dictator General Alfredo Stroessner, who ruled Paraguay with an iron fist for 35 years – continued to be afflicted by poverty, corruption, the marginalization of its aboriginal peoples and an economy based largely on smuggling and drug trafficking. As *The Economist* (2008) put it, "The Colorado party ... has ruled so long that Paraguay sometimes feel like a run-down country club that exists purely for the benefit of party members."

By and large, the results of the Paraguayan elections went largely unnoticed by the international media – just another election in an obscure South American country with a difficult-to-pronounce name. One question that foreign correspondents asked was how close the new president would be to Venezuela, to which the answer was ambiguous.

Only a decade ago – that is, in the late 1990s – the notion that the left would reach power in Paraguay would have been considered somewhere between ludicrous and preposterous. In the new environment of the Latin America of the first decade of the twenty-first century, it is taken as a humdrum event. The reason is that the left has been winning almost everywhere in the region, so much so that it has become "the expected

Which way Latin America? Hemispheric politics meets globalization, Cooper and Heine, eds, United Nations University Press, 2009, ISBN 978-92-808-1172-8

outcome" whenever presidential elections are held (see Cheresky, 2007). A quick look at a map of South America in mid-2008 reveals that at least eight of the continent's 10 countries are ruled by the left or left-of-centre coalitions. To these one could add several other governments in the broader Latin American region, like those of Presidents Daniel Ortega in Nicaragua, René Préval in Haiti, Leonel Fernández in the Dominican Republic and Martín Torrijos in Panama.

Yet, as a significant number of contributions in this volume attest, the left should not be looked upon as a homogeneous or monolithic entity. Some elements of the old left have morphed considerably, and a very different left has emerged. The new left (or centre-left) extends across a continuum that includes the Workers' Party in Brazil, the Frente Amplio (Broad Front) in Uruguay, the Concertación in Chile and "Kirchnerism" in Argentina, and their respective governments (Vilas, 2006: 239–243). These significant departures from the first wave of democratic governments that came into power after the region's transition to democracy in the 1980s have by no means been confined to the ideological sphere. What we are looking at is a much deeper transformation in Latin American politics, one that goes well beyond the alternation in power between right and left, affecting the very way in which politics is practised and by whom.

At one level, this collection is an attempt to add what we think is a necessary modification to this commonly accepted template about Latin American politics and society. Yes, the left in Latin America has made substantive gains. In both its causes and effects, however, this trend is far from a simplistic one. In structural terms, the left has been a beneficiary of the release of disciplines imposed in the bipolar world. Leftist political parties can no longer be immediately condemned and marginalized as agents of international communism. In societal terms, the left has been able to establish itself as the voice of those forces whose priority it is to close the equality gap between an increasingly expectant – and politically demanding – citizenry and the holders of economic privilege and power. In political terms, the left became the beneficiary in some parts of the region simply by its established credentials as the force of opposition in more robust democratic systems. Facilitated by growing discontent with the record of incumbents – specifically, the failure to deliver on jobs, incomes and services – the left came into office as much by default as by its own performance.

The changes demonstrated by the rise of the left are also cultural. Much as in the United States, where Barack Obama's election as president has been described as "historic", something similar could be said about what has happened in Latin America in this decade: electorates are reaching out beyond the traditional white, male, Europeanized élite on which they relied to rule them to a new, much more representative generation of leaders. President Luiz Inácio Lula da Silva of Brazil – now into his second term, with approval ratings of 80 per cent and widely considered among the most effective Brazilian presidents ever – is a former trade union leader and metalworker who lost one of his fingers on the factory floor. Evo Morales, a native Aymara and high school dropout, is the first Bolivian president in many decades to have been elected with an absolute majority of the vote and thus has a legitimacy none of his predecessors enjoyed.[1] Michelle Bachelet of Chile was the first woman elected to a presidency in the Southern Cone, followed in October 2007 by Cristina Fernández de Kirchner in Argentina, whose main rival in those elections happened to be another woman, Elisa Carrió.[2]

Some of the left's success does indeed play out in a personalistic and populist character, as represented by Venezuela's President Hugo Chávez. A good deal of *chavismo* represents a classic expression of the *caudillo* (leader) in Latin American politics. For some observers, Chávez is the generational successor of Fidel Castro as the burr under the US saddle. For others, Chávez is another representation of the left-oriented but nationalist big military man "on horseback" who comes in to clean up the mess left by a corrupt and closed élite.

As the left increases its presence in the region, the formal "rules of the game" of Latin American politics are also being rewritten: at least three countries (Bolivia, Ecuador and Venezuela) are in the process of developing new constitutions and another (Chile, during the 2000–2006 presidency of Ricardo Lagos) undertook significant, if not necessarily radical, reforms to its existing charter. Simultaneously, and again contrary to the conventional wisdom, "Most Latin American countries were better placed in 2007 than they had been at any time in the previous quarter of a century" (Reid, 2007: 312).

From outside the region, observers have had notorious difficulty in explaining these momentous changes, as they do not respond to the conventional wisdom on what politics should look like in the supposedly post-ideological era after the Cold War. One suggestion is that there are really no differences between right and left in this day and age, and that, while candidates might engage in some platform posturing and sloganeering on the stump, at the end of the day governments will do what they always have: muddle through as best they can and try to hold on to power, by no means an easy task even in post-military-coups Latin America. This position, of course, is untenable: the very notion of no more ideologies is itself an ideological position. Ideologies change and adapt themselves to new circumstances – if the world changes, so will ideologies. But that does not mean that all political parties embody the same programmes and values. Although the differences are smaller than they were, say, 30 years ago, there is still significant variation between right and left, and especially so in Latin America, where the right is closely identified with the military dictatorships that ruled from the 1960s to the 1980s.

A second suggestion is that, although the differences between right and left might still hold, no "rise of the left" actually exists. According to surveys conducted by Latinobarómetro, the region's main polling firm, the vast majority of respondents tend to locate themselves closer to the centre than to either extreme of the political spectrum (*The Economist*, 2006). Accordingly, although eight South American countries are ruled by left or left-leaning parties and the vast majority of the 500 million Latin Americans find themselves under governments ostensibly identified with the left, the "rise of the left" is nothing but a myth. This view misses the point. For the purposes of increasing our understanding of the direction in which Latin America is going, the main issue is not what survey data tell us about where respondents place themselves on an abstract ideological continuum, but for whom they vote once they have the chance to do so. And the answer to that question seems to be quite obvious so far.

A third approach has been to take "the rise of the left" as given and move on to the next stage – that is, to make distinctions between the various types of left, especially between the "populist" left and the "pragmatic" left. Jorge G. Castañeda, a contributor to this volume and one of the region's sharpest analysts, has been at the forefront of this approach, which underlines the many differences existing in the government programmes and policies followed by, say, Chávez's Venezuela and Kirchner's Argentina, on the one hand, and Bachelet's Chile and Lula's Brazil, on the other (see Castañeda, 2006). These differences are real, but, strictly speaking, should be a second-order concern, as it were.

The main question is a different one: why this upsurge of the left?

This question is especially pertinent since earlier victories of the left in Latin America had been few and far between and tended to end badly, as the cases of Juan Bosch in the Dominican Republic in the 1960s, Salvador Allende in Chile in the 1970s and Alan García in Peru in the 1980s attest. Indeed, never before in the almost two centuries of the region's independent history has the left achieved its current ascendancy, reaching power in some countries, such as Ecuador and Uruguay, for the first time. Moreover, many observers believe the left will remain in government for quite some time, often alternating with the right but always present, as opposed to its earlier decades, if not centuries, of confinement to the political wilderness.

Democracy and the Washington Consensus

To explain why this new wave of change is happening is by no means easy. For the first time, democracy as a form of government has established itself throughout the region. Universal suffrage is amply recognized, there are free and fair elections, a free press, *alternancia* in power and, as a rule, recognition of and respect for civic and political rights. This is by no means an inconsiderable achievement. As recently as 1979 there were only three functioning democracies, in the full sense of the term, in Latin America; today, democracy is the norm. The region has come a long way.

Yet it is also true that Latin American democracies, as opposed to those of the North, exist in societies marked by both poverty and inequality. In fact, as Guillermo O'Donnell (2004) has pointed out, democracy in Latin America has followed its own path, one that figures poverty and inequality quite prominently, which in turn affects its dynamics and performance. And this relates to the feebleness of the social, economic and, in many cases, legal rights of vast sections of the population.

Over the past 20 years or so, then, there has been a steady expansion of democratic institutions and political rights in the region, quite apparent to all and easily measurable through a variety of indicators. We have also seen the application of a certain type of economic programme, known as "structural adjustment", which held the promise of ending, or at least dramatically reducing, poverty and inequality – a goal which people were willing to make significant sacrifices to attain.

The notion became widespread that there was only one economic model and one type of economic policy: that many key policy decisions ultimately were technical ones and should be removed from the political sphere (i.e. from democratic controls), and that the discipline of markets was in the end more significant than the discipline of democracy. For 15 years the region went through a veritable catharsis of economic reforms, which succeeded each other in various cycles and in which almost no government felt free from engaging – this was, after all, the "Washington Consensus", and the penalties for those willing to depart from it were high.[3] These reforms had a number of beneficial effects, including the establishment of macroeconomic equilibria and the stabilization of economies that had often reeled under three-digit inflation rates. These accomplishments cannot be dismissed lightly. Yet by focusing almost exclusively on cutting back the size of the state (as opposed to enhancing its effectiveness), they also often weakened the state's capacity to perform its essential functions. The concept of a "lean and mean" state became only too true for many Latin Americans, with a state apparatus reduced not just to a bare-bones structure, but to an unwillingness and inability to provide the security and essential public services that citizens expect (see Hershberg and Rosen, 2007).

The conceptual promise of the neoliberal adjustment model thus did not translate into widespread benefits. The average incomes of urban workers, with the exception of those in Chile, stagnated or fell (Portes and Hoffman, 2003: 65). Not only did the distance between the haves and have-nots grow in general terms, but issues of marginality among the indigenous populations were exacerbated – economic resentment is tightly woven into the politics of identity. Still, rather than returning to the rejected formulas of the past (military coups, above all else), Latin America has attempted to find other solutions to these problems. In some cases the torrent of distress has brought with it alternative forms of rebelliousness (Williamson, 2006: 268–272) – as in Bolivia, where in 2003 protests over gas prices and exports resulted in the removal of President Gonzalo Sánchez de Lozada (see McPherson, 2006: 120–121).

It is in this context that, in the course of the current decade and contrary to the prognostications of the prophets of "the end of ideology", this upsurge of the left in Latin America has taken place. This poses a paradox. One would expect protest votes leading to first-time wins by the left in periods of great economic turmoil or recession. Yet for most of this decade Latin America has been undergoing an economic boom. In 2007, its fifth consecutive year of growth, the region's economy expanded by 5.6 per cent, clocking the highest amount of foreign direct investment since 1999 (US$95 billion), while foreign reserves increased markedly to 3.5 per cent of the region's GDP, foreign debt continued to fall (as a share of GDP) and unemployment dropped from 8.6 to 8.0 per cent (ECLAC, 2008).

Thanks to the mid-decade surge in commodity prices, Latin American – especially South American – exports reached hitherto unseen levels. Studies show a close alignment between the business cycles of China and India and those of Latin American countries, indicating that the region has benefited especially from the high and steady growth rates of the two Asian giants (see Heine, 2006; World Bank, 2006; Rosales and Kuwayama, 2007). Here, psychologically, as well as practically, the statist ethos – and domestic politics and society more generally – meets head on with globalism in all its diversity. As Robertson (1992) puts it neatly, globalism (or globality) is as much a question of social consciousness or, one could add, of mental state as of concrete connections. Trade and investment flows, along with cultural affinities and senses of solidarities, have all moved intensely out into the global sphere (Scholte, 2005).

Globalism plays out not only in outside-in fashion with respect to Latin America but also in an inside-out manner. One distinguishing feature of the new Latin American leaders is their global reach – Brazil's Lula embodies this trajectory, as does Venezuela's Chávez. Furthermore, these statist expressions are just the ripple on top of the currents of Latin America's globalism, which can be found across the board from major companies to the multifaceted expressions of civil society activism.

Roots of political change

Various interpretations have been offered of the precise nature of the current Latin American left. One is that, at a time when the rest of the world has dismissed protectionism and heterodox economic policies as unsuitable, Latin America appears to be returning to the failed policies of the 1960s. A standard argument is that Asia is forging ahead because Asian nations are closely attuned to the spirit of the times, while Latin American countries are once again losing the chance to make the Great Leap Forward to becoming developed societies.[4] Yet this is not true. Far from going back to inflationary and inward-looking policies, most Latin American governments today have embraced export-led development and are well aware of the need to keep inflation under control.

Another school of thought subsumes this emerging trend under an even earlier Latin American phenomenon, found in the 1940s and 1950s: that of populism, with its promise of easy and irresponsible redistributionism. In fact, in standard political rhetoric, in many ways "populism" has come to replace "communism" as the new threat of choice looming over the region, especially since "terrorism", the threat of choice elsewhere, is hardly present in Latin America. The truth is that populism, as defined in its Latin American expression of many decades ago, has lost its social basis of support, which was made up of multiclass urban coalitions based on import-substitution industrialization – *strictu sensu*, the only populism one can find in the region today is that of Venezuela under Chávez, which is really petro-populism, fuelled and made possible by that country's extensive oil reserves and the skyrocketing price of oil that occurred during the better part of the first decade of the twenty-first century.

Neither of these characterizations holds up. Instead, they skim over the surface of a very real, region-wide phenomenon without addressing its underlying social and economic causes. If one does that, instead of limiting oneself to the content analysis of political discourse, one finds that these changes – politically much more of a tsunami than a light breeze – are the fallout of 15 years of the dogmatic ramming through of economic reforms, none of which has made much of a dent in the region's underlying problems, including its massive inequality and the huge gaps between social classes. One could debate endlessly whether it is the reforms themselves or the manner in which they were applied that are at fault, but the fact is that vast sections of the population feel their lives are not improving and are demanding change.

Some hard evidence confirms this proposition. According to one study, the index of economic reforms – a composite index that looks at international trade policies, tax policies, financial policies, privatizations and capital accounts, all related to the Washington Consensus and measured from 0 to 1 – shows a steady upward trend from 0.58 in the 1980s to an average of 0.83 between 1998 and 2003 (UNDP, 2004: 39–41). Yet what do these reforms – which have often implied the closing of whole sectors of industry, the firing of hundreds of thousands of public employees and the turning over to private hands, sometimes for a pittance, of public enterprises built up over many decades – have to show as a result? Are Latin Americans better off than they were in 1980?

The numbers suggest they are not. In 1980, when the index of economic reforms was 0.55, per capita income was US$3,739 (in constant 1995 dollars); 20 years later, with the index of economic reforms at 0.83, per capita income stood almost unchanged at US$3,952.

Poverty, however, did go down: affecting 46 per cent of the populations of 18 countries in 1990, the poverty rate fell to 41.8 per cent between 1998 and 2001, almost all of it explained by poverty reduction in Brazil, Chile and Mexico. Yet the absolute number of Latin Americans below the poverty line went up in those years, from 190 million in 1990 to 209 million in 2001. Poverty even increased in relative terms in some areas: in the Southern Cone from 25.6 to 29.4 per cent; in the Andean nations from 52.3 to 53.3 per cent; and in Central America from 45.2 to 51.2 per cent.

At the same time, inequality in the region, as measured by the Gini coefficient, increased from 0.554 in 1990 to 0.58 in 1999; in contrast, the world average in the 1990s was 0.38 and that of developed countries was 0.33. This inequality also expresses itself in the gap between the high- and low-income sectors of society: in 1990 the top decile of Latin Americans had 25.4 times the income of the lowest-income decile; by 1999 the gap had widened to 27.4 times, the highest income inequality in the world. In turn, growing inequality is related to the employment situation. Contrary to the predictions of those who believed reforms would usher in an era of plentiful jobs, nothing of the sort has occurred – as a rule, both unemployment itself and the informal sector grew in the 1990s, although this has changed in the past couple of years.

There should be nothing surprising, then, about the upsurge of the left in Latin America. It is, in many ways, a quite logical, predictable reaction by those who feel left behind, who are tired of waiting for reform programmes to deliver the goods. The moment economists start talking about the "third generation" of reforms as those that will *really, truly* make a difference, one realizes why voters have become tired of such promises.

Engaging the world

How is the region responding to the challenges arising from the international environment? In negotiating this complex and rapidly changing world, has there been an effort to "circle the wagons", as it were, and hark back to the protectionism of yore? Or, on the contrary, have Latin American countries made a point of reaching out beyond their traditional diplomatic partners and tried to become, if not fully global players, at least actors on a wider stage? If the latter, how well have they fared? Are Latin American countries actually benefiting from globalization or are they paying inordinate costs as a result of it?

This is a central question asked in this book, and the various contributors provide somewhat different answers. Before getting to them, however, there are some general propositions about Latin America's international interactions.

- Of all regions in the world, Latin America, because of its geographic isolation (surrounded as it is by two of the world's largest oceans), traditional subordination to the United States and distance from the Eurasian landmass (traditional centre of world conflict), has been a strategically secondary region.

- This has meant a somewhat parochial international perspective, one confined to North America and Western Europe, with little attention being paid to the rest of the world. A quick survey of where Latin American countries have the majority of their embassies (overwhelmingly in Europe) is good evidence as to where international priorities lie.

- There have been exceptions: Cuba in the 1970s and 1980s, and, somewhat intermittently, Brazil. Yet, by and large, Latin American countries, for most of their close to 200 years of independent history, have been reluctant to reach out beyond the "safe" boundaries of North America and Western Europe in their foreign policy, diplomacy and international economic relations.

- As a consequence, Latin American nations have also been, as a rule, relatively absent from international debates about global issues. Though there are exceptions to this – like the Law of the Sea Treaty and the Antarctic Treaty, and where Brazil has been at the forefront of deliberations on the global environment and the role of the Amazon region – there are not many more issues in this category. The reluctance of some Latin American countries in the not-too-distant past to stand for election to the UN Security Council (even when, according to the rotation principle, it is their "turn" and they would have a good chance of being elected) is a good example of this international "shyness"; this reluctance springs from a sense that little can be gained, except headaches, by engaging with global issues on an international platform like the Security Council.

It is against this background that the changes which have taken place in the course of the present decade stand out. In many ways, it has been a period in which Latin America has "come out" in the world scene, starkly raising its international profile.

Regionally, this has been made possible by two interrelated phenomena.

On the one hand, the 1990s saw a revival of regional (and particularly subregional) integration schemes, which many considered had been discarded for good in the 1980s. From the founding of Mercosur in 1991 to a renewed impetus of the Andean Community, the Central American Common Market and CARICOM, a "new regionalism" came to the fore. Very different from the one seen in the 1960s with ALALC (the Asociación Latinoamericana de Libre Comercio) and the Andean Pact, this was an "open regionalism", inspired partly by the experience of ASEAN. Based on export-led development (as opposed to import-substitution industrialization), it looks at the region as a base from which to export to and interact with the rest of the world. These various subregional schemes have fallen short of "blending" into the Free Trade Area of the Americas (FTAA) that was announced with such fanfare at the Second Summit of the Americas in Santiago, Chile, in April 1998. Yet they have provided a somewhat larger base than the nation-state for Latin American countries to engage in relatively unimpeded trade and investment flows across the region.

The 1990s also saw the rise of Latin American political cooperation, to a degree not seen beforehand. Regional summit diplomacy became an established feature, with the Rio Group, the Ibero-American Summits, the Americas Summits (with a somewhat different profile) and, last but not least, the UNASUR summits – which overlapped with those of the various subregional integration schemes, leading to what some observers have referred to as "summit inflation". The point, though, is that Latin American leaders have started to interact regularly in a great variety of forums, thus developing a distinct regional diplomatic identity that has been largely absent until now.

These various "collective action" schemes came into their own with a special impetus after 9/11. If the end of the Cold War meant that Latin

America's strategic significance for the United States (rather low to begin with) was even further diminished, the actions of Al Qaeda in September 2001 entailed the disappearance of the region from the radar screens of the White House and the State Department. Paradoxically, precisely because it was the one region in the world not involved in an attack planned in Central Asia, financed from West Asia, with "trial runs" in East Africa undertaken by personnel trained in Western Europe and the United States, Latin America became a leading diplomatic casualty of the "war on terror".

This marginalization, however, was not without its benefits. With the emergence of Asia as a major growth pole in the world economy, Latin American nations started to realize that their traditional "US and Euro-centric" outlook on world affairs was anachronistic, and that ignoring global issues was no longer an option.

Latin America's growing density of international linkages is thus marked by a steady increase in *regionalism* as a foreign policy platform, growing *diversification* away from traditional partners and towards a greater engagement of countries in the global South, and a shift to a position of relative *strength* as Latin American countries got their domestic economies in order and benefited from the 2002–2008 worldwide commodities boom, thus becoming valuable economic partners in their own right.

In terms of foreign policy, Brazil has been by far the most active and ambitious. Its leadership within the G-20+ in the Doha Round from 2003 on, the India-Brazil-South Africa (IBSA) initiative that same year (see Flemes, 2007; Devraj, 2004) and its joining the G-4 (with Japan, Germany and India) in 2006, in an (ultimately failed) attempt to reform the UN Security Council, are all products of this truly global approach to its international relations. The opening of 32 new embassies in the 2003–2008 period, at a time when many countries were closing missions abroad and cutting the budgets of foreign ministries, is also revealing.

More modest, but not without its own accomplishments, has been Chile's approach to foreign relations, putting international economic policy front and centre. With 54 FTAs, more than any other country in the world, Chile has made access to foreign markets a key component of its foreign policy, having signed agreements with the United States, the European Union, China and Japan, among other countries, and in so doing increasing its exports from US$9 billion in 1990 to US$69 billion in 2008. Chile also joined APEC (in 1994) and has been invited to join the OECD (in 2008), showing precisely the sort of diplomatic initiatives that are necessary in an increasingly complex and networked international system (see www.direcon.cl).

Something similar can be said about Mexico, the first Latin American country to join APEC (in 1991), the first to join the OECD and the one, after Chile, with the largest number of FTAs.

Globalization and the Latin American response

As Laurence Whitehead, a contributor to this volume, points out in his eye-opening interpretation, Latin America is a particularly "outward-oriented" region, one that is constantly looking to validate domestic policy proposals on the basis of international references and alleged "best practices". Parties and factions compete with each other in the offer of different "modernities", which are often quickly abandoned, leading to a veritable "mausoleum of modernities". The interface between the domestic and the international in Latin American politics is therefore particularly dynamic (Whitehead, 2005).

Much of the conservative argument against the region's current "left trend" is couched in terms of its supposedly running counter to broader "international trends" – in short, globalization. According to this perspective, opening up the economy, privatizing public enterprises and deregulating productive activities (especially the labour market) – all key tenets of the Washington Consensus or, in the words of Birdsall and de la Torre (2001), the "Washington Contentious" – are the only way to respond to the enormous demands of a rapidly changing world economy, and those countries that stray from it do so at their peril.

We have already examined what that approach did to Latin American economies and incomes in the 1990s. In fact, what obtains might be exactly the opposite. It might well be that the current political cycle in Latin America overlaps with, and is at least partly a reaction to, a broader international phenomenon: what some authors have referred to as "the collapse of globalism" and others, more modestly, as "the end of liberal globalization" – that is, broadly speaking, the end of globalization as an ideology, though not necessarily as a process (see Saul, 2006; Oppenheimer, 2007–2008). Notions like "the twilight of the nation-state", "global markets in command", "unilateral opening of economies to maximize comparative advantages" and "the ever-rising power of transnational firms" seem increasingly dated at a time when nationalism is reasserting itself almost everywhere; when the forceful presence of the state is behind the rise of new giants China and India; when the collapse of the Doha Round – the first such international trade round to fail since the Second World War – is proof positive that key actors are not necessarily willing or able to move towards a more liberalized and non-subsidized international trade regime; when the fabled FTAA, which was designed to come to fruition in 2005, is nowhere near in sight; and when the electorates of France, the Netherlands and even Ireland have rejected the proposed EU Constitution and thrown a spanner into the process of European integration.

A central tenet of globalism was that the scope of politics was being reduced: there would be no margin for political choice and discretion in a world ruled by abstract economic forces, in the face of which politicians were essentially impotent. In response, the message that Latin American electorates have been sending is that they no longer buy this view and are ready for a change. They want choice. And it is not a coincidence that President Rafael Correa of Ecuador, elected in November 2006, did his doctoral dissertation in economics at the University of Illinois on the subject of globalization and its impact on Latin America.

Choice means alternatives to the single-minded goal of moving, in effect, from a market economy to a market society, in which democratic choice is reduced to a minimal expression, a society of citizens replaced by one of consumers. And this, of course, is critical to Latin America's central predicament: the coexistence of electoral democracy with widespread poverty and inequality. There *are* different ways to reduce poverty and inequality, alternatives to "trickle down" that would remove or at least alleviate the social fractures and divisions that plague so many countries of the region. And this requires a certain kind of politics, one that evaluates different kinds of economic policies, that is built on a strong state able to protect the weaker sections of society – which, in Latin America, encompass 40 per cent of the population – and that engages the world not in a defeatist manner, resigned to accept whatever the forces of globalization bring, but creatively and proactively.

There are many ways to combine the roles of the state and the market, and each country has to come up with its own approaches and solutions. But persistent demands for better welfare programmes, greater social justice, political inclusion and greater equality and dignity for the working man and woman and for disadvantaged groups provide the basis for much political mobilization.

The challenge and the hemisphere

It is, then, to foster understanding of the forces, domestic and international, that have led Latin America to this momentous process of change that this volume has come into being.

The introductory section is formed by three *tour d'horizons*. In the lead chapter, Laurence Whitehead argues, with his usual flair, that the dominant metanarratives of our understanding of Latin America are exhausted; that instead of illuminating the regional scene they condemn us to navigating in a fog. For the United States, the absence of a strong metanarrative that can act as a helpful guide is highly detrimental to its reputation in the region. Although Whitehead sees the US image in the region as still marginally positive, he adds that its "credit rating has dropped sharply". For Latin America, the absence of a compelling meta-narrative is equally negative. Instead of reinforcing a collective logic, autonomous activity is encouraged, with an upsurge of "parochial clashes of interests". Rather than aiming for an overly ambitious new metanarra-tive, though, in a call we believe the contributors to this volume have heeded, Whitehead argues for more detailed research in key issue areas, in both comparative politics and international relations.

Michael Shifter, on the other hand, underscores the degree to which the hemispheric consensus extant in the 1990s has evaporated. For that he blames, as many do, the role of figures like President Chávez in Vene-zuela, but also Washington's failings, its double standards on democracy and human rights after 9/11 and the growing distrust in US domestic politics of free trade and globalization – something that became espe-cially apparent in the 2008 Democratic primaries. Shifter, nonetheless, is upbeat about Brazil and how its long-in-the-making stabilization and progress under Presidents Cardoso and Lula have led it to the economic momentum that forecasters say will put it among the world's dominant economies by 2050. In this, other members of the select BRIC group (Brazil, Russia, India, China) – into which Brazil was thrust by Goldman Sachs in its 2003 report – will play a key role through their steady and growing demand for the country's (and the region's) raw materials.

The foundational debate on the prospects and nature of the left in Latin America is taken up by Jorge G. Castañeda and Marco A. Morales. They contrast the sort of anti-US, authoritarian left present in Venezuela under Chávez with the market-friendly one extant in Chile under Bache-let. They also emphasize the distinction between them with respect to "the means to accede to and remain in power". One works within the confines of democracy and respects the rule of law, whereas the other takes on institutions it deems to be inconvenient. Although Castañeda and Morales admit that there are examples of both types enjoying politi-cal success, they believe the future is brighter for the more moderate variant, which is more likely to be able to attract support from across the political spectrum.

Regional and global influences

Moving to Latin America's interaction with the global political economy, Sidney Weintraub and Annette Hester reveal that there are many tensions among countries in the region when it comes to energy sources and the energy market. The push of the United States for energy independence and the pull of Latin American sensitivity and resistance are a problematic mix – yet, despite their differences, Venezuela has continued to supply the United States uninterruptedly with some 15 per cent of its oil imports, and Caribbean nations have benefited considerably from Venezuela's policy of supplying them with oil at cut-rate prices. But there are also differences among Latin American, and especially South American, countries on how best to deal with energy supply and demand. Chile, one of the fastest-growing and most dynamic economies in the region, does not have any oil and gas supplies to speak of. Its neighbours have plenty of gas, but Bolivia refuses to sell to Chile, Peru might follow suit and Argentina, running out of gas supplies for its own burgeoning domestic demand, is violating existing contracts with Chile and cutting off its supplies.

Brazil's recent discovery of major offshore oilfields, on the other hand, with their potential for launching that country as a major oil producer, has come to underscore the irony of a region that could be self-sufficient in energy but cannot "get its act together" to take advantage of its endowments, with the consequent opportunity costs for all involved.[6] Brazil, in any event, is very much at the forefront on this particular issue with a publicly owned but publicly traded company, Petrobras, that is well managed and able to generate the capital it needs for prospecting and investment in new fields. In stark contrast, the Mexican oil company Pemex, hampered by bureaucratic controls and the financial needs of the Mexican government, which gets some 40 per cent of its revenues from Pemex, has little room for allocating a larger share of its funds to further exploration in the Gulf of Mexico. In a testament to the foresight of its energy policies, Brazil is also at the forefront in terms of alternative energy sources, with its development of biofuels and sugar-based ethanol (a much more efficient source of fuel than the corn-based one used in the United States) in a programme that started in the early 1980s and is now flourishing, given Brazil's seemingly limitless amount of land for such crops.

Energy, of course, has become in many ways the key driver of the international agenda these days, and it has changed the distribution of power – away from the transnational corporations, which had many more trump cards in their hands when the main driver of this agenda was globalization *per se*, and towards the nation-state, whose demise has been heralded so often, but which stubbornly refuses to exit the stage. As energy sources, by definition, are to be found in particular territories, they are bound to fall more easily under the control of sovereign states than the regular production of goods and services, which can be shifted quite easily from one country to another. Yet in the past oil and gas companies tended to develop as enclaves, giving few benefits to the populations of the countries in which they operated, thus generating considerable ill will. It is no coincidence that perhaps the three most militant left-nationalist governments in South America today – those of Bolivia under Evo Morales, Ecuador under Rafael Correa and Venezuela under Hugo Chávez – are to be found in oil- and gas-rich states, which have made the recovery of those resources and the channelling of the benefits to be derived from them to their populations a key priority. So-called resource nationalism is not a random phenomenon; it emerges from specific conditions that allow it to mature and develop. In South America, it is the Andean nations that have had particular difficulty in adapting to the demands of a rapidly changing world economy; not surprisingly, now that demand for some of the commodities with which they are richly endowed is picking up, they quite legitimately want to make the most of it (see Rosenberg, 2007). The notion that somehow it would be in their best interest to let foreign companies dispose of these resources more or less freely is embedded in a less-than-Aristotelian logic.

Nicola Phillips's chapter focuses on Sino-Latin American relations, which have generated considerable interest among specialists in the past few years. She acknowledges the complementarity of the Chinese and Latin American economies, but stresses the vulnerabilities this entails. Mexico and Central America, with their specialization in manufacturing, have been especially affected by Chinese competition; in fact, in 2006 China displaced Mexico as the second-largest exporter to the United States (after Canada). Phillips also points out that the structural rise of China as "the world's factory" will further reduce the opportunities for Latin American industrialization, while its seemingly inexhaustible demand for raw materials, perhaps perversely, will keep the countries of the region "stuck" in their condition as producers of commodities, preventing them from moving up the manufacturing value chain.

Jorge Heine takes a different tack on this issue in his analysis of Indo-Latin American links, a much newer issue. Although the volume of trade between India and Latin America is much lower than that between China and the region (US$10–12 billion versus US$100 billion in 2007), Sino-Latin American trade was at a similar low level as recently as 2001. With a particular focus on Brazil and Chile, which have taken the lead in relationships with India, Heine stresses the actual and potential benefit that "playing the India card" entails. This alludes to sheer volume of trade, enhancement of commodity prices, foreign-exchange earnings and, not least, the benefits of technological transfers and job creation resulting from the Indian information technology sector, one the world's most dynamic – quite apart from opening up the foreign policy options available to Latin American nations.

Anthony Payne's focus is the Commonwealth Caribbean, a subregion with features of its own but whose *problématique* interlocks with that of the broader hemisphere. In some way, debates in the Caribbean reinforce its sense of apartness, as underscored by the focus on reinvigorating CARICOM as a driver towards a single market and external tariff. On the other hand, the creation of the Association of Caribbean States (ACS), which brought together all 25 states of the wider Caribbean Basin into a new body, shows the creative interaction between the Caribbean and Latin America – although the ACS has not lived up to the full potential expected of it by its founders. However that may be, a vigorous debate is taking place in the Caribbean today about its competitive opportunities and vulnerabilities in the global political economy. Much of this debate underlines the structural constraints of the region – only Trinidad and Tobago has the natural resources endowment of its South American neighbours. Still, as part of the English-speaking world and with its geographical and climatic attractions, the Caribbean has some advantages across the spectrum of the services sector that might allow it to overcome its present predicament.

Institutions and values

The third section of the book deals with the institutional fabric that allows, or impedes, collective action in the region. Andrew F. Cooper's contribution traces the rise and ebb of innovative practices within the Organization of American States (OAS), a major beneficiary of the opening of policy space that was created by the end of the Cold War and the spread of democratic norms throughout the region. At the top of the OAS's achievements is the Inter-American Democratic Charter, formally approved in 2001, an instrument that has stood the region in good stead not only in specific crises – such as the collective response to the 2002 coup in Venezuela – but also as a beacon to show other regions the way. Yet as quickly as the norms and instruments of the collective defence of democracy took hold, they became frayed. As Cooper depicts, the promise of an innovative, networked form of multilateralism faded, with a concomitant return to a "club diplomatic culture" and a stronger onus on sovereignty and non-intervention. A stalled OAS has been caught between the interests of the United States – always an awkward champion of innovative initiatives – and those of Venezuela, as under Chávez it became increasingly confident in its defiant stance.

Dexter Boniface's chapter strengthens the perception of an OAS overwhelmed by present circumstances. But he makes the distinction between what he takes to be the still-robust (albeit far from perfect) reaction to external threats to democratic rules and a weaker response to internal challenges through elected leaders who resort to more indirect means to abuse power. Faced with this new form of instability, the OAS is wanting, Boniface finds, lacking both a repertoire of tools it can deploy and the leverage it needs. He thus calls for a renewed effort to find creative instruments with which both states and non-state actors can monitor threats to democracy in the Americas, with firmer criteria for determining when intervention is needed.

Election monitoring might be the most visible success story of regionally oriented multilateralism, and that is the subject of Sharon Lean's contribution. This activity encompasses a range of actors, not just governments, and has become a growth area, increasingly regulated and wider in scope. One constraint it faces is that it can be done by invitation only. Still, it is very much a success story, reflecting well the routinization of democratic procedures in the region. In this context, the need to embed further and refine the standards of election monitoring cannot be overstated.

Balancing national interests

The final section of the book resituates the analysis at the national level, with a number of pivotal country studies. Arturo Santa-Cruz complements Lean's chapter in detailing the trajectory of Mexico's transition to democracy, from the "boring" stage of Vicente Fox's election in 2000 to the "exciting" one of Felipe Calderón in 2006. But he also takes up two topics put forward by other contributors. One is the negative effect of US post-9/11 security policies as they have applied to Mexico, of which the gigantic wall being built on the US-Mexican border might be the most egregious example. The other topic is the increased projection of Mexican democracy abroad, now that an *alternancia* has occurred and Mexico has ceased to be a one-party-dominant state.

On the first issue, Mexico's geographic "advantage" in being situated next to the world's leading power – though one is reminded of the famous phrase, "poor Mexico, so far from God and so close to the United States" – is in some ways diminished by the increasingly shrill, some would say paranoid, debate on immigration and border security in the United States. On the second issue, Mexico comes out as a much more resolute champion of democracy than it has ever been in the past: its push for a non-permanent seat on the UN Security Council in 2009–

2010 and its sustained emphasis on democracy-promotion activities abroad are big departures from Mexico's foreign policy traditions. In Santa-Cruz's view, however, the full test of Mexico's new diplomatic efforts will come in the domestic arena, as the competitive, some would say divisive, nature of Mexican politics will ensure that policy agendas with such high stakes will not remain unaffected by intense partisan debates.

The best-known figure in Latin American today is President Hugo Chávez of Venezuela. What are the implications of his so-called Bolivarian Revolution for the rest of the region? How seriously should he be taken? Does he represent a return to the past, mixing personalism with populism and an authoritarian streak with the politics of confrontation? Or does he embody the wave of the future in Latin American politics, a harbinger of things to come?

Thomas Legler makes the case for looking in greater detail at the policies Chávez has implemented, and the way he has astutely used oil to reward his friends through initiatives such as Petrocaribe and more ambitious ones like the Banco del Sur, designed, according to some, to replace the International Monetary Fund with a more "friendly" financial institution in the region. Chávez has also forged close links with other regional leaders: both the new presidents of Bolivia and Ecuador and the "old" ones of Cuba and Nicaragua. At the same time Chávez, as shown in a number of regional polls, is far from universally popular in the region, and voters in several presidential elections, including those in Peru and Mexico in 2006, turned partly against the candidates he supported. Chávez has had an impact, but he is far from being the *caudillo* to whom other countries are looking for leadership – indeed, Venezuela's inability in 2006 to obtain widespread regional support for its candidacy to fill a non-permanent seat in the Security Council, a quest it ultimately lost, reflects those tensions and contradictions. If anything, Chávez's regional influence has been largely magnified by the international media, which see him as a caricature of the Northern image of a Latin American leader and are happy to give him coverage that extends well beyond his actual regional standing.

Luiz Pedone's contribution picks up one of the most fascinating bilateral relationships in the region – that between Brazil and Venezuela, Lula and Chávez. Though a trade union man and the leader of a left party, the Partido dos Trabalhadores (Workers' Party) – the very possibility of whose election in November 2002 generated a run on the Brazilian currency and a sharp fall in the São Paulo stock market index – Lula has shown himself to be a modernizer and a leader committed to both economic growth and proactive social policies, who has continued to expand and further develop many of the policies initiated by his predecessor, Fernando Henrique Cardoso (1994–2002). The Bolsa Família (Family Scholarship) is one of the most successful social programmes in the region, allowing Brazil to cut down its extreme income inequality despite the fact that its growth rate has been by no means spectacular.

Internationally, Lula has become a "buffer" statesman in high demand, respected and cheered at both the World Social Forum in Porto Alegre and the World Economic Forum in Davos, and one who had an excellent relationship with both George W. Bush and Hugo Chávez. Brazilian foreign policy has always had a worldwide perspective, but Lula has been especially active in reaching out to Africa and Asia, in the G-20+ within the Doha Round and in the India-Brazil-South Africa (IBSA) initiative, all testimony to Brazil's critical and constructive role in building up what Heine has referred to as the "New South".

Brazil has also taken a lead role in MINUSTAH, the UN Stabilization Mission in Haiti, extant since 2004 and the first UN peacekeeping operation with a majority of Latin American troops (of which Brazil has posted the largest number and the general in command of the 7,000 "blue helmets"). Haiti is the subject of the final chapter, by Yasmine Shamsie, who touches upon both bilateral and multilateral efforts to cope with "the Haitian imbroglio". Her main focus, however, is on Haiti's development challenges. Shamsie examines the complexities of Haiti's relationship with its donors and the possibility of reviving export-processing zones, which, in the 1980s, showed such promise that some observers saw the possibility of building up Haiti into "a new Taiwan". The outlook for Haiti is not a happy one, although some observers see a "window of opportunity" with the government of René Préval, whose main concern has been to stabilize both the economy and the polity, and with the international (and the Latin American) community firmly committed to making things work. Shamsie is especially enthused about new approaches that could tap into hitherto relatively unexploited resources, such as remittances and the Haitian diaspora more generally, to kick-start development projects.

Which way Latin America?

It has become somewhat fashionable in certain circles to point to the differences that exist among Mexico and Central America, the Caribbean, the Andean area and the Southern Cone – let alone Brazil, in some ways a world of its own – to deny the very existence of Latin America as a region about which meaningful characterizations can be made.[7]

This volume, however, focuses on the many common strands and challenges that exist in Latin America and the Caribbean today, and looks at the region's complex interface with the rest of the world. As several of the republics in Latin America approach the bicentennial of their independence from Spain in 2010, they also find themselves grappling with the best way to promote development and greater social equity in a context of relative democratic stability and international peace. The formal launching in May 2008 of UNASUR, the Union of South American Nations, a long-in-the-making project spearheaded by Brazil and whose first president *pro tempore* is Michelle Bachelet of Chile, might be dismissed as simply another smoke-and-mirrors exercise attempting to prove the existence on paper of something that does not exist in reality: South American regional integration. Or it might be seen as a subregional response to something that now might never come into being: the FTAA.

There is little doubt, however, that throughout the region a tectonic shift is taking place. Citizens, social movements, political parties and leaders, after taking a fresh look at the traditional functioning of their own polities and faced with a post-9/11 world obsessed with security concerns of little relevance to Latin America, are searching for new, more inclusionary approaches and tools to raise themselves and their countries by their bootstraps. To characterize this search as an anachronistic attempt to roll the region back to the past shows little understanding of what this process is all about. To the contrary, what many Latin American leaders are trying to do – and the enormous dynamism of the region's links with China and India is a good example – is to respond to the challenges presented by a rapidly changing world order by opening themselves up to new perspectives and new ways to interact with this environment without being washed away by the powerful waves of globalization. We hope this collection of essays contributes in a small way to enhancing understanding of that process.

Notes

1. About the upsurge of indigenous movements and parties in the region in the course of this decade see van Cott (2005); on Morales and his project see Dunkerley (2007).
2. For the rise of female leaders in Latin America see Inter-American Dialogue (2008); Buvinic and Roza (2004); Heine (2007).
3. For a recent comparative assessment of the effects of the Washington Consensus see Grugel, Riggirozzi and Thirkell-White (2008).
4. For an argument along these lines see the series of columns by Andres Oppenheimer in *The Miami Herald*, 18–24 January 2007, but especially the one entitled "While Latin America Nationalizes, India and China Open Up" (18 January 2007). In fact, India has been much more reluctant to follow the mantra of the Washington Consensus to "open up, privatize and deregulate" than almost all Latin American countries; yet its growth has averaged 8 per cent from 2003 to 2008. In other words, the lessons of India in this, if there were any to be drawn, would be exactly the opposite to those of Oppenheimer!
5. A useful text on Latin American populism is Coniff (1999).

6. In April 2008 the Brazilian government announced that, in addition to the Tupi oilfield discovered in 2007 (some 300 km off the coast of Rio de Janeiro, with an estimated 5–8 billion barrels of oil) a new oilfield named Carioca had been found, with an estimated 33 billion barrels of oil. With these and other nearby new oilfields, Brazil's total reserves could reach 80 billion barrels, putting it at par with Venezuela as the country with the fifth-largest oil reserves in the world – more than such traditional producers as Russia and Nigeria. These oilfields are some 5,000 m underwater and will demand massive investments and state-of-the-art technology to drill, but there is little doubt that they will considerably strengthen Brazil's hand as a player on the international energy scene. See Endres (2008).

7. This has become especially common in Mexico, whose government officials often talk publicly and in official discourse about Mexico's "being torn between the United States and Latin America", as if Mexico were not an integral part of the latter. Some take this even further, arguing that "Latin" America never existed in the first place, the very denomination being an invention of the French designed to split the region from its Hispanic roots. The semantics can be debated, but there is little doubt that, historically, culturally and behaviourally, there is such a thing as a Latin American identity which distinguishes Latin Americans from, say, Europeans or Africans.

REFERENCES

Birdsall, Nancy and Augusto de la Torre (2001) *Washington Contentious: Economic Policies for Social Equity in Latin America*, Washington, DC: Carnegie Endowment for International Peace.

Buvinic, Mayra and Vivian Roza (2004) "Women, Politics and Democratic Prospects in Latin America", Sustainable Development Department Technical Paper No. WID-108, Inter-American Development Bank, Washington, DC.

Castañeda, Jorge G. (2006) "Latin America's Left Turn", *Foreign Affairs* 85 (May–June), pp. 28–43.

Cheresky, Isidoro, ed. (2007) *Elecciones presidenciales y giro político en América Latina*, Buenos Aires: Manantial.

Coniff, Michael, ed. (1999) *Latin American Populism*, Tuscaloosa and London: University of Alabama Press.

Devraj, Ranjit (2004) "India, Brazil, South Africa Ready to Lead Global South", *Inter Press Service News Agency*, 5 March.

Dunkerley, James (2007) "Evo Morales, the 'Two Bolivias' and the Third Bolivarian Revolution", *Journal of Latin American Studies* 39(1), pp. 133–166.

ECLAC (2008) *Informe preliminar sobre las economías de América Latina y el Caribe*, Santiago: UN Economic Commission for Latin America and the Caribbean.

Endres, Alexandra (2008) "Die brasilianische Hoffnung", *Die Zeit*, 12 June.

Flemes, Daniel (2007) "Emerging Middle Powers' Soft Balancing Strategy: State and Perspectives of the IBSA Dialogue Forum", Working Paper No. 57, German Institute of Global and Area Studies, Hamburg.

Grugel, Jean, Pia Riggirozzi and Ben Thirkell-White (2008) "Beyond the Washington Consensus: Asia and Latin America in Search of More Autonomous Development", *International Affairs* 84(3), pp. 499–518.

Heine, Jorge (2006) "The Asian Giants and Latin America", *The Hindu*, 30 October.

——— (2007) "Women to the Fore: Feminizing Latin Politics", *The Hindu*, 13 December.

Hershberg, Eric and Fred Rosen, eds (2007) *Latin America after Neoliberalism: Turning the Tide in the Twenty-first Century?*, New York: New Press/North American Congress on Latin America.

Inter-American Dialogue (2008) *Women in the Americas: Paths to Political Power*, Washington, DC: Inter-American Dialogue.

McPherson, Alan (2006) *Intimate Ties, Bitter Struggles: The United States and Latin America since 1945*, Washington, DC: Potomac Books.

O'Donnell, Guillermo (2004) "Notas sobre la democracia en América Latina", in UNDP, *El debate conceptual sobre la democracia*, Santiago: UN Development Programme.

Oppenheimer, Andres (2007) "While Latin America Nationalizes, India and China Open Up", *The Miami Herald*, 18 January.

Oppenheimer, Michael F. (2007–2008) "The End of Liberal Globalization", *World Policy Journal* 24(4), pp. 1–9.

Portes, Alejandro and Kelly Hoffman (2003) "Latin American Class Structures: Their Composition and Change During the Neoliberal Era", *Latin American Research Review* 38(1), pp. 41–82.

Reid, Michael (2007) *The Forgotten Continent: The Battle for Latin America's Soul*, New Haven, CT: Yale University Press.

Robertson, Roland (1992) *Globalization: Social Theory and Global Culture*, London: Sage.

Rosales, Osvaldo and Mikio Kuwayama (2007) *América Latina, China e India: Hacia una nueva alianza de comercio e inversión*, Santiago: UN Economic Commission for Latin America and the Caribbean.

Rosenberg, Tina (2007) "The New Nationalization: Where Hugo Chávez's 'Oil Socialism' Is Taking the Developing World", *New York Times Magazine*, 4 November.

Saul, John Ralston (2006) *The Collapse of Globalism and the Reinvention of the World*, Camberwell: Penguin.

Scholte, Jan Aart (2005) *Globalization: A Critical Introduction*, 2nd edn, Basingstoke: Palgrave.

The Economist (2006) "The Democracy Dividend", *The Economist*, 9 December.

——— (2008) "Liberation Politics: Paraguay's Elections", *The Economist*, 17 April.

UNDP (2004) *La democracia en América Latina: Hacia una democracia de ciudadanos y ciudadanas*, Santiago: UN Development Programme.

van Cott, Donna Lee (2005) *From Movements to Parties in Latin America: The Evolution of Ethnic Politics*, New York: Cambridge University Press.

Vilas, Carlos M. (2006) "The Left in South America and the Resurgence of National-Popular Regimes", in Eric Hershberg and Fred Rosen, eds, *Latin America after Neoliberalism: Turning the Tide in the Twenty-first Century?*, New York: New Press/North American Congress on Latin America.

Whitehead, Laurence (2005) *Latin America: A New Interpretation*, New York: Palgrave Macmillan.

Williamson, Robert C. (2006) *Latin America: Cultures in Conflict*, Basingstoke: Palgrave.

World Bank (2006) *Latin America and the Caribbean's Responses to the Growth of China and India: Overview of Research Findings and Policy Implications*, Washington, DC: World Bank.

Part I

The Americas at a crossroads

1

Navigating in a fog: Metanarrative in the Americas today

Laurence Whitehead

The exhaustion of the metanarrative?

In 1979 Jean-François Lyotard introduced the term "metanarrative" (Lyotard, [1979] 1984).[1] It was his argument that, in the post-Enlightenment modern era, knowledge and experience were legitimated through metanarratives (or their variants, "grand narratives" and "master narratives"): master stories that structured and gave meaning to all lesser "stories".[2] He further argued, however, that in contrast with the condition of modernity, the postmodern condition is characterized by increasing "incredulity" towards metanarratives and their inherent claim of explaining the totality of experience. As he put it, "The narrative function is losing its functors, its great hero, its great dangers, its great voyages, its great goal. It is being dispersed in clouds of narrative language elements" (ibid.: xxiv–xxv).[3] Along with other postmodernists after him, Lyotard viewed "incredulity" towards the metanarrative as a positive development because metanarratives not only obscured the heterogeneity of reality (so that identifying them and ceasing to believe them is a way to "see" better) but also did not simply serve to "explain" disparate events and create a coherent account of reality, but rather to *legitimate* existing human knowledge and power relations.

Lyotard's concept of the metanarrative has been uncritically embraced by some scholars in the human sciences and equally forcefully rejected by many others. It operates at such a grand level of abstraction that its critics fault it as immune to falsification. (Some go on to criticize it as yet

Which way Latin America? Hemispheric politics meets globalization, Cooper and Heine, eds, United Nations University Press, 2009, ISBN 978-92-808-1172-8

another metanarrative of the kind it purports to expose.) This chapter adopts a different approach. It explores the utility of Lyotard's hypothesis when applied within a particular spatial and temporal context – namely, the Western hemisphere after the end of the Cold War. This contextualization involves a sharp change of gear. It shifts the argument down from the very general and abstract to a more directly observable and perhaps even testable level of analysis. The stories considered here apply to identifiable places and events (as any compelling narrative will do). Yet this contextualization may still rest on metanarrative assumptions; these more grounded stories may still organize and legitimize power relations and suppress discordant perspectives; they still function as totalizing and teleologically directed interpretations of modernity; and they may still elicit growing incredulity as their unilinearities are exposed and heterogeneous realities crowd back in.

Obviously, these stories are all selective – they cannot encapsulate everything of interest about the development of hemispheric relations since 1990. Here, I use them to highlight major underlying trends and reassess familiar historical patterns from an unfamiliar theoretical perspective. Each story or narrative strand emphasizes a particular set of causal linkages and downplays others: it "maps" the terrain according to a simplifying logic that can be illuminating for some purposes and some users but that is misleading (or disempowering) for others. So, there are always social and political interests associated with the propagation of each successive discourse. But in the space available it is not possible to say much about where each narrative comes from. Other chapters in this volume help to provide that missing context.

This chapter, then, takes the notion of the "metanarrative" as the starting point in considering the ways in which various kinds of "subnarratives" have shaped, and continue to shape, politics, economics and society in Latin America and, more broadly, in the Americas. More specifically, all three subnarratives I examine here can be seen as derivative strands of the grand metanarrative of post-Enlightenment modernity, as posited by Lyotard.

The dominant strand is "optimistic" and "liberal internationalist". In it, human happiness, freedom and progress are achieved through democracy, free markets and rationalized government. It is the strand that was converted from a master narrative into an absolute truth by the "end of history" argument that Francis Fukuyama (1992) proposed. The second strand, the "Marxist strand" or the regional variant of the original, is critical.

The third, neoconservative strand is somewhat different because, unlike the first two, which both offer up "utopias" (liberal liberty and justice or socialist emancipation), neoconservatives offer only a defensive strategy to protect the frontiers of areas of liberty (even as it eats away at them). In this sense, it is a "pessimistic" subnarrative rather than a "critical" one, as it offers no alternative. If one were to give it a label, it would be the neoconservative narrative of the "clash of civilizations" that Samuel Huntington (1996) proposed in response to Fukuyama's millennial enthusiasm. All subnarratives contain dominant dualities or oppositions between what is to be avoided and what is to be pursued – capitalist oppression versus the dictatorship of the proletariat; the state of nature and oppression versus the rule of law and liberal liberty, with an emphasis on free markets. In this neoconservative strand, conflict is understood to be between a free, "civilized", democratic, enlightened "West" and a not-free, totalitarian, unenlightened "Islam". Translated into a more specific policy realm, it poses a conflict between peace-loving free societies and terror networks emanating from that particular "civilizational field". In Latin America it makes its appearance as a new securitized discourse favouring hard-line policing and repression of "undesirables" of all kinds. This strand can still be situated within a metanarrative of modernity, but it is fearful. Despite the neoconservative vision of "spreading democracy" to the dark corners of the earth, it focuses less on progress and "upward movement" (like the liberal internationalist strand and the Marxist one in its heyday) and more on "defensive offensive" action against those it considers to be the "enemy". It is, more than the other two, a subnarrative based on fear.[4]

These three interpretative frames, each providing a different "worldview" or historically based interpretative schema, have all played a role as "ordering" and "legitimating" stories for the Americas and have competed for attention in the region.

I have previously argued (Whitehead, 2005) that Latin America as a large world region has been characterized historically – and, therefore, has specificities that set it apart form other large and "developing" world regions – by an outward-looking, top-down reformist bent. Its élites have tended to look to the core Enlightenment countries to find "maps" to navigate their "territory". They have tended also to opt for élite-led projects in an attempt to reshape or tame that territory to fit more neatly or comply with the normative goals prescribed by those maps, or to deploy a repertoire of post-Enlightenment metanarratives of modernity which have functioned as maps to navigate, make sense of and legitimate the territory.[5] Thus, to give a shorthand example, in the era when the Keynesian and neo-Marxist *dependentista* narratives prevailed, protectionism and state control of resources were preferred and legitimated; and in the era of neoliberal metanarratives, liberalization and privatization are preferred and legitimated. As this example suggests, at some points one narrative strand or map has dominated, shadowing all others;

at other times the narratives or maps appear to be superimposed, so that different "projects of modernity" compete for attention at the same time.

Ultimately, all such maps or narratives have proved to be inadequate. As rival totalizing interpretations, they have all been unable to capture and monopolize the collective imagination of national societies or major regional groupings. Thus, different variants of these narratives or maps have made repeated appearances, without one ever having won over the others permanently.

Never has this overlaying of maps, or fragmentation of interpretative stories, seemed starker than it is today. It is true that, even at the height of the Cold War, many political actors paid little more than lip service to the prevailing ideological orthodoxies, and seized every opportunity to broaden the scope for more parochial initiatives to produce more tangible and immediate benefits. Equally, powerful undercurrents of societal resistance to "metanarrative regimentation" have been reinforced by democratization and the entry of new groups and interests into the collective debate. Economic liberalization, the retreat of the state and the rise and fall of transnational networks and international diasporas have also added to this new pluralism and dispersion of outlooks.

So it is not just the demonstrable failings of successive worldviews that have produced the current need to "navigate in a fog" – broader sociopolitical and socio-economic forces are also pushing in that direction. Whatever the case, liberalism now appears to compete with nationalism, populism and the darker themes of "civilizational" conflict or its local variant, "securitized" discourses of fear; and none seems to dominate over another sufficiently to provide a sense of unity of direction. This certainly appears to be the case since the rise of the neoconservatives in Washington.

The current overlaying of maps or narratives, or the sense that Latin America is navigating "in a fog", may illustrate the more general phenomenon that Lyotard and others say characterizes the "postmodern" world: the end of standardized, mass-produced, unified ways of thinking that accompanies the end of Fordist ways of manufacturing products. It is possible that one of the factors contributing to the lack of credibility of the last dominant metanarrative to operate in the Americas has something to do with postmodern "incredulity", or that the Western hemisphere has definitively lost faith in its integrative geopolitical trajectory and/or identity. Alternatively, it is possible that what is now in place is a new postmodern metanarrative, in the sense that it is more fragmented, more of a collection of *petit récits* than an easily identifiable single whole.

But while I borrow from Lyotard, I take no position on whether postmodern incredulity is more real or more imagined, or on whether the theories of postmodernists are giving rise to new metanarratives adapted to a new phase in human history rather than abolishing them altogether. What I do broadly agree with is that metanarratives structure and order reality by providing maps to navigate the territory; that they give reality a certain meaning and direction; and that, in doing so, they serve to structure and legitimate many other areas of decision-making and political, social and economic action. My interest is to examine how this useful theoretical device works on the ground in the Americas, and the more modest claim I put forward is that, after three successive and competing worldviews have foundered within the span of a generation, there is – at least for the time being and in this particular regional setting – an understandable scepticism about all such comprehensive political schemas.

The question, then, is what guiding principles, shared interests and regional dynamics are available to shape the next stage of the politics of the Western hemisphere (whether cooperative or conflictive), given the rapid sequential exhaustion of three successive strands of narratives? For a while after 11 September 2001, it was possible to believe that the Bush administration might unilaterally impose an agenda for the Americas that was not consensual or responsive to dominant local aspirations. However, the evisceration of the neoconservative alternative to liberal internationalism seems so complete that I work from the assumption that the US neoconservative project has passed beyond the point of no return. But there can be no straightforward return to the liberal internationalist aspirations of the 1990s. Among other reasons, although it has lost credibility and momentum, the logic of the "war on terror" will remain an influence throughout the region, probably for at least another generation. It cannot override other, more rooted regional realities, but nor can it simply be forgotten or undone. While "twenty-first century socialism" is even less plausible as a metanarrative than was its twentieth-century predecessor, it is still a presence to be reckoned with. Thus, in the absence of any credible metanarrative capable of bringing together the diverse political actors in the region, Latin America appears to be "navigating in a fog".

This may be just a temporary interlude. The neoconservative deviation never had much appeal in most of the new democracies of Latin America for understandable reasons (it is too reminiscent of the "national security" dictatorships of the 1970s), and there was broad short-term disaffection with the Bush administration. At the same time, Andean *cosmovisiones*, *globalophobia* and *Castrophilia* do not represent coherent challenges to liberalism, conceived as a broad and all-inclusive framework encompassing mainstream cooperation across the Americas. Thus, in this view, underlying liberal and modernizing assumptions remain in place and can readily be reactivated once this particular anomalous episode of unilateral assertiveness has been reabsorbed; the region's basic liberal metanarrative remains intact, current disarray represents more than a pause before regrouping and with a little good luck and some repositioning in Washington the prior direction of progress can soon be resumed. Perhaps so, but at a minimum this assumption requires some interrogation.

Three narratives that strain "credulity"

The "Marxist" narrative

The failures of the world communist (or at least Soviet) prospectus have been so exhaustively laboured that it suffices to say that Soviet Bolshevism proved a false option as a theory of history, as a system of economic organization, as the hegemonic belief system of a world power and as a project for human liberation. In North America, the failure of this worldview was complete about a half-century before the collapse of the Soviet Union. In Latin America and the Caribbean, what survived into the 1980s was a very selective and filtered version of the original worldview, a minority disposition. But from 1959 onwards these inherent weaknesses were disguised (some would say superseded) by the Cuban revolution, as the doubtful attractions of Russian communism were outshone by the more resonant appeal of Castroism. Although this was very much a minority taste – particularly appealing to students, intellectuals and, later, some Catholic as well as traditional anti-clerical audiences – it was still an eloquent and relatively coherent worldview, structured by its defiance of US hegemony and its privileged alignment with Washington's great rival in the bipolar contest.

Whereas US opinion quickly and uniformly came to view the Cuban model as evidence of Moscow's imperial and totalitarian ambitions, many opinion-makers outside the United States (even those opposed to Castro) were unable to shake off a sneaking admiration for the one leader in the Western hemisphere who always retorted to the hegemonic power, and offered the (remote) promise of an integral alternative to subordinate status within a pan-American strait-jacket. Evidence of the genuine mobilizing power of this metanarrative is provided by Allende's Chile, Sandinista Nicaragua and a range of shorter or less successful experiments in Bolivia, Uruguay, Venezuela and even Grenada.

To summarize, the idea of a Marxist-led movement of popular liberation became a genuine totalizing project in parts of South America in the 1960s and 1970s, and in Central America in the 1980s. The closure of this cycle came not with the fall of the Berlin Wall in November 1989 but in February 1990 with the defeat of the Sandinistas in a genuinely competitive election.[6]

The liberal internationalist "end of history" narrative

In 1989 the Berlin Wall came down and the Soviet utopia dissolved. One of the key doctrinal challenges that had long structured North and Latin American understandings of the world, and the role of the Americas within it, disappeared. In Washington many saw this as the "end of history", the inauguration of a unipolar world in which US-derived ideals of individualism, democracy and market freedom would become universalized. From this perspective, the elimination of the communist option guaranteed the permanent ascendancy of a rival liberal internationalist utopia. Far from inaugurating the eclipse of all utopian projects, the destruction of a false alternative would pave the way for global acceptance of the one right model, the "last best" hope of humanity: an idealized account of the United States writ large.

So, with the fall of the Wall and, later, of the Sandinistas in Nicaragua, many opinion-makers throughout the Western hemisphere concluded that a unipolar metanarrative would prevail without further contest. This was the message conveyed by the Free Trade Area of the Americas (FTAA) project launched by President Bush senior, the North American Free Trade Agreement (NAFTA) and the 1994 Miami Summit of the Americas process initiated by President Clinton. For Latin America and the Caribbean this prospect may have seemed less enticing than from within the Washington Beltway, but, like it or not, the direction of history seemed clear. It seemed best to climb on the bandwagon, join NAFTA, participate in the FTAA and sign up to the Democratic Charter of the Organization of American States (OAS), at least to help protect some otherwise-fragile political rights. Some may have resisted, and the Cuban regime may have stubbornly defied the inevitable but, out of conviction or a prudent sense of realism, the great majority of the political and economic élites of the region repositioned themselves as adherents of the prevailing creed.

Although there was something strained and artificial about the underlying consensus, even at the height of convergence around the time of the Miami Summit of the Americas in December 1994, it nonetheless reflected a powerful metanarrative signalling a coordinated direction of historical change: market liberalization, open regionalism, the reinforcement of liberal constitutionalism and honestly counted and competitive elections. Consumer rights (as opposed to producer rights) gained more traction, both within many domestic markets and through international reinforcement (with the single-market process within the European Union and the hub-and-spoke system of so-called free trade agreements in the Americas, for instance). Not only in the electoral domain but also in other mainly market-related spheres, the longstanding nominal entitlement to individual rights was underpinned by more effective systems of monitoring and enforcement. Although the mass media operated within narrow limits and with a largely anti-political framework, the scope for pluralism of information and opinion was somewhat broadened, at least compared with Cold War orthodoxies. And the internet permitted forms of horizontal communication and political expression from below that may have partly offset the decline of more traditional variants of mass political activism. The various components of the package seemed to fit together as a reasonably coherent and mutually supportive whole. They also offered the prospect of material and symbolic benefits for a wide range of actors, provided they were adept at reinventing themselves in accordance with the new hegemonic script.[7]

The totalizing vision was backed by strong intellectual and research credentials promoted by the Washington-based international financial institutions and the leading centres of modern social science across the region. It was articulated through a powerful media consensus, and backed by the international business community, particularly the financial sector. It was not, however, purely an economic project. The "democratic convergence" component of the liberalization agenda was also powerful. It brought to the fore the National Endowment for Democracy and the OAS. It was a vision that was now broad enough for civilian political leaders of different political persuasions to rally round and use as they competed in elections.[8] (It is worth noting the significant array of former Marxist thinkers, still in search of a transformative doctrine, who recognized in liberal internationalism a functional if reverse equivalent of the movement they had just left.) Hitherto-powerful blocking interests such as military establishments, nationalists and protectionists also disappeared from view with an alacrity that would have aroused suspicion were it not for the fact that the momentum seemed unstoppable in the 1990s. This constituted a vastly broader movement than the previous pro-communist surge. For a time, anyone with any ambition had to climb on the bandwagon, since the outcome seemed preordained, and any who resisted or lagged behind seemed doomed to lose influence and political capital.

But liberal internationalism (and the FTAA process in particular) also ground to a halt. First, the picture just sketched exaggerates the extent of adherence to the new dispensation: Brazil responded to these developments quite differently than Argentina (more slowly and reluctantly);

NAFTA was on offer to Mexico only (and the "tequila" crisis of 1995 immediately exposed the drawbacks and fragilities of that project); and power groups such as the guerrillas in Colombia, the military in Guatemala and the judiciary in Chile interpreted the new opportunities in accordance with their own specific endowments and encumbrances. It took time to understand the full ramifications of the Soviet eclipse and the true extent of the liberal internationalist impulse. It was not only communism that was comprehensively discredited; social democracy sustained heavy damage as well. Globalization demoted trade unions, challenged widespread statist assumptions and reinforced the power of mobile finance capital.

Thus, the post–Cold War political climate in the Americas in the 1990s was more nuanced and complex, and this hegemonic script might have transformed itself into a more broadly based and socially rooted model of liberal internationalism. But, just like the one before it, this post–Cold War metanarrative, perhaps never more than a fantasy or a "road not taken", was superseded by events. Many of those who embraced its tenets with unfeigned enthusiasm are now working hard to reposition themselves as sceptics of neoliberalism or, indeed – to quote the ingenious terminology invented by Ernesto Zedillo just as the movement was going into reverse – as *globalofóbicos*. What happened to explain the crumbling of this second metanarrative?

First, the stampede to join the winning side was so massive and undignified that many early enthusiasts were sure to become disillusioned. One has only to consider the credibility of Argentina's Carlos Menem as the standard-bearer of modern liberties, of Mexico's PRI (Partido Revolucionario Institucional) as the scourge of electoral malpractice, of Carlos Andrés Pérez and Acción Democrática in Venezuela as the enemies of statism and clientelism or of El Salvador's ARENA party as the guarantor of human rights. All this was only temporarily credible with a great suspension of disbelief. In due course, the "inconvenient truths" that were overlooked resurfaced.

Second, the neoliberal model failed to deliver on its promises, at least after the sudden stop of capital flows to emerging markets in 1998. And third, the FTAA inducement depended upon the willingness of the US Congress to continue operating within the broad framework of "liberal internationalism". Even before the end of the Clinton presidency, it had become clear that Congress was more eager to promote counternarcotics victories (Plan Colombia) than greater economic and political liberalization. It turned out that there was more effective protectionist resistance (combined with anti-illegal-immigration sentiment) in North America than in much of the South.

The "civilizational" narrative of war on terror

On top of all these difficulties came the defeat of Gore by Bush, the shock of 9/11 and the attempted coup against the elected president of Venezuela in April 2002. Like the impact of February 1990 in Nicaragua on the Marxist subnarrative, this last incident can be regarded as a defining moment, when the already-tattered liberal internationalist interpretation failed the most visible of reality tests. From then on, the liberal internationalist script was comprehensively displaced by the logic of the "war on terror". Even in the Western hemisphere (where no Islamic terrorism or weapons of mass destruction could be sighted or even concocted), security became the watchword, to the detriment of liberty.

Even so, the liberal internationalist perspective was not yet exhausted, and the neoconservative strand was not a complete repudiation of its precursor. There was certainly some ideological repositioning, as well as a partial rotation of personnel, but the main shift was a move from ungrounded optimism about the world to defensive panic and the fragility of Western civilization. Although the security obsessions of 2001–2008 are neither as broadly based nor as durable as their Cold War liberal precursor worldview, there are substantial groups and activist communities for whom the fear of further mass attacks provides an organizing principle that overshadows all "normal" politics. The US security services provide the core constituency, with a professional interest in promoting this outlook, but there are also powerful business and media interests, and a wide variety of otherwise marginal – mostly conservative – lobbies have gained traction by rallying to the neoconservative banner and catering for the public opinion it serves. For at least the first three years after 11 September 2001, fear of international terrorism controlled much of US popular imagination, including most Republicans, many Democrats and the great bulk of the media. Outside North America, some ingenuity was necessary to join the crusade against such an imprecisely defined evil "other", not least because the source of danger seemed so remote. But the Uribe version of Plan Colombia, the *mano super dura* in El Salvador and various Cuban-American campaigns all mimicked the prevailing mindset, enlisting Washington's patronage for other purposes.

The Washington-based neoconservative bloc was united around a clearly defined and interlocking set of beliefs and prescriptions that, for about five years after the World Trade Center atrocity, seemed capable of generating a coherent set of policies for the United States. Neoconservative policies were assertive, unilateral, military- and security-based and "transformational". They divided the world into loyal (and subordinate) allies and fanatical enemies, squeezing all intermediate positions and overriding the other interests and aspirations of all secondary players.

So long as the US government (the executive, unimpeded by the judiciary and endorsed by Congress) seemed united and confident in its pursuit of this agenda, and so long as it was possible to believe that the proposed global transformation might have some substantive moral content, this narrowly based project seemed almost credible as an alternative metanarrative. But it was always too artificial, intellectually strained and time limited to constitute a genuine alternative to either Cold War liberalism or liberal internationalism.

Had Al Qaeda proved capable of further mass atrocities, such as a dirty bombing in a US city, it may have lasted rather longer as a serious threat. In the absence of such spectacular validation of neoconservative threat perceptions, however, the dismal consequences of their drastic new doctrine in Iraq, Afghanistan, Palestine and Guantánamo sapped support from the neoconservative coalition. Even the US executive began to display fissures, which culminated in the 2006 resignation of Secretary of Defense Donald Rumsfeld from the Pentagon. The Democrats had caved in 2001 and lost the presidential election of 2004, but in November 2006 they recaptured Congress and restored its function as a check on an overweening executive. Even the Supreme Court hesitantly began to defend the rule of law. As these shifts occurred within US politics, it became apparent even to Washington's most loyal allies that US public opinion was no longer so traumatized by the indignity of 11 September and, therefore, it was no longer so obvious that what now seemed a limited Bush-Cheney agenda should be supported.

The many subordinate allies (notably in Latin America and the Caribbean) that had been restrained by public opinion from lending their wholehearted endorsement to neoconservative doctrines now found more room to express their various national priorities. Political attention turned again to problems that had been sidelined in the face of an immediate and existential "terrorist" threat (problems such as environmental degradation and non-terrorist variants of international criminality).[9] But it would be misleading to view this shift as a restoration of the *status quo ante*. Although the neoconservative metanarrative is no longer ascendant, its disruptive effects (and various contextual global and regional changes that have occurred since the 1990s) prevent a straightforward return to the liberal internationalism of the last century.

The disintegration of the neoconservative worldview leaves a void rather than a new unitary schema, for three broad reasons that are general, but also specific to the Western hemisphere.

First, although the neoconservative master narrative may no longer dominate all Western policy priorities, its effects remain in place, as does the lingering legacy of the "war on terror". Although the "with us or against us" psychology of 2002–2005 has faded in the absence of any further major atrocities in the Western hemisphere, it has not disappeared and may be revived by any further incident. There is a permanent element in the institutional shifts precipitated by the "war on terror" (from the State Department to the Pentagon, for instance, or from immigration reform to homeland security, and from international mobility to border controls). It will take years before the memory of Guantánamo fades sufficiently to allow Washington's self-appointed leadership in the promotion of human rights and the rule of law to recover. The unifying dynamic of the Miami Summit process is probably irretrievable, and the OAS Democratic Charter and the Inter-American Commission on Human Rights have been lastingly downgraded.

Second, the alternative policy concerns that were postponed and neglected and the many suppressed or overlooked aspirations of Washington's hemispheric allies are now resurfacing as a discordant cacophony of fragmented and difficult-to-satisfy demands. Energy trends in the Western hemisphere vividly illustrate this point. The "war on terror" has not increased the security of Middle Eastern hydrocarbon reserves, nor has it promoted austerity moves among North American consumers. Consequently, oil prices have reached a new plateau, with serious implications for both the cost of imports and the security of the supply reaching a large number of small, energy-deficient states in the region. The major oil companies face shrinking access to promising prospects outside North America, as taxes contract and exploration rights shift the balance of power towards the state-owned enterprises of Latin America and the Caribbean. Several key state enterprises may find it difficult, however, to maintain and expand production in accordance with external demand and their theoretical resource endowments. In short, hydrocarbon security in the Western hemisphere is becoming more precarious. The neoconservative focus on "terrorism" thus neglected one of the most basic realist objectives: protecting regional supplies and effectively managing energy interdependence. A similar case can be made in several other crucial policy areas. Climate change may pose a far greater existential threat to human security in the Americas than anything Al Qaeda can do. The neoconservatives were interested in concentrating unilateral power to "defeat evil", but not in multilateral cooperation to tackle shared environmental challenges. Another decade is thus elapsing without effective answers to a problem whose consequences have been magnified. As the glaciers disappear and the aquifers are drained, zero-sum conflicts tend to crowd out the space required for constructive cooperation.

Illegal migration, internal displacement and the proliferation of transnational crime networks also fragment the capacity for region-wide policy coordination, both by eroding the legitimacy of the constituted authorities and by shortening the time horizons within which effective action is required. In short, Washington's allies in the hemisphere lack a unifying theme to replace the FTAA and the "war on terror". They have inherited a multiplicity of neglected and pressing problems that tend to pit them against each other rather than generate a collective response.

Third, partly as a result of the first two trends, what is emerging in the wake of a discredited neoconservative metanarrative is not just the reassertion of longstanding but marginalized aspirations; rather, counter-ideologies such as anti-globalization and even "twenty-first-century socialism" have gained credibility with the observable failings of both liberal internationalism and neoconservatism. There is a broader spread of ideological positions or less underlying consensus than before on what should be the regulatory principles governing public policy choices in the Western hemisphere. Thus, for the time being at least, the various governments of the Americas could find themselves "navigating without a map".

One of the effects of this shift is that the United States now has fewer reliable allies and more disaffected (or even hostile) partners to contend with in its own hemisphere. The recent (and perhaps temporary) upsurge of *chavismo* constitutes the most surprising and visible manifestation of this loss of regional consensus, but the phenomenon extends well beyond Venezuela. Economic liberalization and privatization are widely believed to have delivered unequal and, overall, disappointing results in many Latin American countries. Resource nationalism and some variants of state interventionism, therefore, have recaptured some lost ground. The post-2002 rise in most commodity prices has, at least temporarily, eased traditional balance-of-payments constraints, and the surge in demand from Asia has drawn attention to the success of the Chinese and Indian economic models, which are at considerable variance with the prescriptions of the Washington Consensus. Hitherto-authoritative prescriptions emanating from the Washington-based international financial institutions are no longer either so credible or unavoidable, and relatively heterodox policies that were off limits in the 1990s have begun to regain traction not only in Caracas and Quito, but also in Buenos Aires, La Paz and potentially across much of South America (in Mexico and Central America, the scope for economic disengagement from North America is far narrower).

In addition to these macroeconomic shifts, there is also a political mood change and potentially even some scope for geopolitical realignments. The isolation of Cuba has lessened as the moral authority of the United States has diminished (denunciations of prison conditions on the island sound less convincing when made by those in charge of Guantánamo). The attractions of open and inclusive forms of democratization apparently on offer in the 1990s have not always trumped narrower and more security-obsessed *democraduras* favoured by the United States since 2001. Faced with that unappealing variant of democracy, a significant section of opinion – not just in oil-exporting nations or in South America – may prefer alternative socially redistributive projects, notwithstanding the familiar drawbacks of "populism". In short, the current challenge to regional consensus emanating from Venezuela needs to be understood in a broader context. However Chávez fares, his appeal reflects the discredit of the previous hegemonic metanarratives. His "twenty-first-century socialism" may fall far short of constituting a coherent or viable counteroffer to previous versions of *pensamiento único* – in my opinion, it can never achieve the status of an alternative metanarrative (as per pre-1990 communism) – but its significance is more than local and transitory. It confirms the disintegration of regional consensus in the wake of Washington's neoconservative excursus and its collapse.

Conclusion: Who needs a map?

One response to the foregoing analysis is to accept its broad thrust but to dismiss its significance. A "realist" line of response could be that only those few commentators and opinion-formers whose livelihoods depend on parsing the prevailing metanarrative need concern themselves with the exhaustion of such all-encompassing but relatively vacuous discourses, and that, for the most part, pan-American relations and inter-hemispheric bargains and adjustments go ahead on the basis of the same national interest and power-political calculations whatever the ostensible overarching rationale. Small states, weak governments and competitive political actors are always "navigating without a map", no matter how well versed in prevailing rhetoric they seem. On this basis, nothing of importance follows from the exhaustion of successive hegemonic rationalizations, not even from the temporarily embarrassing discredit of the neoconservatives. It is only if US hard power has been damaged by Iraq that any lasting consequences will flow for hemispheric relations.[10]

However, the discredit of these three narrative strands cannot be dismissed as easily as realists might contend. The consequences of conducting hemispheric relations without an underlying consensus on objectives or a master narrative to coordinate the diverse participants need to be considered from two distinct angles. There are consequences for the dominant (or hegemonic) player, and consequences for all secondary actors.

From the standpoint of the US government, although it is no doubt possible to postpone and downgrade hemispheric policies while focusing on more urgent challenges elsewhere, it is neither expedient nor practical to dispense altogether with a strategy for the Americas. From a hard realist standpoint, it might seem sufficient to identify and reward certain unwavering allies and to isolate or sanction any troublesome dissident regimes. That might leave most players free to pursue their own interests within the boundaries set by these two extremes. The dominance and inevitability of US power might speak for itself, without the need for any great metanarrative or ostentatious efforts at regional coordination. But history indicates the limits to such an approach, one that roughly describes US policy prior to the Cuban revolution of 1959.

The assumption that US power speaks for itself was shaken by defeat in Viet Nam in 1975 and the Iranian hostage crisis of 1979, and might come under pressure again if the Middle East situation does not improve. What these precedents suggest is that, after setbacks, it can be very much in Washington's interest to regain the initiative, reset the hemispheric agenda and promote a coordinated set of pan-American initiatives held together by some headline justification (like the Alliance for Progress or the Miami Summit process). Such discursive moves should not be dismissed as inconsequential rhetoric. They create expectations, circumvent obstructions and raise the profile of the United States in its neighbourhood. Although partly declaratory and subject to highly interested and selective interpretation, projects of this kind also commit resources and can engage domestic interests as well as enlisting external cooperation. Although such metanarratives depend heavily on diplomacy and the mobilization of soft power, they also capitalize on the material and even military capabilities of the United States. Only a very narrow construction of the realist position could overlook the great benefits that the United States has derived as a global superpower from its unusually benign relationship with its immediate neighbours (in contrast with Britain and Ireland, or China and Viet Nam, not to mention Russia and its "near abroad"). A century or more of history supports the idea that, at least from the standpoint of the regional hegemon, there is something concrete to be gained from the promotion of an overarching pan-American discourse. Thus continuing to pursue an insouciant stance after the failure of the neoconservatives could carry with it substantial medium-term costs.

An idea of the costs that the United States is already paying for this "turn" can be garnered from the latest survey by the Pew Global Attitudes Project (2007: 3), which reports that anti-Americanism is "deeper but not wider" globally, while, among its oldest allies, "The U.S. image ... continues to decline". As regards Latin America, there is good news and bad news. On the positive side:

majorities in four of the seven Latin American nations included in the survey – including Venezuela (56%) – have a positive opinion of the U.S.... [although] Brazilians (44% favourable, 51% unfavourable) and Bolivians (42% favourable, 52% unfavourable) are somewhat more likely to have a negative opinion of the U.S. than a positive one. (Ibid.: 14)

Views of US culture and technology are also overwhelmingly positive in Latin America (Argentina 50 per cent favourable towards US culture, 51 per cent favourable towards US technology; Bolivia 49 per cent and 71 per cent; Chile 58 per cent and 67 per cent; Mexico 53 per cent and 62 per cent; Peru 50 per cent and 78 per cent; and Venezuela 71 per cent and 76 per cent). Also positive is that

there is generally no gap between how America and its people are viewed. For example, in Mexico about the same number rate the U.S. (56%) and Americans (52%) favourably, and the same is true in Bolivia, Brazil, Chile and Peru. Venezuelans give Americans higher ratings (64% favourable) than they give the United States itself (56% favourable), although both the people and the country are relatively popular. In Argentina, there is a 10-point gap between ratings of Americans (26% favourable) and the United States (16% favourable). (Ibid.: 19)

On the negative side:

The image of the United States has eroded since 2002 in all six Latin American countries for which trends are available. The decline has been especially steep in Venezuela (26 points), Argentina (18 points), and Bolivia (15 points) ... Five years ago, majorities in both [Brazil and Bolivia] felt favourably toward the U.S. Meanwhile, negative views of the U.S. in Argentina, which were clearly evident five years ago, have only intensified. Indeed, the balance of opinion toward the U.S. among Argentines (16% favourable, 72% unfavourable) is worse than in any country surveyed outside the Middle East. (Ibid.: 14)

In Venezuela, "favourable opinions [of the United States] have declined by nearly 30 percentage points since 2002, though a majority (56%) still has a positive impression of the U.S." (ibid.: 8).

While US technology and culture are still viewed in a positive light, Latin Americans have a much more negative view of the prospect of the spread of US ideas, particularly US views of democracy (Bolivia 19 per cent; Chile 24 per cent; Mexico 23 per cent; Peru 29 per cent; Venezuela 37 per cent). As regards views of the US approach to business, these

have also grown more negative in much of Latin America. Distaste for American-style business is up 20 percentage points in Venezuela since 2002, and 15 points in Mexico; it also has increased by 13 points in Argentina, where two-thirds of the public now say they do not care for American ideas about business. The only exception to this trend is Bolivia, where the number of people who dislike American ways of doing business has declined by a modest five points. (Ibid.: 26)

The view of US unilateralism is mixed, "with Argentines overwhelmingly saying the U.S. ignores their interests, while almost two-thirds of Venezuelans say American foreign policy does incorporate their concerns" (ibid.: 21). And as regards the "war on terror", "support has also weakened in the Western Hemisphere, with sharp drops in Venezuela and Canada" (ibid.: 22). Finally, "In each of the seven Latin American countries surveyed, more distrust than trust Bush by margins of at least two-to-one. Confidence is particularly low in Argentina (87% little or no confidence) and Brazil (80%)" (ibid.: 62).

Overall, it would appear that that the United States is living "on credit": its image is still marginally more positive than negative because of better past behaviour and shared values, but its prestige and "credit rating" have dropped sharply over the past few years as a result of its unilateralist turn. Even in the area of values, the fact that "American ideas about democracy" are no longer popular says a lot about the failure of that country to match its democracy-promoting rhetoric with its own behaviour at home and abroad.

For the three reasons discussed above, it will not be easy for Washington to recapture the hemispheric initiative any time soon. No Alliance for Progress or Miami Summit substitute is likely to be on offer, given continuing US fears of terrorism and external threats and the budget constraints imposed by this outlook. Even if some attractive new hemispheric strategic were to elicit the requisite domestic support, the response from potential partners is likely to be more awkward and questioning than on previous occasions. As we have seen, there is less agreement about basic priorities and more diversity of aspirations, and it may prove harder to bring hemispheric partners into line than was the case either during the Cold War or in the optimistic first flush of the post–Cold War era. Some Latin American countries may have interesting alternatives to consider (in Asia and elsewhere).[11] In addition, with the rise of transnational networks, diaspora communities and "intermestic" issues (such as immigration, remittances and drug trafficking), all future attempts to project US priorities into Latin America and the Caribbean will have to contend with powerful feedback and reverse flows. Whereas the Alliance for Progress and even the Miami Summit process could be viewed as reshaping the rest of the hemisphere without altering internal balances within the United States, future initiatives are likely to entail strong and visible consequences *within* the North American heartland.

This may not rule out all further experiments in region-wide coordination, but it will alter their dynamics and raise new barriers. In summary, from a US standpoint, navigating without a map is not cost-free, but charting a collectively agreed course has become more problematic.

From the perspective of the secondary parties involved, a first point to make is that they have a strong incentive to examine the behaviour of the hegemonic power and the changing constraints under which it operates in its region. In some (extreme) cases, the foreign policy analysis of a secondary player may consist of little more than a faithful reproduction of currently prevailing US attitudes and priorities. Even in such cases, however, there is likely to be a significant gap between the original and the imitation, for two main reasons.

First, it is typically very difficult for a secondary player to grasp the relative unimportance of its own position and interests compared to other claims on the superpower's attention. Imitation is almost always an attempt to appropriate something valued in Washington by giving it a local interpretation: "if there is a war on terror, we must recast our security policies to bring us to the forefront of that effort".

Second, by the time a secondary player has locked itself into what it judges to be the core priorities of the hegemonic power, it is liable to find that the debate in Washington has already moved on. (Thus, by the time El Salvador got its troops into the firing line in Iraq, the US public had already begun to lose its appetite for such operations.) In consequence, even the most unconditional backers of Washington's successive orthodoxies find that they cannot simply read from a preordained script. They, too, need independent agency, separate tactics and autonomous analysis. The same argument applies in reverse to those few players whose first instinct is to oppose or reject whatever the United States currently advocates. The Cubans certainly choose their confrontations carefully, having long experience of the costs of indiscriminate opposition. President Chávez may be less discriminating, but he still supplies a large proportion of the crude oil the United States imports, and he must be learning the hard way that some knee-jerk reactions are more counterproductive than others.

In between these two extremes, most governments in the Western hemisphere monitor US trends attentively, trying to avoid unnecessary exposure to issues tangential to their main concerns. They do not always expect to foresee the next lurch from Washington, but they try to build a reputation for prudent adjustments to the main thrust of US policy, accompanied by discreet reservations where a clear need or justification can be demonstrated. The history of Mexico's foreign policy provides a particularly clear example of this pattern – with the uncomfortable experience of chairing the UN Security Council at the time of the Iraq war as a strong reminder of the need for caution.

Following the apparent failure of the neoconservatives, it may be a little harder than before for any of these three categories of players to judge the lie of the land in Washington, and there is probably scope for more indiscipline and confusion. Some governments may conclude that a divided and demoralized United States could be more responsive to prodding or suggestions, but this is unlikely to produce predictable results. For the most part, therefore, the absence of a strong lead from Washington is more likely to produce disarray than a coherent or productive response in the Americas. Countries could find themselves competing against their neighbours for the attention of a distracted and erratic hegemon. Thus Argentina and Brazil disrupt the Southern Common Market (Mercosur) with their rival attitudes towards the United States; similarly with Colombia and Peru inside the Andean Community, and Canada and Mexico in NAFTA.

Navigating in a fog is not, however, just a matter of competing for the attention of an otherwise-involved United States. There are almost two-score nations and political jurisdictions in the Western hemisphere, and their external relations involve bilateral ties with immediate neighbours, subregional groupings, international organizations and linkages with extra-continental partners, as well as a "hub-and-spoke" focus on the United States. These other dimensions of external policy can be of considerable importance, particularly in South America. When there is a Cold War in progress, or a continent-wide thrust towards liberal convergence or even a global security threat like the one that emerged after 9/11, all other concerns can be ordered and reshaped in accordance with the dominant international rationale. But if there is no coherent general framework that can structure the foreign policy priorities of a secondary state, then each player is liable to proceed according to an independent and uncoordinated logic. Argentina may decide that Uruguay's proposed pulp-and-paper plant constitutes an external threat dwarfing other concerns. Bolivia may make it a matter of state policy to deny natural gas to Chile. Nicaragua may revive its territorial claim to the holiday islands of San Andrés and Providencia, long administered by Colombia. The congress of Peru may redraw its maritime boundaries to the detriment of the interests of Bolivia and Chile. Such issues are not new by any means, but in a context in which other, more unifying, collective projects have gone into abeyance, they are likely to rise to the surface and generate more heat.

So, with the United States distracted and parochial clashes of interests on the upsurge, does navigating in a fog imply the loss of all capacity for cooperative agreement in the Americas? Not necessarily. The key point is that, without an overarching regional project, framework or normative consensus – indeed, a metanarrative – and in the absence of strong and credible direction from Washington, regional or subregional agreements are likely to be more varied, competitive and looser, less stable. There may still be scope for a "Bolivarian Alternative", particularly if lubricated by Venezuelan oil revenues. The structural conditions promoting subregional integration schemes such as the Andean Community, Central American integration and Mercosur may remain in place, but each of these arrangements may be subjected to increased counter-pressures and international turbulence. The forces driving transnational cooperation in the Americas will not disappear, but they are likely to encounter more headwinds (to extend the nautical metaphor). Such driving forces include the pressing need to coordinate major infrastructure projects to permit the countries of the Americas to respond to the physical demands of globalization; the impossibility of effectively tackling region-wide issues such as deforestation, water scarcity, pollution or the control of international trafficking except via international agreements; and the growing influence of international diasporas.

Finally, there is the question of shared underlying values. Despite the (perhaps temporary) exhaustion of all three successive master metanarratives in the hemisphere, major areas of convergence still unite the countries of the region and differentiate the Western hemisphere from other regions. There are shared liberal ideas about the separation of powers, individual rights, freedom of expression, gender and tolerance of cultural differences, and shared religions and linguistic traditions. In terms of political practices, elections, decentralization, rotation in office, democracy and perhaps even popular sovereignty are shared values. Admittedly, such ideas and practices are variously interpreted in different parts of the region, and many find counterparts in at least some other large regions.

The diversity of interpretations and multiplicity of external reference points help to explain the absence of a single consensus, *pensamiento único*, or permanent metanarrative for the whole hemisphere. The common ground is sufficient, however, to generate a certain degree of tacit agreement and, indeed, regional cooperation, even in the absence of a directing hegemonic power or compelling master narrative. Despite the frictions between nations, the Western hemisphere has an exceptionally long history as a zone of peace (and the role of the military has been downgraded accordingly). Despite contending with many inequalities and injustices, the Inter-American Commission on Human Rights and the various ombudsmen still enjoy prestige and exert influence because of the shared aspirations they embody. Pan-American and subregional institutions may be relatively weak but they are also persistent, and reflect widespread preferences for negotiated solutions to disputes between nations. Thus, while the nations of the Americas may currently find themselves navigating in a fog, they are in familiar waters and have a patrimony of common navigational skills on which to draw.

Notes

1. The term makes its appearance in Lyotard's *The Postmodern Condition* (published first in French in 1979 and in English translation in 1984), which many consider to be the cornerstone of postmodern philosophy. The report was prepared in response to a request by the Conseil des universités du Québec to frame the debate about the possible impact of the use of computers in higher education.

2. At the heart of the Enlightenment metanarrative was a great quest that would lead man to ever-greater heights of happiness, prosperity and progress through reason and scientific knowledge. This grand narrative of post-Enlightenment modernity has various strands: the scientific metanarrative, which explains the world in Newtonian terms as being governed by laws that, once uncovered, will permit us to know all there is to know about the world; the philosophical metanarrative, consisting of belief in the possibility of finding a unifying philosophy that explains all of existence; and other critical strands, the most notable being the Marxist, with its binary opposition between capital and labour, but also the feminist one, for which the principal ordering reality is patriarchy, and even the Freudian one, for which the ordering principles are super ego, ego and id. Terms such as "capitalism", "liberalism" and "fascism", among other such "essentially contested concepts", can equally be seen as shorthand for what are complex metanarrative strands. An earlier pre-Enlightenment example of a metanarrative is that provided by religions such as Christianity, with its offer of the hope of life after death and redemption from sin in this world.

3. The cause of postmodern "incredulity", in Lyotard's view, was the rise in the postmodern era (that is, after the Second World War) of cybernetics, or the computerization of knowledge and language and information-processing technology, with which knowledge came to be legitimated differently than in the past. It should be noted that Lyotard did not argue that metanarratives had disappeared (a view often attributed to him), but that they were increasingly hard to swallow and, further, that we should pay attention to their function of legitimating action and power relations.

4. There is another contender, the "Bolivarian Alternative". It is also a critical subnarrative with authoritarian-populist overtones that rejects liberal internationalism and has some currency in South America. If one were to place it within a wider context, this strand may be seen as part of the broader reaction against globalization (with the United States as the worst offender and thus the great enemy, or "Great Satan"). The anti-globalization movement shares some of the discursive elements of the anti-hegemonic Marxism of the past, and can be seen as the new battle-cry for those disaffected with today's hegemonic metanarrative strands. In the absence of a unifying ideological outlook, however, its features are much more dispersed and incoherent. They include nationalist and populist reactions and, as Olivier Roy (2004) argues, it can also include deterritorialized Islamic fundamentalist reactions that focus hatred on the perceived centre of deracination, the United States. That the Bolivarian Alternative is unlikely to provide a solid alternative, however, is revealed clearly in the 2007 survey of the Pew

Global Attitudes Project, which shows that Hugo Chávez is "widely mistrusted" throughout Latin America:

> While most respondents in Venezuela (54%) express at least some confidence in Chávez to do the right thing in world affairs, 45% say they have little or no confidence in him. Elsewhere in the region, views of Chávez are far more negative. In Chile and Brazil, about three-quarters express doubts. (Pew Global Attitudes Project, 2007: 64)

Less surprisingly, "in the United States, a 55% majority expresses little (17%) or no confidence (38%) in Chávez's leadership, while just 18% say they have some or a lot of confidence in him" (ibid.: 65).

5. It is no accident that all three of the interpretative strands exerting their influence on the post–Cold War Western hemisphere are eminently part of the Western post-Enlightenment canon: contrary to what Huntington says, and as argued elsewhere, Latin America is very much a part of the West (the "far west", as Alain Rouquié said). This is not just because the local hegemon, the United States, is at the core of that canon, but also because Latin America's élites (and its citizens more variably) have always identified themselves as being part of the West. For more details see Whitehead (2005). The images of the map and the territory are drawn from Alfred Korzybski (1995), who warns that "the map is not the territory".

6. A representative overview of a large, but now largely superseded, literature can be found in Jorge G. Castañeda (1994), which is as much an exhibit as an analysis of the phenomenon it addresses.

7. This point is developed more fully in Whitehead (2008).

8. It is also worth noting that this interpretative strand has the power of one that is not a "virgin" strand – it is not the first era of political or economic liberalism in the region. The region's struggles for independence drew quite explicitly from the French and American Revolutions, which are at the core of the post-Enlightenment political and philosophical metanarrative. In the nineteenth and early twentieth centuries, Latin America was more fully integrated into the world economy than any other part of the so-called developing world. So today's "democracy and free markets" have powerful historical antecedents. One interesting difference between the democracy and free market metanarratives of the past and today is that the current version has a certain "performative" aspect to it reminiscent of Lyotard's notion of "performativity". The technocratic mania associated with this liberal phase seems to illustrate Lyotard's broader point that performativity is taking the place (at least in part) of other metanarratives. More specifically, it suggests that performativity is colouring the new liberal orthodoxy in so far as the notion that good *técnicos* can resolve any issue from the top down and that progress can be quantified and measured (much as international financial institutions currently measure performance) was an integral part of the 1990s' interpretive frame.

9. The Pew Global Attitudes Project (2007: 2), for instance, "finds a general increase in the percentage of people citing pollution and environmental problems as a top global threat"; in Latin America, such "worries have risen sharply", with many people blaming "the United States – and to a lesser extent China – for these problems and [looking] to Washington to do something about them". Further, "AIDS and other infectious diseases continue to be viewed as … a major concern in Latin America" – thus, "AIDS and infectious diseases are cited most frequently as global dangers in Venezuela (58%) and Mexico (54%)" (ibid.: 34).

10. While it is possible that US hard power has been damaged by unsuccessful military operations in the Islamic world, this is not what is under discussion here. It remains

an open question whether, and how severely, the neoconservative moment may have altered Washington's capacity for global leadership.

11. It is interesting to note that China's growing power is generally viewed benignly in Latin America. As the Pew Global Attitudes Project (2007: 42) reports, while "there are prominent exceptions to this general rule [in Mexico, 55 per cent see China's economic development as a threat] ... [t]his is in sharp contrast to views in ... Latin America" more generally, as well as in Africa and Asia.

REFERENCES

Castañeda, Jorge G. (1994) *Utopia Unarmed: The Latin American Left after the Cold War*, New York: Vintage.

Fukuyama, Francis (1992) *The End of History and the Last Man*, New York: Free Press.

Huntington, Samuel P. (1996) *The Clash of Civilizations and the Remaking of the World Order*, New York: Simon & Schuster.

Korzybski, Alfred (1995) *Science and Sanity: An Introduction to Non-Aristotelian Systems and General Semantics*, 5th edn, Fort Worth, TX: Institute of General Semantics.

Lyotard, Jean-François ([1979] 1984) *The Postmodern Condition: A Report on Knowledge*, Theory and History of Literature 10, Minneapolis, MI: University of Minnesota Press.

Pew Global Attitudes Project (2007) *Rising Environmental Concern in 47-Nation Survey: Global Unease with Major World Power*, Washington, DC: Pew Research Center, available at http://pewglobal.org/reports/pdf/256.pdf.

Roy, Olivier (2004) *Globalized Islam: The Search for a New Ummah*, New York: Columbia University Press.

Whitehead, Laurence (2005) *Latin America: A New Interpretation*, New York: Palgrave Macmillan.

——— (2008) "International Dimensions Revisited: Their Current Role in Latin America", in Jorge I. Domínguez and Michael Shifter, eds, *Constructing Democratic Governance in Latin America*, Baltimore, MD: Johns Hopkins University Press.

2

Managing disarray: The search for a new consensus

Michael Shifter

Western hemisphere relations look fundamentally different towards the end of the first decade of the twenty-first century than they did at the beginning of the final decade of the twentieth century. The shift to civilian, constitutional rule and the end of the Cold War made the early 1990s a heady time in the Americas. It was common to talk about "collective" responses to democratic crises, about the march towards a hemisphere-wide free trade arrangement and about widespread, enthusiastic support for a market economy.

In 2008, in contrast, such references would not only fall flat, they would indeed provoke laughter. *Convergence and Community: The Americas in 1993*, the report produced by the Inter-American Dialogue in the early 1990s aimed at influencing the Clinton administration policy towards Latin America and the Caribbean, has the ring of a distant era (Inter-American Dialogue, 1992). In less than 20 years there have been profound and unexpected changes – in the United States, in Latin America and in inter-American affairs.

There is perhaps no more striking measure of the wide gap between the two moments than the first and Mar del Plata Summit of the Americas meetings. The 1994 meeting in Miami – the first of its kind since Montevideo in 1967, over a quarter-century earlier – was characterized by enormous optimism and goodwill. Aside from ambitious, lofty rhetoric, what emerged most concretely from the gathering was a common commitment to pursue a Free Trade Area of the Americas (FTAA) by 2005. Yet by the November 2005 summit in Mar del Plata, Argentina, that commitment

Which way Latin America? Hemispheric politics meets globalization, Cooper and Heine, eds, United Nations University Press, 2009, ISBN 978-92-808-1172-8

had largely unravelled and the FTAA was on life support. The assembly of Western hemisphere heads of state was full of discord and marked by a sour, acrimonious mood.

In retrospect, the hyperbolic pronouncements in the mid-1990s were probably unfounded, the product of wishful thinking. Conversely, today's disagreements are mostly manageable and less fundamental than those that dominated inter-American relations during the Cold War. Nonetheless, the shift in attitude over just a decade is dramatic, while the task of repairing the damage and rebuilding trust is daunting.

The United States: Hypocrisy and anxiety

Washington has belatedly and grudgingly acknowledged this change in the tone of inter-American affairs, with Latin America's resistance often cited as the principal source of the problem. The common view is that Latin America has been reluctant to open its markets fully and vigorously apply free trade principles. Most governments, the argument goes, have resisted proceeding very far down the road of institutional reform. US officials also attribute the paralysis of the hemispheric agenda to populist backsliding, as exemplified by the election of Hugo Chávez in 1998. The confrontation and tension over a wide range of issues raise doubts in Washington about whether Latin America is prepared to tackle the ambitious economic and political goals that were outlined in the mid-1990s.

As we will see below, there is a measure of truth to such claims. However, changes in the United States are equally, if not more, responsible for the unravelling of the hemispheric agenda. Perhaps most fundamental are the creeping doubts about the tenets of free trade and globalization. The first clear indication of such questioning came in 1998, when Congress denied President Bill Clinton the "fast-track" authority to negotiate free trade agreements that are not subject to its amendments. Whether unfounded or not, the view began to take hold in the United States that the North American Free Trade Agreement (NAFTA), negotiated with Mexico and Canada, had been detrimental to US workers. Thus, by the late 1990s, the political backlash to free trade was already gathering steam in the United States.

As we enter the latter part of the first decade of the new century, that anti-trade sentiment has become even more pronounced. The free trade constituency in Bill Clinton's Democratic Party had virtually vanished in the same party a decade later. A 2007 Pew Center survey reveals sobering results about attitudes towards key elements of globalization: whereas only 59 per cent of Americans generally support free trade, those numbers are substantially higher in Canada (82 per cent), Chile (88 per cent), Mexico (77 per cent), Peru (81 per cent) and even Venezuela (79 per cent) (Pew Global Attitudes Project, 2007). In 2005 the free trade agreement with the Central American countries and the Dominican Republic (CAFTA) passed Congress by just one vote. In 2008 an agreement with Panama was facing some difficulty and a free trade deal with Colombia appeared severely troubled, if not dead. In an era of economic uncertainty and anxiety, the free trade sceptics are multiplying and gaining clout in both political parties.

Against that altered political reality, it becomes increasingly difficult for Latin Americans to take seriously exhortations to lower their tariffs and open up their markets. In addition, there has been little relaxation of substantial US subsidies for key agricultural products such as cotton, sugar and orange juice. Instead, political interests have become even more entrenched and powerful in the United States, as evidenced by Farm Bills that expand subsidies rather than roll them back. US protectionism has become the chief sticking point in negotiations, particularly with Brazil, rendering a hemisphere-wide agreement virtually unthinkable for the foreseeable future.

US preaching on democracy and the rule of law also acquired an increasingly hollow ring after the 1994 Summit of the Americas, when it seemed the collective will to respond to interruptions of constitutional rule reached its high-water mark. Despite their considerable limitations and lack of teeth, the Washington-backed responses of the Organization of American States (OAS) to democratic crises in Haiti (1991), Peru (1992) and Guatemala (1993) were more vigorous than they had been towards comparable breakdowns historically (Cooper and Legler, 2006). It is tempting to start from the post-9/11 period (and subsequent abuses associated with the Iraq war) when tracing the decline of US credibility on democracy and the rule of law, but this trend can be discerned even in the late 1990s. After all, the Clinton administration basically stood with the Peruvian regime led by Alberto Fujimori and Vladimiro Montesinos even after it became clear that it was a mafia state, unspeakably corrupt and a major human rights violator (Palmer, 2006: 65–68).

Still, US hypocrisy and double standards on democracy and human rights became especially salient after the terrorist attacks in New York and Washington on 11 September 2001 (the same day the Inter-American Democratic Charter was approved in Lima, Peru). The abuses reported at Guantánamo, Cuba, touched a very sensitive nerve in Latin America, as did the outrages at Abu Ghraib (Shifter, 2006a). Indeed, the military adventure in Iraq itself showed a disdain for international norms and standards that did not go unnoticed in Latin America, where the United States has long pushed these same norms and standards. For many Latin Americans, Washington's friendly relations with autocratic regimes like those in Pakistan and Egypt in the name of fighting terrorism evoked the Cold War: similar justifications were made for backing Pinochet's Chile or Videla's Argentina in past decades.

Two other US decisions substantially undercut its claims to moral authority. The first concerns the refusal of many Latin American governments to sign Article 98 of the International Criminal Court, which would exempt US citizens in their countries from prosecution. Refusal to sign led to US sanctions of military aid programmes, a source of considerable irritation in US-Latin American relations. Latin Americans wondered how Washington could square a commitment to the rule of law with such a blatant exception, ostensibly on no other grounds than "American exceptionalism" – the notion that US motives are inherently pure and therefore should be exempt from normal regulations (Lipset, 1996).

The second issue that further eroded Latin American confidence in the US commitment to democracy was Washington's response to the April 2002 military coup in Venezuela. In a statement immediately following the coup, the Bush administration scarcely disguised its delight at the overthrow of Hugo Chávez, who was returned to office, however, just 48 hours later. Though the administration rectified its position at a special OAS meeting shortly thereafter, the damage had been done. In a foreign policy context in which "regime change" was an option, Latin Americans understandably wondered whether they might be the next in line (Shifter, 2002).

Finally, it is difficult to imagine anything resembling a hemispheric consensus or goodwill in light of the US debate on immigration. As in the trade debate, anxiety about globalization – in this case, the influx of peoples – generated a strong nationalist reaction, including some ugly name-calling and a "wall" along the 2,000-mile US-Mexico border. The crackdown on illegal immigration intensified in 2007 throughout the United States, making the early days of even the Bush administration – when there was serious talk of a comprehensive immigration deal – seem like a distant era (Shulman, 2007). As President Bush found out in his March 2007 visit to Latin America, US immigration policies are not watched only in Mexico or Central America but are followed closely throughout the region – even as far away as Uruguay. Indeed, the immigration controversy could well pose the most formidable obstacle to restoring inter-American trust in the future.

Latin America: Fragmentation and pragmatism

With the end of military governments and hyperinflation in Latin America, it was widely believed that the ground had been laid for more profound political and economic transformation in the region. The notion was that political and economic order would be accompanied by more robust and effective courts and political parties, along with thoroughgoing social reforms in such areas as education and healthcare. Authoritarianism and financial chaos would no longer be impediments to broad-based, equitable and democratic development. Not only would Latin American governments cooperate more with the United States, they would also enjoy better and more productive relations among themselves.

In some respects the theory worked. Elections have become routine – happily, a tough habit to break – in almost every country in the region. As the comparative Latinobarómetro survey has consistently shown, democracy remains the preferred political model and system for most Latin Americans (*The Economist*, 2006). Moreover, inflation has been held substantially in check. Greater fiscal discipline and prudent economic management have contributed to higher growth rates since 2003, resulting in a welcome reduction in extreme poverty in a number of countries, according to the UN Economic Commission for Latin America and the Caribbean (CEPAL, 2007). Latin American integration has also progressed, reflected in a variety of trade deals and increased investment among countries, not to mention unprecedented internal migration and remittance flows.

At the same time, however, institutional reforms have been disappointing at best. The performance of political parties has generally declined, while social policies aimed at alleviating poverty and inequality have been woefully inadequate. What is most striking about the region in the twenty-first century is the high degree of social discontent and frustration that one finds in country after country. Acute social and even geographic polarization was clearly revealed in the results of the particularly intense 2006 election cycle (Castañeda and Navia, 2007). In Mexico, Peru, Ecuador, Bolivia, Venezuela and Brazil, huge internal divisions were on display that pose a significant challenge for effective governance.

The same accelerated forces of globalization that have helped generate high growth rates and increased financial flows in Latin America have also strained relatively weak institutions. Greater access to information technology has been a fundamental change in Latin America, leading to heightened demands and expectations for a larger share of the national wealth. Increased political participation by previously excluded and marginal groups has no doubt contributed to a greater democratic opening. The region's indigenous populations – particularly significant in such countries as Bolivia, Guatemala, Peru, Ecuador and Mexico – are playing more prominent political roles, as are Afro-Latin Americans and women.

Globalization, of course, also has had a much darker side, which has contributed to enormous fragmentation and uncertainty throughout Latin America. Since the height of consensus and convergence in the mid-1990s, there has been a notable rise in the level of crime and insecurity in almost every major urban centre in the region. In poll after poll this problem, along with unemployment, ranks as the most critical public concern (*The Economist*, 2006). Following Colombia's experience in the 1980s and 1990s, drug-fuelled violence has now reached crisis proportions in Mexico and major Brazilian cities such as São Paulo and Rio de Janeiro. The explosion of Latin America's illicit economy – not only drugs but other manifestations of criminality as well – makes effective political integration extremely difficult (Shifter, 2007a).

In this context, the rise of Hugo Chávez over the past decade is hardly surprising. The Venezuelan president is a symptom of the severe underperformance of the region's economy and traditional political institutions. His emergence stems from the dramatic deterioration of Venezuela during the "lost decades" of the 1980s and 1990s, when the country lost some 40 per cent of its national income and bitter social resentment spread. Venezuela's major political parties and other élite sectors proved ill-equipped to deal with growing demands for change. Chávez succeeded in putting his finger on a fundamental grievance, felt by many in Venezuela and, indeed, throughout Latin America, that has become the basis of his appeal (Shifter, 2006b). Chávez's principal innovation has been the social mission programmes – ranging from subsidized food to healthcare and literacy training – that have helped bring down poverty levels in recent years. Social inequality and the need for greater distributive justice are unquestionably higher on the Latin American policy agenda in 2008 than they were in the mid-1990s.

Indeed, more than any other political figure today in Latin America, Chávez embodies the antithesis of the "convergence" thesis advanced in the aftermath of the Cold War. He has posed a sharp challenge to the three main tenets that were reflected in the framework of the 1994 summit: a supposedly shared commitment to market economics, democratic politics and better cooperation with the United States. Chávez, in contrast, has assigned a greater role to the state in the economy, rejected the notion of "liberal" or "representative" democracy that had been so enthusiastically embraced at the Miami gathering and, most notably, defied the United States while seeking to construct a counterweight to US power (Coppedge, 2003: 165–192).

As the leader of a major oil producer who came to power when oil was around US$10 a barrel, Chávez is, of course, an exceptional case in Latin America. Other regional leaders, even sympathizers like Bolivia's Evo Morales, Ecuador's Rafael Correa and Nicaragua's Daniel Ortega, face more serious constraints than Chávez in their economic and political decision-making. But almost all Latin American leaders feel a markedly greater concern for the social agenda than before, as well as a desire for greater elbow-room or independence from the United States. Even the most enthusiastic defenders of the Washington Consensus have come to acknowledge that the agenda set forth in the early 1990s was incomplete and that social priorities failed to get the weight they deserve (Birdsall and de la Torre, 2001).

Other political currents that have gained ground in Latin America similarly reflect this marked shift towards the social agenda. The 2002 election of Luiz Inácio Lula da Silva of the leftist Workers' Party in Brazil had enormous symbolic significance, not only for Latin America's largest country but also for the region as a whole. Lula's more moderate, pragmatic brand of "leftist" politics and surprisingly cordial relationship with George W. Bush offered the promise of a more social democratic alternative in the region. Lula's re-election in 2006 signalled the relative success of his formula, which blends market mechanisms with a strong social orientation. The centrepiece of his social agenda is the bolsa familia income transfer programme, which began under his predecessor, Fernando Henrique Cardoso of the Social Democratic Party, and has succeeded in reducing poverty (Castañeda, 2006).

The succession of democratic governments in post-Pinochet Chile best represents this pragmatic political tendency, which has continued under the socialist governments of Ricardo Lagos and Michelle Bachelet. These various administrations have managed to bring down poverty levels with policies encouraging market integration, government interventions when appropriate and a variety of free trade agreements, including with the United States. In November 2005 Chile became the first Latin American country to sign a free trade agreement with China.

Even governments that have never been accused of being part of the so-called pink tide are putting more emphasis on the social question than governments did in the 1990s. It is noteworthy, for example, that the Mexican government of Felipe Calderón of the Partido Acción Nacional (PAN, or National Action Party) identified the fight against poverty as its highest priority. Calderón in fact has built on a programme expanded under his predecessor, Vicente Fox, called Oportunidades, which was later adopted in Brazil and is now touted for its success in reducing poverty. In addition, the administration of Colombia's hard-line President Álvaro Uribe has sought to combine a focus on enhancing security with expanding spending on social and anti-poverty programmes. In the early part of the twenty-first century this is an inescapable priority for any Latin American government confronting acute inequalities and dealing with heightened demands by emerging social groups (Shifter, 2006c).

Consumed by national social and governance agendas, most Latin American leaders have been unable to fulfil the promise of regional integration – an opportunity made even more viable because of the relative disengagement of Washington from the region in recent years. Part of the mid-1990s' optimism had to do with the sense that subregional groups would flourish and expand. Many hoped, for example, that NAFTA would not only succeed in spurring trade and investment but also evolve into a much deeper and more multifaceted integration scheme (Pastor, 2004). Adding to the optimism was the example of the Mercosur trading group, involving Brazil, Argentina, Uruguay and Paraguay, which initially surpassed expectations in trade terms. The notion that this arrangement could begin to approximate in some respects the European Union was also seriously considered. Even the Comunidad Andina de Naciones (CAN, or Andean Community of Nations), though weaker than NAFTA or Mersocur, appeared poised for greater development in the overall environment of integration and cooperation.

Today, the idea of thriving subregional arrangements remains a distant vision. Such arrangements have, at best, stalled. Political constraints and lack of both imagination and will have prevented a deepening of cooperation on a variety of issues. To be sure, Latin American trade and investment have continued at a relatively high rate and accords have multiplied, but existing arrangements appear to have provided little added value and offered scant interest in cooperating more systematically. Just as Chávez is a symptom, rather than a cause, of the challenge to democratic politics and market economics, so he plays a similar role with respect to integration schemes. His decisions and behaviour are instructive and reveal a wider hemispheric setting of considerable disarray and flux.

In 2005 Chávez decided to leave the CAN because two of its members, Colombia and Peru, had signed free trade agreements with the United States. He then sought to join Mercosur, in keeping with his notion of constructing a South American counterweight to US hegemony in the region. As of this writing, it is still not clear if Venezuela will be accepted into Mercosur, despite the substantial resources it undoubtedly would bring to the table. Mercosur's reluctance is partly due to the Brazilian Senate objecting to Chávez's decision in early 2007 not to renew the licence of a private Venezuelan TV station, RCTV. At the same time, at the urging of Correa of Ecuador and even Colombia's Uribe, Chávez has expressed interest in rejoining the CAN. All of this manoeuvring reflects the kind of fluid hemispheric relations that characterize the region and defy the notion that Latin America is sharply divided among distinct ideological blocs. Indeed, in 2007 both Lula and Argentina's Néstor Kirchner invited Calderón to consider joining Mercosur (Pérez de Eulate, 2007). Mexico, which had long been viewed as firmly in the North American orbit and an improbable Mercosur member, is also clearly looking to diversify its ties throughout the Americas.

Two further examples illustrate the growing divisions and notable lack of consensus in hemispheric relations. The first was the election of the secretary-general of the OAS in 2005. In that case, the United States backed two candidates, a former Salvadoran president and then a Mexican foreign minister, before agreeing to the consensus candidate, former Chilean foreign and interior minister José Miguel Insulza. In that vote, the United States initially was reluctant to support a candidate who seemed to have the enthusiastic backing of its adversary, Hugo Chávez. That short-sighted posture proved costly for inter-American comity, and in the end Secretary of State Condoleezza Rice had to clean up the mess that others in the US government had made. The hemisphere's tremendous political fragmentation was also on display at the United Nations in 2006, when there was a prolonged voting deadlock between Guatemala and Venezuela over which would occupy one of the two non-permanent Latin American seats on the Security Council. In the end, Panama was the compromise choice, but, again, only after a high degree of acrimony had divided the region.

In this context of political disarray at the regional level, there have, of course, been enormous strides in integration in such spheres as migration, remittances, trade and investment. It is the realm of politics that has been most problematic and has impeded a more vigorous hemisphere-wide arrangement that would provide greater stability and strength to compete more effectively in the global economy. In place of effective cooperation, the region has witnessed a marked pragmatism, an interest in exercising as many options as possible in an effort to assert national interests. In the case of energy producers, most especially Venezuela but also Bolivia and Ecuador, this has resulted in what is often described as "resource nationalism": an attempt to renegotiate deals with foreign investors to get the most favourable terms possible. Nonetheless, in the energy area, where a number of countries face severe difficulties, there has been a notable lack of cooperation in dealing with such a fundamental shared challenge.

Global connections: Adjusting to new realities

In light of the past 15 years of experience in hemispheric relations, it clearly seems wise to temper expectations about what can be achieved in terms of inter-American harmony and cooperation. The somewhat exhilarating days appear to have been an interregnum – the product of an unusual confluence of circumstances and a break in the historic mix of conflict and accommodation in the Americas.

At the same time, however, it is important to avoid complacency and becoming resigned to the current state of disarray and discord. Latin America has made noteworthy strides in a variety of areas, especially in macroeconomic performance and regular elections. In the past few years, moreover, poverty has declined in a number of countries, and even inequality has been slightly reduced (CEPAL, 2006: 26–27). Most impressively, Latin America is increasingly connected to the global economic order and plays an important role in international politics. That presence is likely to become even more pronounced in the years ahead.

For many in the United States, in particular, it remains difficult to grasp fully these shifting circumstances. At least through most of the twentieth century, Latin America was regarded by the United States as its strategic preserve or "back yard" and largely an appendage of US foreign policy. That traditional mindset persists, despite the palpable and often dramatic changes one sees in the region.

Venezuela and Brazil amply illustrate such changes. Venezuela under Chávez has been active not only in regional politics but on the global stage as well. Motivated in part by anti-US belligerence, Chávez has increasingly worked on the international stage with such leaders as Russia's Vladimir Putin and Iran's Mahmoud Ahmadinejad. The latter has made several visits to Latin America, not only to Caracas but also to Nicaragua, Bolivia and Ecuador, where he attended the inauguration of Rafael Correa in January 2007. Flush with money thanks to record oil prices, Chávez has particularly sought to overcome Venezuela's vulnerability to Washington on two key fronts: energy and security. He has made shifting the bulk of Venezuela's oil exports to China a high priority (at present, the United States buys about 60 per cent of the country's exports). Though the technical and economic obstacles to such a strategy are huge, for Chávez the political benefits are compelling. And to protect himself against possible US military action, Chávez has bought billions of dollars worth of Russian arms, including 24 jet fighters, 53 helicopters and 100,000 assault rifles (Chivers, 2007).

As a regional power, Brazil, too, is increasingly influential and active on the global stage. In a 2003 report from Goldman Sachs (Wilson and Purushothaman, 2003), Brazil was identified as one of the BRIC countries – along with Russia, India and China – that could well become the world's four dominant economies by 2050. Brazil's chief foreign policy priority is securing a permanent seat on the UN Security Council. Its projection on the international scene was evident during the Cardoso years (1994–2002) and has continued under Lula. The production of sugar-based ethanol and other biofuels is of primary emphasis and a centrepiece of its foreign policy.

In a curious way, economically expanding regional powers like China and India, hungry for energy and other raw materials, are not only helping to fuel the region's overall growth but, as a consequence, also contributing to rising demands and expectations on the part of Latin America's more politically active social groups. China's imports from Latin America have been most impressive, growing at some 60 per cent per year and in 2006 reaching an estimated US$60 billion. Following Chile's example, Peru, another significant copper exporter, could well be next in line for a free trade accord with China. To be sure, the impact of such economic powerhouses as China and India on Latin America is ambivalent and differentiated, with Mexico and Central American countries deriving fewer benefits and, in fact, facing growing competition for their products (Domínguez, 2006). These nuanced relationships underscore Latin America's myriad global dimensions.

One area highly germane to Latin America that has long had a global character is the drug problem. In recent years the drug trade's international connections have become even more pronounced, while traffickers and others involved in the trade are more sophisticated and adaptable than ever. Yet the US-led war on drugs has essentially been on automatic pilot, failing to recognize or come to grips with the obvious flaws in its unilateral, supply-side approach. Even though the results have been palpably disappointing and the costs huge and mounting, there has been little serious public debate about alternatives to the current anti-drug policy. Such alternatives might reasonably highlight demand and harm reduction, but also more serious multilateral approaches with political muscle behind law-enforcement cooperation, rather than every government looking to Washington. To be sure, the legalization or decriminalization option might be most viable in the long term, given the damage that is being done, but that approach appears politically unfeasible in the near future (Nadelmann, 2007).

The difficulty of making progress on the drug question underlines the domestic political constraints that often stand in the way of more effective inter-American cooperation. Unfortunately, drug policy appears frozen for the time being and public opinion in the United States, as indicated above, is moving perceptibly against the tenets of free trade and globalization. The immigration debate, as well, has been almost entirely driven by US internal politics, and the result has been the inability of Congress or the executive to tackle an untenable situation – one that could well roil inter-American relations for the next decade. It is instructive, and immensely dispiriting, that, in the congressional debate on the immigration proposal in 2007, there was hardly any consideration given to the possible implications of any decision for US-Latin American, or US-Mexican, relations.

One potentially positive factor that is likely to change the outlook on immigration over the longer run is simply the growing political role of the Latino population in the United States. Having already surpassed African Americans as the largest minority group, the more than 44 million Latinos in the United States are voting in greater numbers than before, and will probably exercise greater political influence in the coming years. Despite the often-fierce backlash from varied hard-line sectors in the United States, the trend towards greater Latino political muscle is unlikely to be reversed. The imperatives of the US economy are too great and the cultural connections are too profound to stem this tide.

Conclusion

The challenge for the United States will be to remain engaged in hemispheric affairs and committed to a policy agenda that not only has greater appeal throughout the Americas but also best advances US interests (Shifter, 2007b). A withdrawn and uninterested attitude towards the region, or an insistence on being in control, has proved not just unproductive but also self-defeating. It makes sense for other governments to take the lead on critical questions where cooperation is essential: trade, democracy, drugs and the environment. Eventually, the challenge of reincorporating Cuba into the inter-American system will also need to be addressed. The huge baggage the United States carries limits its effectiveness in promoting such an agenda. Brazil, Mexico and Canada might well take the initiative in energizing a serious hemispheric policy discussion on these and other issues.

Although lofty goals about finding a new convergence in the Americas should be downplayed, it is vital to explore ways of enhancing greater cooperation on specific policy questions. That task remains as compelling as it was nearly two decades ago.

REFERENCES

Birdsall, Nancy and Augusto de la Torre, with Rachel Menezes (2001) *Washington Contentious: Economic Policies for Social Equity in Latin America*, Washington, DC: Carnegie Endowment for International Peace/Inter-American Dialogue.

Castañeda, Jorge G. (2006) "Latin America's Left Turn", *Foreign Affairs* 85(3), pp. 28–43.

Castañeda, Jorge G. and Patricio Navia (2007) "The Year of the Ballot", *Current History* 106(697), pp. 51–58.

CEPAL Development Division and Statistics and Economic Projections Division (2006) *Social Panorama of Latin America 2006*, Santiago: Comisión Economica para America Latina y el Caribe.

——— (2007) *Estudio económico de América Latina y el Caribe 2006–2007*, Santiago: Comisión Económica para América Latina y el Caribe.

Chivers, C. J. (2007) "Chávez's Bid for Russian Arms Pains U.S.", *New York Times*, 16 August.

Cooper, Andrew F. and Thomas Legler (2006) *Intervention without Intervening?: The OAS Defense and Promotion of Democracy in the Americas*, New York: Palgrave.

Coppedge, Michael (2003) "Venezuela: Popular Sovereignty vs. Liberal Democracy", in M. Shifter and J. I. Domínguez, eds, *Constructing Democratic Governance in Latin America*, Baltimore, MD: Johns Hopkins University Press.

Domínguez, Jorge I. (2006) "China's Relations with Latin America: Shared Gains, Asymmetric Hopes", China Working Paper, Inter-American Dialogue, Washington, DC.

Inter-American Dialogue (1992) *Convergence and Community: The Americas in 1993*, Washington, DC: Inter-American Dialogue.

Lipset, Seymour Martin (1996) *American Exceptionalism: A Double-Edged Sword*, New York: W. W. Norton.

Nadelmann, Ethan (2007) "Think Again: Drugs", *Foreign Policy* (September/October), pp. 24–35.

Palmer, David Scott (2006) *U.S. Relations with Latin America During the Clinton Years: Opportunities Lost or Opportunities Squandered?*, Gainesville, FL: University Press of Florida.

Pastor, Robert A. (2004) "North America's Second Decade", *Foreign Affairs* 83(1), pp. 124–135.

Pérez de Eulate, Mariano (2007) "Fuerte impulso de Kirchner para que México se acerque al Mercosur", *Clarín*, 31 July.

Pew Global Attitudes Project (2007) "World Publics Welcome Global Trade – But Not Immigration", Pew Research Center, Washington, DC.

Shifter, Michael (2002) "Democracy in Venezuela, Unsettling as Ever", *Washington Post*, 21 April.

——— (2006a) "The Divided States of the Americas", *Current History* 105(688), pp. 51–57.

——— (2006b) "In Search of Hugo Chávez", *Foreign Affairs* 85(3), pp. 45–59.

——— (2006c) "A New Politics for Latin America?", *America* 195(20), pp. 18–25.

——— (2007a) "Latin America's Drug Problem", *Current History* 106(697), pp. 58–64.

——— (2007b) "South America and the US: How to Fix a Broken Relationship", statement before the House Committee on Foreign Affairs, Washington, DC, 19 June.

Shulman, Robin (2007) "Immigration Raid Rips Families; Illegal Workers in Massachusetts Separated from Children", *Washington Post*, 18 March.

The Economist (2006) "The Latinobarómetro Poll: The Democracy Dividend", *The Economist*, 7 December.

Wilson, Dominic and Roopa Purushothaman (2003) "Dreaming with BRICs: The Path to 2050", Global Economics Paper No. 99, October, Goldman Sachs, New York, available at www2.goldmansachs.com/ideas/brics/book/99-dreaming.pdf.

3

The emergence of a new left

Jorge G. Castañeda and Marco A. Morales

The prognosis for the future of the left in Latin America was certainly not very positive at the beginning of the 1990s. While the European left had been able to rethink and update itself accordingly and become a full-fledged player in the electoral arena, the Latin American left did not seem close to coming to terms with its *aggiornamento*. On the contrary, it typically still adhered to a nationalistic and anti-American discourse, reluctant to embrace more liberal macroeconomic and trade strategies, refused to commit itself fully to the defence of human rights and democracy and was only beginning to engage seriously in a process of trading arms for votes as a means to achieve power (Castañeda, 1994).

It should not be a surprise that, by 1990, the left had been able to gain power in only three countries in the region: Cuba, Nicaragua and Chile. The first two cases were the result of armed revolts where the standing governments were overthrown and replaced with revolutionary ones by violent means. In Cuba the ascent of the left was marked by the entry of Fidel Castro into Havana in 1959, and in Nicaragua by the defeat of the Somoza government in 1979, although the Sandinistas were to be defeated at the polls in 1990 in the first fully democratic elections since they took power. Chile was a different case. The socialists had been elected to office in 1970 and were overthrown in a military coup in 1973. They returned to power in 1989 as part of the coalition of parties, Concertación, that won the first democratic election after the Pinochet dictatorship.

In the nearly two decades that followed, nine countries have elected or re-elected parties that identify themselves with the left or the centre-left.[1]

Which way Latin America? Hemispheric politics meets globalization, Cooper and Heine, eds, *United Nations University Press, 2009, ISBN 978-92-808-1172-8*

These parties have been in power in Chile since 1990, Venezuela since 1999, Brazil since 2003, Argentina since 2003, Uruguay since 2005, Bolivia since 2005, Nicaragua since 2006, Peru since 2006 and Ecuador since 2007. It is unlikely that the presence of the left will be diminished anytime soon, since governments in these countries are scheduled to remain in power at least until 2010.[2] This means that more than half the countries in continental Latin America – and 60 per cent of the population (ECLAC, 2006) – will until 2010 be governed by parties identified with the left.

As the numbers suggest, the surge of the left was slow during the 1990s, when only two countries elected leftist governments, and in one of them – Chile – the left was part of a coalition of parties, and not formally *in* power. Yet it must be noted that, for the most part, the successful surge of leftist parties into power after 2000 had been "cooking" during the 1990s. Many of these parties were becoming more successful at the polls because they were able to learn consistently from past experience and build more successful electoral coalitions that would eventually take them into office.

Since there is no doubt about the surge of the left in Latin America – particularly during the past two years – our aim in this chapter is to provide a more detailed account of some interesting puzzles this trend underscores. Are all governments from the left comparable? If not, is it useful to classify them into narrower categories? What has led to this surge in governments from the left? Why are these governments not enacting a more radical agenda? Our answers are but hypotheses in need of further empirical verification, and new evidence arises every day. Yet our review of the available evidence suggests there are interesting trends worth noting, and some of them give clear hints as to where to look for answers.

Left swerves

Our assessment must begin somewhere. Let us briefly recount some peculiarities of the countries that have elected governments from the left since the 1990s. It is worth pointing out two initial patterns. First, wherever the left was re-elected, it consistently managed to increase its previous vote share. Second, newly elected governments from the left were, for the most part, the result of a progressive build-up of votes from previous elections.

- *Chile.* Although the Chilean socialists have been part of the Concertación coalition since 1989, it was only in 2000 that they formally acceded to power; Ricardo Lagos was the first member of the party to hold office in the post-Pinochet period. Michelle Bachelet, the current president, is also a socialist. Thus in two of the four periods that the Concertación has been in power, the left has held the presidency. Bachelet won the Chilean presidency in January 2006 with a comfortable 7 per cent advantage in a run-off election.[3] With this feat, she overcame the setback suffered by Lagos in 2000 when he was nearly defeated by the rightist Joaquín Lavín. Significantly, despite being forced into a run-off election, Bachelet managed to increase Lagos's share of the vote by 2 per cent in this last round.

- *Venezuela.* Hugo Chávez first came to power after winning the 1998 election. Controversial as his terms have been, the fact remains that on 3 December 2006 he was re-elected for the second time,[4] defeating the social democratic candidate, Manuel Rosales, by more than 3 million votes (about 25 per cent of the vote).[5] Remarkably, Chávez has increased his share of the vote in every election since he first took office, amassing 56 per cent of the vote in 1998, 60 per cent in 2000 and nearly 63 per cent in 2006.

- *Brazil.* Luiz Inácio Lula da Silva has been president since 2003, and in 2006 managed a leisurely re-election. After an intense two-way campaign against Geraldo Alckmin of the PSDB (Partido da Social Democracia Brasileira), Lula was re-elected in the 29 October run-off, when he gained a 20 per cent lead. Interestingly, his 48 per cent of the vote in the first round was higher than the 46 per cent he obtained in the first round in 2002 and much higher than in his previous unsuccessful electoral bids: 32 per cent in 1998, 27 per cent in 1994 and 16 per cent in 1989.[6]

- *Argentina.* Cristina Fernández de Kirchner managed to win the 2007 presidential election under the Frente para la Victoria label – a spin-off of the Justicialista party – that had led her husband into office in 2003. Her 45 per cent of the vote[7] made a run-off election unnecessary, and more than doubled her husband's share of the vote four years earlier. Néstor Kirchner had been elected president in 2003 with 22 per cent of the vote. Since neither candidate obtained 45 per cent of the vote as required by the 1994 constitutional reform, a run-off between him and Carlos Menem was inevitable. Foreseeing his defeat, however, Menem declined, effectively giving the presidency to Kirchner. It is hard to assess the electoral growth of the left in Argentina during this period; rather, a series of *ad hoc* fronts and divisions within parties associated with the left have been the signature of Argentine politics.

- *Uruguay.* Tabaré Vázquez was elected in 2005 as the candidate of the leftist coalition Frente Amplio, with 51.7 per cent of the vote;[8] in his previous unsuccessful bids he had obtained 45.9 per cent (1999) and 30.6 per cent (1994).

- *Bolivia*. Evo Morales, the coca-leaf-grower leader and founder of the Bolivian Movimiento al Socialismo (MAS), was elected president in 2005 with 53 per cent of the vote[9] – a historical achievement considering that his closest competitor trailed him by 25 per cent – a share more than double the 20 per cent he obtained when he ran in 2002. In just two elections, MAS and Morales became the main fixtures of the left in Bolivia.
- *Nicaragua*. Daniel Ortega, the reloaded leftist ex-guerrilla leader of the Frente Sandinista de Liberación Nacional, was elected president in 2006 with 38 per cent of the vote.[10] After 16 years out of power and three losing presidential candidacies, Ortega decided to reinvent himself and campaign on a more moderate platform: he no longer opposes the Central America-Dominican Republic-United States Free Trade Agreement, he is willing to maintain diplomatic relations with the United States, he rejects the seizing of private property, as he did in the 1980s, and he has even taken a clear step to the right by openly declaring his opposition to abortion. Despite winning the election, Ortega suffered a relative electoral setback, obtaining nearly 4 per cent fewer votes than in his 2001 bid.
- *Peru*. Alan García became president for the second time in an unexpected comeback in 2006, when, despite having been out of office for 16 years, he defeated the populist Ollanta Humala by a mere 5 per cent of the vote in a run-off election; he also managed to increase his share of the vote by 4.8 per cent from his last candidacy in 2001.[11] García had left office in 1990 facing severe hyperinflation, economic turbulence and a surge in violence. A change in his discourse was necessary, and he thus openly supported the US-Peru Trade Promotion Agreement and advocated fiscal soundness. But he also engaged, inevitably, in populist promises: the death penalty for terrorists and cuts in the wages of ministers and members of Congress.
- *Ecuador*. Rafael Correa won the 2006 election with 56.67 per cent of the vote in a run-off against the rightist candidate Álvaro Noboa.[12] After a close outcome in the general election, in which he ran under a populist and pro-Chávez platform, Correa was forced to reinvent himself and become more moderate if he was to win the run-off. He distanced himself from Chávez, promised to maintain the Ecuadorian dollar economy and played down the threat of debt default.

An unusual confluence of elections occurred in 2006, providing a number of simultaneous observations that might help us detect more patterns related to the surge of the left in Latin America. Three countries (Venezuela, Chile and Brazil) confirmed the left in power, but three countries (Nicaragua, Peru and Ecuador) also joined the ranks of the left. García and Ortega are the celebrated comebacks of the season, and both accomplished this by becoming "moderate" versions of themselves: Ortega by distancing himself from his Marxist-guerrilla past, and García by running away from his populist past. Correa, as well, had to moderate his tone in order to win the run-off election that made him president of Ecuador. Furthermore, of the nine countries that went to the polls during 2006, only Colombia and Mexico elected governments from the right, and in both cases the defeated left fared better than ever before. In broad terms, these elections showed three important traits. First, for every election won by a party from the right, the left won three. Second, except for Nicaragua, every party from the left increased its share of the votes, even when its candidate did not win the presidency. And third, except for Venezuela, the moderate left – i.e. the modern, reformist and internationalist version – fared better in the polls than the radical left.

Moving left even while keeping right

Contrary to the trend in other countries, Mexico and Colombia not only avoided electing a leftist candidate in 2006, but chose to confirm their conservative governments: in Colombia by re-electing Álvaro Uribe, and in Mexico by electing the PAN candidate, Felipe Calderón. In both cases, however, the left scored better than ever, and by a large margin.

- *Mexico.* Andrés Manuel López Obrador, the populist candidate from the leftist PRD (Partido de la Revolución Democrática), lost by a razor-thin margin of less that half a percentage point (roughly 240,000 votes) to the right-of-centre PAN candidate, Calderón.[13] After months of leading in the polls, López Obrador became a victim of his own rhetoric, his implausible populist platform and his incomprehensible reluctance to distance himself from Hugo Chávez. Still, he managed to accomplish what no other candidate from the left had ever done: a real possibility to win the presidency. It is interesting to note that López Obrador more than doubled the share of the vote obtained by Cuauhtémoc Cárdenas, the PRD's presidential candidate in 1994 and 2000.[14]
- *Colombia.* The right-of-centre incumbent, Uribe, was re-elected with a surprising 62 per cent of the vote.[15] Like most of the leftist presidential candidates running that year, the candidate from the Polo Democrático Alternativo, Carlos Gaviria, came in second with a remarkable 22 per cent of the vote, almost a fourfold increase from the 6 per cent the left obtained in 2002 and surpassing for the first time Colombia's other traditional party, the Liberals.

Thus, Latin American voters seem to prefer candidates who run on leftist platforms, and the left seems to have developed the ability to select appealing candidates. This was the case in Chile, Brazil, Ecuador, Nicaragua, Peru and Venezuela. Aside from Hugo Chávez, neither of the extreme populist candidates – López Obrador in Mexico and Humala in Peru – could win an election: moderation does pay off. Former radical leaders who had previously been voted out of office were voted in again under a moderate facade, and the need to attract votes in a run-off election forced Ecuador's Correa to moderate his stance in order to win. Both Ortega and García had to reinvent themselves in order to create sufficient majorities, and in both cases their margin of victory was narrow. Ortega had to distance himself from his Marxist revolutionary rhetoric of the past by promising not to seize lands, as he had done just before losing the presidency in 1988; he also advocated issues typical of the right, such as a pro-life stance. García also had to overcome his leftist reputation by moving his rhetoric closer to the social democratic centre, but here he was helped by the radicalism of his opponent, Humala.

Are Latin Americans turning left?

As witnesses to and students of the rise of the left, we have two related questions before us. First, why do we find significant differences among the leftists elected to power? Second, what can explain the recent surge of the left in Latin America? We suspect the two answers are related.

The standard argument is that Latin America's poverty and inequality explain the electoral surge of the left. After all, if the left advocates redistribution and social equality, it is only natural that the poorest – the majority in Latin America – would support it (Cleary, 2006). Unfortunately for this argument, poverty and inequality are not new features to the continent. According to World Bank estimates, Latin America is the most inequitable region in the world (Machinea, Bárcena and León, 2005). If we were to gain some traction explaining the surge of the left in Latin America, we would also need to explain why it was only in the 2000s that the left began to receive so many votes, and it did not do so before. So other factors, coupled with poverty and inequality, must explain the surge of the left since the 1990s. And for the story to be plausible, at least one of these factors must also explain why the left gave up arms and embraced the polls. After all, there would be no "turn to the left" in Latin America if there were no viable candidates competing from the left.

We need to keep in mind that, for the left to be elected to power, leftist candidates must be coming who appeal to voters. A surge of the left can be due to the participation of more candidates with appealing traits and discourse or to a change in the tastes of a sufficient proportion of voters, or a combination of both. We have observed that Latin American parties of the left have been able to provide "quality" candidates. But have the

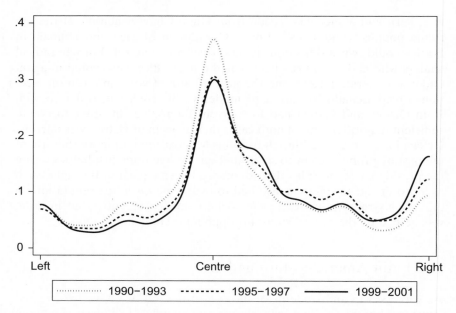

Figure 3.1 Latin American voter identification by ideological position, 1990–2001
Source: World Values Survey, 1990–2001.

ideological tastes of Latin American voters changed at all during this time?

For the 1990s, data from the World Values Survey for Argentina, Brazil, Chile, Mexico, Peru and Venezuela allow us to take a closer look at possible ideological shifts among Latin Americans.[16] Figure 3.1 shows that, if we look at roughly the beginning (1990–1993), middle (1995–1997) and end (1999–2001) of the decade, no trend is visible of individuals moving to the left. If any shift appears, statistical tests confirm it was to the right – that is, during the 1990s Latin Americans did not tend to identify themselves particularly with the left; instead, we see an ideological shift to the right.

Was this apparent shift to the right only temporary, and did the actual shift to the left occur only after 2000? To explore this matter, we use data from Latinobarómetro for all Latin American countries to compare the beginning (2001) and the middle (2005) of the present decade.[17] Figure 3.2 shows clearly that during the first half of the decade there was a consistent shift to the left in all Latin America, which is also confirmed by statistical tests.[18] This is the result of larger shares of individuals in most countries identifying themselves with the left and centre-left in 2005 than

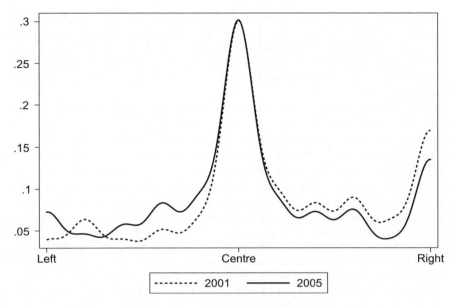

Figure 3.2 Latin American voter identification by ideological position, 2001–2005
Source: Latinobarometro, 2001/2005

in 2001. The exceptions to this trend are Colombia and Costa Rica, where public opinion swerved to the right, and Argentina, El Salvador, Nicaragua and Paraguay, where average citizens continue to identify with the centre as they have for the past five years.

That is, while Latin Americans tended to identify more with the right during the 1990s, this trend seems to have reversed during the first half of the 2000s. This nicely corresponds to the period in which governments from the left have been successfully elected to office. Unfortunately, it would be irresponsible to claim that Latin Americans elected governments from the left *because* they identified with the left. It might be the case that they began to identify with the left *as a result* of successful leftist governments. And we must also keep in mind that a majority of the successful candidates from the left during the 2000s had been unsuccessful during the 1990s but had steadily increased their share of the vote on every bid. So the answer is unclear, and the use of complex statistical methods to solve this controversy satisfactorily is beyond the scope of this text.

It is important to note that the trend does not imply that Latin Americans have shifted *radically* towards the left in the past five years. As the preliminary release of Latinobarómetro surveys for 2006 shows, most countries in the region have average placements around the centre of the ideological scale (Latinobarómetro, 2006). Only Costa Rica and Honduras are placed slightly to the right, while Chile, Bolivia, Uruguay and Panama have placements slightly to the left. Yet all of them are in close proximity to the centre.

The related puzzle is that, once elected to office, the candidates from the left – the moderate versions of it – have not implemented extreme policies but have governed with an agenda similar to that of their conservative predecessors. This might be the result of the natural bureaucratic inertia that slows down the implementation of different policies, or it might well be the result of insufficient legislative majorities that impede drastic budgetary changes to finance new policies. But an additional, plausible explanation can be found in the ideological changes illustrated above. In each country a plurality of voters elected candidates from the left, and it is to them that presidents have needed to cater in order to remain in power. Evidence suggests that successful candidates from the left typically are those who have built larger support coalitions that go beyond the left and usually reach to the right as well (Morales, 2008). That is, the more successful candidates from the left are those who have been supported by more ideologically diverse groups of voters.

This might also contribute to a more robust explanation of the middle-ground path most governments of the left have taken in Latin America: by their expressed self-identification, fewer individuals would agree with radical changes towards the left and, whether the more moderate versions of leftists share this preference or not, the fact is that they are constrained by their constituencies. Furthermore, if governments from the left agree to play by the rules of the democratic game, they will simply be bound by their constituencies not to enact more radical policy changes. But if governments from the left start violating the rules of the game as a *modus operandi*, then they can put in place much more radical policies. Remarkably, that is what we observe in practice.

Not all lefts are created equal

The question lingers: are there one, two or more lefts in Latin America? During the past decade and a half we have witnessed an increase in the number of elected governments that subscribe to the tradition of the left. The phenomenon must be understood, but is our object of interest the same in all cases? We argue that it is not – that the differences between cases suggest the need for at least two categories (Castañeda, 2006). Their origins are divergent: some sprang from a historical left that updated itself to accede to power and remain there, while others appeared with a flamboyant and appealing populist discourse. Their means to accede to and remain in power are also at conflict: some subscribe to the limits of the democratic game and the rule of law, while others tend to trample on institutions when they become inconvenient for their immediate needs. The ultimate long-term goals of their policies are also different: some look for immediate results to cement their support and allow them to remain in power, while others willingly assume the costs today for policies that will have long-lasting effects tomorrow in those areas they care about the most–poverty and inequality.

The striking – and convenient – conclusion one can draw from these distinctions is that they show overlaps that strongly suggest the adequacy of a dichotomous classification. The labels convey information about the distance between the poles. So it is irrelevant whether the labels are "good" versus "bad", "right" versus "wrong" or "modern" versus "old"; the point is that the two discriminating extremes in this spectrum provide a robust frame for analysis. Are two categories enough or do we need more (Schamis, 2006)? Taxonomies are schematic by definition. They are supposed to capture certain commonalities of a given population. But a taxonomy with as many classifications as there are cases simply cannot help to improve our understanding of the phenomenon we observe.[19] We could subject a dichotomous classification to another subdivision and refine the contours of the differences between groups. Yet parsimony is better appreciated when new schemes fail to improve our understanding of the rise of the left in Latin America. So we will not discard refinements from the outset, but simply point to the trade-off involved in adding complexity to models while gaining little explanatory power in return.

Grouping Chávez, Kirchner and Morales at the opposite pole to Lula, Bachelet and Vázquez is not without challenge. The former do belong to a different category, it is argued, because they are the ones who have delivered on their promises (Weisbrot, 2006) and the only ones who have responded to "long-ignored needs and building much-needed human capital" (Álvarez Herrera, 2006). Be that as it may, the core question is not whether they reduced poverty by a certain percentage or whether they implemented direct transfers to the poorest or whether their motives agree with their discourse. The relevant question has to do with the *sustainability* of these policies. That is, for how long can poverty be reduced as a result of direct transfers to the population without the use of additional instruments to help people overcome poverty and remain out of poverty afterwards? If poverty-reducing policies are based on the availability of cash, it is only natural that when the flow of these funds stops so will the programmes, and consequently poverty might go back to its previous level.[20] Furthermore, it is inevitable to ask if financing these direct cash transfers is the best use of resources to tackle poverty. After all, if there are better uses for these funds, do elected leaders not have – at the very least – a moral obligation to engage in them?

Making this distinction, as exemplified above, clarifies – rather than obscures (Cleary, 2006) – the actual trend we see in the region: both types of left have come to power, but it is the moderate versions of the left that are being more successful at winning elections. Are Hugo Chávez and Evo Morales anomalies? It is hard to say without better-defined counterfactuals, and that is beyond the scope of this text. Yet the evidence mentioned earlier suggests that the rise of the left is a result of its appealing to a critical mass of voters. Given voters' ideological shifts, more moderate policies just might be needed to gain office.

Following the same line of reasoning, we also subscribe to the explanation that it is not so much institutions as voters who determine the winner in an election.[21] A country might have somewhat stable democratic institutions – think of Mexico in 2006 – but the candidate from the left who cannot appeal to a sufficient number of voters due to a radicalized discourse is highly unlikely to win the election.[22] Was it a stable institutional framework or his ability to alienate more centrist voters that kept López Obrador out of office? We tend to think it was the latter.

Analysts might choose to question the basis for a distinction or, jeopardizing their credibility, impose some value-charged "ulterior motives" on the taxonomy (Borón, 2006). The latter simply adds nothing to our understanding of the rise of the left; the former opens a venue for potentially profitable discussion. By claiming that there is only one left and, therefore, only one surge to be explained, we would necessarily have to assume that the same factors affect all countries in exactly the same manner. Somehow it does not make intuitive sense to make this assumption when explaining the rise of Chávez, Morales, Bachelet and Lula. Clearly, if distinguishing between cases shows beyond all reasonable doubt that the factors explaining the rise of some cases are equally applicable to the rest, then we might confidently conclude that distinguishing between cases with certain common features would strengthen our confidence in a single "left wave" in Latin America. For the time being, however, we would not advise throwing out the baby along with the bathwater.

A closer look at the countries that have chosen the left

It makes sense to look more closely at the countries that have elected or re-elected governments from the left to see if anything in them suggests they differ from the rest of Latin America. For descriptive purposes, we use the convenient term "cluster of the left" for countries that have had governments identified with the left since 1990. If there is nothing different about these countries, we should not observe any radical differences when we compare this cluster with the rest of Latin America. Yet evidence strongly suggests that there is something peculiar about them.

Latinobarómetro's latest analysis of the attitudes of Latin Americans in 2006 shows some intriguing trends in terms of attitudes (Latinobarómetro, 2006). The numbers are interesting *per se*, but become even more revealing when we aggregate and compare them. For instance, while 41 per cent of Latin America's population think the elections in their countries are not fraudulent, the number rises to 47 per cent in the cluster of the left and to 65 per cent in countries with a modern left: Chile, Uruguay and Brazil. The story is similar when we look at the proportion of individuals who think their countries are democratic. On average, only 36 per cent of Latin Americans think their country is democratic, but this number is a bit higher (39 per cent) in the cluster of the left and higher still (43 per cent) in the countries with a modern left. And when asked if their governments act for the good of the people, only 26 per cent agree with the statement, but the number is higher (28 per cent) in the cluster of the left and even higher (35 per cent) in the countries governed by the modern left. Finally, and perhaps most relevant, 38 per cent of Latin Americans are satisfied with how democracy works in their own country; in the cluster of the left the number rises to 40 per cent and in countries governed by the modern left to 48 per cent.

As a group, therefore, it seems clear that voters in countries that have elected governments from the left have attitudes that differ from those in the rest of Latin America – differences that seem to crystallize in satisfaction with their institutions and the way these institutions work.

It is obviously hard to draw strong conclusions with aggregate data for a single point in time. But it would be naïve to deny that the data suggest differences in attitudes in countries that have preferred to be governed by the left: voters there seem to be more content with their system and with the results of their governments. We cannot know if it is the government from the left that has made them more content with the system, or if they were previously content with the system and elected a government from the left for this reason. Yet these numbers do certainly suggest that we should not just ignore differences within the left.

A new left emerging?

The preceding lines naturally lead to a series of conclusions regarding the surge of the left and the nature of the parties from the left that have been elected to office. There has indeed been a surge of the left in Latin America, and the number of parties identified with the left that have been elected has increased since the 1990s. But the surge that we saw concentrated between 2003 and 2006 is clearly the final stage of a process that had been brewing during the previous decade. Nearly all the parties from the left that are currently in power increased their share of the vote in election after election until finally winning and, for the most part, they have sustained this growth once in office. Interestingly, however, the recent elections have underscored that, with some notable exceptions, parties from the left that present "quality" candidates fare much better when these candidates are moderate and avoid a radical rhetoric.

The parties from the left differ in their origins – some are updated versions of the old Latin American left with a long-term vision; others are populist versions of the left that seek power with short-term goals. They are also more successful in countries where voters hold a particular set of opinions. Voters in countries where governments from the left have been elected are, in general, more satisfied with their institutions than are voters in other Latin American countries.

The differences between these two types of parties from the left are perhaps best illustrated by their different policies. The parties from the moderate left did not come to power to implement radical changes in policy; rather, they have adapted policies that have worked well in other countries or have tried to enact their own "interpretations" of a somewhat different model. Yet it seems to be the case that these moderate versions of the left have adapted particularly well to the constraints that are desirable in a well-functioning democracy. That is, by virtue of the need to appeal to broader constituencies, which implies reaching out to the ideological spectrum beyond the left, these parties seem to be naturally constrained by the incentives of the democratic game. The left needs to remain in power in order to maintain policy continuity, and one way to do that is by minimizing the risk of losing the next election. This is easily achieved by not implementing radical reforms that might alienate voters, and by producing some of those desirable results that made the left an attractive alternative in the first place. It seems only natural that the very features of the moderate left lead to long-term results.

Unfortunately, the same logic does not apply to the populist variants of parties from the left, especially as these tend to be centred around the figure of a charismatic leader, not around the party *per se*, and hinge on short-term results to remain in power. To an extent, the updating and institutionalization of one variant of the left has served to safeguard against a broader surge of populism. At the same time, the ability of this left to define its agenda more clearly has enhanced its attraction to voters and its chances of achieving long-term goals. It is fortunate, then, that Latin

American voters do not seem to be fooled that easily by radical and populist candidates, but have tended to prefer a more moderate course.

Notes

1. If we consider Costa Rica's Oscar Arias to have been on the centre-left due to his party's social democratic credentials, and if we align the party platform of Panama's Martín Torrijos also with the centre-left, this number rises to 11.
2. In 2009 five countries in Latin America are scheduled to hold presidential elections: El Salvador, Panama, Honduras, Chile and Uruguay. Unless the left loses the presidency in Chile or Uruguay – which seems unlikely at the time of writing – the ratio of left to right governments is unlikely to be altered.
3. Official results from Chile's Servicio Electoral.
4. It would actually be his second full term since the new constitution entered into force in 2000. But he had served for two years as president after being elected in 1998 for the first time.
5. Preliminary results from Venezuela's Consejo Nacional Electoral.
6. Official results from Brazil's Tribunal Superior Electoral.
7. Official results from Argentina's Dirección Nacional Electoral at the Ministry of the Interior.
8. Official results from Uruguay's Corte Electoral.
9. Official results from Bolivia's Corte Nacional Electoral.
10. Official results from Nicaragua's Consejo Supremo Electoral.
11. Official results from Peru's Oficina Nacional de Procesos Electorales.
12. Official results from Ecuador's Tribunal Supremo Electoral.
13. Official results from Mexico's Instituto Federal Electoral.
14. While it may never be known for certain how many votes Cárdenas got in 1988, he obtained around 18 per cent of the vote in both 1994 and 2000.
15. Official results from Colombia's Registraduría Nacional del Estado Civil.
16. European and World Values Surveys Four-Wave Integrated Data File, 1981–2004, v.20060423, 2006. The European Values Study Foundation and World Values Survey Association. Aggregate File Producers: ASEP/JDS, Madrid, Spain/Tilburg University, Tilburg, the Netherlands. Aggregate File Distributors: ASEP/JDS and ZA, Cologne, Germany.
17. Latinobarómetro databases for 2001 and 2005 that include representative samples for Argentina, Bolivia, Brazil, Colombia, Costa Rica, Chile, Ecuador, El Salvador, Guatemala, Honduras, Mexico, Nicaragua, Panama, Paraguay, Peru, Uruguay and Venezuela are available from the corporation's website for analysis; see www.latinobarometro.org.
18. The same results hold using only data for Argentina, Brazil, Chile, Mexico, Peru and Venezuela.
19. One of the clearest examples of this preference can be found in Corrales (2006).
20. This is not a very popular perspective on this debate, where most accounts seem to care only about immediate results. For alternative formulations see Stiglitz (2006) and Cardoso (2006).
21. For the opposite view see Da Nóbrega (2006).
22. It could also be argued that López Obrador nearly won the election, but this is more a function of the effective number of candidates competing. Had there been a run-off between Calderón and López Obrador, we could have seen a reshuffling of votes from the

excluded candidates to those in the run-off. We need to point out, however, that there were three-party contests as well in 1994 and 2000, but Cárdenas was never as close as López Obrador to winning an election.

REFERENCES

Álvarez Herrera, Bernardo (2006) "A Benign Revolution", *Foreign Affairs* 85(4), pp. 195–198.
Borón, Atilio (2006) "Vargas Llosa y la democracia: Breve historia de una relación infeliz", *Pensamiento Crítico*, 7 November.
Cardoso, Fernando Henrique (2006) "Populism and Globalization Don't Mix", *New Perspectives Quarterly* 23(2), p. 63.
Castañeda, Jorge G. (1994) *Utopia Unarmed: The Latin American Left after the Cold War*, New York: Vintage Books.
——— (2006) "Latin America's Left Turn", *Foreign Affairs* 85(3), pp. 28–43.
Cleary, Michael (2006) "Explaining the Left's Resurgence", *Journal of Democracy* 17(4), pp. 34–49.
Corrales, Javier (2006) "The Many Lefts of Latin America", *Foreign Policy* 157, pp. 44–45.
Da Nóbrega, Mailson (2006) "Latin America, Two Lefts or Two Tendencies?", *Tendencias Weekly*, 20 June.
ECLAC (2006) *Statistical Yearbook for Latin America and the Caribbean, 2005*, Santiago: UN Economic Commission for Latin America and the Caribbean.
Latinobarómetro (2001) *Informe Latinobarómetro 2001*, Santiago: Latinobarómetro, available at www.latinobarometro.org.
——— (2005) *Informe Latinobarómetro 2005*, Santiago: Latinobarómetro, available at www.latinobarometro.org.
——— (2006) *Informe Latinobarómetro 2006*, Santiago: Latinobarómetro, available at www.latinobarometro.org.
Machinea, José Luis, Alicia Bárcena and Arturo León (2005) *The Millennium Development Goals: A Latin American and Caribbean Perspective*, Santiago: UN Economic Commission for Latin America and the Caribbean.
Morales, Marco A. (2008) "Have Latin Americans Turned Left?", in Jorge G. Castañeda and Marco A. Morales, eds, *Leftovers: Tales of the Latin American Left*, New York: Routledge.
Schamis, Hector E. (2006) "Populism, Socialism and Democratic Institutions", *Journal of Democracy* 17(4), pp. 20–34.
Stiglitz, Joseph (2006) "Is Populism Really So Bad for Latin America?", *New Perspectives Quarterly* 23(2), pp. 61–62.
Weisbrot, Mark (2006) "Left Hook", *Foreign Affairs* 85(4), p. 200.
World Values Survey (2008) *European and World Values Surveys Four-Wave Integrated Data File, 1981–2004*, available at www.worldvaluessurvey.org/.

Part II
The new economic challenges

4

Competing for energy

Sidney Weintraub and Annette Hester

Energy policy in Latin America is driven more by cross-country animosities than by cooperative efforts. The outstanding example of long-lasting resentment is Bolivia's inability to come to terms with the loss of its access to the sea following its defeat by Chile in the nineteenth-century War of the Pacific. Bolivia is still unwilling to ship natural gas to Chile or use a Chilean port to liquefy Bolivian natural gas for shipment to Mexico and the United States. Argentina has ceased shipping natural gas to Chile because of a lack of supplies, while Peru is reluctant to sell natural gas to Chile. Instead of relying on its neighbours, Chile is now building a regasification facility to receive liquefied natural gas (LNG) from Indonesia and other distant locations.[1]

The inability of Latin American and Caribbean (LAC) countries to sustain regional energy cooperation is similar to what happened in the trade field. Examples of trade contention are manifold: the Latin American Free Trade Association was dissolved in 1980 after 21 years of existence because it proved impossible to lower internal tariffs; the idea of a Free Trade Area of the Americas was greeted enthusiastically when proposed in 1994, but has become moribund because of disagreement over the gradual removal of the internal protection necessary to make free trade possible; and the Southern Common Market (Mercosur, whose core members are Argentina, Brazil, Paraguay and Uruguay) has long been beset by conflicts over protective measures by Argentina and Brazil that have prevented formation of the customs union that was originally envisioned. Even though it would be inconsistent with the nominal customs

Which way Latin America? Hemispheric politics meets globalization, Cooper and Heine, eds, United Nations University Press, 2009, ISBN 978-92-808-1172-8

union of Mercosur, Uruguay has flirted with signing a free trade agreement with the United States because of the burdens placed on its exports to Brazil and Argentina.[2] Mercosur's original plans were grand; the follow-through has been discordant. Trade among Mercosur countries has nevertheless increased because of their high economic growth over the past five years, stimulated largely by the high prices received for their commodities because of increased demand from China and India. High growth of gross domestic product (GDP) normally engenders increased imports.

This lack of cohesion goes mostly unnoticed by the United States. US practice has long been to ignore LAC countries other than at times of perceived crisis; this neglect was notable after 11 September 2001, when official attention became centred on the Middle East. The disregard for the region is particularly disconcerting because Western hemisphere countries supply about 50 per cent of US oil and oil-product imports and 95 per cent of its natural gas imports. The largest US oil supplier is Canada (which also supplies the bulk of its natural gas imports), but Mexico and Venezuela are also important sources (see fig. 4.1).

Thus, in this chapter, we deal primarily with the lack of energy cooperation in the hemisphere and the economic cost this imposes on the region. Understanding the existing choke points in the hemisphere is essential for the analysis that follows, in which we suggest areas where cooperation might be pursued. The inability to sustain trade cooperation

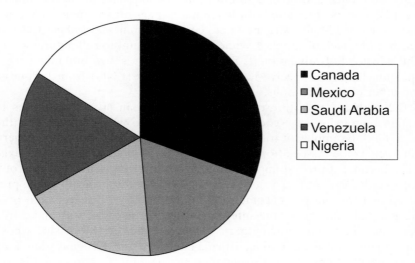

Figure 4.1 US oil imports by source country, January–October 2007
Source: US Department of Energy, Energy Information Administration, available at http://tonto.eia.doe.gov/dnav/pet/pet_move_impcus_a2_nus_ep00_im0_mbbl_m.htm.

has also been economically costly for LAC countries. Explanations given in the trade field, ranging from dependency theory to deploring the so-called Washington Consensus allegedly imposed from outside, have their counterparts in today's energy practices based on political grievances. National policies have not been optimal in either field for stimulating LAC economic growth.

Oil and natural gas production and consumption in the hemisphere

In 2006 the United States imported a net total of more than 13 million barrels a day (bbl/d) of oil (both crude and oil products), equal to about 66 per cent of US oil demand. Importantly, while demand has been increasing, domestic production is in decline. The implication is that, all other factors remaining constant, US dependency on foreign supplies will increase. The Western hemisphere's 50 per cent share of US oil imports is thus significant both because proximity reduces shipment costs and because an extensive infrastructure network exists, especially in North America. In addition, the quality of Mexican and Venezuelan exports of crude oil is such that most of it can be refined only in the United States and not, for the most part, at home or in other countries. Looking only at the hemispheric share of US imports can be misleading, however, because the market for oil is global, and specific arrangements between suppliers and markets are generally less important than the global relationship between supply and demand. Nonetheless, the significant increase in demand for oil from China and India, their growing pre-occupation with security of supply and the concentration of oil assets in the hands of national oil companies make global market equilibrium delicate.

US natural gas consumption in 2006 was 619.7 billion cubic metres (bcm) and total imports were around 116 bcm, of which about 86 per cent came from Canada. Imports of LNG in 2006, in contrast, amounted to only 16.56 bcm, 75 per cent of which came from Trinidad and Tobago; another 17 per cent was delivered by pipeline from Canada and Mexico. Offshore imports of LNG are likely to grow considerably, based on estimates of declining production of natural gas in the United States, Canada and Mexico (North American Energy Working Group, 2005), although pipeline-delivered LNG from North American sources might be significant if the Alaska pipeline and the related Mackenzie Valley pipeline come to fruition and if there is a significant increase in production from unconventional sources, especially in Canada, where unconventional gas is still largely untapped.

In 2006 Canada exported 2.3 million bbl/d of oil to the United States, representing about 17 per cent of US crude-oil imports. Most of this was unconventional oil from oil sands, production from which could increase significantly in the next decade, although serious environmental and labour constraints will likely dampen current high projections.

Mexico is also a significant oil producer, but the country has only about 10 years of proven reserves based on current production levels, due primarily to insufficient investment in exploring the deep waters of the Gulf of Mexico.[3] In addition, Mexico's imports of oil products and natural gas are growing.

Brazil, in part because of its development of ethanol as a transportation fuel, is now self-sufficient in oil, but the country is still dependent on natural gas imports from Bolivia. Argentina, until a few years ago, was an important producer and exporter of natural gas to Chile, but price controls under the government of President Néstor Kirchner stifled investment. Argentina has now signed a long-term contract to receive natural gas from Bolivia, which has large proven reserves. Unless more discoveries are made, however, Bolivia will find it difficult to meet its domestic needs as well as its commitments to Brazil, Bolivia's largest foreign market, let alone fulfil its new contract with Argentina.

Colombia supplies its own oil needs and has a modest residue for export; it also has considerable coal reserves. Ecuador has the third-largest proven oil reserves in Latin America, but the country has been beset in recent years by political turmoil, and uncertainty will continue at least until President Rafael Correa's intentions become clearer. Peru has considerable proven gas reserves, but these are in an environmentally sensitive area close to the Amazon, and issues related to ecological damage have yet to be fully resolved.

Venezuela has the highest conventional oil reserves in the LAC region, about 77 billion barrels, plus even more non-conventional extra-heavy bitumen reserves. Despite the animosity between President Hugo Chávez and the United States, 60 per cent of Venezuela's exports are sent to the United States because US refineries – including several owned by Venezuela – are equipped to handle Venezuela's heavy oils. (See tables 4.1 and 4.2 for a summary of oil and natural gas production, consumption, trade and proven reserves in the Western hemisphere.)

The meaning of cooperation

Two Latin American countries, Venezuela and Ecuador, are members of the Organization of Petroleum Exporting Countries (OPEC). OPEC countries cooperate with each other to control the prices they receive

Table 4.1 Oil and natural gas production, consumption and trade, Western hemisphere, 2006

| | Oil *(thousands of barrels per day)* | | | | |
| | | | Trade | | |
	Production	Consumption	Imports	Exports	Balance
United States	6,871	20,589	13,612	1,317	−12,295
Mexico	3,683	1,972	421	2,102	1,681
Canada	3,147	2,222	1,130	2,330	1,200
South and Central America			1,178	3,681	2,503
Venezuela	2,824	565			
Brazil	1,809	2,097			
Argentina	716	442			
Colombia	558	230			
Ecuador	545	180			
Trinidad and Tobago	174				
Peru	116	160			
Chile		248			
	Natural gas *(billions of cubic metres)*				
United States	524.1	619.7	116.4	20.9	−95.5
Canada	187.0	96.6	9.4	99.8	90.4
Argentina	46.1	41.8	1.8	6.1	4.3
Mexico	43.4	54.1	10.8	0.1	−10.7
Trinidad and Tobago	35.0		0.0	16.3	16.3
Venezuela	28.7	28.7			
Brazil	11.5	21.1	9.5	0.0	−9.5
Bolivia	11.2		0.0	10.8	10.8
Colombia	7.3	7.3			
Chile		7.6	5.6	0.0	−5.6
Peru		1.8			

Source: BP (2007).

for their oil sales by limiting or expanding supply. Yet cooperation in the Western hemisphere need not – indeed, should not – result in the formation of a cartel or take the form of a commitment not to compete. The importance of Canada as a significant producer of unconventional oil provides considerable assurance against a cartel covering the entire hemisphere.

Cooperation and competition can be reinforcing phenomena. A good example of this kind of synergy can be seen in the field of international trade, where rules of conduct are agreed to by countries in the World Trade Organization (WTO) or in specific bilateral trade agreements in

Table 4.2 Proven reserves of oil and natural gas in Western hemisphere, end 2006

	Proven reserves	
	Oil *(billions of barrels)*	Natural gas *(trillions of cubic feet)*
Canada, oil sands	163.5	
Venezuela	80.0	152.3
United States	29.9	209.2
Canada, excluding oil sands	17.1	58.8
Mexico	12.9	13.7
Brazil	12.2	12.3
Ecuador	4.7	
Argentina	2.0	14.7
Colombia	1.5	4.3
Peru	1.1	12.0
Bolivia		26.1
Trinidad and Tobago		18.7

Source: BP (2007).

which they set a framework for what is considered fair competition. For example, the WTO generally proscribes government subsidies to promote international sales of manufactured goods, in order to permit undistorted price and quality competition to take place. As another example, international cooperation provides time-limited monopoly pricing for patents in order to promote inventiveness and prevent the stifling of originality. As still another example, the International Energy Organization, part of the Organisation for Economic Co-operation and Development (OECD), was created as a counterbalance to OPEC in order to provide reliable energy data and project the likely future direction of oil production, prices and sales to facilitate oil trade.

We envisage hemispheric cooperation as including the following types of actions to facilitate energy trade:

• reaching agreement on the construction of infrastructure, including oil and gas pipelines to encourage trade between countries, gas liquefaction facilities to export gas and regasification facilities at the import end
• providing accurate figures on oil and gas production and reserves to permit forward planning
• providing time for commentary by other countries when national oil and gas regulations are written or altered – a sensitive area in many countries given the independence of regulatory agencies
• cooperation on defining standard measurements for reporting emissions and ongoing consultation on environmental policy.

Most of these kinds of cooperative activities are already well developed between Canada and the United States and, to a large extent, between Mexico and the other two, but they are less solid between LAC countries. The formation of the North American Energy Working Group in 2001 facilitated cooperation among the three North American countries and has led to the joint publication of valuable energy data and projections that make planning easier with respect to, for example, natural gas, particularly proposed and approved LNG terminals in the three countries. Moreover, pipeline and cross-national electricity infrastructure is much more extensive in North America than in LAC countries, in part because Canada and the United States are richer than the LAC countries, but also because habits of cooperation between the two countries have a long history and solid institutional base.

Impediments to energy cooperation

Impediments to energy cooperation are of various types: historical, ideological, nationalistic, populist and combinations of these. As noted above, Bolivia's unwillingness to ship natural gas to Chile is based on its nineteenth-century loss of access to the sea, but it also reflects uncertainty about the way Bolivia's government, under the leadership of Evo Morales, wishes to handle that country's hydrocarbon resources.[4]

In Mexico, in contrast, the impediment to energy cooperation is the near impossibility for the government to change the constitution to permit private equity investment in oil, most natural gas ventures and electricity generation, even if it wished to do so. Popular support for public operation of these activities has been built into the psyche of most Mexicans by the glorification of the expropriation of foreign oil properties 60 years ago – indeed, Lázaro Cárdenas, president in 1938 when the expropriation took place, is one of Mexico's revered heroes. A constitutional change might be possible, however, if Mexico ran out of oil or faced an energy crisis that substantially raised electricity costs to non-competitive levels. There is much inexact talk outside Mexico that Pemex (Petróleos Mexicanos, the national oil company) will have to be privatized to attract foreign investment. In fact, Pemex does not have to be privatized to enter into joint ventures with private companies, foreign or domestic, any more than would other national oil companies, such as Brazil's Petrobras, Norway's Statoil or Saudi Arabia's Aramco. Unlike in Mexico, however, potential investors can "book reserves" to support energy investment financing in other countries with national oil companies.

In Argentina, President Néstor Kirchner set limits on the prices producers could charge for natural gas in order to build his political popularity, an action that, quite naturally, stifled exploration investment in that country.[5] In Venezuela, impediments to energy cooperation are President Chávez's animosity toward the United States and his affinity with Fidel Castro; these are largely ideological, but his own ego plays a role as well.

Individual country situations

Beyond the general analysis provided above, the details of energy policy are unique in each country. Some countries seek cooperation while others resist it, not always with the intention to be recalcitrant but sometimes because national conditions encourage such behaviour, as in Mexico.

The United States

The importance of the United States cannot be overstated when discussing hemispheric energy issues, since in 2006 it consumed almost 21 million bbl/d of oil – close to 25 per cent of global consumption.

In recent years there has been significant official emphasis on energy "security", a term that is rarely defined precisely and is often conflated with the need for energy "independence", something that surely will not be possible for many decades, if ever. The US need for imported energy, particularly oil and gas, must thus be an element of US foreign policy, not a separate consideration – indeed, in 2006 an independent task force of the US Council on Foreign Relations cited the folly of seeking oil independence as its first major point (Deutch and Schlesinger, 2006: 14). This empty talk of energy independence, coupled with neglect of the region that provides about half of US imported oil, has been imprudent.

Only recently has the US government emphasized the search for alternatives to gasoline, particularly ethanol, in order to reduce dependency on imported oil for transportation needs and to respond to growing environmental concerns. The United States has now overtaken Brazil to become the world's largest producer of ethanol, using corn as the raw material (in Brazil the feedstock is sugarcane). Brazilian ethanol production no longer needs direct subsidies; US ethanol production, in contrast, is highly subsidized, and it is unlikely ever to be economical without subsidies. In addition, the United States charges heavy import duties (54 cents per gallon, plus a 2.5 per cent tariff) on ethanol imports from Brazil. A more rational policy would be for greater cooperation among

Brazil, the United States, the European Union and Canada to improve ethanol and other biomass technologies. Cooperative research would also be valuable to assess the price impact of the growing use of food and feed crops to produce biofuels.[6]

Ethanol now provides about 3 per cent of the energy used to power transportation in the United States, compared with 40 per cent in Brazil. Even if the United States were to accelerate the development of ethanol technology, it would take decades to make a significant effect on reducing the US demand for gasoline. Moreover, the adoption of ethanol as a significant transportation fuel requires dedicated pipeline and distribution systems and the production of flex-fuel vehicles capable of handling either gasoline or alcohol at the pump. Still, the United States is making some modest progress in reducing gasoline demand now that corporate average fuel economy standards have been broadened in recent energy legislation.[7]

As energy prices have risen, the United States has become more efficient in energy usage – GDP per unit of energy use rose by 20 per cent from 1994 to 2003 (World Bank, 2006) – but much more could be done if energy security were truly a major national goal.

Finally, the intersection of environmental and energy policies is sure to gain importance in the near future. Proposed environmental legislation, currently being discussed in the Senate, singles out varied energy production by source and seeks to "tax" production that is heavily associated with emissions.

Canada

The relationship between Canada and the United States is the major exception to the hemispheric picture of lack of cooperation. Indeed, the US-Canadian economic and energy relationship is more intimate than that between any other two countries in the hemisphere. Total US two-way trade is greater with Canada than with all other countries in the hemisphere taken together, despite Canada's modest population of about 33 million compared with 560 million in the LAC countries. Canada is the largest foreign supplier of oil, oil products, natural gas and electricity to the United States. When the North American Free Trade Agreement (NAFTA) was negotiated, it included a provision that Canada would supply the United States with a proportional share of oil set at a certain percentage of its production even in times of shortage in Canada, although this commitment has never been tested in practice. Mexico essentially omitted making any commitments on oil in NAFTA.

Counting what is believed to be recoverable oil from the oil sands in the Western Canada Sedimentary Basin, Canada's proven reserves are 178 billion barrels, second only to those of Saudi Arabia. In 2006 Canada's total oil production was 3.15 million bbl/d, although, as in the United States, conventional sources are in decline. Meanwhile unconventional production has risen dramatically, from 430,000 bbl/d in 1996 to 1.22 million bbl/d in 2006. Moreover, according to the Alberta government's own projections,[8] oil-sands production could top 3 million bbl/d per day by 2020 and possibly even 5 million bbl/d by 2030.[9]

These two factors – a commitment to energy cooperation and the resource base of the oil sands – together make Canada the most reliable hemispheric supplier of oil to the United States.

The development of Canada's oil sands took a combination of persistence, favourable legislation on taxes and royalties, much investment and the good fortune of high oil prices to make Canada's unconventional oil competitive. It also required constant upgrading of technology, something that will be needed in the future as well. The early stages of oil extraction were largely a mining operation to remove the overburden to get at the bitumen below. Future production will require heating the bitumen underground, *in situ*, to get it to flow to where it can be gathered. Some 80 per cent of total production is expected to come from *in situ* operations.

Canada will have to solve major problems to meet its publicly announced production goals. The quantity of water necessary to extract and upgrade the oil is immense, toxic emissions are high and the cost to heat the underground bitumen, now done by expensive natural gas, ultimately may become prohibitive. Considerable technology improvements will be both costly and imperative. Canada ratified the Kyoto Protocol environmental obligations, but cannot meet them largely because of its oil-sands operations.[10]

Mexico

Despite its large current oil production and exports, Mexico is a less reliable oil supplier than Canada because it has devoted less funds to exploration and has not maintained its production/reserve ratio in recent years. In 2006 Mexico produced 3.7 million bbl/d of oil, 1.7million bbl/d of which was exported to the United States, amounting to 12 per cent of US oil imports. Unless augmented, however, Mexico's proven oil reserves will last only about 10 years at current production and replacement rates. The lack of funds for exploration is due to high taxation by the federal government of the gross revenues of Pemex; the federal government relies on these taxes to finance 40 per cent of its general budget.

As a result, Pemex has had losses in most years since the early 1990s. Because of high world oil prices, the federal government has been able to provide additional funds to Pemex during the past few years – even though Mexican oil is sold at a discount because of its relatively low quality – but there have been few important oil finds despite this extra revenue. Mexico enacted new legislation in 2007 that is expected to increase tax collection by 1 per cent of GDP in 2008 and about 2 per cent of GDP in subsequent years. This increased tax revenue will enable the government to reduce its take from Pemex, although modestly.[11]

Mexico could expand exploration and reserves in four different ways. First, it could collect even more taxes, but the intense battle required in 2007 to change the tax laws is most unlikely to be repeated during President Felipe Calderón's remaining time in office until the end of 2012. Second, it could allow Pemex to go deeper into debt; something that few in Mexico think is a sound option. Third, Mexico could accept private investment in joint ventures with Pemex, as other national oil companies do in Latin America and elsewhere. Fourth, Mexico could get lucky and hit it rich, although this would be like winning a lottery and cannot be described as policy. None of these is a "solution" that has a high probability of success in the near term (that is, during the current administration), and an oil and electricity crisis could arise in the medium term (say, during the six-year term of the next president).

The difference between the way that Pemex must operate and the way independent oil companies, many from the United States, operate can be seen in the Gulf of Mexico. Promising oil and gas possibilities exist in the deep waters of the Gulf, and drillings in this area now account for about two-thirds of total US Gulf oil output. Indeed, as figure 4.2 shows, the US part of the Gulf is replete with exploratory drillings, while the Mexican part has practically none. Deep-water exploration can cost as much as $100 million per well for each exploratory effort, but Pemex cannot afford this without assurance of success each time, which is not the way oil exploration works. Consequently, Pemex has no solid experience in deep-water drilling; by contrast, Petrobras, the Brazilian national oil company, has developed this expertise to good advantage in deep waters off the Brazilian coast. Indeed, in an auction held in August 2007, Petrobras was the highest bidder for 34 of 40 blocks in the US portion of the Gulf of Mexico (Petrobras, 2007).

Venezuela

Because of high oil prices, President Chávez of Venezuela has ample funds to play a prominent role in Latin America and elsewhere. Venezuela provides oil at concessionary prices to Cuba and other countries in

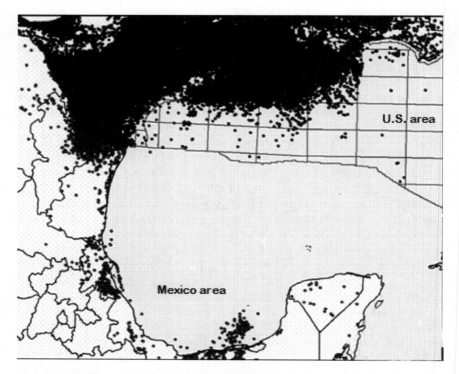

Figure 4.2 US and Mexican drilling in the Gulf of Mexico
Note: Each dot represents a drilling.
Source: Weintraub and Fernández de Castro (2007: 122); reprinted with permission.

the Caribbean, and has bought Ecuadorian and Argentine bonds to assist those countries. Chávez has talked frequently of shifting his major oil exports from the United States to China, but he has been unable to take this very far because the refining capacity for Venezuela's heavy oil does not exist in China. This must be frustrating for Chávez as he railed against the United States and President Bush in particular, as he did in his address at the opening of the UN General Assembly in September 2006. By the same token, Chávez's constant attacks, his close relations with Cuba and his courting of other anti-American oil producers, such as Iran, are frustrating for the US government because answering in kind merely gives more weight to his pronouncements.

Data on Venezuela oil production are unreliable; the government says that oil production is in excess of 3.3 million bbl/d, but analysts believe the 2006 figure was 2.8 million bbl/d (BP, 2007). Petróleos de Venezuela

SA, the national oil company, is less efficient than it was before Chávez came to power because many employees were fired in February 2003 after a strike by officials and workers failed in its effort to force Chávez from office. Chávez was re-elected president for another six-year term in December 2006.

Chávez has proposed construction of a 5,600-mile mega-pipeline for natural gas going from Venezuela, across sensitive terrain in the Brazilian Amazon and down to Argentina, with spurs that could serve Brazilian cities and Uruguay as well. The cost of such a project could be as high as US$30 billion – depending on construction delays. It is most unlikely that the mega-pipeline project will come to fruition, however, because Venezuela does not produce enough natural gas to fill it (its gas reserves are associated with oil and would require considerably more oil production than Venezuela now wants if oil prices are to remain high), the environmental consequences could be severe and the cost of the gas in the Southern Cone would probably be higher than imported LNG. Lately, Chávez has put this project on the back burner and instead is touting the possibility of delivering LNG to Uruguay and Argentina.

Venezuela is not making provisions for a sharp fall in oil and gas prices. Instead, its high oil revenues are being invested in state-sponsored industries for cotton, steel, cement, pulp and paper and other activities; they are also being used to create jobs and substitute for imports, as well as to finance Chávez's foreign escapades. Before Chávez, Venezuela prospered when oil prices were high but suffered when they were low because little was set aside for the bad times. Chávez, however, is behaving as though oil prices will remain high for as long as he is around – and he obviously plans to be around for a long time.

Bolivia

Evo Morales, elected president in 2005, promised in his campaign to renegotiate oil and gas contracts and to nationalize private companies operating in these activities in Bolivia. He has kept his promise – more or less – but he has had to backtrack from time to time because of resistance from Brazil and because he realized that Bolivia's national oil company, Yacimientos Petroliferos Fiscales Bolivianos, lacked the expertise to do all that was expected of it. Morales has close ties to Venezuela's Chávez and has apparently relied on him for advice on renegotiating prices for gas exports. There is a difference, however, between Venezuelan oil, which can trade as a commodity wherever there are refineries to receive it, and Bolivian gas, which must go by pipeline to neighbouring countries unless some of it is converted into LNG. The two countries to which Bolivia can export large amounts of gas are Brazil and potentially Argentina. As noted earlier, Bolivia refuses to sell gas to Chile unless Chile provides an outlet to the sea.

Foreign oil companies, particularly in the downstream sector, were nationalized in spectacular fashion on 1 May 2006 when troops were sent to seize at least 56 fields, including the largest operations, those of Petrobras and Repsol-YPF. Taxes and royalties were raised from 50 to 82 per cent for the largest fields, and the companies were given 180 days to comply or leave the country. The reaction in Petrobras, especially to the use of troops, was furious, but Brazil's President Luiz Inácio Lula da Silva was more conciliatory. Petrobras said it would sue over the contract annulment, but discussions have continued on gas prices because of Brazil's need for Bolivian gas and Lula's desire not to alienate Bolivia.

Morales is burning many bridges, and these may have to be rebuilt in the years ahead. Petrobras plays a large role in Bolivia; before its gas facilities were nationalized, Petrobras's operations accounted for some 20 per cent of Bolivia's GDP. New investment in Bolivia from Brazil ceased for a while, but is now under discussion once again because of Brazil's need for Bolivian gas. Brazil is speeding up development of gas finds in the deep waters of the Santos Basin off its Atlantic coast to provide gas to São Paulo state, and is planning to build regasification facilities to reduce future reliance on Bolivia.

Morales, in internal speeches, has been critical of the United States, which led to reluctance in the US Congress to extend import preferences to Bolivia that were due to expire in December 2006; in the end, the trade preferences were extended to all four Andean countries that enjoyed them (Bolivia, Colombia, Ecuador and Peru). Moreover, separatist sentiment has grown in Santa Cruz and other Bolivian departments that dominate the country's gas production and exports.[12]

Ecuador

Political instability has been a hallmark of the Ecuadorian situation for several decades. The country has had seven presidents since 1996 (11 if a triumvirate that lasted only hours and a president who was deposed after one day are counted). This political turmoil has gone hand in hand with Ecuador's troublesome relations with private investors. In May 2006, for example, the government terminated a contract with Occidental Petroleum (Oxy) and seized its assets, alleging breach of contract. Oxy, with support from the US government, is seeking the return of its assets and US$1 billion in damages. Ecuador has also had disputes with Texaco, now part of Chevron. ExxonMobil and BP have long since abandoned the country, and EnCana of Canada sold its assets there to a Chinese company in 2005. In 2005 private companies accounted for 62 per cent of oil production, while production by Petroecuador, the national oil company, has fallen by 50 per cent in the past 10 years.

In March 2006 the Ecuadorian legislature attempted to raise the tax on oil production to 60 per cent of all "excess" profits. The then president, Alfredo Palacio, vetoed the legislation, but a second version, which became law, increased the tax to 50 per cent of excess profits. The price of Ecuador's Oriente crude, which provided the baseline for what was deemed excessive, was $45 a barrel.

The United States had been negotiating a free trade agreement with Ecuador, but put the negotiations on hold after Oxy's assets were expropriated. Nevertheless, Ecuador was included in the US extension of Andean trade preferences enacted in December 2006. Relations between Ecuador and the United States are now largely in suspense because of the policy platform on which President Rafael Correa was elected in November 2006. He has said he intends to reschedule Ecuador's foreign debt, something that does not build investor confidence; he has also proposed renegotiation of oil contracts to increase the government take. It is uncertain which of these plans will be promulgated.

Brazil

Brazil differs from the other South American countries discussed thus far in several key respects. For one, it is home to half the population of South America. Furthermore, its oil and gas policies have, for the most part, been well thought through, and the operations of Petrobras, the national oil company, have largely been professional.

In the past few years Brazil has become self-sufficient in oil, thanks to a combination of new production and the use of ethanol alongside gasoline for transportation. However, the country must import large amounts of natural gas – about 15 million cubic metres a day, mostly from Bolivia. New discoveries have been made in waters as deep as 3,500 metres in the offshore Campos, Santos and Espirito Santo Basins, and large investments are being made to bring this gas to market. In November 2007 Petrobras announced the discovery of a large oil and gas find of 5–8 billion barrels of light oil, with associated gas, in the Santos Basin at depths of 5,000–7,000 metres, which if substantiated would significantly increase Brazil's current proven reserves of 12 billion barrels. The technology for bringing the oil and perhaps even the gas from Tupi (as the field is called) to market must still be worked out, however, and is likely to take years to accomplish.

The contrast between what Petrobras has been able to do at Tupi and the inability of Pemex to drill in much shallower waters in the Gulf of Mexico is a vivid example of the difference in the development of these two national oil companies.

Although the government has a majority of the voting shares, Petrobras also has private shareholders and many private companies have entered into joint ventures with it. Pemex, by contrast, has no joint ventures for the exploration and production of oil. The Mexican government – or at least that cohort of the government that favours a change in Pemex's structure – has sponsored trips by legislators to Brazil to learn more about how Petrobras is run.

Conclusions

The Western hemisphere offers much potential in terms of energy production and trade. However, unless policies that foster collaboration are put in place, this potential will be unrealized. For instance, Trinidad and Tobago contemplates increasing shipments of LNG to the United States, and therefore needs to know in advance that ample regasification facilities will be available at the US end. Chile and Brazil contemplate constructing regasification facilities to assure adequate supplies of natural gas in the future, and thus must nail down where the LNG will come from. Much investment in exploration and production as well as enlarged pipeline facilities will be needed for Bolivia to meet its contract to increase natural gas shipments to Brazil and Argentina. The infrastructure involved in these cases is both costly and time-consuming to build, and it takes at least two parties for construction to move ahead. Similarly, the economic production of ethanol will require upgraded technology of a kind that can be used by many countries. Developing the least costly and most secure techniques for carbon dioxide sequestration when coal is used for generating electricity will also require cross-country cooperation.

Such examples of essential cooperation are self-evident. It is less obvious but equally necessary for countries to estimate their future energy needs and how these will be supplied. It might take a decade or more to bring a new oil and gas find to market, as is likely to be the case for Brazil's Tupi exploitation. It might take decades to perfect sophisticated battery technology for motor vehicles. The same is true for other alternative energy technologies, such as wind and solar power on a large scale.

In this vein, energy planners must make judgements today about which foreign suppliers of various kinds of energy will be reliable in the next decade or two. Their estimates need to take into account levels of proven oil and gas reserves, the degree and location of exploration activities, levels of technological sophistication in the various energy-producing countries and other physical aspects. The nature of the politics in potential supplier countries and the maturity of their institutions are also important considerations in judging future reliability.

Canada, because of its determination to develop the oil sands and because of its mature institutions, must be considered a reliable supplier – indeed, the most reliable in the hemisphere, and perhaps globally, for the United States. Mexico, because of the way Pemex is used to fund the federal budget and because of political impediments to private investment, cannot be considered a reliable supplier, even domestically. Brazil should be able to take care of its own oil and gas needs, although not necessarily its electricity generation requirements, over the medium term, but its large population could mean that Brazil does not become an important exporter of either oil or gas. At present, Venezuela's politics make it an uncertain source of oil and gas, at least for the United States, but its politics are likely to change over the next decade or two and estimates about the country's reliability over the medium term must, therefore, factor in many contingencies. In Bolivia and Ecuador, too, politics and immature institutions make them uncertain suppliers over the medium term. Colombia's reliability as a supplier over the medium term is hampered both by its uncertain oil reserves, even for its own use, and by the ongoing activities of the anti-government guerrilla movement. In Peru, promising natural gas finds face environmental sensitivities.

With these considerations and the discussion in the rest of the chapter in mind, a number of key conclusions emerge. First, for the United States, the objective of energy independence is a chimera, and the more it is repeated by senior government officials, from the president on down, the less likely the authorities will be to institute the policies necessary to foster cooperation with other countries in the hemisphere. At the same time, those countries are annoyed by US calls for energy independence for itself without regard for hemispheric energy independence – although, in fact, neither objective is feasible.

Second, it is a fool's game for the United States to distance itself from the rest of the hemisphere in terms of foreign policy generally. Since the United States depends on the region for half its oil imports and practically all its imports of natural gas, energy policy should be seen as a critical component of foreign policy.

Third, although it might be possible to find alternative sources for transportation fuels and electricity generation, it would take time to bring about significant changes in US energy usage. Thus, decisive action is needed now. Moreover, since the development and testing of alternative sources of energy are costly endeavours, cooperation would ensure their speedier delivery and faster adoption.

Fourth, given the increased importance of environmental issues and their intersection with energy issues, collaboration and discussion are essential as new policies are contemplated.

Finally, the problems that hamper energy cooperation are primarily political. The politics takes many forms – historical, ideological, nationalistic – and can be generated both within and between countries. Whatever its basis, however, the lack of energy cooperation in the hemisphere is economically costly.

Notes

1. The facility will not be fully functional for several years, however, and Chile lacks natural gas for generating electricity in the interim. As a strategic matter, Chile has learned that it cannot rely on its neighbours – for example, as Argentine natural gas production declined, that country reneged on a contract specifying that Chile would receive its proportional share.
2. Uruguay and the United States have agreed to negotiate a trade agreement, but there is no decision as to whether it will be for free trade or to reduce trade restrictions to promote greater interchange.
3. This estimate comes from President Calderón's annual *Informe*, delivered in September 2007.
4. Presidents Bachelet of Chile and Morales of Bolivia have been holding talks on a practical solution amenable to both countries that would provide a basis for Bolivia to ship natural gas to Chile by pipeline. See Viscidi (2007).
5. There has been some relaxation of energy price controls, especially at the consumer level, but this is by no means complete. If Bolivia is unable to deliver in a few years on its long-term natural gas supply contract with Argentina, and this is clearly possible, the controls that Argentina imposes on the prices that producers can charge would probably give way.
6. At the beginning of 2008 corn was trading in Chicago at US$4.66 a bushel, close to an 11-year high, and soybeans at US12.51\frac{1}{2}$, a 34-year high (Flood, 2008).
7. The US energy bill approved in December 2007 separates automobile and light-duty truck standards, but the average new fleet fuel standard will reach 35 miles per gallon by 2020.
8. In Canada the provinces have jurisdiction over mineral resources.
9. See the website of Alberta Energy, www.energy.gov.ab.ca/OurBusiness/oilsands.asp.
10. Much material on the environmental effects of oil-sands exploitation is published by the Pembina Institute; see www.pembina.org.
11. The main aspect of the fiscal reform enacted in late 2007 is a new unitary tax that will be levied at a rate of 16.5 per cent in 2008, rising to 17.5 per cent in 2010. The key motivation is to capture taxes not collected under Mexico's regular income tax of 28 per cent, but with fewer exemptions. Companies will pay the greater of the two taxes. The greater collections of 1–2 per cent of GDP should permit the federal government to reduce its tax take from Pemex.

12. At the time of writing there is discussion in both the US Congress and the executive branch about extending trade preferences for Bolivia and Ecuador because of what are seen as anti-American comments by the presidents of the two countries. Venezuela does not now get these preferences. Peru will not need them after its free trade agreement with the United States goes fully into effect. Colombia may need an extension of the preferences if the US Congress delays approval of its free trade agreement with the United States.

REFERENCES

BP (2007) *BP Statistical Review of World Energy*, June, London: BP.

Deutch, John and James R. Schlesinger, chairs (2006) *National Security Consequences of U.S. Oil Dependency*, Independent Task Force Report 58, Council on Foreign Relations, Washington, DC.

Flood, Chris (2008) "Wheat and Corn Prices Poised for Further Rise", *Financial Times*, 11 January.

North American Energy Working Group (2005) "North American Natural Gas Vision", Experts Group on Natural Gas Trade and Interconnections, Washington, DC, January.

Petrobras (2007) *Investor Relations*, No. 24, Rio de Janeiro, September.

Viscidi, Lisa (2007) "Bolivian Minister: Private Sector to Help Raise Natgas Output", *Oil Daily*, 17 October.

Weintraub, Sidney, and Rafael Fernández de Castro (2007) "Mexico", in Sidney Weintraub, ed., *Energy Cooperation in the Western Hemisphere*, Washington, DC: Center for Strategic and International Studies.

World Bank (2006) *World Development Indicators*, Washington, DC: World Bank, available at http://publications.worldbank.org/WDI.

5

Coping with China

Nicola Phillips

Few would question the contention that the extraordinary economic expansion of China since 1978 carries profound consequences for global development. As much in relation to the advanced industrialized economies as to developing economies, observers have absorbed themselves in seeking answers to key questions arising from China's emergence on the world stage. Does the Chinese economy represent a threat or an opportunity? Is China poised to become an economic powerhouse capable of rivalling the global economic position of the United States? Does the Chinese development model represent an alternative that will challenge the prevailing neoliberal orthodoxy, or a path that is unique to China and cannot be replicated elsewhere? Is Chinese development based on an economic model so replete with contradictions and dislocations that it cannot escape eventual implosion?

The short answer to each of these huge questions is quite simple: in many ways, it is too early to tell. Yet, at the same time, the emergence of China has already had an appreciable impact on the context in which development strategies are formulated and, indeed, on the broader prospects for development in every region of the world, inasmuch as it has been pivotal to a redrawing of global production and value chains and to a restructuring of the global division of labour and patterns of global demand and terms of trade.

For Latin America and the Caribbean, these changes, together with a set of shifts in multilateral and bilateral arrangements, have put in place a series of fundamental development dilemmas at a time when the region's

Which way Latin America? Hemispheric politics meets globalization, Cooper and Heine, eds, United Nations University Press, 2009, ISBN 978-92-808-1172-8

development performance has been notably fragile. In 2005 and 2006, despite overall growth figures of around 5 per cent and terms of trade for commodities that were more favourable than they had been for some time, Latin American and Caribbean growth lagged appreciably behind emerging economies in Africa, Asia and Eastern Europe (ECLAC, 2006: 27). Except in certain pockets, particularly those fuelled by high oil prices and high demand for the region's commodity exports, other indicators of social and human development were uninspiring and overall levels of inequality remained the highest in the world. At the same time, a range of development strategies have been rendered obsolete or profoundly threatened by a combination of shifts towards multilateral liberalization, the bilateral elimination of margins of preference, the emergence of disabling competition from China and India in third markets and, with it, the sharpening of the already profound limits to the global competitiveness of Latin American and Caribbean economies.

In short, I argue that we are seeing a contraction of existing and potential development spaces for Latin America and the Caribbean of an order that prompts a set of serious questions about the basis on which the region's economies can pursue their effective insertion into the global production and value chains and the transnational division of labour.

I elaborate this argument in four sections. In the first, I offer an overview of emerging trade and investment relationships between China and the economies of the Latin American and Caribbean region. In the second section, I examine the significance of the emergence of China for the region's development strategies and developmental prospects. In the third, I reflect on the early impact of these emerging arrangements on the existing economic relationship between Latin America and the United States. In the fourth section, I seek to inject a challenge into these understandings of the emergence of China based on national economies, and I argue instead for a focus on transnational capital and global production and value chains. In the conclusion, I pull together arguments about the panorama for Latin American and Caribbean development in this light.

Emerging Sino-Latin American patterns of trade and investment

The implications of China's economic expansion for the global economy relate in many ways to the sheer size of the Chinese economy. Using purchasing power parity calculations, China now has the second-largest economy in the world, behind the United States; using official exchange rates, it is the fourth largest. With a population of 1.3 billion people, the potential Chinese consumer market is the largest in the world. The growth of China's gross domestic product has averaged around 9.5 per cent since the mid-1980s, and in 2006 was 10.7 per cent (World Bank, 2007). There is every expectation that, if this trajectory is maintained (as it is widely assumed it will be), China will overtake the United States as the world's largest economy, the only question being when in the next 50 years or so this will happen. It is currently the third-largest trading nation in the world, with its share of world trade standing at close to 6.5 per cent in 2005. Around 40 per cent of China's gross national product now rests on exports, with the bulk of the export sector sustained by foreign investment of various forms.

China's economic rise has generated a new panorama for global commodity markets, given the vast expansion in Chinese demand for energy (including oil), minerals and agricultural products. At the same time, trade in manufactured goods has already been transformed by expanding Chinese production based on very low labour costs – by some estimates, around 3 per cent of equivalent costs in the United States. Chinese overseas investment has also increased, particularly in connection with the strategy of securing supplies of commodities and energy. Of equal global significance is the manner in which US debt is financed largely by China's purchase of US treasury bills, which acts simultaneously to constrain interest rates in the United States and facilitate the Chinese strategy of keeping the currency low – a process seen in the United States and elsewhere as one of unabashed currency manipulation.

Quite apart from these indicators of size, weight and emerging role in the global economy, the expansion of China is of significance for the potential consequences of its contradictions and effects. The most often noted of these is the pronounced environmental deterioration caused by the rapid processes of industrialization and urbanization. Despite double-digit growth, per capita income in China has not improved and is still only around half of Russia's, and unemployment has gradually increased (Breslin, 2005: 736). The "underbelly" of Chinese growth is seen also in the social and political dislocations caused by mass migration from the countryside to explosively expanding urban areas, placing what many see as unsustainable pressure on services, infrastructure, employment and the environment. The social consequences of the most rapid process of urbanization in history are potentially staggering under these circumstances, and have already led observers to talk about the "Latin Americanization of China" (Gilboy and Heginbotham, 2004).

A range of other tensions in the Chinese economic model are noteworthy when thinking about the consequences of Chinese expansion for the global economy, including the massive problem of debt and non-performing loans in the financial and banking sectors, patterns of massive duplication of production and competitive urbanization and the consequences for rural populations. One concern that is voiced particularly frequently is the potential impact of a Chinese financial collapse on emerging markets, as well as for the US and wider global economies, as a result of potentially severe alterations in the US debt and interest-rate situation. In this sense, the emergence of China is significant not only for its intervention in global markets and, potentially, its ideological appeal across the developing world, but also for the potential regional and global consequences of the often massive economic, social and environmental dislocations implicated in its model of growth and expansion.

It is in this context that we need to locate a discussion of the emerging relationship between China and Latin America. At face value, the growth in Chinese trade with Latin America can be said to have boomed over the past five years, with total trade increasing from around US$200 million in 1975 to US$12.6 billion in 2000, US$26.8 billion in 2003 and US$50.5 billion in 2005. The annual average growth of Sino-Latin American trade also leapt between 2000 and 2005 to around 27 per cent. It must be noted, of course, that when a boom starts from a very low base, arresting levels of expansion do not necessarily mean significant levels of overall trade: Sino-Latin American trade is equivalent to only 10 per cent of US-Latin American trade, and China accounts for only 4 per cent of total Latin American trade; in contrast, the United States and Canada together account for 50 per cent of the whole region's trade, and considerably more than that of particular countries within it. One must not get carried away with the scale of commercial interactions between China and Latin America, even though the increase and dynamism of bilateral trade are very striking.

Between 1999 and 2004 Chinese exports to Latin America increased just over threefold and imports from Latin America just over sevenfold (Dumbaugh and Sullivan, 2005: 2), and a Chinese trade deficit with Latin America has prevailed consistently. Mexico is the most significant destination for Chinese exports, absorbing around 24 per cent of the total to the region, followed by Brazil at around 20 per cent. Again, the annual average growth rates of exports to these countries over the 2000–2005 period are arresting: respectively, 35.5 per cent and 31.6 per cent (Dussel Peters, 2006: 12). Conversely, the pattern of Chinese imports from Latin America is dominated by Brazil, Chile and Argentina, with the former accounting for around 37.4 per cent in 2005, while Mexico accounted for only 8.3 per cent of the total from the region. At the end of 2005, China had become the second-largest export market (behind the United States) for Chile, Peru and Cuba, and the third largest (behind the European Union) for Brazil (see table 5.1).

Table 5.1 Sino-Latin American trade: Exports to and imports from China as percentage of total, selected countries, 1995 and 2005

Country	Imports from China as a share of total imports (%)		Exports to China as a share of total exports (%)	
	1995	2005	1995	2005
Argentina	3.5	6.5	2.8	8.8
Brazil	2.7	6.8	3.5	8.3
Chile	3.2	8.1	2.3	11.3
Colombia	0.7	5.6	1.3	0.9
Mexico	0.9	3.1	0.7	1.1
Peru	2.8	8.6	7.3	11.1
Venezuela	0.5	3.8	0.0	1.7

Source: International Monetary Fund, *Direction of Trade Statistics*, presented in Jenkins, Dussel Peters and Moreira (2006).

As for the nature of Latin American exports to China, around 75 per cent are raw materials, foodstuffs and natural-resources-based manufactured goods, concentrated particularly in copper, iron ore, nickel, soy, pulp, fishmeal and sugar. Copper represents around 44 per cent of Chilean exports to China, around 57 per cent of Argentina's exports are oilseeds and Brazilian exports are dominated by oilseeds and mineral ores, as well as timber and soybeans (Dussel Peters, 2006: 15). In terms of imports from China, an overwhelming proportion – around 90 per cent – consists of manufactured products, the bulk of which are labour-intensive, low-technology and low-value-added goods (see Lall and Weiss, 2005; Jenkins, Dussel Peters and Moreira, 2006). Key products here are textiles and apparel, footwear, machinery and plastics. The technology component of Chinese exports is rapidly increasing, however, and such sectors as automobiles, auto parts, steel, telecommunications and electronics are becoming steadily more significant in the overall export profile of the Chinese economy, as well as in the profile of its exports to Latin America.

Sino-Latin American foreign direct investment (FDI) starts from a similarly low base and has also shown a striking increase, if not as dramatic as that of trade. Latin American FDI in China appears to have increased to an arresting degree, reaching around 13 per cent of total FDI flowing into China in 2003. The vast bulk of this investment, however, comes from the tax havens of the Cayman Islands and British Virgin Islands, the latter now representing the second most significant source of investment in China. As such, this is not investment by firms and actors from Latin America itself – indeed, it is likely that Hong Kong and Taiwanese investment, channelled through these tax havens, accounts for most of these flows (Breslin, 2005: 744). In reality, Latin American investment in China is minimal, as is Chinese investment in Latin America as a share of overall FDI to the region. Chinese FDI in Latin America has been increasing visibly since the start of the 2000s, particularly in railways, oil and gas exploration, communications satellites and construction. But Chinese investment in Africa, Asia and North America has been greater than in Latin America, and it should also be noted that China itself accounts for only a tiny proportion of total global FDI flows.

This aggregate regional sketch tells us little, however, about the real significance of China's economic presence in Latin America. The implications vary considerably across the region. With broad brushstrokes, the region can be divided into Mexico and Central America on the one hand and most of South America on the other. This is unsurprising, given the nature of production structures and economic profiles across the region. The Mexican and Central American model rests on the integration of these countries into vertical flows of trade in manufactured goods associated with assembly and processing activities, especially in sectors such as textiles and apparel. Like China, Mexico has also come to specialize in temporary imports for processing and re-export. Mexico and much of Central America and the Caribbean thus have export and production profiles that bring these countries into considerably greater competition with China in third markets, to the extent that the dominant perception of Chinese economic expansion is one of profound threat. Indeed, Mexico's trade deficit with China stood at some US$4.5 billion in 2005, by far the highest in the region. Moreover, as we will see, China has displaced Mexico as the main trading partner of the United States, particularly in the textiles and apparel sectors (ECLAC, 2006: 55). The pronounced dependence of these countries on the US market means that this displacement carries profound consequences for the development model currently prevailing in Mexico and Central America.

Conversely, the overall South American profile is one of capital-intensive industry associated with the processing of natural resources, these activities being characterized by low levels of domestic value-added (Phillips, 2004). Within this model, countries such as Argentina and Paraguay remain largely dependent on agriculture, while Chile and most of the Andean countries remain dependent on natural resources and higher-value-added natural-resources-based products in sectors such as copper, minerals and fishing. In the case of Venezuela, the key export is oil and oil-related products, and Chinese involvement with Venezuela has revolved largely around its potential as a supplier of energy resources. Thus South American exports are seen, in the most general terms, to be complementary to Chinese production structures, and an extension of trade and investment relations is often touted, again in the very broadest of terms, as a positive development for this part of the region.

Brazil is something of an exception, given the importance of manufacturing in its production and export profile, and the scale of competition with China is correspondingly perceived to be much greater. It is significant that primary products represent 60 per cent of Brazil's exports to China, but only 31 per cent of its exports to the rest of the world (Jenkins, Dussel Peters and Moreira, 2006: 12), indicating a lack of both competitiveness and market access for Brazilian manufactured exports in China. Factor endowments are crucial in this scenario – above all, China's vast supply of cheap labour, which translates into average wages around three times lower than in Brazil. The much higher levels of government intervention in the Chinese economy yield easy access to credit from state banks, in stark contrast to the Brazilian model; despite developmentalist streaks in Brazilian strategies that differentiate it from the majority of other Latin American countries, the extent of Chinese state support for industrialization outstrips any similar promotion measures in a broadly neoliberal region (ibid.: 15).

The developmental implications of Sino-Latin American trade and investment

If these trajectories continue, the implications for Latin American development are potentially profound. For South America, the economic relationship revolves around Chinese demand for raw materials, energy and resources-based products. Exports to China have expanded vigorously, a welcome trend for South American exporters and governments. Moreover, Chinese demand has pushed up world prices for primary products following decades of decline in prices, with important positive implications for the terms on which the major resources-based economies of South America are participating in world trade. At the same time, other Asian governments appear to be following the Chinese lead in clamouring to secure supplies of raw materials from Latin America and Africa.[1] The results of this explosion in demand are already evident: Latin America and the Caribbean as a region achieved the second-largest increase in exports in 2005, after China, explained by the South American economies' specialization in commodity exports and flows of trade in oil and oil-related products (ECLAC, 2006: 31).

Nevertheless, it is the concentration of these exports in traditional resources-based sectors that represents the more troubling panorama for Latin American development, especially when put in the context of the

Table 5.2 Composition of Chinese trade with ASEAN and LAIA countries, 2004, percentage shares of trade flows of each group of products

Category	Group	Imports (%)	Exports (%)
Primary	ASEAN	9.0	9.0
	LAIA	13.3	0.9
Resources-based manufactures	ASEAN	15.6	11.1
	LAIA	7.8	3.4
Low-technology manufactures	ASEAN	5.0	4.1
	LAIA	2.4	2.2
Intermediate-technology manufactures	ASEAN	6.2	8.4
	LAIA	1.2	3.1
High-technology manufactures	ASEAN	19.5	8.3
	LAIA	0.6	1.7
Other	ASEAN	4.7	3.2
	LAIA	0.6	0.5

Source: Adapted from ECLAC (2006), based on data from the UN Commodity Trade Statistics Database.

longstanding inability of the majority of South American countries to compete in global markets for manufactured high-technology products, as well as the increasing dominance of China in the United States and other markets. In terms of its global trade profile, Brazil, as noted, is a rather different case, but here again debate has centred around the recognition that Chinese interest in the Brazilian economy is essentially about raw materials. The pertinent issues here are twofold. First, as table 5.2 shows, patterns of Chinese demand for raw materials from Latin America are based almost entirely on primary products, the demand for processed products and resources-based manufactures being focused significantly more on economies of the Association of Southeast Asian Nations (ASEAN). In this sense, South American economies are subject to sharp competition from Asian economies more generally, and are locked into the lower-value-added ends of commodity and production chains. The higher one goes in the hierarchy of technological content for raw-materials-based products, as table 5.2 shows, the greater the gap between the representation of ASEAN and Latin American Integration Association (LAIA) economies in supplying Chinese demand.

Second, the competition from China in industry and manufacturing means that any incipient space for upgrading the industrial competitiveness of South American economies is being further squeezed, so that existing structures of dependence on natural resources and raw materials are likely to be reinforced as a result of China's economic expansion. The extent to which this reinforcement will constitute a serious long-term development problem for the region remains a matter of some speculation, but it is nevertheless worth noting that debates about development in Latin America have, for the past half-century, revolved precisely around the imperative of breaking the region's dependence on raw materials for export, especially given the dislocating effects of the so-called Dutch Disease (the deindustrialization of a country's economy associated with a rise in natural resource exploitation) and other structural problems associated with such a model. The celebration of the export opportunities provided by the emergence of China consequently has something of a strange ring to it, in that most of the long-established anxiety about this form of dependence on raw materials appears curiously to have disappeared from contemporary discourse. Yet, given what we know from both theory and past experience, the new strategy that is crystallizing around Chinese demand for raw materials is without question inauspicious for the region's economies.

For the northern part of the region, the competition from China takes a different form, inasmuch as the potential is for the disruption of existing development models based on low-value-added, low-cost manufacturing with preferential access and a competitive niche in the US market. For Central America and the Caribbean (and, in part, for Mexico), the main competition from China is felt in the textiles and apparel sectors. China is now the largest exporter of apparel outside the Organisation for Economic Co-operation and Development (OECD), accounting with India for the bulk of apparel exports from non-OECD to OECD countries. Through the 1980s and 1990s, the Central American and Caribbean textiles and apparel sectors benefited from a combination of the provisions of the Multi-Fibre Arrangement (MFA) and the strong inclination in the United States towards outsourcing functions at the lower-value-added end of the production chain. The ending of the MFA and the gradual lifting of restrictions under the terms of the Agreement on Textiles and Clothing, together with the multilateral lifting of import restrictions on Chinese apparel exports under the terms of China's accession in 2001 to the World Trade Organization (WTO), have positioned exporters in the Caribbean Basin (including Mexico) among the most visible losers in the global textiles and apparel industries (Heron, 2006). They are now exposed increasingly to the full force of competition from textiles "giants" like China, India, Bangladesh, Pakistan and so on – a competition that is waged primarily on the terrain of labour costs, as table 5.3 shows.[2]

In late 2005 some of the force of this competition was diverted as the United States and European Union negotiated with China sets of quota restrictions on imports of Chinese apparel. The side-effect of this protection of US and EU domestic markets is a certain temporary sheltering of

Table 5.3 Cost of manufacturing a dress shirt for the US market, selected countries

Country of origin	Total manufacturing cost (US$)
China	1.12
Nicaragua	1.50
Dominican Republic	1.70
Honduras	1.70
Guatemala	1.80
El Salvador	1.85
Costa Rica	2.00
Mexico	2.20
United States	5.00

Note: Amounts shown assume that it takes 20 minutes to cut, sew and finish a dress shirt for the US market.
Source: Devlin, Estevadeordal and Rodríguez-Clare (2006).

the smaller textiles and apparel exporters in Mexico, Central America and the Caribbean from the potentially devastating effects of a free trade regime in these sectors. The issue remains unresolved, however; the quota arrangement with the United States came to an end in 2008, and it remains clear that China's position in the WTO points in the direction of the eventual achievement of unfettered market access for apparel exports.

At the same time, the production-sharing arrangements that stemmed from the promotion of outsourcing by the United States (as in the case of the Caribbean Basin Initiative, for example) are coming to an end in any case, but are also challenged by the lifting of the MFA, as a result of which US and other retailers have access to direct imports from the big Asian suppliers. For Caribbean Basin producers, this represents a severe squeezing of the niche they formerly occupied in supply chains and the US market. Furthermore, in any case, given the provisions of production-sharing arrangements that make duty-free exports contingent on the use of fabrics and yarns manufactured in the United States, the textiles and apparel industries in the Caribbean Basin were always located at the low-value-added ends of the supply chain and were constrained to import raw materials at much higher prices from the United States, even when they were available from Asian economies at much more competitive costs. The Central American Free Trade Agreement goes some way towards protecting the position of Central American countries in the US market, but, taken together with the multilateral elimination of quotas, the terms of the agreement have been calculated to signify a potential 50 per cent cut in the expansion of Central American textiles and clothing exports to the United States (Hilaire and Yang, 2003: 15–16).

More generally, the impact of competition from China on Mexico has been felt in the decline of the manufacturing sector in terms of its share in overall gross domestic product and employment. Mexico continues to export more intermediate- and high-technology-intensive manufactured goods (Jenkins, Dussel Peters and Moreira, 2006: 23), so the competition between China and Mexico in third markets has thus far been concentrated in low-technology products. As noted earlier, however, the technology component of Chinese exports is rapidly increasing. Across the region, steel, automobiles and electronics are the sectors in which Chinese competition is likely to emerge forcefully. China probably became a net exporter of steel by the end of 2006, with potential for extremely rapid growth over the coming years.[3] In the automobile sector, much of the development strategy in areas such as Guangdong province in the Pearl River delta hinges on achieving global prominence as a major car and auto-parts manufacturer. Companies such as Honda already have joint ventures in China aimed at feeding that country's explosive boom in car ownership; similarly, Chinese manufacturers have expressed intentions to purchase the technology of major companies such as Daimler and BMW (Jubany and Poon, 2006: 9) and thus develop China's ability to compete on the front line of global car production. Again, given the prominence of this sector in countries such as Mexico and Brazil, not to mention the United States itself, China's rise in this area portends a significant reordering of the regional automobile industry.

The final point to make concerns the diversion of investment from Latin America and the Caribbean that has already become evident. Total flows of FDI to the region grew more slowly in 2004 and 2005 than did flows to China, Asia or even Africa (ECLAC, 2006: 32), and the movement of China into sectors previously attractive to FDI in many Latin American economies is ominous for the region's position on the global investment map.

What we are seeing, then, is a squeezing of development space for Latin America and the Caribbean that, in its various forms, is uniformly inauspicious. The location of the region in global production and supply chains is increasingly, and apparently ineluctably, premised on the supply of primary products, with few prospects for competing with ASEAN countries in the supply of resources-based manufactures. Oil from countries such as Venezuela also fits into this picture. Brazil is perhaps different in this respect, but still its capacity to achieve greater representation in global manufacturing chains and in the export of processed products to China is hampered by all the aforementioned constraints on competitiveness *vis-à-vis* the Chinese economy and the competing Asian suppliers. Chile, as usual, is something of an outlier given the extent of its competitiveness in resources-based manufactures and the considerably greater degree of diversification it has achieved over the past 30 years or so. In the Caribbean Basin, including Mexico, the picture is dominated by profound competition in third markets, especially in manufacturing and sectors such as textiles and apparel, but also by the absence of options for inserting their economies into alternative supply and production chains in the manner of those of South America.

Latin America and the United States

What does all this mean for the economic relationship between the United States and Latin America? One argument often advanced relates to the way in which the impact on Latin America and the Caribbean of the slowdown in the US economy and the weakening of US demand is compensated by the expansion of demand in China and its impact on commodity prices (ECLAC, 2006: 27–28). Other arguments see the surge in Latin American – especially South American – economic interest in China as a reflection of the languid state of contemporary relations between the United States and Latin America.

Quite apart from the commercial opportunities arising from the opening up of a market of this size and the particular pattern of demand that attends the Chinese model of industrialization, China is often presented as filling a developmental gap left by the United States (Roett, 2005). US investment in Latin America has been steadily declining as US corporations have focused their strategies predominantly on the emerging markets of Asia (including China). Moreover, the burgeoning US deficit precludes any serious rectification in the short term of the neglect that many perceive as having characterized US engagement with the region in recent years. In this context, the potential of Chinese investment in infrastructure, in particular, has often been noted as valuable for many Latin American economies. Venezuela and other energy-producing countries have been a particular focus in this regard, with significant Chinese investment in exploration, refining capacity and transportation infrastructure.

Such interpretations of China's importance for Latin America clearly have something to offer, but cannot be pushed too far. The simplest reason is that the economic relationship with the United States remains by far the most important for the region. Table 5.4 indicates levels of trade reliance on the United States in 2005 by country, and the disparities in this reliance between, for example, some of the large Southern Cone

Table 5.4 Trade dependence on the United States, selected countries, 2005

Country	Exports to the United States (US$ million)	Exports to the United States as proportion of total exports (%)	Trade balance with the United States (US$ million)	Trade balance with the world (US$ million)
Mexico	183,351	85.8	65,089	−7,559
Honduras	3,309	75.6	154	−106
Nicaragua	991	63.0	401	−619
El Salvador	2,051	60.6	272	−3,332
Guatemala	2,694	50.1	29	−3,431
Ecuador	4,950	46.5	4,107	420
Costa Rica	3,177	44.8	−119	−2,717
Panama	973	14.8	−1,009	−2,000
Dominican Republic	4,325	77.9	−26	−1,544
CARICOM	9,167	52.2	2,330	1,052
Cuba	0	0.0	−361	−2,970
Venezuela	32,587	58.8	25,987	29,674
Colombia	8,849	41.8	2,843	1,988
Peru	5,173	30.4	3,052	4,917
Uruguay	761	22.4	489	−474
Brazil	22,472	19.0	8,918	44,758
Chile	6,248	15.8	1,821	9,142
Bolivia	383	14.0	59	1,007
Argentina	4,321	10.8	1,357	11,320
Paraguay	54	3.2	−774	−1,564

Source: ECLAC (2006).

economies and some of the smaller economies in the Caribbean Basin – especially, it should be noted, those economies dominated by the "off-shore" development model of export assembly, particularly in the textiles and apparel sector. While aggregate figures for the region as a whole do show some offsetting by China of the effects of slowdown in the United States, this mechanism does not work for the majority of the most dependent economies in the north of the region. At the same time, Chinese investment in Latin America is still profoundly limited; trade is far more important – indeed, the developmental implications of China's rise reside predominantly in the arena of trade, rather than in investment, although even then, as noted above, China accounts for only 4 per cent of total Latin American trade. In short, the notion that China fills either the gap in US investment in the region or the limitations of the region's access to the US market finds little justification, inasmuch as the main economic relationship for Latin America and the Caribbean remains overwhelmingly with the United States, with but a handful of exceptions in the Southern Cone.

The most pressing concern, in this light, relates to the potential displacement of Latin American competitiveness in the US market. The possibilities for export diversification have been celebrated, for widely disparate reasons, in various countries of South America that operate with *relatively* less pronounced structures of dependence on the US market (Argentina, Brazil, Chile), but the "threat" arising from China in the US market has been felt keenly in many Latin American economies. Table 5.5 gives an indication of this displacement by comparing the US import-value market share for China and the major Latin American economies in various key sectors between 1981 and 2001. As noted, a massive displacement of Mexican exports in the US market has already occurred, particularly in garments and textiles, toys, furniture and electronic value-chain products (Dussel Peters, 2006: 19). Similar patterns obtain for Central America and the Caribbean, along with the important emergence of China in other sectors – such as automobiles, steel, electronics, telecommunications and so on – that carry implications for Latin American exports to the United States and for US overseas investment. The potential (further) diversion of investment away from the Americas to Asia is seen as a considerable challenge to Latin American development prospects and strategies, alongside displacement in US markets, and there is certainly enough evidence to suggest that these perceptions are not ill-founded.

It is in part for this reason that many countries in Latin America – particularly in Central America but also in the Andean region, where levels of dependence on the United States are relatively more pronounced – have been eager to enter into bilateral trade negotiations with the United States. The further effect of China's emergence, however, might well be to diminish the possibility of the success of such negotiations, particularly given the decline in public and political support in the United States for trade agreements since the start of the decade, uniformly attributed to the emerging "threat" from the Chinese economy and to what is perceived as the negative experience of the North American Free Trade Agreement (NAFTA). Undoubtedly, the steady growth in the US trade deficit – which reached record highs in 2005 and 2006 (more than US$765 billion in the latter year), fuelled primarily by rising Chinese imports – has sharpened still further the political sensitivity of the trade agenda. Much, but not all, of this sensitivity is related to pronounced concerns about the impact of trade on the US labour market, an aspect to which the Americas are particularly vulnerable given the parallel salience of the immigration issue in US politics (Phillips, 2007a). In this

Table 5.5 US import-value market share, selected countries, 1981, 1991 and 2001

Industry	China (%)			Argentina (%)			Brazil (%)			Chile (%)			Mexico (%)		
	1981	1991	2001	1981	1991	2001	1981	1991	2001	1981	1991	2001	1981	1991	2001
Food	1	2	3	3	2	1	13	5	2	1	2	4	9	11	12
Beverage/tobacco	0	0	0	0	1	1	2	4	2	0	1	1	4	5	14
Crude materials	3	2	3	1	0	0	2	3	5	1	1	2	3	5	4
Mineral fuels	0	1	0	0	0	1	0	0	1	0	0	0	8	9	8
Animal/vegetable oils	0	0	0	1	5	1	9	3	1	0	0	0	0	4	2
Chemicals	1	2	3	1	0	0	2	1	1	0	0	0	3	3	2
Manufactured materials	1	3	9	1	0	0	2	2	2	1	1	1	2	4	7
Machinery	0	2	7	0	0	0	1	1	1	0	0	0	4	7	16
Misc. manufacturing	2	15	26	0	0	0	2	2	1	0	0	0	4	4	10
All	1	4	9	0	0	0	2	1	1	0	0	0	5	6	12

Source: Devlin, Estevadeordal and Rodríguez-Clare (2006: 112).

sense, an important implication of the emergence of China for Latin America could materialize through the mechanisms of US domestic politics and domestic reactions to China, with the effect of progressively compromising the possibilities for safeguarding the region's most important economic relationship, particularly under the additional pressures of multilateral liberalization commitments.

There is, moreover, a dimension of the discussion about the relationship between the United States and Latin America and the Caribbean – and, indeed, about development strategies – that is fundamental but often overlooked. That dimension relates to the profound pressures for migration that emerge at the intersections of longstanding processes of deindustrialization and deruralization, the constraints on agricultural trade, the effects on particular sectors of competition from China and the continuing failure of the development orthodoxy to produce growth and development. The short-term implications of trade liberalization and increasing labour flexibility, as well as the widespread decimation of rural economies, are felt particularly in levels of unemployment and underemployment, downward pressures on wages, the consequent reinforcement of wage differentials with the major receiving countries and patterns of internal migration. In many cases, the last of these effects is associated with the development of manufacturing activity and the concentration of FDI in the major urban centres or, in some cases – such as Mexico and other Central American and Caribbean economies – into border regions where export-processing zones absorb migrants from displaced rural communities. Indeed, research demonstrates a strong correlation between internal migration and subsequent international movements.

While not ignoring the extensive social networks that are well understood to be central to individual decisions to migrate, the overall panorama of development failures and the divergence of wage levels continue to define what we traditionally would have called the "push factors" associated with migration to the United States. The signs are clearly that such pressures are sharpened in countries most affected by the shifts in sectors such as textiles and apparel, manufacturing and so on. Moreover, the restructuring of the US economy as a result of shifts in the transnational division of labour and the competition waged from China and Asia on labour costs has generated a situation in which competitiveness has come to depend on the massive import of labour, particularly of the low-skilled and illegal varieties, in both the services sector and agriculture (Phillips, 2007b).

Thus, the restructuring of global and regional economies that is conditioned increasingly by China's emergence has meant that traditional forms of dependence on the US economy have been given a new twist.

Table 5.6 Remittances from the United States, selected countries, 2004

	Amount (US$ million)	As percentage of GDP (%)	As percentage of exports (goods and services) (%)	As percentage of total FDI (%)	As percentage of net official development assistance or official aid (%)
Argentina	270	0.2	0.7	6.6	296.7
Bolivia	422	4.8	16.6	363.8	55.0
Brazil	5,624	0.9	5.2	40.0	1,973.0
Colombia	3,857	3.9	19.8	126.4	757.8
Costa Rica	320	1.7	3.7	51.6	2,461.5
Dominican Republic	2,438	13.2	26.3	378.0	2,802.3
Ecuador	1,740	5.7	19.9	150.0	1,087.5
El Salvador	2,548	16.1	59.2	546.8	1,207.6
Guatemala	2,681	9.8	58.2	1,729.7	1,229.8
Haiti	1,026	29.1	218.8	14,657.1	422.2
Honduras	1,134	15.4	37.0	387.0	176.6
Jamaica	1,497	16.9	38.4	248.7	1,996.0
Mexico	16,613	2.5	8.2	95.6	13,729.7
Nicaragua	810	17.9	49.0	324.0	65.7
Peru	1,360	2.0	9.4	74.9	279.3
Trinidad and Tobago	93	0.7	1.6	9.3	−9,300.0[a]
Uruguay	105	0.8	2.6	33.8	477.3
Venezuela	259	0.2	0.6	17.1	528.6

a. This minus percentage arises as the figure for aid to Trinidad and Tobago in 2004 was −1 (US$ million).
Source: Author's calculations, based on primary data on remittances from the Inter-American Development Bank (www.iadb.org/mif/remittances) and on primary data on GDP, exports, FDI and aid from World Bank (2006).

That dependence has come to centre on the US market not only as a destination for Latin American and Caribbean exports and a source of investment, but also increasingly as a source of employment. The issue of remittances adds a further dimension to this new dependence, the scale of which is indicated in table 5.6. What we are seeing, in a nutshell, is the substitution of the "offshore" development model across the Caribbean Basin with one based on the "onshore" provision of labour to the US economy and the concrete, purposeful elaboration of development strategies based on the concept of "remittance economies". The debate surrounding migration and remittances is considerable, and there is insufficient space here to assess it fully. The point to bring out is simply that the elaboration of development strategies concretely around remittances is clearly an emerging result of the severe squeezing of competitiveness and development options in the region, and an indication of the consolidation of a new transnational political economy of dependence on the United States.

In all of the above ways, the emergence of China, far from filling gaps left by US policy or investment patterns and far from offsetting dependence on the US economy, has acted to reinforce and deepen the centrality of the relationship of Latin America and the Caribbean with the United States to the development prospects of the region's economies and societies.

Global production and value chains and the new transnational division of labour

Thus far, the picture I have sketched of the emerging relationship of Latin America and the Caribbean with China, its implications for development and its consequences for the region's relationship with the United States has relied upon stylized depictions of national economies interacting with one another and a similarly stylized treatment of the rise of China. This line of analysis – which is entirely dominant in the academic and policy literature – is useful but misses a crucial point: that the story of the emergence of China, as such, is not one of a single national economy but, rather, one of a particular phase in global capital accumulation driven by mobile transnational capital. Transnational capital has "landed" in China as a result of the particular set of factor endowments that I have already mentioned, facilitated by the internal economic reforms undertaken by the Chinese government from the late 1970s onwards. As such, it is misleading to talk about the emergence of "China"; rather, we are seeing the consolidation of a particular phase in the evolution of global production and value chains, driven by the strategies of transnational capital, within the territorial boundaries of the Chinese economy. William I. Robinson (2006) captures this well in his reference to China not just as the "industrial workhouse of the world" but as the "workhouse of transnational capital".

Let me illustrate this argument briefly with the example of the Chinese computer industry. Around 75 per cent of China's computer-related products are, in fact, produced by Taiwanese companies, and around 70 per cent of Taiwanese computer-related products are based on so-called original equipment manufacturing (OEM) contracts with foreign firms, overwhelmingly from the United States and Japan. As such, we need to understand China's computer industry – and, indeed, other sectors – as representing only the final stage in a global production process that is not adequately represented by bilateral investment figures that show Taiwan as the source of investment in China or by bilateral trade figures that show China as the exporter to the rest of the world (Breslin, 2005: 744–748).

It is thus problematic to talk about the emergence of "China" and its implications for other economies in the world. Rather, like these "other" economies, the growth of the territorially defined "Chinese economy" is associated with the strategies and structures of transnational capital, and what happens within the territorial borders of the Chinese economy represents an integral dimension of evolving global production and value chains. Inasmuch as it is, by extension, a pattern of growth fuelled primarily by the production and investment strategies of companies in the developed world, which, in turn, are premised largely on demand in markets in the developed world (ibid.: 745), the dominant parameters of the debate – about China as a threat to the United States, for instance – are misplaced. The focus rests uniformly on the extent of Chinese exports to the United States and the US trade deficit with China, without due recognition of the profile of investment in the underlying production processes, in which US capital is fully imbricated.

The ramifications of this argument are extensive, but I focus here on those that are relevant to our present purposes. By focusing on the role of US firms in the production processes that fuel Chinese growth, and consequently exports "from" China, one can draw a more complex but vastly more revealing picture of the implications of China's rise for Latin America and the Caribbean. First, the development dilemmas experienced by the region in this context arise not so much from China itself as from the region's particular mode of insertion into *global* production structures. Concentrating on "China", therefore, misses a key point about the demands of competitiveness and the particular place of Latin American and Caribbean economies in the global economy as a whole. Second, "competition" from China is fuelled, in a variety of sectors, by investment from the developed world, including the United States. This suggests both that inferences of China's filling of developmental gaps left by the United States are simplistic and misplaced, and that US production and investment strategies are pivotal to the development predicament in which many Latin American and Caribbean countries find themselves. Third, assertions – such as those made frequently by President Hugo Chávez of Venezuela, among others – that a focus on China represents an alternative to traditional forms of *economic* dependence on the United States clearly underestimate the role and stake of US interests in Chinese industrialization, whether directly or via more circuitous routes such as OEM investment in the Taiwanese computer industry. In this sense, notions of "China", "the United States", "Taiwan" and so on in trade and investment statistics reveal little about the importance of global production networks and the location of Chinese industrialization – and, indeed, Latin American and Caribbean economies – within these global processes.

Conclusion

What emerges most forcefully from this discussion is that the rise of China does not cause but, rather, throws into relief the huge development problems of the Latin American and Caribbean region, especially the long-term and insidious process of deindustrialization in which the region continues to be mired, the profound problems of regional and global competitiveness of the majority of export sectors and products, the continued lack of higher-value-added production capabilities and the pronounced dependence on the US market at a time when preferential arrangements are being systematically dismantled under WTO auspices. It also raises a set of key questions about the future trajectory of Latin American and Caribbean development and the directions that development strategies can – or, indeed, should – take.

There is a compelling argument to make that, to a greater or lesser extent, the foundations of many of the most established development strategies are being challenged in quite fundamental ways by the latest phase of global capitalist restructuring, which is manifested most clearly in the emergence of China. Perhaps the most salient of these foundations is the notion of geographical advantage, which, particularly in the northern part of the region, has long shaped a set of development strategies based integrally on proximity to the United States and its markets (see Wise, 2007). While geographical proximity clearly continues to define many of the "newer" development strategies – migration and the emergence of remittance economies, illicit and illegal activity (notably the drugs trade), tourism-based strategies – the emergence of China has clearly weakened, if not completely dismantled, the notion in matters of trade and investment.

If these arguments are correct, Latin American and Caribbean development strategies require a much fuller reorientation than has hitherto occurred towards a prioritization of debates and strategies focusing on insertion into global (rather than regional) production and value chains, as well as the transnational division of labour. The question then is how to do this in the wider context of the squeezing of the global development space available to the Latin American and Caribbean region that I have identified and elaborated in this chapter. Perhaps the more pressing question still is how the region can aspire to address the profound social problems that continue to characterize it in a global context in which, not least as a result of the nature of Chinese development, competitiveness apparently is cast more and more as a social "race to the bottom".

Notes

1. Park Yong Soo, president of the state-run Korea Resources Corporation, is reported to have stated that "within a few years there is likely to be a 'war' to develop raw materials … [and] China is challenging aggressively" (Rohter, 2004).
2. It should be noted that the competitiveness of Asian producers is also associated with the frequent use of "unfree" labour, including child labour, alongside the more general sources of competitiveness associated with the sheer abundance of low-cost, relatively highly skilled workforces in countries such as China and South Korea, strong production capacity in the manufacturing of both cotton and man-made fibres and close trade and investment links between China and South Korea, Taiwan and Japan (Nathan Associates, 2002, cited in Heron, 2006: 7).
3. This issue has been identified by the three NAFTA partners as one that requires joint action, and a trilateral working group has been set up under the auspices of the North American Security and Prosperity Partnership (Jubany and Poon, 2006: 9).

REFERENCES

Breslin, Shaun (2005) "Power and Production: Rethinking China's Global Economic Role", *Review of International Studies* 31(4), pp. 735–753.

Devlin, Robert, Antoni Estevadeordal and Andrés Rodríguez-Clare (2006) *The Emergence of China: Opportunities and Challenges for Latin America and the Caribbean*, Washington, DC: Inter-American Development Bank.

Dumbaugh, Kerry and Mark P. Sullivan (2005) *China's Growing Interest in Latin America*, Washington, DC: Congressional Research Service, 20 April.

Dussel Peters, Enrique (2006) "What Does China's Integration to the World Market Mean for Latin America? The Mexican Experience", paper presented at conference on Responding to Globalization in the Americas: The Political Economy of Hemispheric Integration, London School of Economics, London, 1–2 June.

ECLAC (2006) *Latin America and the Caribbean in the World Economy, 2005–2006*, Santiago: UN Economic Commission for Latin America and the Caribbean.

Gilboy, George J. and Eric Heginbotham (2004) "The Latin Americanization of China?", *Current History* 103 (September), pp. 256–261.

Heron, Tony (2006) "The Ending of the Multifibre Arrangement: A Development Boon for the South", *European Journal of Development Research* 18(1), pp. 1–21.

Hilaire, Alvin and Yongzheng Yang (2003) "The United States and the New Regionalism/Bilateralism", IMF Working Paper WP/03/206, International Monetary Fund, Washington, DC, October.

Jenkins, Rhys, Enrique Dussel Peters and Mauricio Mesquita Moreira (2006) "The Economic Impact of China on Latin America – An Agenda for Research", paper presented at Seventh Annual Global Development Conference, pre-conference workshop on "Asian and Other Drivers of Global Change", St Petersburg, FL, 18–19 January.

Jubany, Florencia and Daniel Poon (2006) *Recent Chinese Engagement in Latin America and the Caribbean: A Canadian Perspective*, Ottawa: Canadian Foundation for the Americas (FOCAL), March.

Lall, Sanjaya and John Weiss (2005) "China's Competitive Threat to Latin America: An Analysis for 1990–2002", *Oxford Development Studies* 33(2), pp. 163–194.

Nathan Associates (2002) *Changes in the Global Trade Rules for Textiles and Apparel: Implications for Developing Countries*, Arlington, VA: Nathan Associates.

Phillips, Nicola (2004) *The Southern Cone Model: The Political Economy of Regional Captialist Development*, London: Routledge.

——— (2007a) "The Limits of 'Securitization': Power, Politics and Process in US Foreign Economic Policy", *Government and Opposition* 42(2), pp. 181–212.

——— (2007b) "Migration as Development Strategy? The New Political Economy of Dispossession and Inequality in the Americas", IPEG Papers in Global Political Economy 27, British International Studies Association, International Political Economy Group, Aberystwyth, May.

Robinson, William I. (2006) "Latin America, State Power and the Challenge to Global Capital: An Interview with William I. Robinson", *Focus on the Global South*, Bangkok, 21 November, available at www.focusweb.org.

Roett, Riordan (2005) "Relations between China and Latin America/the Western Hemisphere", statement before Subcommittee on Western Hemisphere, House International Relations Committee, US Congress, Washington, DC, 6 April.

Rohter, Larry (2004) "China Widens Economic Role in Latin America", *New York Times*, 20 November.

Wise, Carol (2007) "Great Expectations: Mexico's Short-lived Convergence under NAFTA", Working Paper 15, Centre for International Governance Innovation, Waterloo, ON, January.

World Bank (2006) *World Development Indicators*, Washington, DC: World Bank.

World Bank (2007) *East Asia & Pacific Update: Ten Years after Asia's Financial Crisis*, Washington, DC: World Bank, April, available at http://siteresources.worldbank.org.

6

Playing the India card

Jorge Heine

On 2 June 2006 Jindal Steel and Power announced it had secured the rights to the El Mutún iron ore deposits in eastern Bolivia near the Brazilian border, one of the biggest in the world, with reserves of 40 billion tonnes. This entailed an investment commitment of US$2.1 billion, the largest ever by an Indian company in Latin America and the largest foreign direct investment (FDI) project in Bolivia ever. Over eight years, the project is to generate a pellet plant with production of 10 million tonnes a year, a sponge iron plant producing 6 million tonnes a year, a steel plant producing 1.7 million tonnes a year and a power plant with a capacity for 450 megawatts. It is also expected to create some 12,000 jobs.

The investment announcement took place only a month after the partial nationalization of a number of oil and gas fields in Bolivia, which many greeted as the "kiss of death" for FDI in that country. Revealingly, after an international tender for El Mutún, the only company willing and able to meet the Bolivian government's requirements was Jindal. Many predicted that the deal, given its many complexities (not the least of which was the price of the gas provided for it by Bolivia), ultimately would fall through. Yet on 18 July 2007 the formal contract for the deal was signed in Santa Cruz in the presence of President Evo Morales.[1]

From the Rio Grande to Tierra del Fuego, Indian companies are moving into Latin America and investing in many areas, from oil to information technology (IT), from pharmaceuticals to the automobile industry. That this is happening precisely at a time when Latin America has been moving to the left strikes many as odd. Yet it responds to the very real

Which way Latin America? Hemispheric politics meets globalization, Cooper and Heine, eds, United Nations University Press, 2009, ISBN 978-92-808-1172-8

complementarities between the Indian and Latin American economies, complementarities that have only recently come to the fore and triggered this increase in investment and trade flows.

The irruption of India and China into the world economy is one of the defining features of the early twenty-first century. The two Asian giants share a number of features, not the least of which are their territorial and demographic size and the aggressiveness with which they are importing commodities – matched only by the zeal with which they are flooding world markets with their own products. Comparisons between "the dragon and the elephant" have become a staple of many studies and publications.[2] Analyses of their interaction with other regions, including Latin America, are often undertaken along the same paired comparisons (see, for example, Santiso, 2006; Cesarini, 2007; Rosales and Kuwayama, 2007). And there is a good reason for this. As one study puts it:

> today China and India's share of world exports is 50 per cent larger than LAC's [Latin America and the Caribbean's] share, whereas in 1990 the reverse was true. In the late 1980s LAC had a trade-to-GDP ratio roughly equal to the trade-to-GDP ratio of China, and two times larger than the trade-to-GDP ratio of India. By 2004, the trade-to-GDP ratio of China was 35 per cent larger than the trade-to-GDP ratio of LAC, and India's trade-to-GDP ratio was only 14 per cent smaller than LAC's. (Lederman, Olarreaga and Perry, 2006: 3)

Yet India often gets short shrift, being overshadowed by the sheer size of the Chinese trade and investment figures.

The purpose of this chapter is to examine the ties between Latin America and India, which, while still of lesser significance than those with China, are growing fast, have a number of distinct features and are part and parcel of the broader set of opportunities available to Latin American nations in the new century's globalized economy. The chapter begins with a survey of the background of Indo-Latin American relations, current trade and investment flows and complementarities. It then takes stock of the degree to which the region and India have moved closer on the diplomatic front, followed by some concluding observations.

From the NICs to the BRICs

Latin America and India are not only in different neighbourhoods, as it were, but have also been members of different clubs.[3] In addition to the considerable distance between South Asia and the Western hemisphere – an obstacle for trade, tourism and other exchanges – the two have also been part of very different international groupings. India was a founder and leader of the Non-Aligned Movement, a largely Afro-Asian lot, of which very few Latin American countries were full and active members. The latter have tended to stick to themselves in various regional bodies, and even those few that, in the 1990s, joined entities such as Asia-Pacific Economic Cooperation (APEC) in an effort to build bridges across the Pacific did not run into India there. What used to be known as the British Commonwealth has been another significant reference point for New Delhi, albeit one where, by definition, no Latin Americans are to be found.

Moreover, the inward-looking, import-substitution development strategies that most Latin American countries and India followed from the 1950s to the 1970s were not conducive to trade diversification, and in the 1980s Latin America's debt crisis put paid to any hopes of such a thing happening then. In the early 1990s, therefore, not surprisingly, trade between India and Latin America was negligible, reaching less than US$0.5 billion in 1991–1992. Yet the moment both sides started opening up their economies, trade increased significantly, albeit from a very low base, with Indian exports to Latin America growing 11-fold over the next 10 years: by 2004 interregional trade had reached US$3 billion (see fig. 6.1). In comparison, in 2003 Chinese-Latin American trade reached US$30 billion, with Chile alone exporting more to China than the value of all Indo-Latin American trade put together.

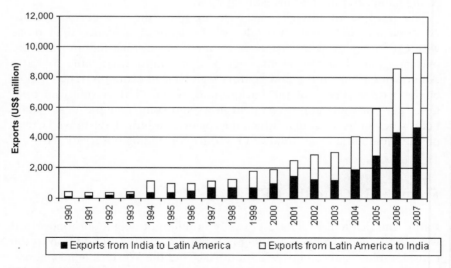

Figure 6.1 Trade between Latin America and India
Sources: International Monetary Fund (2008); Euromonitor (2008).

Other obstacles continue to hinder Indo-Latin American trade and investment: shipping links between Latin America and India are few and far between, negotiating the Indian bureaucratic maze (not only in New Delhi but also at the state level) is no easy task and India has been unwilling, for understandable reasons, to expose its agricultural sector – precisely one area where Latin America has some significant comparative advantages – to unfettered competition from abroad. The result has been a reluctance in Latin America to undertake the effort to make the most of the enormous potential of the Indian market.

These practical difficulties have been buttressed by the expectation, rarely explicitly articulated, that any major effort to strengthen Indo-Latin American links would be bound to fail, as have most past attempts at South-South cooperation. According to this reasoning, in marrying "weakness with weakness" – as evidenced in the experiences of the Non-Aligned Movement, the G-77 and its latest (also frustrated) expression, the G-15 – these perhaps well-intentioned but ultimately futile initiatives lead nowhere.[4]

In the harsh post–Cold War world, where economics trumps and economic diplomacy reigns, the key challenge for developing countries is to find markets for their goods and services and reliable sources of FDI. These tend to be found in North America, Europe and Japan, and that is where energies ought to be directed. South-South relations are all well and good, but the real action lies elsewhere – or so the reasoning goes. Collective action among developing countries not only fails to serve this purpose, but in fact might be counterproductive: since each country must look out for its own interests, the last thing any of them would want to do is antagonize those on whom they ultimately depend for trade, FDI and development assistance.

Yet two developments have thrown a monkey-wrench of sorts into all this. One was the rise in the 1980s of the so-called newly industrializing countries (NICs) – emerging economies such as Brazil, Indonesia, Mexico, Egypt, Nigeria and South Korea that managed to grow at high rates and significantly expand their manufacturing base, becoming attractive trade partners with markets of their own. The other development was the irruption of East and Southeast Asia into the world economy. With their outstanding economic performance, Taiwan, Singapore, Malaysia, Thailand and South Korea quickly joined the ranks of middle-income nations, thus belying the notion, as dependency theory had once postulated, that it was impossible for countries of the global South to leave underdevelopment behind.

East and Southeast Asia quickly became the world's fastest-growing region and one that was impossible for Latin America, traditionally fixated on Europe and the United States, to ignore. While Atlantic Coast nations such as Argentina and Brazil historically have focused on their ties to Western Europe, their Pacific Coast neighbours quickly grasped this major shift in world geoeconomics and saw the then somewhat sleepy APEC as a key tool with which to latch on to it. Mexico was the first to join, in 1991, followed by Chile in 1994 and Peru in 1999. APEC was to blossom into a key entity which has brought together many of the world's largest non-European economies.

In the 1990s Latin America and the Caribbean increased its market share of world exports from 4.5 per cent to 5.6 per cent. In so doing, two distinct subregional patterns emerged. On the one hand, Mexico and some Central American and Caribbean countries became increasingly integrated into the manufacturing circuits of US industry, as *maquiladoras* (assembly plants) moved steadily south of the Rio Grande. In South America, on the other hand, countries made the most of their rich natural resources endowment, and products such as cereals, coffee, wood and its derivatives and minerals such as copper, oil, tin, iron and nickel became their main exports. The enormous demand for natural resources coming from East Asia, a highly populated but, as a rule, natural-resources-poor part of the world, became an obvious magnet for Latin American commodities.

Whereas Japan had been a significant trading partner for Latin America for quite some time, it was only in the 1990s that China, South Korea, Taiwan and other East Asian countries came on to the radar screens of Latin American exporters and entrepreneurs, having by then established themselves as key trading partners. As one study put it, "although the Asian countries together absorb between 8 and 13 per cent of the region's external sales, depending on whether or not Mexico is included in the calculations, these sales are especially significant for Chile, Peru, Ecuador, Argentina and Brazil, which sell between 8 per cent and 32 per cent of their total exports to these countries" (ECLAC, 2004: 6).

With India's emergence as a regional-*cum*-global economic power – a process that started in the 1980s but became apparent to Latin Americans only at the turn of the century – that country became the natural next focus, after Japan and East and Southeast Asia, of Latin America's "look East" policy.

The reasons, then, for Latin America to put India on the front burner of its foreign policy and international economic policy agenda have less to do with "the spirit of Bandung" than with "the spirit of Cancún" – the site of the August 2003 Doha Round ministerial meeting of the World Trade Organization (WTO), where the G-20+ was born and Brazil and India took the lead in bringing many developing countries together on a common agenda for agricultural issues.

The argument here is twofold. On the one hand, in the international division of labour, where, for good or ill, South America has emerged as a key supplier of agricultural and mineral resources, the rapidly industrializing and quickly growing Indian economy is demanding commodities in such volumes that South American producers are sometimes not able to keep up. In marked contrast to the already-mature Western European and North American markets, the Indian economy is not only growing at a high rate, but its hitherto smallish foreign trade sector (US$364 billion in 2007) is also becoming much more sizeable (projected to reach US$500 billion in 2010), giving an additional impetus to import demand. Thus, whereas the notion of setting up production facilities to supply the Chinese market has already taken hold in Latin America, and many businesses are acting accordingly, doing the same for the Indian market is only now beginning to be considered, and Latin American businesses are thus missing out on many extant opportunities.

Conversely, India's increasingly diversified industry, which is moving away from its earlier almost exclusive focus on the domestic market to take on the international one, is finding that Latin America provides a natural outlet for many products, from traditional ones such as textiles and garments to newer ones such as cars, pharmaceuticals, chemicals and IT, where Indian products are highly competitive on both quality and price.

Competition or complementarity?

Thus, despite the distance between India and Latin America, many factors seem to be pulling the two regions together, with both having much to gain. Yet concern has been expressed in some sectors that "unfair" competition from China and India might adversely affect jobs and industry across Latin America. The evidence is mixed, but one study concludes that "since the mid-nineties there has been a rising correlation of business cycles between LAC and the two Asian economies" (Lederman, Olarreaga and Perry, 2006: 8). That is, far from hampering Latin America's growth, the rise of China and India has had a largely positive impact.

The current boom that the region, poised in 2008 for its sixth consecutive year of growth, is enjoying is partly related to the upswing in commodity prices. South America is one of the richest regions in the world in terms of natural resources – only the Middle East and North Africa have a higher, largely oil-based, natural resources index – and both China, "the world's factory", and India, "the world's service centre", are gobbling up natural resources at an incredibly fast rate. Indeed, over the past 15 years their share of world consumption of many commodities has doubled, reaching a total of as much as 25 per cent in some cases. As one recent study puts it:

> China is *Chile's* second largest export market [it has now become its first]; for example, China imports one fifth of its copper and 45 per cent of its wine and grapes from Chile. *Brazil* alone provides some 45 per cent of China's soybean imports, with another 23 per cent of soy products coming from Argentina. In 2005, 80 per cent of fish meal came from Peru and from Chile. (Arnson, 2008: 1)

For countries like Chile, Peru and Argentina, exports to China represent between 10 and 12 per cent of total exports, in some cases up from less than 1 per cent in 1990. Mexico and Central America, with export profiles more oriented towards manufacturing, are in a different situation, in which competition with Chinese products, in particular, is quite real. In fact, China recently replaced Mexico as the second-largest exporter (after Canada) to the United States. On the other hand, Chinese investment in Mexico is huge, reaching US$28 billion in 2004.

In short, the complementarity of the Chinese and Indian economies with those of South America is quite straightforward, with the latter producing many of the commodities and raw materials the former need to sustain their 8–10 per cent growth rates, and South American markets providing a ready-made outlet for Chinese and Indian manufactured goods, services and IT. In the cases of Mexico and Central America, the challenge is to tap into the FDI and innovation possibilities that China and India are offering to spur their own growth.

In both cases, however, the policy implications are clear. The steady economic growth at high rates of the two most populated countries on earth over the past quarter of a century has given a considerable impetus to the economies of a number of Latin American countries, especially since 1990, in terms of export volumes and international commodity prices. The all-time-high price of copper (which in early 2008 reached US$4 a pound, four times what it was in 2004) is but one example, with the contribution of China and India to the growth in world demand for "red gold" totalling 25 per cent over the 1990–2004 period, and even more since then (World Bank, 2006).

One concern, however, is that this heightened demand for Latin America's natural resources could have the negative effect of "locking in" the region into the production of commodities, as opposed to products (including manufactures) with greater added value. In that sense, the irruption of China and India as global economic players could actually *harm* Latin America by standing in the way of its industrialization (see Phillips in this volume). This argument, however, should be examined at various levels. First, as mentioned above, the growing Chinese and Indian demand for commodities has increased volumes of trade between these countries and Latin America, which has helped the region maintain a positive balance of trade over the past few years. Second, the steadily rising demand for raw materials is also leading to higher prices for them, thus generating an additional benefit for Latin American producers. Third, the growth of key Asian markets has allowed Latin America to diversify its exports away from traditional markets in North America and Western Europe – in 2007, 40 per cent of Chile's exports went to Asia, with China displacing the United States as Chile's number one export market and India displacing Germany as its number 10.[5]

Thus it is difficult to sustain the notion that, somewhat perversely, these trends are harmful to Latin America "in the long run". In fact, the considerably increased volumes and prices of a number of key exports as a result of the growth of China and India have meant a foreign exchange bonanza for Latin American countries, allowing them to pay off their debt, increase their reserves and, in some cases, lay the seeds for an eventual "sovereign wealth fund".[6] Some countries have managed this unexpected wealth better than others; yet these resources, if wisely invested in infrastructure, innovation and industrial policies, could well lay the foundations of a second phase of export development, one that adds more value to these commodities and generates more jobs. Whether or not that happens – and the reluctance among Latin American finance ministers to do anything that smacks of "industrial policy" and "picking winners" might stand in the way of any programme along those lines – to blame China and India for these trends would mean jumping several links in the causality chain.

On the other hand, there is no reason why Latin American countries could not aim at increasing their own share of manufactured products exported to China and India. Thus, whereas China imports a larger share of commodities from Latin America than from ASEAN (Association of Southeast Asian Nations) (13.3 per cent versus 9.0 per cent), the reverse is true for manufactured products based on natural resources imported from ASEAN (15.6 per cent versus 7.8 per cent), which indicates there is considerable room for the growth of exports of more value-added products from the region. India, for its part, sources a larger share of its commodities from ASEAN (16.1 per cent) than from Latin America (6.8 per cent), and the gap between manufactured products based on natural resources imported from ASEAN (14.5 per cent) and those from Latin America (3.9 per cent) is larger than in the case of China. This seems to offer quite a bit of room for the expansion of Indo-Latin American trade

(Lederman, Olarreaga and Perry, 2006). Indeed, such trade is growing very quickly (although from much a lower level than that with China), having more than tripled from US$3 billion in 2003 to some US$11 billion in 2007. This volume, while much lower than the US$100 billion in Sino-Latin American trade in 2007, equals the level of that trade in 2000 – meaning that the volume of Latin America's trade with India is only seven years behind that with China, by no means an insurmountable gap.

Brazil and India: Joining forces on the world stage

If the economic complementarity of Latin America and India is clear, are there reasons to expect greater political cooperation between the two, despite their distance apart and their very different security and foreign policy concerns?

An interesting case is provided by the growing links between Brazil and India. A 2003 Goldman Sachs study (Wilson and Purushothaman, 2003), coining the term BRIC – for Brazil, Russia, India and China, projecting that, because of their sheer territorial and population size among other factors, they would be the leading economies of the twenty-first century – put Brazil and India in a very different category than the one many observers had perceived them to be in until then. Russia, of course, cannot very well be placed in the South, and China always stands somewhat apart. Brazil and India, however, have taken on with great verve the role of leading the New South – that is, the post–Cold War developing world, which finds itself trying to sort out the twin challenges of globalization and regionalization.[7] This effort has expressed itself in several initiatives, most prominently IBSA and the G-20+.

IBSA, which has received little attention in the North, brings together India, Brazil and South Africa – three key actors in Asia, Latin America and Africa – to develop a common agenda and share matters of common concern. The project was originally mooted by South African President Thabo Mbeki in January 2003, and has since evolved into a significant trilateral dialogue among key Southern countries (see FRIDE, 2007; John de Sousa, 2008). IBSA was initially greeted with considerable scepticism in many quarters as just another short-lived developing country "talk shop". Crystallized for the first time at a foreign affairs ministers' meeting in Brasilia in June 2003, IBSA focused originally on UN Security Council reform and the Doha Round WTO negotiations. Over the years since then it has institutionalized itself, moving from regular ministerial meetings to presidential summits, paying considerable attention to "hard" matters such as trade and transportation and generating quite an ambitious agenda. In the words of Indian Prime Minister Manmohan Singh,

	Key entities	Size	Strategy	Priority	Economic position
Third world	NAM, G-77	Large	Defensive	Aid	Weak
New South	IBSA, G-20+	Small	Proactive rule-maker	Trade	Strong

Figure 6.2 From third world to New South
Source: Author's elaboration.

"IBSA is a unique model of transnational cooperation based on a common political identity. Our three countries come from three different continents, but share similar world views and aspirations" (quoted in FRIDE, 2007: 2). The three summits held so far – Brasilia, September 2006, Pretoria, October 2007, and New Delhi, October 2008 – have been critical in signalling support at the highest level for a project viewed with distrust not only in the North but also within sectors of the bureaucracies of the three participating countries.

As Figure 6.2 indicates, IBSA also signals the transition from the Old ("third world") South, based on large, somewhat unwieldy entities whose central platform was the demand for greater international aid and cooperation, to the New South, anchored in smaller but more focused bodies. The former spoke from weakness, the latter from strength – undergirded by the increasing economic weight of its members. The former wanted aid, the latter simply trade. The former thrived on confrontation, the latter on negotiation.

In this regard, the commonalities that are brought to the table by the IBSA members are worth noting. These are all democratic nations, with multi-ethnic and multicultural populations and long traditions of dialogue and peaceful conflict resolution. And it is by no means a coincidence that this group should have emerged when it did, precisely at a time when a rearranging of the rules of world order is being demanded, both at the United Nations and at the international financial institutions.

Significant differences exist among India, Brazil and South Africa. India is an emerging global player, a nuclear power with outer-space capabilities and the second-largest population on earth. Neither Brazil nor South Africa finds itself in these categories – although they occasionally foray into global issues, they are largely middle powers that play leading roles in their respective regions. Nonetheless, all three are committed to multilateralism and the rule of international law. This is reflected in UN peacekeeping, where India is the country that historically has committed the largest number of troops (some 70,000 so far), and where Brazil (in Haiti) and South Africa (in Central Africa) lately have taken on this role in their respective regions with special enthusiasm.

The G-20+, the group that emerged after the August 2003 Doha Round meeting in Cancún and was designed to deal with agricultural issues within the WTO, is another case of Indo-Latin American cooperation. The group, half of whose members are from Latin America, is led by Brazil and India. Despite their divergent interests in the agricultural negotiations – Brazil takes an assertive position, keen to have greater access to international markets, whereas India's stance is defensive and protectionist – they have managed to maintain a common front *vis-à-vis* the demands of the United States and the European Union, and have brought a degree of technical capability and command of the issues to the negotiations that developing nations had rarely shown in previous international trade rounds.

Chile and India: Economics in command?

If partnerships between countries such as India and Brazil are in many ways "natural", the degree to which rewarding and mutually beneficial relations can be developed between India and smaller Latin American countries seems to be an open question, given their obvious differences in size.

Chile, the quintessential Latin American "middle power", provides a good reference point, and a look at how economic links with India have evolved should illuminate broader issues on emerging trends in Indo-Latin American relations. No country on earth is further away from India than Chile, yet Chile exports more to India than any other Latin American country, to the tune of US$2.2 billion in 2007 – for its part, India traded more with Chile (US$2.5 billion) that year than with either Pakistan or Bangladesh.[8] Chile, in that sense, reflects well both the enormous opportunities that India's emergence as an economic powerhouse presents and the challenges it entails.

As table 6.1 shows, Chilean exports to India have increased exponentially over the past decade, and especially over the past five years, when they rose almost 10-fold from US$230 million in 2003 to US$2.2 billion in 2007. This has also meant a growing trade surplus for Chile, one that increased from US$151 million in 2003 to US$2 billion in 2007. Since copper – the price of which tripled from 2003 to 2007 – accounts for most of the increase, it would be easy to dismiss Chile's trade surplus as a fluke or one-time occurrence, caused simply by favourable terms of trade. But that would be a mistake. Part of the reason copper prices have risen, of course, is rising demand from China and India, and as the two Asian

Table 6.1 Bilateral trade between Chile and India (US$ million)

Year	Chilean exports	Chilean imports	Trade difference	Total trade
1997	74.4	66.0	8.3	140.5
1998	50.1	66.8	−16.7	116.9
1999	99.3	55.1	44.2	154.4
2000	124.5	70.1	54.3	194.6
2001	117.8	75.2	42.5	193.0
2002	179.7	82.1	97.6	261.8
2003	222.3	70.5	151.8	292.8
2004	426.1	100.1	326.0	526.2
2005	493.1	134.6	358.5	627.7
2006	1,727.7	164.5	1,563.2	1,892.2
2007	2,221.5	207.7	2,013.8	2,429.2

Source: Data from www.direcon.cl.

Table 6.2 Chile-India trade, 1991–2007 (US$)

	Copper	Non-copper	Copper	Non-copper	Number of exported products
	US$ million		%		
1991	7.6	0.3	95.79	4.21	5
1992	9.0	6.6	57.88	42.12	8
1993	13.4	6.6	61.78	38.22	25
1994	51.4	11.2	81.49	18.51	19
1995	77.5	7.6	91.06	8.94	21
1996	81.3	13.6	85.71	14.29	23
1997	65.8	8.1	89.09	10.91	26
1998	23.7	9.6	82.25	17.75	20
1999	87.6	13.2	86.90	13.10	30
2000	115.0	9.5	92.38	7.62	35
2001	108.0	9.8	91.71	8.29	32
2002	160.3	19.4	89.20	10.80	83
2003	192.7	29.6	86.68	13.32	70
2004	395.5	30.5	92.84	7.16	88
2005	447.4	45.6	90.75	9.25	93
2006	1,676.6	51.1	97.04	2.96	103
2007	2,102.2	109.3	95.06	4.94	134

Source: Data from www.direcon.cl.

giants continue to industrialize and develop their infrastructure, their demand for commodities and metals, including copper, is likely to continue unabated. Yet Chilean exports of copper to India have risen much faster than for the rest of Chile's leading export markets (see table 6.2) – so much so that, between 1996 and 2006, India jumped from being Chile's twenty-fifth-largest export market to being its eleventh largest, and in 2007 displaced Germany in tenth spot.

This enormous increase in Chilean exports and the high trade surplus the country has been running with India might reasonably have led to concerns about a negative Indian reaction and the consequent introduction of tariffs or non-tariff barriers to Chilean exports. In fact, quite the opposite has been the case: on 8 March 2006 India signed a preferential trade agreement with Chile, the first with any Latin American country, which took effect in August 2007 (see Heine, 2007).

On the other hand, the degree to which copper became such an overwhelmingly dominant product within Chile's export basket to India (up to 97 per cent of the value of all exports in 2006, from 86 per cent in 2003) raises the obvious question, mentioned above, about the potentially negative impact of India's demand for South American commodities and raw materials. To what extent does it condemn South American nations to a "third world-first world" relationship – where there are substantial differences in the size, strength, intent and desire of the parties involved (see fig. 6.2) – with India, in which the latter sells manufactured and intermediate products in return for basic commodities with little or no value added?

Again, what is interesting to note here is that, although copper has been the driving force behind Chile's exports to India, this does not mean that other products are absent. While the numbers are still small, non-copper exports have also grown (from a little under US$10 million in 2001 to US$51 million in 2006) from a very limited basket of 32 products to a still-limited but more respectable one of 103. Far from crowding out other exports, therefore, the steep increase in Chilean copper exports to India has gone hand in hand with that of other products, including such perishable ones as fresh fruit, of which Chile contributed around a third of India's total imports of US$25 million in 2007.

The complementarity of the Chilean and Indian economies, however, is not limited to trade; it is also reflected in investment flows. Chile's Innovation Council has identified business process outsourcing (BPO) and knowledge process outsourcing (KPO) as priority areas to be actively promoted, and the Indian IT industry has been receptive. Tata Consulting Service, India's largest IT company, bought Chilean BPO Cromicrom in 2005 and now has a total of 2,000 employees in Chile, servicing Chilean and regional markets; Evalueserve, another Indian IT company, albeit one doing KPO, also set up shop in Chile in 2006 to do "near-shoring" – that is, providing services to US clients in real time, taking advantage of the fact that Chile is on Eastern Standard Time.

Thus although the driving force of the tremendous increase in Indo-Latin American economic relations over the past few years has been India's demand for raw materials and commodities – oil, iron, soya and copper, among others – and the need to sell its own manufactured products – cars, chemicals, pharmaceuticals, garments and textiles, to name a few – one cannot reduce trade and investment between India and Latin America to that pattern and conclude that it can provide only further impetus to Latin America's "deindustrialization". A passive, complacent attitude on the part of Latin American governments and businesses certainly could lead to such an outcome. But if, on the contrary, a proactive, assertive policy to make the most of the opportunities that India offers is pursued, the results could be very different, as the case of Chile clearly shows.

Conclusion

The rise of the Asian giants has been a defining factor of the first decade of the twenty-first century, changing both its geopolitics and, even more so, its geoeconomics. For Latin America, and especially for South America, this has had a number of effects. First, it has increased the demand for Latin American exports, particularly of commodities, which have risen dramatically. Second, it has contributed to a rise in prices of the region's leading exports, thus benefiting it even further. Third, it has allowed the region to diversify its export markets, traditionally confined to the United States and Western Europe. Fourth, it has widened the region's foreign policy options.

A body of literature has arisen on the implications of growing Sino-Latin American links, which are of longer duration and greater significance than Indo-Latin American ties. Yet little analysis has been undertaken of the latter, with many commentators tending to conflate the effects of the rises of China and India for the region. This can be explained by the sheer magnitude of the trade figures between China and Latin America. The time has come, though, to stop treating China and India for these purposes as "Chindia", as it were, and instead to examine the significance for Latin America of India on its own. Although the land of Gandhi shares a number of attributes with that of Mao, there are also some significant differences between the two.

Given India's somewhat lower growth rate than China's, much attention has been paid to the disparities in the value of their respective exports and FDI, the implication being that these constitute some sort of qualitative difference, with India in the role of China's "poor relation", as it were. Yet this view is quite short-sighted. On both fronts, despite the somewhat different economic models that both "giants" follow, India is catching up.[9] On the other hand, India is a democracy, with a vibrant civil society, a free press and institutions, both political and financial, that guarantee a degree of stability and predictability one can hardly expect in more closed societies. For economic purposes, India's economy is driven by the private sector, which means that its investment decisions are made mainly by private companies strictly for business motives. Though long oriented largely towards the domestic market, Indian companies are now taking on the world market, including Latin America.

Indian leaders, less flamboyant than their Chinese counterparts, have undertaken nothing as spectacular as Chinese President Hu Jintao's November 2004 visit to Chile, Argentina, Brazil and Cuba, in which he promised US$100 billion worth of Chinese investments in the region in the course of the coming years – though little has since materialized. Nonetheless, Indian companies such as Essar, Bajaj Motors, Reliance, TCS, Jindal Steel and Power and others have been quietly scouting the region for opportunities and, in many cases, moving forward with significant investment projects.[10]

For Latin America, India offers not just a huge export market but also a potentially significant source of FDI and technology transfer; it also provides a way for Latin America to diversify its foreign policy options. Brazil, better than any other country in the region, has grasped that point, and the result has been its involvement in IBSA, the G-20+ and, to some degree, the G-4. For India, on the other hand, Latin America represents both a source of the raw materials it so badly needs and a market for its manufactured products, some of which would be rather difficult to place in Northern markets. Importantly, however, Latin America also represents a platform on which India can display its newly found global role as it frees itself from the shackles that, until the early 1990s, had prevented it from taking on the international responsibilities expected of a country of its size and historical trajectory.

Notes

1. See Jindal Steel and Power press releases, 2 June 2006, 19 July 2007.
2. *The Economist* makes such comparisons regularly.
3. This section draws heavily on Heine (2005).
4. I am indebted to Ambassador Shankar Bajpai, chairman of the Delhi Policy Group and one of India's foremost foreign policy thinkers, for this expression. For some of his reflections on India's changing role, see Bajpai (2006).
5. For a detailed breakdown of Chile's trade figures see www.direcon.cl, the official website of the Chilean Foreign Ministry Directorate of International Economic Relations.

6. In early 2008 Chile had some US$20 billion in accumulated reserves deposited in various accounts in New York and was taking steps towards the formal establishment of a sovereign wealth fund. It is estimated that these reserves should reach US$30 billion by the end of 2008. Chile's fiscal surplus was 4.5 per cent of GDP in 2007.

7. Not surprisingly, President Luiz Inácio Lula da Silva is the only Latin American president ever to have visited India *twice*, first in January 2004 (when he was chief guest at India's Republic Day celebrations) and again in June 2007, during his second term. In turn, Indian Prime Minister Manmohan Singh's only official bilateral visit to Latin America during his term in office so far (2004–2008) was to Brazil, in September 2006, though he later visited Havana for the XIV Non-Aligned Summit that same month. The other Latin American presidents to visit India between 2003 and 2008 are Ricardo Lagos of Chile (January 2005), Hugo Chávez of Venezuela (March 2005) and Felipe Calderón of Mexico (September 2007).

8. All figures used here are from www.direcon.cl.

9. Indian exports increased from 7 per cent of GDP in 1990 to 21 per cent of GDP in 2005; this is very similar to the Chinese case, where exports increased from 6 per cent to 21 per cent of GDP in the first 15 years of reforms. I am indebted for this point to my colleague at the Centre for International Governance Innovation, Manmohan Agarwal.

10. One should mention, however, the Latin American tour undertaken in April 2008 by President Pratibha Patil, India's first female head of state, in which she visited Chile, Brazil and Mexico accompanied by a significant business delegation. As a measure of the growing ties between India and Latin America, 17 permanent missions from Latin America and the Caribbean were to be found in New Delhi in April 2008, up from 12 in 2003. So far, missions have been established by Argentina, Brazil, Chile, Colombia, Costa Rica, Cuba, the Dominican Republic, Ecuador, El Salvador, Guyana, Mexico, Panama, Paraguay, Peru, Suriname, Trinidad and Tobago, Uruguay and Venezuela. By way of comparison, only 13 Latin American and Caribbean permanent missions were to be found in Moscow in 2006.

REFERENCES

Arnson, Cynthia (2008) "Introduction and Acknowledgments", in Cynthia Arnson, Mark Mohr and Riordan Roett, eds, *Enter the Dragon? China's Presence in Latin America*, Washington, DC: Woodrow Wilson International Center for Scholars/Johns Hopkins University School for Advanced International Studies.

Bajpai, K. Shankar (2006) "India Engages with the World", paper presented at Eleventh Prem Bhatia Memorial Lecture, New Delhi, 8 May.

Cesarini, Sergio M. (2007) "La seducción combinada: China e India en América Latina y el Caribe", Centro Argentino de Estudios Internacionales, Buenos Aires.

ECLAC (2004) *Latin America and the Caribbean in the World Economy 2002–2003*, Santiago: UN Economic Commission for Latin America and the Caribbean.

Euromonitor (2008) *Countries & Consumers Database*, available at www.euromonitor.com/countries_consumers.aspx.

FRIDE (Fundación para las Relaciones Internacionales y el Diálogo Exterior) (2007) "IBSA: An International Actor and Partner for the EU", Activity Brief 17 (October), FRIDE, Madrid.

Heine, Jorge (2005) "Beyond Neruda and Tagore: The Challenge of Indo-Latin American Relations", *World Affairs* 9(2), pp. 72–89.

——— (2007) "Acuerdo comercial con India", *El Mercurio* (Santiago), 20 August.

International Monetary Fund (2008) *Direction of Trade Statistics Database*, available at www.esds.ac.uk/aandp/access/login.asp.

John de Sousa, Sarah-Leah (2008) "Brasil, India y Suráfrica, potencias para un nuevo orden", *Politica Exterior* 121 (January–February), pp. 165–178.

Lederman, Daniel, Marcelo Olarreaga and Guillermo Perry (2006) "Latin America's Response to China and India: Overview of Research Findings and Policy Implications", in *Latin America and the Caribbean's Response to the Growth of China and India: Overview of Research Findings and Policy Implications*, Washington, DC: World Bank.

Rosales, Osvaldo and Mikio Kuwayama (2007) "América Latina al encuentro de China e India: Perspectivas y desafíos en comercio e inversión", *Revista de la CEPAL* 93 (December), pp. 85–108.

Santiso, Javier (2006) "Realismo mágico? China e India en América Latina y Africa", *Economía Exterior* 58, pp. 59–69.

Wilson, Dominic and Roopa Purushothaman (2003) "Dreaming with BRICs: The Path to 2050", Global Economics Paper No. 99, October, Goldman Sachs, New York, available at www2.goldmansachs.com/ideas/brics/book/99-dreaming.pdf.

World Bank (2006) *Latin America and the Caribbean's Response to the Growth of China and India: Overview of Research Findings and Policy Implications*, Washington, DC: World Bank.

FURTHER READING

Das, Gurcharan (2002) *The Elephant Paradigm: India Wrestles with Change*, New Delhi: Penguin.

Dickerson, Marla (2007) "Latin America Attracts Indian Investors", *Los Angeles Times*, 10 June.

Friedman, Thomas (2006) "Are Latin Americans Going to Emulate India or Get Addicted to China?", *New York Times*, 21 June.

Gandhi, P. Jegadish (2007) *India and China in the Asian Century: Global Economic Power Dynamics*, New Delhi: Deep and Deep.

Granguilhomme, Rogelio (2007) "El turno de India en la estrategia de México para Asia", *Foreign Affairs en Español*, January–March.

Hamm, Steve (2007) *Bangalore Tiger: How Indian Tech Upstart Wipro is Rewriting the Rules of Global Competition*, New Delhi: McGraw-Hill.

Kamdar, Mira (2007) *Planet India: How the Fastest Growing Democracy is Changing the World*, New York: Scribner.

Luce, Edward (2006) *In Spite of the Gods: The Strange Rise of Modern India*, London: Little, Brown.

OECD (2007) "Trade for Development: China, India and the Challenge of Specialisation", in *Latin American Economic Outlook 2008*, Paris: OECD.

Viswanathan, R. (2005) "India's Energy Quest in Latin America", *The Hindu*, 31 March.

—— (2005) "Acquisition of Strategic Reserves Abroad: Why Latin America Is the Obvious Destination", *Business Line*, 6 July.

Whelan, Carolyn (2005) "India Discovers Latin America", *Fortune Magazine*, 8 August.

7

Repositioning the Commonwealth Caribbean

Anthony J. Payne

The Commonwealth Caribbean's current crisis of development is perhaps the gravest it has faced in the post-independence era. The crisis has been generated by the region's failure to establish for itself a viable role within the wider context of the contemporary neoliberal globalization of the world economy. The Caribbean is actually no stranger to globalization. It has had a long and direct relationship with the modern world economy, and its distinctive characteristics as a region derive in large part from the extent, intensity, velocity and impact of its interactions with the core countries of the world system over the past 500 years.

The most recent period has been debilitating. Over the past 20 years or so, neoliberalism has come to shape both the practice and the theory of Commonwealth Caribbean development, rendering the former largely acquiescent in the face of powerful external forces and the latter predominantly defensive and compromising in the face of similar powerful external arguments and ideologies. That said, the development debate in the region has not been extinguished entirely. It has been kept alive largely by what one might call the *técnicos* of the Commonwealth Caribbean – principally either professional policy-makers working for national governments or regional organizations or politicians offering themselves to their electorates on the basis of their managerial competence rather than the sheer inspiration of their leadership. They have been industrious and imaginative, but they have not shaped a new paradigm. By definition, *técnicos* work within the established political parameters of an era, and globalization has meant that these continue to be set outside the region.

Which way Latin America? Hemispheric politics meets globalization, Cooper and Heine, eds, United Nations University Press, 2009, ISBN 978-92-808-1172-8

The context here is that, by the late 1990s, the stark neoliberal certainties of the previous decade had come to be replaced in Washington by the so-called post–Washington Consensus (PWC) (Broad and Kavanagh, 1999; Fine, 2001; Payne, 2005). Prompted by their sense that the rapid spread of globalization was generating its own instabilities and a period of consolidation was required, several key global thinkers sought to add a number of new ideas to the core of the original Washington Consensus in a series of attempts to rescue it from its own inadequacies. These new ideas were various, but included at different times and in different hands an awareness of the role of social capital in economic performance, promotion of the concept of "good governance", the partial rehabilitation of the state (albeit the "lean and mean" state of neoliberal provenance) and the strengthening of regional and global institutions. In a nutshell, the PWC was an attempt to legitimize globalization by mitigating some of its worst excesses. Its colour was thus paler than that of its predecessor, its tone more muted, its generalities perhaps worthier; but it was still recognizably neoliberal at root, and much of the old orthodoxy was still present. It was also still firmly rooted in Washington, especially in the World Bank. Within the Commonwealth Caribbean, this new global consensus became the intellectual framework within which leading *técnicos* endeavoured to adjust the region's relationship with globalization. In particular, it shaped the main contours of the three major policy debates about development that were conducted in the region between the mid-1990s and the mid-2000s.

The first of these debates concerned the case for closer Caribbean integration, and elaborated on the longstanding regional formula of simultaneous "deepening" and "widening". Some of the thinking on the strategy of "deepening" sought to address past failures and focused primarily upon ways of delivering the renewed commitment of the Caribbean Community (CARICOM), post-1989, to the establishment of a single internal market and a single external tariff. Other continuing agendas included the idea of a common currency, improved regional air and sea transport, easier intra-regional capital movement, a regional judicial service and the establishment of an assembly of Commonwealth Caribbean parliamentarians. It cannot be said that these projects were conceptualized in new or exciting ways, but this did not mean that the proposals themselves were not sensible enough. The question of "widening" arose because some questioned whether even the CARICOM grouping of countries was too small to meet the challenges of a fast-changing global economy. This perception had led to the creation in 1994 of a new body, the Association of Caribbean States, composed of the 25 states of the wider Caribbean Basin. The association, however, was set up with too few resources and too weak an institutional base to make a significant impact on regional policy-making. Its contribution, at best, has been to remind a frequently insular Commonwealth Caribbean that it shares a sea and many common problems with others, and that joint policy platforms, in principle, can be agreed across the basin as a whole.

The second debate centred upon the notion of "strategic global repositioning" (SGR), a phrase coined by Richard Bernal, Jamaican ambassador to the United States during most of the 1990s. He advanced this concept in a series of presentations from 1996 onwards, defining it as:

> a process of repositioning a country in the global economy and world affairs by implementing a strategic medium to long term plan formulated from continuous dialogue of the public service, private sector, academic community and the social sector. It involves proactive structural and institutional transformation (not adjustment) focused on improvement and diversification of exports and international economic and political relations. Achieving SGR requires changes in both internal and external relations. (Bernal, 2000: 311)

A lot was packed into this formulation – perhaps too much. Bernal had a set of ideas that underpinned SGR, but tailored his emphasis according to the focus of the audience he was addressing. Essentially, the strategy was to effect an accommodation with globalization in order to realize the opportunities the process was deemed to offer. It required disparate and demanding actions: abandoning the traditional mindset; diversifying exports; adjusting proactively; improving human resources; supplementing the skills pool with overseas nationals; developing strategic corporate alliances; creating a business-facilitating environment; improving physical infrastructure; modernizing international marketing; and garnering capital, technology and skills (Bernal, 1996: 7–14). Although SGR obviously assigned a vital role to a dynamic private sector, it also envisaged an important redefinition of the capacity and purpose of the Caribbean state, with a view to making it more "effective" and generally bringing it into line with the "good governance" modalities of the PWC. The concept of SGR unquestionably struck a chord with mainstream Commonwealth Caribbean political leaders and was widely embraced, especially by Owen Arthur (1996, 1999), the prime minister of Barbados, who gave it voice in a number of forceful speeches delivered in the latter part of the 1990s.

The third debate extended beyond the region and explored the associated notions of smallness and vulnerability as defining features of the policy predicament not only of the Commonwealth Caribbean but of other similarly placed countries, too. These arguments were first raised in 1997 in a study prepared by the Commonwealth Secretariat. Subsequently, they were taken forward in an academic direction by efforts to devise a composite vulnerability index that measured and ranked countries according to their vulnerability, and in a policy direction by the work of a Commonwealth Secretariat/World Bank joint task force that reported in 2000. The Commonwealth Caribbean *técnico* community followed these discussions closely and, indeed, contributed to them. The policy objective to which they gave rise was the notion that small, vulnerable countries should be granted "special and differential treatment" in all their dealings with the international community, especially in relation to aid and trade.

Some fundamental problems emerged, however, to confront this discourse (Sutton, 2000). The composite vulnerability index was generally, although not completely, persuasive in revealing the vulnerabilities of small Commonwealth Caribbean and similar countries (Atkins, Mazzi and Easter, 2000). However, that was not enough to overcome the political obstacles that existed among external donors and within international organizations to the idea of treating more favourably countries that were not among the poorest in the world. By the same token, the joint task force did not support the view that the special characteristics of small states were sufficiently distinctive or disadvantageous to merit the creation of a new "country category" (Commonwealth Secretariat/World Bank Joint Task Force on Small States, 2000). The report thus fell back upon the itemization of measures that small, vulnerable countries could and should undertake to help themselves. The result has been that the concept of "special and differential treatment" has come to the fore and been widely adopted by Commonwealth Caribbean and other small states in their pleas to various international forums without the evidential case for the campaign ever quite winning the acceptance of sceptics, let alone opponents.

As I have indicated, these various contributions to the ongoing discussion of Commonwealth Caribbean development sought to feed off and, of course, enter the wider global policy debate. It is notable, however, that for a long period the global community evinced little apparent concern about the anxieties that existed in the Commonwealth Caribbean about the region's potential marginalization within the context of globalization. That attitude changed only in early 2005, when the World Bank published two major studies of the region. One was a massive and detailed empirical account of the economic challenges facing the region (World Bank, 2005b); the companion piece focuses on the even-smaller countries grouped together within the Organization of Eastern Caribbean States (World Bank, 2005a).

Although the many recommendations in the two reports are too wide-ranging to be summarized succinctly, the Bank's broad message is stark and unconcealed: the abiding impression of the region's economy is "one of under-fulfilled potential and concern for the sustainability of past accomplishments". Key phrases include "Formidable challenges lie ahead" and "So it cannot be business-as-usual". The Bank sees no future in agriculture for export and only a limited future for industry. Economic growth depends on competitiveness, which means services, notably information and communication technology (ICT) enabled products and services, offshore education, health services and niche education. The route to a viable services-based economy, according to the Bank, necessitates "a pro-active approach", comprising "greater integration within the CARICOM region", "an orderly dismantling of preferences in return for increased financial and technical support", "improving the investment climate", "making the public sector more cost-effective" and "improving the quality and effectiveness of human resources" (World Bank, 2005a, 2005b).

These familiar precepts of neoliberalism drive the two World Bank reports, highlighting again and again the sheer extent of the security of the authors "in their 'paradigm' ", as well as the harsh fact that the Bank, in effect, was seeking to impose a "one-size-fits-all" model" on the region (Sutton, 2006b: 60). What is more, if the bibliography and the various studies that accompany the reports are to be believed, the World Bank proceeded in substantial ignorance of the plethora of other work done on the Caribbean development problem by the region's own *técnicos* – at least, the two studies cite very little of it. In a telling comment delivered to a meeting of the Caribbean Development Forum in Barbados in June 2005, Clive Thomas (2005), a leading academic from the University of the West Indies (UWI), argued that the World Bank reports betray a failure by their authors "to pay proper and respectful regard to the institutional memory of the region's discourses on economic matters".

Nevertheless, what emerges strongly from this brief survey of recent thinking about the development of the Commonwealth Caribbean is a broad argument about the need for a "repositioning" within globalization. All positions in the debate acknowledge this, albeit with different emphases, but none explores it fully and satisfactorily: they do not sensitively balance the specific realities of the Commonwealth Caribbean region – and the extensive debate about them that has unfolded within the region – with the significance of global political and economic trends and the attendant debate about these trends that has been generated within the global policy community. The closest approximation to such an analysis is Bernal's notion of "strategic global repositioning". But – perfectly understandably, given his quasi-political role and considerable public responsibilities – Bernal has not been able to unpack precisely enough the welter of arguments he has woven together around SGR. These arguments can helpfully be separated into three connected agendas that relate, in turn, to competitiveness, diplomacy and governance.

The SGR agenda

Competitiveness

The Caribbean has a long history of engagement with competition issues, stretching back as far as sugar, slavery and mercantilism, all of which were invoked in the "pure plantation economy era" as either essential for prosperity or a significant constraint on it. The existence of a contemporary debate on what to produce, how to produce it and how to trade it is nothing new, and serves as an uncomfortable reminder to the region that progress and transformation are slow and the past weighs heavily on the present. Bernal (2002: 26–27) neatly captured this in the title of his keynote address to a private sector summit on competitiveness: "The Future Is Not What It Was for the Caribbean". In this talk, he argued for the "imperative for change" to "consolidate and improve existing production lines while reorienting the economy towards new types of economic activities for both the national and global markets". A brief audit of key sectors of the Commonwealth Caribbean economy in relation to current and anticipated competitiveness reveals the kinds of difficulties to which Bernal referred.

It is now widely recognized, for example, that the future for most extra-regional export agricultural products, notably sugar and bananas, is bleak in the extreme. Minerals are buoyant only in Trinidad and Tobago, with its booming oil and gas sector (Pantin and Hosein, 2004: 180); by comparison, the bauxite/alumina industry has lost the importance it formerly had in Jamaica, although it remains significant, and is struggling in Guyana. Industry, once considered the key to the region's development, has not met expectations, with its share of regional gross domestic product (GDP) dropping from 38 per cent in the 1960s to 25 per cent in the 1990s. Services have thus been the most important driver of growth in the Caribbean in the past 40 or so years, and now account for 62 per cent of regional GDP. Yet in this sphere, too, there are problems: tourism offers an increasingly "mature" product in an ever more price-competitive global market, while the financial services sector, although well established in countries that were early entrants to the business, does not have much capacity to spread to new sites given the recent enactment of onerous new international standards and regulations.

The future prosperity of the region thus depends on the successful development of new services. The report of the Caribbean Trade and Adjustment Group (2001) recommends information, entertainment and health export services, while the World Bank (2005b) highlights ICT-enabled products and services, offshore education and health services. Critical to such prospects is a cheap and efficient telecommunications sector, which has been undergoing modernization in recent years, including the introduction of more competition. Also of key importance are highly educated and well-trained human resources, which, at one level, the Commonwealth Caribbean seems well placed to provide, since access to education is better in the region than in most parts of the non-industrialized world. In rankings that measure years of schooling, however, the average ranking for Caribbean countries has fallen from forty-seventh place out of 92 countries in 1970 to fifty-second in 2000 (ibid.: para. 63), and there is a problem with school completion rates. The pass rates for mathematics and English in the Caribbean Examinations Council secondary examinations remain very low, and the proportion of the population in tertiary education, at 15 per cent in 2000, is below the Latin American average of 24 per cent (ibid.: paras 64–65).

There is manifestly a great deal to be done, including substantial structural transformation, before the Commonwealth Caribbean can be said to be "competitive" in global terms. The required mix of policies includes macroeconomic rigour, big changes in private sector practices (Wint, 2004), astute trade policy decisions and serious investment in ICT (infoDev, 2005). The magnitude of the task is well understood in the region, but whether the leadership and the vision are there, and in common, to carry it through is a more open question. The official discussion on competitiveness has largely been technical and from the top down, but what is clear is that the massive improvement needed can be achieved only if there are sweeping and costly changes in the domestic economy, supported by matching regional and international actions. There needs to be widespread understanding and support for such an imperative, which, at a minimum, suggests a competitiveness policy (and, by extension, a development policy) that goes well beyond technical fixes.

Diplomacy

The question of how to conduct external relations in an era of sweeping and fundamental changes within the world order has preoccupied the Commonwealth Caribbean for at least the past 15 years, and has gradually generated a greater realization of the importance of the role that effective diplomacy must play in the region's overall development strategy. Cedric Grant (2000) described how CARICOM's leaders, alarmed by the build-up in the early 1990s of an array of different trade negotiating arenas, moved in a series of uncertain *ad hoc* steps to establish, first, an informal interlocutory group of heads of government, and then a more formal Prime Ministerial Subcommittee on External Negotiations. In 1997 a new institution, the Caribbean Regional Negotiating Machinery (RNM), was established to handle these various interlinked negotiations. The heads of government took the view that the region's existing means

of "foreign policy coordination" within CARICOM required reinforcement, and accordingly conceived of the RNM as a kind of special project
that would be endowed with a limited lifespan coterminous with the
length of the various negotiations and would operate in subsidiary fashion within the domain of the existing Caribbean Community Secretariat.

Appointed as the RNM's first head was the influential figure of Shridath Ramphal, former Commonwealth secretary-general. He imposed
his own considerable persona on the design of the RNM, which thence-
forth worked in distinctive, and often provocative, style to push the region's leaders to adopt proactive, rather than conventionally reactive,
approaches to the prospect of change in the international trading regime
(Ramphal, 1997a, 1997b, 1998). Although this is not the place to review
in full the RNM's work over the past decade, the institution unquestionably was given a most difficult brief, and it is not surprising that, at times,
its capacity has been fully stretched in order to cope. Ramphal stood
down as chief negotiator after the conclusion of the World Trade Organization (WTO) Ministerial Conference in Doha in November 2001 and
was replaced by Richard Bernal. Trade diplomacy continues in relation
to the Doha Round of multilateral trade negotiations, the region's economic partnership agreement with the European Union and a range of
bilateral agreements – although discussion of the prospective Free Trade
Area of the Americas (FTAA) has now stalled, thereby reducing at least
some of the resource problems initially posed by the simultaneity of so
many negotiations.

In a review of the organization of trade-negotiating capacity at the
Caribbean regional level, Dunlop, Szepesi and Van Hove (2004: 5) offer
the following well-judged summary:

> The pooling of scarce resources and capacity at regional level appears a logical
> and appealing answer for developing countries that face a multitude of trade
> negotiations, but it is far from a straightforward exercise. Within most regions
> economic interests among its [sic] members diverge. Setting up a system of dis-
> tributing the costs and benefits of the trade liberalisation is difficult, more so for
> developing country regions ... the region can only go as fast as its members, so
> trade capacity support is needed at both national and regional level. The insti-
> tutional set up, role and mandate of the regional negotiating machinery re-
> mains a major challenge, and will evolve according to the deepening of the
> regional integration process. A fine balance needs to be struck between effi-
> ciency and negotiating strength on the one hand and concerns of participation
> and ownership by the members on the other.

It is thus accepted that, despite the best efforts of Ramphal and others
and notwithstanding the novelty of the RNM concept, the Commonwealth Caribbean has not fully honed the diplomatic structure it needs
to have at its disposal in the complex world of globalization. It could,

and should, do more, but it is as well to concede one obvious truism that cannot be managed away – namely, the fact that the Commonwealth Caribbean is involved in negotiations with the biggest, most powerful and most ruthless countries in the world. The United States and the European Union regard the Doha Round as fundamental to their own economic and political interests, and they have played their hands self-ishly. Within the FTAA, the United States did not hesitate to use the po-tential carrot of offering separate arrangements to particular countries and was quite prepared at one sticky point in the talks to seek behind the scenes to undermine Bernal's standing with CARICOM heads of government (Lewis, 2005: 77). Within the economic partnership agree-ment process, the European Commission has yet to rein in the tough tac-tics of its trade negotiators. Moreover, in all these processes, Latin American countries are rivals much more than allies. The problem of confronting massively disproportionate power in all their diplomatic dealings is one that small Caribbean countries cannot escape, even when acting collectively.

Governance

The importance of "good governance" for economic and social develop-ment has been explored within the Commonwealth Caribbean in various reports, conferences and academic studies over the past few years. The main focus of attention has been whether the system of governance in-herited at independence is any longer "fit for purpose" in maintaining democracy, delivering development and coping with globalization. In this debate, the opening shots were fired in a study by Patrick Emmanuel (1993). He identified the key areas of concern as the electoral system and relations between parliament and the executive and between the public service and local government, and recommended "more representative electoral systems, more virile parliaments, less authoritarian executives, more responsive bureaucracies and more decentralised networks of rep-resentation and administration". He also argued that there was "growing evidence, especially among the large generation of youth, of alienation from both formal and informal political institutions" and a "feebleness of will towards genuine change" that threatened the "legitimacy and au-thority of governance itself let alone any specific system of governance" (ibid.: 108, 111), thereby raising the prospect of sudden, violent and un-predictable change.

This has not happened, but the areas Emmanuel identified have been the staples of much of the subsequent discussion. They resurfaced, for ex-ample, in a paper by Selwyn Ryan (1996) for the UN Development Pro-gramme, where he identifies as major threats to "good governance" in the region, *inter alia*, a "spoils system" in which the winners of elections monopolize all the perks of office, a parliamentary system in which accountability and controls are weak and a judicial system that is finding it difficult to deal with increases in crime, corruption and drug taking. Ryan (1999) further developed these observations a few years later in a monograph in which he considers the experience of government in most Commonwealth Caribbean countries and reflects on the need to reform the Westminster system as the model of governance. Ryan points to failing political parties, bureaucracies under stress, judicial systems in crisis and the erosion of the "culture of civil discourse" as undermining the political system and leading to increasing apathy, anomie and violence. These problems are compounded, in his view, by other region-wide practices of the political élite; chief among them authoritarian leadership styles, adversarial politics (political and ethnic tribalism), the cultivation of political patronage and the encouragement of zero-sum attitudes in government in which "winner takes all".

At the same time, a sense of proportion needs to accompany this analysis. While the identified shortcomings are serious, they have not yet proved fatal. There is still faith in the Commonwealth Caribbean's capacity to reform the Westminster-Whitehall system incrementally. Ryan (ibid.: 347–349) himself takes this line, as does the Organization for American States (OAS) Unit for the Promotion of Democracy, which examines the relationship between the "Westminster system" and "good governance" and concludes "there [are] serious and substantial reforms that would go a long way toward correcting or at least alleviating imbalances and deficiencies of the current system" (OAS, 2002).

Attention here has focused in the main on public sector reform – by which is meant the implementation of the "new public management" paradigm (CARICAD, 1995) – and on the further and deeper involvement of civil society organizations in governance mechanisms (Brown, 2002). Neither of these strands of reform has been completely successful, however, and the governance debate in the region can best be described as being "in recess" (Sutton, 2006a). The debate should be revived, but in a manner that gives greater prominence to the development dimension and provides a broader interpretation of the elements of "good governance". This will mean both more deliberative and purposive action by the state at the national and regional levels and, more generally, a reconsideration of the role of the state in the region. In so doing, the Commonwealth Caribbean must look beyond what Clive Thomas (1998) has described as "the post colonial development state" and the successor "neoliberal state" to a new form of state with greater involvement of civil society organizations, a more supportive public sector and a wider vision. It must also be a more "proactive" state, given the generally weak record of the private sector outside of a small number of enclaves in relatively few countries. The key here is to build capacity in state management and planning and to deliver more effective and efficient public services to citizens.

Conclusion

Where does all this lead by way of conclusion? At the outset of this chapter I highlighted the importance of Bernal's case about the Commonwealth Caribbean's need for "strategic global repositioning", and argued that his formulation of this concept has not been given sufficient critical scrutiny within the region, which thus has remained underdeveloped, both intellectually and politically. I also identified competitiveness, diplomacy and governance as the formative elements of strategic global repositioning, and I have endeavoured to illustrate that problems within these three areas manifestly constitute the most pressing, and intractable, aspects of the Commonwealth Caribbean's current development *problématique*. What is striking, however, is that the analysis of what needs to be done in each sphere points strongly in the same broad policy direction. What emerges is an overriding need to create in the Commonwealth Caribbean a "CARICOM developmental state" – the functional equivalent of the kind of East Asian "developmental states" concept that was so crucial in the 1980s and 1990s to breaking the impasse of underdevelopment in that part of the world. In the remainder of the chapter, I set out briefly what is meant by this notion.

The concept of a "developmental state" has been endlessly debated in the academic literature, but Leftwich (2000: 167) classically defines it as "a transitional form of the modern state ... whose political and bureaucratic elites have generally achieved relative autonomy from socio-political forces in the society and have used this in order to promote a programme of rapid economic growth with more or less rigour and ruthlessness". Although "developmental states" are sometimes viewed as being necessarily authoritarian in their politics, this is not a defining feature and so does not preclude the idea of a democratic variant. The point is that the political and economic élites have to be sufficiently distanced from the push-and-pull of interest-group politics to have the autonomy to chart a coherent development strategy – to identify and back the economic sectors that have growth potential ("picking winners"), to manage external market relations with the rest of the global economy ("selective seclusion") and generally to give strategic direction to a country's development ambitions. The key task is "getting the control mechanism right" (Amsden, 1989), rather than "getting prices right", the mantra of the neoliberals. It is also considered vital, however, that the relative autonomy of the élites be "embedded" (Evans, 1995), meaning they should be well enough enmeshed with business and other potential development partners in the society that their proposed policies command legitimacy.

Like all development models, this package of characteristics obviously emerged at a particular time and in a particular place. It cannot be transferred in a simplistic way. At the same time, this does not mean that important lessons cannot be learned and key elements of the model subsequently adapted for use in other parts of the world. However, with only a small number of exceptions (Griffith, 1991; Gayle, 1993), theorists concerned with Commonwealth Caribbean development have ignored the "developmental state" model, most presuming that it somehow does not apply to a region with as great a commitment to democracy as to development. Interestingly, the idea was picked up again by Nikolaos Karagiannis, a research fellow at UWI in Jamaica. He concedes that, as he puts it, it would be "wrong to consider that Japanese economic policy-making could, or indeed should, be transplanted to Caribbean economies which are characterised by different historical and cultural circumstances, and different socio-political characteristics". But what is important to learn from East Asia, he argues, is "how to approach development problems – i.e. the *strategic* approach" (emphasis in original), the point being that, in his view, "governments may still pursue strategic industrial policy in a globalising world economy" (Karagiannis, 2003: 25, 9).

The latter general point, which in a way is really what SGR has always been about, is important but needs to be framed somewhat differently. Karagiannis focuses exclusively on the nation-state as the potential vessel within which to pursue strategic developmentalism. While it is the case that all Commonwealth Caribbean countries need to focus hard on the issue of competitiveness, improving their development diplomacy and taking their interest in the reform of governance further than they have done thus far, these goals will be extraordinarily difficult to deliver at the national level alone. Considered as separate entities, all Commonwealth Caribbean countries, even the largest and most populous like Jamaica and Trinidad and Tobago, are too small to acquire and sustain the necessary steering capacity. In a further manifestation of the politics of smallness, Commonwealth Caribbean state machines are also, inevitably, too close to the pull of societal pressures to establish the kind of relative autonomy that is at the heart of the classic conception of a "developmental state". In short, however much one might wish it, the region is not going to give birth to a flock of "mini-developmental states" at the national level. In that sense, at least, it is right to conclude that the various East Asian national experiences cannot be transferred to Caribbean states.

However, the crucial missing element in the discussion of the "developmental state" concept in the context of the Commonwealth Caribbean has been the CARICOM dimension. CARICOM remains, in essence, a weak version of the intergovernmentalism that was all that was possible politically in the region in the years after the collapse of the West Indies Federation in 1962, qualified only by the *ad hoc* creation of the RNM and the eventual establishment of a Caribbean Court of Justice. It may be, though, that another opportunity to reshape the basis of Commonwealth Caribbean regional governance is in the midst of presenting itself. In July 2003, on the thirtieth anniversary of the original signing of the CARICOM treaty, the CARICOM heads of government met in Jamaica. Aware, as they put it, that "the current geopolitical and geostrategic environment is significantly different from that which existed ... in 1973" and that "the process of globalisation and economic liberalisation continues to pose significant challenges for the economically fragile and vulnerable member states of the Community", they adopted the Rose Hall Declaration on Regional Governance and Integrated Development. In this statement, they agreed to establish a CARICOM Commission, answerable to them but specifically charged with deepening the regional integration process in matters such as the creation and functioning of a single market and economy, as well as in "other areas ... as the Conference of Heads may from time to time determine" (CARICOM, 2003). It was no more than a commitment of principle, but a CARICOM Commission was something that had never been promised before in the region, and in that sense the Rose Hall Declaration was a momentous and potentially seminal decision.

Everything, of course, depended (and still depends) on what ensues. The heads of government set up a Prime Ministerial Group on Governance, chaired by Ramphal, the former RNM head, to elaborate on the details of the proposal. This group did its work – including identifying an income stream to support the commission that would be derived from a percentage allocation of the import duties gathered by all CARICOM states – and reported to a further gathering of leaders in February 2005. They apparently felt they had too little time to consider such a major change, however, and bypassed the matter. The heads of government considered it again at another summit in February 2006, at which a further "technical working group" was appointed, led by Vaughan Lewis, a UWI academic and former prime minister of St Lucia. This group reported to yet a further CARICOM heads' meeting in February 2007 (Lewis, 2006). Lewis endorsed the commission proposal, but instead of moving immediately to adopt the report, the leaders established a process of further consultation and additional comment, including proposals for alternative models of governance. These were to be channelled through Edwin Carrington, as CARICOM secretary-general, and included in an interim report to be considered by the heads at their next meeting in July 2007. Clearly, therefore, there has already been some slippage of time and perhaps some waning of intent since Rose Hall.

It should be stressed, however, that the establishment of a CARICOM Commission, with a new tier of three or four ex-regional politicians appointed as commissioners, will not be transformative in itself. But a commission that built itself up into something akin to a "CARICOM developmental state" might well be. What this would involve in detail requires more argument and research, but at the very least it would mean reviving the secretariat as the administrative base of the commission, fully incorporating the RNM as the external affairs division, deftly integrating a range of other regional mechanisms of functional cooperation into the ambit of the commission and, critically, setting up a new and dynamic economic planning bureau to plan the region's overall development strategy, including addressing fundamental questions of production. The commission would need to be protected from day-to-day pressures from the region's political leadership, it would need to be seen to offer the career of choice to the brightest and most energetic of the region's technocrats and it would need to work closely with the regional private sector and key civil society organizations.

The Commonwealth Caribbean, at long last, might be on the verge of setting up a CARICOM Commission, but it must beware of doing too little too late once again. What is needed is an ambitious vision of what the commission can become, and a sense that the creation of a regional "development state" is both desirable and feasible if the Commonwealth Caribbean is to engineer for itself a viable position within a globalized world economy. Since the West Indies Federation ended in 1962, the region has, in effect, wasted a generation. It partially redeemed itself with the establishment of CARICOM in 1973, but it now needs to seize the Rose Hall moment, to establish and properly fund a CARICOM Commission and to charge it with nothing less than charting all aspects of a region-wide development strategy capable of coming to terms with globalization.

Acknowledgements

This chapter draws directly on a longer study co-authored with Paul Sutton and published in June 2007 as a Centre for International Governance Innovation working paper under the title *Repositioning the Caribbean within Globalisation*. I am grateful to Paul for allowing me to derive from it this shorter version of the argument.

REFERENCES

Amsden, Alice H. (1989) *Asia's Next Giant: South Korea and Late Industrialization*, Oxford: Oxford University Press.

Arthur, Owen (1996) *The New Realities of Caribbean International Economic Relations*, St Augustine, Trinidad and Tobago: University of the West Indies, Institute for International Relations.

―――― (1999) "Keynote Address by the Prime Minister of Barbados", presented to Twenty-third Annual Miami Conference on the Caribbean and Latin America, Miami, 9 December, mimeo.

Atkins, Jonathan P., Sonia Mazzi and Christopher Easter (2000) *A Commonwealth Vulnerability Index for Developing Countries: The Position of Small States*, London: Commonwealth Secretariat.

Bernal, Richard (1996) "Strategic Global Repositioning and Future Economic Development in Jamaica", North-South Agenda Papers 18, University of Miami, North-South Center, Miami, April.

―――― (2000) "The Caribbean in the International System: Outlook for the First Twenty Years of the 21st Century", in Kenneth Hall and Denis Benn, eds, *Contending with Destiny: The Caribbean in the 21st Century*, Kingston, Jamaica: Ian Randle Publishers.

―――― (2002) "The Future Is Not What It Was for the Caribbean", address to Private Sector Summit 2002, Competitive Private Sector Development: An Imperative for the Future, Bridgetown, Barbados, 4 March.

Broad, Robin and John Cavanagh (1999) "The Death of the Washington Consensus?", *World Policy Journal* 16(3), pp. 79–88.

Brown, Deryck (2002) "The Private Sector as a Social Partner: The Barbados Model", in Selwyn Ryan and Ann Marie Bissessar, eds, *Governance in the Caribbean*, St Augustine, Trinidad and Tobago: University of the West Indies, Sir Arthur Lewis Institute of Social and Economic Studies.

Caribbean Trade and Adjustment Group (2001) "Improving Competitiveness for Caribbean Development", CRNM/CTAG/Final Report/Rev2/08/01, Washington, DC.

CARICAD (1995) "Report of a Working Group on Public Sector Reform and Administrative Restructuring in the Caribbean Community", Caribbean Centre for Development Administration, Bridgetown, Barbados, mimeo.

CARICOM (2003) "Rose Hall Declaration on Regional Governance and Integrated Development", CARICOM Statements and Declarations, available at www.caricomlaw.org/doc.php?id=23.

Commonwealth Secretariat/World Bank Joint Task Force on Small States (2000) "Small States: Meeting Challenges in the Global Economy", Final Report, Washington, DC, March, mimeo.

Dunlop, Adam, Stefan Szepesi and Kathleen Van Hove (2004) "Organising

Trade Negotiating Capacity at the Regional Level: A Caribbean Case Study", ECDPM Discussion Paper 54, European Centre for Development Policy Management, Maastricht, September.

Emmanuel, Patrick (1993) *Governance and Democracy in the Commonwealth Caribbean: An Introduction*, Bridgetown, Barbados: University of the West Indies, Institute of Social and Economic Research.

Evans, Peter B. (1995) *Embedded Autonomy: States and Industrial Transformation*, Princeton, NJ: Princeton University Press.

Fine, Ben (2001) "Neither the Washington nor the Post-Washington Consensus: An Introduction", in B. Fine, C. Lapavitsas and J. Pincus, eds, *Development Policy in the Twenty-first Century: Beyond the Post-Washington Consensus*, London: Routledge.

Gayle, Dennis J. (1993) "Applying the East Asian Development Model to the English-Speaking Caribbean", in Jacqueline Anne Braveboy-Wagner, W. Marvin Will and Dennis J. Gayle, eds, *The Caribbean in the Pacific Century: Prospects for Caribbean-Pacific Cooperation*, Boulder, CO: Lynne Rienner.

Grant, Cedric (2000) "An Experiment in Supra-National Governance: The Caribbean Regional Negotiating Machinery", in Kenneth Hall and Denis Benn, eds, *Contending with Destiny: The Caribbean in the 21st Century*, Kingston, Jamaica: Ian Randle Publishers.

Griffith, Winston H. (1991) "The Applicability of the East Asian Experience to Caribbean Countries", in Yin-Kann Wen and Jayshree Sengupta, eds, *Increasing the International Competitiveness of Exports from Caribbean Countries*, Washington, DC: World Bank.

infoDev (2005) "Executive Summary", in *Improving Competitiveness and Increasing Economic Diversification in the Caribbean: The Role of ICT*, Washington, DC: infoDev, available at www.infodev.org.

Karagiannis, Nikolaos (2003) "Towards a Caribbean Developmental State Framework", paper presented to Development Strategy Forum, Caribbean Development Bank, Bridgetown, Barbados, 15–17 January, available at www.cdb.org.

Leftwich, Adrian (2000) *States of Development: On the Primacy of Politics in Development*, Cambridge: Polity Press.

Lewis, Patsy (2005) "Unequal Negotiations: Small States in the New Global Economy", *Journal of Eastern Caribbean Studies* 30(1), pp. 54–107.

Lewis, Vaughan (2006) "Managing Mature Regionalism: Regional Governance in the Caribbean Community", Report of Technical Working Group on Governance appointed by CARICOM Heads of Government, Georgetown, Guyana, available at www.caricom.org.

OAS (2002) *Westminster in the Caribbean: Viability Past and Present, Prospects for Reform of Radical Change*, Washington, DC: Organization of American States, available at www.upd.oas.org.

Pantin, Dennis and Roger Hosein (2004) "Competitiveness in Small, Open, Mineral Based Economies: The Case of Trinidad and Tobago", in Lino Briguglio and Gordon Cordina, eds, *Competitiveness Strategies for Small States*, Valletta and London: Island and Small States Institute/Commonwealth Secretariat.

Payne, Anthony (2005) *The Global Politics of Unequal Development*, Basingstoke: Palgrave Macmillan.

Ramphal, Shridath (1997a) "The West Indian Society – A Recipe for Strength and Growth", opening address to Seventeenth Caribbean Insurance Conference on Securing Our Future, Bridgetown, Barbados, 2 June, mimeo.

––––– (1997b) "Keynote Address", presented at Ninth Annual Private Sector Conference of the Caribbean Association of Industry and Commerce, Kingston, Jamaica, 26 June, mimeo.

––––– (1998) "The Negotiations: Process and Preparation", paper presented at Free Trade Agreement of the Americas Seminar for Bahamas Public and Private Sector, Nassau, Bahamas, 6 March, mimeo.

Ryan, Selwyn (1996) "Democratic Governance and the Social Condition in the Caribbean", in *Governance and Democratic Development in Latin America and the Caribbean*, New York: UN Development Programme.

––––– (1999) *Winner Takes All: The Westminster Experience in the Caribbean*, St Augustine, Trinidad and Tobago: University of the West Indies, Institute of Social and Economic Research.

Sutton, Paul (2000) "An Agenda for Small States in the Opening Years of the Twenty-First Century", paper presented to Special CDB Discussion Forum, Caribbean Development Bank, Bridgetown, Barbados, 26 January, mimeo.

––––– (2006a) *Modernizing the State: Public Sector Reform in the Commonwealth Caribbean*, Kingston, Jamaica: Ian Randle Publishers.

––––– (2006b) "Caribbean Development: An Overview", *New West Indian Guide* 80(1/2), pp. 45–62.

Thomas, Clive (1998) "Globalization, Structural Adjustment and Security: The Collapse of the Post-Colonial Development State in the Caribbean", *Global Development Studies* 1(1/2), pp. 67–84.

––––– (2005) "The World Bank's 'A Time to Choose': Comment", paper presented to Caribbean Forum for Development, Bridgetown, Barbados, June.

Wint, Alvin (2004) "Jamaica in International Competition", in Lino Briguglio and Gordon Cordina, eds, *Competitiveness Strategies for Small States*, Valletta and London: Island and Small States Institute/Commonwealth Secretariat.

World Bank (2005a) "OECS: Towards a New Agenda for Growth", Report 31683-LAC, World Bank, Washington, DC, 7 April.

––––– (2005b) "A Time to Choose: Caribbean Development in the 21st Century", Report 31725-LAC, World Bank, Washington, DC, 26 April.

Part III

A fresh multilateral impetus

8

Renewing the OAS

Andrew F. Cooper

Entering the new millennium, the Organization of American States (OAS) appeared to be on the cusp of transformation, particularly in terms of its promotion of a democracy agenda. In declaratory terms, much progress was made in the evolution of a "democratic solidarity paradigm".[1] The inter-American system's emerging democracy norms and parameters for collective action became enshrined in the historic Inter-American Democratic Charter (IADC), signed on 11 September 2001. In operational terms, the OAS has built up a sizeable record of interventions in defence of democracy against authoritarian threats or setbacks during the past 15 years that includes Peru (1992, 2000), Guatemala (1993), the Dominican Republic (1994) and Paraguay (1996, 1999). The 2000 Peru initiative deserves special recognition, in that it took shape – with a high-level OAS mission and the establishment of a *mesa*, or table of dialogue – in a manner that would have been unthinkable a decade earlier (Cooper and Legler, 2006). In 2003 the OAS also organized a tripartite mission – along with the Carter Center and the UN Development Programme – to facilitate dialogue between Venezuela's polarized political forces. Although this effort did not achieve its more ambitious aim of bringing about national reconciliation, in May 2003 the tripartite mission helped broker an agreement between the government of Hugo Chávez and the opposition Coordinadora Democrática for an electoral solution to the political crisis.

With these conditions in mind, it was possible to put a positive spin on the organizational trajectory of the OAS. Traditionally viewed as weighed

Which way Latin America? Hemispheric politics meets globalization, Cooper and Heine, eds, United Nations University Press, 2009, ISBN 978-92-808-1172-8

down by structural constraints, the OAS was for the first time allowed space and capacity for agency. As the director of the Americas programme at one leading US think-tank asserted as late as November 2004: "The OAS represents multilateralism that works. It is the key element of the inter-American system. With the decided support of the member states, it is poised to move ahead in serving the citizens of the hemisphere" (DeShazo, 2004).

In terms of style, the OAS seemed to be well on its way towards shifting from a quintessential club-type entity to an organization embracing a more expansive, networked form of multilateralism. Club multilateralism engages with issues such as democratic promotion only to the extent that this activity allows the *status quo* to be managed more effectively. Highly protective of the prerogatives of states (the members of the club), club multilateralism is content with the framework of the sovereignty-protected system. Central to the dynamic of networked multilateralism, by way of contrast, is the desire to effect change within the corpus of the domestic political system. Far more diffuse in its make-up – with room to operate for non-state as well as state actors – networked multilateralism is quite willing to challenge the norm of non-intervention.[2]

Still, as quickly as this type of scenario enveloped the workings of the OAS, the central debate shifted to other concerns about multilateralism in the Americas. In part these concerns reflected embedded issues of organizational capacity, but they were also an extension of the measure of polarization taking hold within the OAS. Far from a sense of consensus, the OAS has become a site of divergence about the rules of the game for the organization.

The United States, traditionally the dominant member of the OAS, was ambiguous about the shift from a club to a networked form of multilateralism, since this mode of operation made it far more difficult for the United States both to socialize and to discipline the OAS. But the alternative scenario was far more divisive, in that it constituted a direct challenge to US leadership of the OAS. Whereas the United States anticipated benefits as well as complications from the shift to a networked approach, a clash about rules increasingly became a win/lose struggle between the United States and its allies versus Chávez of Venezuela and his allies. Rather than a contest about organizational style, it became one about who makes the collective rules for the OAS and for what reasons. If networked multilateralism has made the dominance of the United States more awkward, it has also been fundamentally compromised by what could be seen as an "anti-hegemonic" force with no interest in what the United States considers to be consensus orientation or acceptable behaviour (Cox, 1992).

The nature of the club

In defining the OAS as a classic "club", it is informative to point to a number of core characteristics that determine both the institution's strengths and its weaknesses at the point of transition. The first of these is the enhanced profile of the role of OAS secretary-general since César Gaviria took over the position in 1993. As Gaviria was intellectually willing to take risks in pushing forward the democracy agenda, he must take a good deal of the credit for the turnaround of the OAS (Gaviria, 1998). Bureaucratically, Gaviria injected some new blood into the organization: rather than accept the notion that the OAS was the preserve of the older generation, Gaviria surrounded himself with a "kindergarten" of talented younger advisers.

Operationally, Gaviria was willing to bend the restrictions of club multilateralism. While technically beholden to member states, he exercised considerable operational leadership in both Peru and Venezuela in a way that undoubtedly enhanced the prestige and authority of his office, independent of the weight of member states behind him. In addition to numerous fact-finding and consultative trips and press statements, Gaviria expanded his "good offices" by centralizing control over secretariat activities to promote democracy and taking personal charge of facilitating dialogue in polarized Venezuela from November 2003 to May 2004.

Yet, by interjecting an element of personalization into its culture, Gaviria expanded the scope for criticism of the OAS's modalities, particularly with respect to his intervention in Venezuela. After all, Gaviria was the former president of Colombia, a country with which Venezuela had considerable tensions over operations by Colombian guerrillas along their shared border. To his critics, Gaviria's rationale for taking on the position of facilitator was merely that of self-promotion: a bid for the Nobel Peace Prize, a high-level UN position or, perhaps more far-fetched, re-election as secretary-general of the OAS. To his supporters, however, Gaviria combined genuine concern for the promotion of a "newly focused" OAS and fear of the spillover effect in the hemisphere (more precisely in the Andean region, including Colombia) of the breakdown of order in Venezuela. In case any doubts remained about his personal commitment to the mission, the secretary-general moved both physically and psychologically to Caracas for approximately six-and-a-half months.

In the post-Gaviria era, however, transition problems have added to the OAS's organizational vulnerabilities. In a touch of profound irony for a region so often associated with corruption – and for an organization that took the lead in producing the Inter-American Convention Against Corruption, the first anti-corruption treaty in the world – the consensus choice to succeed Gaviria, former Costa Rican President Miguel Ángel Rodríguez, was forced to step down in October 2004 after only three weeks in office over charges that he had accepted kickbacks during his 1998–2002 presidential term.

A second determining characteristic of the OAS in transition, which has attracted some considerable attention, involves the issue of material resources. The organization remains in a weak financial position: its total budget hovers around US$80 million and the level of its "Regular Fund" has remained unchanged for a good many years. Its operations and programming are further hurt by the fact that a significant number of its members are in arrears on their annual contributions. Even at the moment now viewed as the high-water mark for the organization's promotion of a democracy agenda, this was a significant problem. At the end of 2001 the accumulated arrears of the United States, Brazil and Argentina were calculated at US$35.7 million, US$6.4 million and US$3.7 million, respectively (OAS, 2001b; see also OAS, 1999a; *Financial Times*, 2000). The operations of the Unit for the Promotion of Democracy (UPD) and, more recently, the Department for the Promotion of Democracy have been especially affected by this budgetary shortfall. The UPD must fund what has become an ambitious array of hemisphere-wide democracy-enhancing activities, from democratic institution-building, election monitoring and technical assistance to de-mining in Central America, on a 1999 annual budget of just US$3.5 million, supplemented by an anticipated US$10–15 million in external funding (OAS, 1999c). Its election observation missions, a cornerstone of its operations, are funded precariously by voluntary contributions at the national level instead of by a permanent fund within the OAS (OAS, 1999b).

While necessary, this focus on personal leadership and funding is, however, far from sufficient to capture the restrictive underpinnings of the OAS as a club. In stripping the culture of the OAS to its basics, three components must be privileged. One is the respect that the organization continues to accord to intergovernmentalism, although it might have bent this orientation in several of its interventions – moves that signalled the potential for progress toward networked multilateralism with a greater intensity of operation and diversity of actors. But there has been no clear break in the primacy of the club rule that, ultimately, it is states that decide on courses of action. Indeed, one of the many paradoxes built into the OAS has been that, amid the space opened up for faster response and the inclusion of civil society, the legitimacy of the OAS as a club has increased because of its stature as a club of democracies, rather than as an institution full of dictatorships and military regimes.

The second distinctive component of the OAS is the exceptional standing of the United States, not only the dominant personality within the club but also the most prone to throwing its weight around to maintain "order" therein. Dating back to the Monroe Doctrine and the Roosevelt Corollary, the United States has consistently let its intentions be known to the other members. This trend was further consolidated during the Cold War years, via the 1964 Mann Doctrine that justified coercive methods to curtail the influence of the Soviet Union in the region (Payne, 1996). What is more, the United States has shown an ongoing willingness and capacity to act on its intentions in a manner – following the typology laid out by Tesón (1996: 30–31) – that subordinates *soft* intervention (involving diplomatic discussion, examination and recommendatory action) to *hard* intervention (entailing the use of coercive diplomatic measures, such as economic sanctions) and even *forcible* intervention (through the use of force, such as military invasion).

This proclivity of the United States to act as the policeman of the Americas produced the backlash among the other members that constitutes the final major trait of the OAS: the members' overarching concern that the principles of non-intervention and sovereignty be respected. All the governments of the hemisphere fear the imposition of values that represent merely a marker of US interests. The mechanisms of collective defence, therefore, have been for the most part directed against the United States itself.[3]

The uneven post–Cold War role of the United States

Even released from the confining pressures of the Cold War, the United States serves as an ambiguous (or even hypocritical) advocate of democracy in the Americas. Its baggage of heavy-handed intervention has tended to be juxtaposed with a perceived lack of interest in creating an authentic democratic community. The administrations of neither Bill Clinton nor George W. Bush can be said to have engaged in a longer-term, forward-looking vision for democracy in the Americas. Rather, the United States has alternated between a search for a new model of economic and social interdependence and the instinct to use a realist framework. The Clinton administration clearly lacked a longer-term, more progressive, post–Cold War vision for the hemispheric agenda in which the consolidation of democratic solidarity would become the present-day equivalent of the Kennedy administration's Alliance for Progress. To the extent that democracy in the hemisphere figured significantly in the first George W. Bush administration, it was almost exclusively as a reaction to problems within the Americas with potentially serious repercussions for US security interests, whether directed against Cuba or Cuban influence, drug trafficking or illegal immigration, as witnessed in the push for the June 2002 Inter-American Convention Against Terrorism.

To be sure, the US level of tolerance of the types of democratically elected governments it deems to be acceptable and the repertoire of tools to be used to promote democracy in the region have been augmented. With a redefinition of the stakes involved and the absence of a common enemy, one of the side-effects of the end of the Cold War was a fragmentation of bureaucratic interests. In the competition between the Pentagon and the State Department, as well as between the intelligence and drug-enforcement agencies, space opened up for "soft" diplomatic techniques to a degree never previously allowed. The ascendancy of the State Department in articulating Latin American policy during the Clinton years was reflected in the prominent roles of Under Secretary of State Thomas Pickering and Peter Romero, acting assistant secretary of Western hemispheric affairs, at the OAS General Assembly held in Windsor, Ontario, in 2000 and in the initiation of the Peru initiative.

The role of the United States as a supporter of the IADC provides further evidence of this trend. Until the last decisive moment, the United States cannot be said to have been the "maker" of the Democratic Charter; rather, distracted by the complexity of changing administrations, the United States assumed a secondary position in the early part of the negotiations. The start of the initiative coincided with a wholesale change in bureaucratic personnel, with the Clinton team being replaced by Roger Noriega and Otto Reich.

But if not the "maker", neither was the United States the "breaker" of the IADC process. At the April 2001 Summit of the Americas in Quebec City, US President Bush and his advisory team did not hold up the paragraph on the charter due to the lack of text. On the contrary, the United States perceived the benefits of having the charter in place not only as locking in representative democracy in countries such as Peru but also as another potential tool for any crowbar diplomatic efforts directed at cases like Haiti or, potentially, Venezuela or even Cuba.[4]

From the perspective of civil society, US groups were at the forefront of the monitoring (and lobbying) effort to strengthen the wording of the charter. Dr Jennifer McCoy (2001), director of the Latin American and Caribbean programme at the Carter Center in Atlanta, arguably was the most prominent of these activists, but the campaign was joined by a number of other well-known non-governmental organizations (NGOs), including the National Democratic Institute, once consultations began.[5]

It must be emphasized that, when it mattered most, Secretary of State Colin Powell made a decisive contribution to the IADC that ultimately ensured its success. Although he had been absent in the long prelude to the special OAS meeting that finalized the charter on 11 September 2001,

Powell did what was necessary to bring the IADC into existence amid the unfolding spectre of tragedy in the United States. Instead of leaving right away for Washington, Powell stayed in Lima for the number of hours it took to have the charter passed with decisive and unanimous approval. For a moment, at least, the need for an endorsement of a multilateral commitment – and for democratic solidarity with the United States – trumped all other priorities (OAS, 2001a).

To highlight the "soft" aspects of US behaviour is not to suggest that these features are fully embedded. Amid the expanding of the US repertoire of techniques to be used within the Americas, a reversion to harder tools could be found as well. To calls for OAS intervention, the United States flexed its muscle by making more tangible threats to reduce or suspend bilateral assistance outright.[6]

The US stance on Venezuela revealed that an even more reactionary style had been built into US foreign policy concerning the defence of democracy. In stark contrast to most of the rest of the Americas, the United States appeared to support the overthrow of Chávez during the crisis surrounding the April 2002 coup. Senior Bush administration officials had met several times with key opposition figures in the months prior to the coup. White House spokesman Ari Fleischer and then National Security Advisor Condoleezza Rice remarked that Chávez had provoked his own downfall. While the Bush administration had many reasons for wanting to remove the Chávez government – such as its harsh criticism of the US fight against terrorism, its close ties with Cuba, its apparent support for the FARC (Revolutionary Armed Forces of Colombia) guerrilla group in Colombia and its refusal to allow the United States to fly drug interdiction flights over Venezuelan territory – the apparent US support for the coup was at odds with its stature as a promoter and signatory of the Inter-American Democratic Charter.[7]

The US current dilemma concerning the Americas

In terms of its current role within the OAS club – and indeed its location within the Americas more generally – the United States has become caught in a deep and apparently entrenched dilemma: its political and psychological position does not allow it to act as a "normal" state within its own back yard. Whatever its true motives, the United States remains cast as the bully of the Americas. At the same time, it cannot easily act unilaterally in the post–Cold War era, even though it might have new obsessions – namely, the putative new "axis of evil" between Venezuela and Cuba – that provoke it to act in this fashion. As former US diplomat Wayne Smith has put it with graphic effect, "Castro has the same effects on U.S. administrations that the full moon has on werewolves. But the 'werewolf' effect now applies to Chávez as well" (cited in Forero, 2005).

These limitations do not mean that the United States is powerless to act in specific cases where the regional "order" is jeopardized. One classic case where the United States got its way was Haiti in 2004 (Bogdanich and Nordberg, 2006). Not only did it avoid the presence of a UN stabilization force that would have propped up Jean-Bertrand Aristide, but it was able to remove Aristide in a way that put the stamp of legitimacy on the process by extracting a letter of resignation from him.

On the main game evolving in the Americas, nonetheless, the United States has become more circumscribed in what it is able to achieve. Its verbal attacks on Chávez have been strong enough to arouse some considerable tensions in the region. Rather than buttressing the US position, however, this campaign highlights the extent to which the United States has lost its grip on the hemisphere. Instead of reinforcing the pivotal role of the United States, the counteroffensive has lent some credence to the notion that the United States has become the "odd state out" within the OAS club. As Peter Hakim (2006) has put it cogently, "Throughout the region, support for Washington's policies has diminished. Few Latin Americans, in or out of government, consider the United States to be a dependable partner."

On the losing end: Electing a new OAS secretary-general

Two snapshots of recent events highlight the extent to which the United States has lost control of the Americas in the context of the workings of the OAS. The first showcases the US missteps in its attempt to impose its favoured candidate to replace first César Gaviria, then Miguel Ángel Rodríguez, as secretary-general of the OAS.

Rewinding this episode, it would be difficult to think of a messier and more counterproductive scenario for the United States. Instead of seeking to find a credible consensus candidate – to which it could attach itself as part of a winning constellation – the United States put the onus on a narrow rewarding of geopolitical loyalty. Its first choice was the controversial president of El Salvador, Francisco Flores, a politician whose reputation was made and marred on the international stage by two political decisions: first, alone among the leaders in the region, Flores supported the coup to oust Venezuela's Chávez in April 2002; second, Flores took an active "followership" stance in the US-led coalition of the willing in the Iraq war – even to the point of sending troops to Iraq.[8] As a reward for supportive behaviour, this bid was doomed to fail, particularly as the rival candidate, José Miguel Insulza, Chile's interior minister, possessed strong credentials for the position. An experienced and pragmatic political scientist/politician from a pro-market state that had successfully negotiated a free trade deal with the United States, Insulza appeared a picture-perfect candidate for the United States to back, even if only on the second attempt. Yet, rather than rallying behind this alternative, the United States tried to stymie his bid.

The US second choice for secretary-general, Luis Ernesto Derbez, Mexico's foreign minister, was a marked improvement in terms of electoral calculus. His curriculum vitae included acting as chair of the agricultural negotiations at the World Trade Organization meeting in Cancún, Mexico. He was also the original choice of Canada, the other partner of the North American Free Trade Agreement (NAFTA), as well as the fallback preference of the Central American states. Nonetheless, these strengths were overwhelmed by a number of weaknesses. In a hemisphere increasingly dominated by governments from the left, he was a conservative politician from Fox's Partido Acción Nacional with a background as a World Bank economist. Additionally, Derbez's image as the candidate from the NAFTA and soon-to-be Central America Free Trade Agreement countries isolated him from the South American "core" countries – excepting only Peru and Bolivia, which had their distinct historical reasons for mobilizing against any candidate from Chile, and Colombia, the closest US ally in South America.

As a sidebar, one can add that this dual image of the Derbez candidature pushed support away from him in Mexico itself. Many of the Mexican political élite distanced themselves from this campaign on a combination of personal/partisan/foreign policy rationales. Rather than working to buttress Mexico's image on the global stage, the bid was viewed as individualistic status-seeking at odds with Mexico's diplomatic tradition. It looked too much like a reassertion of US authority, locking Mexico into a North American hub and cutting into its capacity to take independent positions on a wide variety of issues. The late Adolfo Aguilar Zinser – Mexico's ambassador to the United Nations in 2002 and 2003, whose profile had risen because of his role in the Security Council proceedings on Iraq and because of his firing by Fox over a statement he made contending that the United States considered Latin America to be its "back yard" – publicly criticized Derbez's candidacy on these grounds. Derbez was called before the Mexican Congress to explain his position, with the Federal Chamber of Deputies asking him to withdraw from the race (see Cevallos, 2005; *El Universal*, 2005a).

Nor, as this complicated campaign progressed, did the United States raise its game in terms of its public commitment to democracy in the region or its level of private diplomatic skill in gaining support for its preferred candidate. On the one side, the US opposition to Insulza seemed to contradict its concern with the promotion of democracy. The Chilean minister had an impeccable democratic record, including a stint of 16 years in exile (between Italy and Mexico) in opposition to the Pinochet regime. The US resistance to his candidacy was therefore usually deemed to be ideological in nature. Such suspicions were increased by US references to Insulza's call for the reinstatement of Cuba in the OAS and Chávez's lobbying for his election. Even when cast in this fashion, though, the opposition to Insulza seems misguided. At odds with any image that he was a Cuban apologist, Insulza got into a public row with Castro. After being called a "silly little man" by the Cuban leader, Insulza replied that "the worst favour we could do ourselves is to get involved in a war of words with someone who has spoken so many words throughout his lifetime" (Agence France-Presse, 2005a).

On top of this issue, neither Insulza nor the Chilean government had been implicated in any underhand tactics in the campaign. Although then Chilean President Ricardo Lagos met with Chávez as part of the lobbying effort, Chile dissociated itself with both the purported actions (favourable oil deals) and the words of the Venezuelan leader: "The North American imperial power is trying to make itself the owner of the OAS again, because it can see the OAS slipping out of its hands" (quoted in Tobar and Richter, 2005). As its ambassador to the United Nations denoted, Chile appeared to run a clean campaign: "Chile has a policy on democracy and human rights that it doesn't change for votes" (*The Economist*, 2005).

In complete contrast, the United States pursued a muscular campaign on behalf of Derbez. In terms of actors, Defense Secretary Donald Rumsfeld went on a mission to the Americas in March 2005 to do some arm-twisting. In terms of targeting, the United States was accused from the start of using strong-arm tactics on the Caribbean states to bring them into line with its position. It was only when Condoleezza Rice as secretary of state became more fully engaged in this issue that the United States smoothed over the cracks in terms of both its own diplomatic approach and the political divide within the Americas. In an attempt to regain some sense of initiative, Rice persuaded Derbez to withdraw from the campaign, avoiding what would have been a final decisive but divisive vote. Then, as part of a four-country consultative trip to the Americas in April 2005, she nudged Insulza to make at least some token statements that could be construed as support for an interventionist regime on democracy.

Even this attempt at pragmatism – with the appearance that the United States had become the deal-maker – was severely undermined by the "hard" voices within the Bush administration. An e-mail message by Roger Noriega, the assistant secretary of state for the Western hemisphere, subsequently leaked to the *New York Times,* ratcheted up the interpretation of the Insulza declaration from pragmatic compromise to an outright US diplomatic triumph with the exhortation that Insulza "was [making] a public statement alluding to the Chávez threat" (Rohter, 2005; see also Lobe, 2005).

Misplaying the Americas agenda: The Fort Lauderdale OAS General Assembly

The US performance as host of the thirty-fifth OAS General Assembly in Fort Lauderdale, Florida, in June 2005 embellished the manner in which it had misplayed the extension of the democratic agenda. The overall tenor of the US approach was to impose – not negotiate – its preferences on the other members of the club. On the economic front, the welcoming address by Bush focused on the benefits of open markets, as if the Washington Consensus remained fully intact (Sanger and Brinkley, 2005). On the security front, the focus remained centred on US security interests (terrorism/drugs) rather than on poverty, which preoccupied the vast majority of members. For some leaders – President Luiz Inácio Lula da Silva of Brazil stands out in this regard – this alternative agenda arose out of a genuine commitment to social issues. For others, especially as they watched the upheavals in Ecuador and Bolivia provoked in large part by the privatization of water and natural gas, a strong element of convenience took hold. In either case, they had some major incentives for resisting the US recipe for action.

In more specific terms, the United States used its opportunity as the convener of the event to try to isolate Chávez and the export of his Bolivarian social model beyond Venezuela to the wider neighbourhood. The obsession of the Bush administration with the Venezuelan leader – what the *New Statesman* termed its "red rag" (Hilton, 2005) – increased as Chávez consolidated his hold on power and, with that greater confidence, his role as the voice of the counter-consensus in Latin America. Taming this ascendant force became public job number one in the Americas, infamous as it was, in tandem with the longstanding US *bête noire*, Fidel Castro, in what Otto Reich (2005) depicted as the "Cuban-Venezuelan axis".

While the goal was clear, the means to achieving it were strictly limited. Whatever the extent of US involvement in the April 2002 coup against Chávez, it was a tactic not to be repeated. Furthermore, economic sanctions were a decidedly two-edged sword in the case of Venezuela. As a leading producer of energy at a time of massive price increases, Venezuela had a number of strong cards to play in any escalation of the conflict between itself and the United States: it could continue to reward states that supported it diplomatically, and it could divert supply away from the US market.

Faced with these boundaries, the United States turned to the IADC as the prime mechanism to single Chávez out and target Venezuela for intervention. The earliest and most persistent source of opposition to the introduction of the charter had been framed in the terms that it would operate as a device for replacing the Chávez government.[9] Venezuela stood out at the Quebec Summit as the one country ready and willing to go on record as having reservations about the document. This stance, understandably, was in large part politically motivated, as Chávez and his government perceived Venezuela as being the leading candidate for intervention on the basis of the IADC. However, the normative base for these objections needs referencing as well: the contradistinction between representative and participatory democracy.

The US use of this tool to isolate Chávez had the additional paradoxical advantage of targeting the state that had been the first beneficiary of the charter in practice, since, as mentioned above, the IADC had proved to be the main mantra of rallying a defence from both inside and outside Venezuela against the 2002 coup. If, in many ways, the charter was a success during its first major test, many of its lessons were unintended ones. In terms of its target country, the IADC had produced not only its most critical opponent but also its most grateful beneficiary.

What got in the way of this rationale for deploying the charter against Chávez were the flaws in the diplomatic style used in this effort. At odds with the OAS "club culture" concerning consensus, the United States pushed forward its initiative on the IADC with little or no consultation, adding to the notion of its being a "rogue" player. In the words of Arturo Valenzuela, a former Clinton National Security Council adviser and director of Georgetown University's Center for Latin American Studies: "To put forward this initiative, which has much merit, as a proposal from the United States instead of broaching it as a consensual idea is, up to a point, damaging to the initiative" (quoted in Agence France-Presse, 2005a). The respected observer Michael Shifter added: "The United States made the classic mistake of not effectively or widely consulting Latin American nations before putting forward the proposal" (cited in Barclay, 2005).

Further weakening its credibility, the US initiative included little attention to detail about the way a supposedly upgraded charter would work in practice. Initially, it appeared that the new mechanism would be designed to act as a monitoring device (Noriega, 2005). Subsequently, the focus shifted to its use as a tool to aid fragile democracies. As Secretary of State Rice put it at the General Assembly, "There are clearly some troubled democracies in Latin America. Governments that fail to meet this crucial standard must be accountable to the OAS. We must replace excessive talk with focused action" (cited in Daniel, 2005).

The suggestion of such a mandate accentuated the image of the initiative both as a reactive instrument that would allow the United States to recapture its momentum after the Insulza victory and as an apparatus intended to serve US, and not necessarily hemispheric, interests. Indeed, without massaging the proposal to temper sensitivities in the region, the United States opened itself up to a severe diplomatic backlash. On grounds of principle, this negative reaction was a foregone conclusion. States with a long tradition of standing up for the norms of sovereignty and non-intervention – and against anything that smacked of US contravention of these norms – were adamant in their opposition to the US initiative to upgrade the charter. Any thought of ratcheting up the IADC to allow "police-like" instead of preventive activities was unpalatable to Brazil. So was the issue that "outsiders" would evaluate democratic standards (Rapoza, 2005; *Brazil Report*, 2005). In a similar vein, Mexico rejected any new architecture that would tilt the OAS away from being a club of equals to one that would allow some members to become arbiters or to impose their will on others. As a presidential spokesman noted, "We are not in agreement with any tutelage from anybody" (*El Universal*, 2005b).

In operational terms, there was vigorous resistance to any attempt to draw up a list of "offenders" to be targeted by the OAS. Such a list was viewed as objectionable not only for the normative reasons noted above but also because a move to list-making would play to the sore feelings of many states in the region about other punitive lists the United States had drawn up on drug-enforcement issues and human rights violations. As one critic from the Inter-American Dialogue, Daniel P. Erikson, summarized, "They've watched the U.S. government developing lists for years. They don't go down very well" (quoted in Richter, 2005).

Rather than acting as a catalyst for mobilization, then, the US initiative had the unintended consequence of taking attention away from Venezuela and placing it on the United States itself (Brinkley, 2005a; Hester, 2005). Indeed, Chávez took full advantage of this reaction by playing up the theme that the target of supervision should be reversed: "If any government needs monitoring, it is that of the United States" (Agence France-Presse, 2005b).

Reining in networked multilateralism

It is one thing to regard the quelling of the US initiative on the IADC as a victory for club multilateralism – from this angle, the failure of the initiative was a straightforward rejection of the notion that the United States had the power to impose its authority over other OAS members, including Venezuela, through "soft" means. It is another thing entirely to suggest that this episode also means a substantive setback for networked multilateralism in the Americas.

The model of networked multilateralism is based on the premise of an enhanced role for NGOs. Indeed, what was innovative about the introduction of the IADC was the galvanizing effect that NGOs from both the North and the South had on the process. Any state-based opposition to the charter was premised on the notion that this mechanism was too intrusive. The fundamental concern of the societal groups, in contrast, was the lack of clarity and substance in the text (see Cameron, 2002). Set against this background, it seems likely that NGOs would favour any initiative that upgraded the charter and translated words into action. The so-called Friends of the Inter-American Democratic Charter included not only NGO-friendly former politicians such as Jimmy Carter but also members of civil society, most notably from Peru, the original "home" of the charter. As part of its own plan of action, this group wanted non-state actors to be able to communicate directly with the Permanent Council, traditionally the preserve of government envoys.[10]

The NGOs' distress arising from the IADC episode was due to their feeling contaminated by the initiative's strong association with US interests. At the core of the original initiative, as advocated by Noriega, was the proposal to establish a committee – which would hear from trade unions, lawyers, citizens' groups and NGOs with concerns about their own governments – to monitor the quality of democracy among the states of the region (Brinkley, 2005b). Initiated with little or no consultation, this component put the NGOs in an awkward position. Many in the NGO community had sought to add teeth to the IADC – during the original negotiations, Peru had suggested that the Inter-American Commission on Human Rights perform the function of external oversight – but this form of external validation had come up against the norms of non-intervention and sovereignty, as the OAS members clung to their state-based prerogatives. Other members of the NGO community used the opportunity to attack the *bona fides* of the US government in introducing the measure. One US-based NGO representative stated, for example, that the initiative was "an unwise and unjustified extension of the Democratic Charter, which could be subject to political manipulation ... It would be better for the United States to resolve its differences with Venezuela through normal diplomatic channels, rather than trying to amend the Inter-American Democratic Charter so that it could be used for political purposes" (Weisbrot, 2005).

The spillover effect of the US initiative was renewed resistance not only to the IADC but also to the legitimacy of NGOs' involvement in the process as part of the extension from club to networked multilateralism. Exposed to unwelcome scrutiny as "allies" of the US government in expanding the charter, advocates of maintaining the OAS as a tight, state-based club used the opportunity to claw back gains the NGOs had made in the exercise of inter-American multilateralism. This clash, in turn, was intensified by an open dispute between the United States and Venezuela over what an authentic NGO looked like. For example, the Bush administration supported the presence of the Venezuelan group Súmate (Join In) as an NGO and even invited the group's leader, María Corina Machado, to the White House. The Chávez government, however, regarded the group as an opposition movement and a backer of the 2002 coup. In a vigorous counterattack, then Venezuelan Foreign Minister Alí Rodríguez Araque accused the United States of misusing the NGO accreditation process by granting NGO privileges to groups that acted as political parties. Extending this argument, Rodríguez made it clear that he was sceptical about most forms of NGO participation in any schemata that amounted to networked multilateralism: "The organization is called Organization of American States and not organization of the civil society" (BBC Monitoring, 2005).

The shifting contest about club rules

Since these two setbacks for the United States, the form of contested multilateralism in the OAS has shifted appreciably. As the form of networked multilateralism has been frustrated, the contest between the United States and Chávez's Venezuela over club ownership has intensified. The degree to which US leadership has been eroded is to a considerable extent a reflection of how that country has lost the geopolitical script and the tools of influence within the Americas. But it is also a sign of how Chávez's "anti-hegemonic" campaign has become a polarizing force not only at the mass level but also within the confines of the OAS club.

The November 2005 Summit of the Americas in Mar del Plata, Argentina, signalled the extent of this divide. Chávez was strident in his opposition to the US political/economic agenda and vowed to bury the proposed Free Trade Area of the Americas. Other countries were drawn to take sides, as witnessed by the vituperative post-summit exchanges between Mexico City and Caracas that culminated in an expulsion of ambassadors. Nor, it may be added, did this situation improve right away with the handover of power in Mexico from Vicente Fox to Felipe Calderón. After Calderón told a Davos panel that countries with prejudices against free trade agreements belonged in the past, Chávez called Calderón a *caballerito* (*Latin American Weekly Report*, 2007).

Moreover, this intra-regional ideological battle is likely to escalate. Chávez has accused the United States of making it difficult for Venezuela to obtain spare parts for its US-made F-16 fighters and has threatened to share the aircraft with Cuba and China. He has played the energy card in cultivating other Latin American leaders of various left-wing orientations who have also moved offside with the United States. Chávez held "unity talks" with Argentina's Néstor Kirchner, promoting both Venezuela's entry into Mercosur and a number of energy accords, and he has reached out to solidify ties with the Bolivian and Ecuadorian presidents, Evo Morales and Rafael Correa.

Beyond the internal challenge presented by Chávez, the US disconnect with the region has made it easier for China to make headway from the outside. In response to China's requests, many Latin American nations – including Argentina, Brazil, Chile, Peru and Venezuela, but significantly not Mexico – have conferred on China the status of market economy. China has also designated many nations throughout Latin America and the Caribbean as official tourist destinations for Chinese citizens. As well, in November 2004 China announced a US$10 billion energy deal in Brazil, while Brazil's state-owned oil company, Petrobras, and China's National Offshore Oil Corporation are reportedly studying the feasibility of joint operations in exploration, refining and pipeline construction around the world. China is also exploring energy deals in Ecuador, Bolivia, Peru and Colombia, as well as offshore projects in Argentina. Assertive Chinese commercial interests were also demonstrated at the Asia-Pacific Economic Cooperation meeting in Busan, South Korea, at which China and Chile signed a free trade agreement, the first between the Asian giant and a Latin American country (Varela, 2005). "It is essential that the leaders be able to put all of our political will and to instruct the negotiators that it is necessary to succeed," former Chilean President Ricardo Lagos told a chief executives' gathering alongside the summit (CNN World Business, 2005).

The US mix of passivity and aggressiveness has not proved a menu for effectiveness in the region. Its "hard" actions of the past, while still available, are doled out only as part of occasional side plots and not in the pursuit of any strategic main game. Neither has the United States compensated for this instrumental deficiency by any constructive display of legitimacy-enhancing "soft" power (see Nye, 1990). When given a chance to share responsibility, as on the election of the OAS secretary-general or building a creative coalition around an upgraded IADC, the United States has fumbled the ball. Rather than boosting its authority, it has diminished its reputation and its ability to work in coalition with other states of the region.

Tactically, the United States has demonstrated an ability to refine the diplomatic skills needed to meet the challenges of the emergent geopolitical realities. One sign of a revamping along these lines was the appointment of Tom Shannon, an experienced State Department official, as assistant secretary of state for Western hemisphere affairs. The new US position that the countries of the region should focus on human development – by investing in people through poverty alleviation and jobs – reflects this turn towards a more prudent form of statecraft.[11] Another signal was the Bush administration's self-declared "year of engagement" with the region and its charm offensive, complete with trips to selected countries by Shannon and Nicholas Burns, the undersecretary of state for political affairs, as preludes to a major tour by Bush himself in March 2007.

A further adjustment is the push by the United States to extend its influence among key members of the club. As an early sign of this trend, Bush stopped for a "working visit" in Brazil on his way home from the 2005 Summit of the Americas in Mar del Plata. Even though Brazilian President Lula has had his own numerous disputes with the United States, this move towards a rapprochement was based on the recognition that Brazil has become the pivotal country in a shaky region. In declaratory terms, Bush acknowledged that Lula "occupies a unique position in the hemisphere". In operational terms, the United States has signalled new flexibility on issues important to Brazil, such as the recent offer in the context of Bush's trip to make substantial cuts in tariffs on farm trade. In return for these overtures, with some hopes of success (Oppenheimer, 2007), the United States hopes that Brazil will help rein in Chávez and stabilize neighbouring democracies.

Even with these initiatives, however, the most likely scenario is a long moment of deep psychological frustration. Even apparent diplomatic victories for the United States showcased this mood, as witnessed most dramatically at the United Nations (a site Chávez used to castigate Bush as the "devil"). Although the United States was able to fend off Venezuela's bid for a seat on the Security Council, it did so only after 47 rounds of balloting, the choice of a compromise candidate (Panama) over its own choice (Guatemala) and the use of heavy-handed tactics in this draining struggle (LaFranchi, 2006).

Inevitably, the OAS has not just been caught up in this contested atmosphere but is in danger of being immobilized by it, as evidenced by the manner in which the OAS straddled the US–Chávez conflict up to and during the June 2007 OAS General Assembly meeting in Panama. Although there were some tentative signs that the OAS might criticize the Venezuelan government for its refusal to renew the broadcast licence of the private television channel RCTV, at the meeting the OAS adopted a cautious form of club multilateralism. Secretary-General Insulza emphasized the organization's "conciliatory role" consistent with the rules of "dialogue and consensus" (*Jurnalo*, 2007).

In public, the majority of OAS members followed a similar approach. The United States found it could muster almost no support for a proposal that Secretary-General Insulza establish a concerted OAS mission to investigate the RCTV case. Secretary Rice's claim that this was a vital case of "freedom of speech" was countered by Venezuela, which used a mix of defensive (sovereignty-oriented) and offensive tactics (for example, it proposed that, if the OAS were to designate a commission, its first task should be to look at the US military prison in the Guantánamo Bay naval base or the situation on the US-Mexican border). Equally, the United States, invoking the support of various NGOs (such as Reporters Without Borders) on this issue, was weakened by the fact that the main lobbying of the OAS was carried out by former employees of RCTV.

Amid this polarization, any hope that the OAS will be able to extend the shift from club to networked multilateralism becomes unrealistic. On the contrary, the question turns on whether the OAS will even be able to continue as a club. Already there are signs of disengagement by major members. Notably, neither Brazil nor Mexico – states on which the United States has placed great weight – sent representation at the foreign minister level to the OAS General Assembly in Panama. In this atmosphere, the main consensus-oriented club game of the OAS will become even more difficult to achieve. Encouraged by its ability to counter the United States on a wide dossier of cases, the Chávez government has no incentive to play by the traditional rules. Indeed, even if it became the target of OAS action, Venezuela would probably walk away from that institution, as it has from international financial institutions.

For its part, the United States has shown little will or ability to learn how to operate effectively in a club in which it is still a major member but no longer the dominant one. Both its past baggage and the unevenness of its current approach have led the United States to become increasingly out of synch within this regional club. The pivotal test will be how it adjusts to this sense of diminished status. It is one thing for the United States to be stymied on specific issues, but quite another to feel it is losing the club it was able to shape to its own needs and interests for so long. This sense of loss might spark a creative response, although the thrust of this rethinking might direct the United States towards *ad hoc* solutions – with an emphasis on new forms of coalitions of the willing as opposed to a renewal of the OAS. It might also, however, stimulate the United States to take a more muscular approach to reclaim ownership. How the US response plays out will determine not only what type of club (if any) the OAS will be but also the overall pattern of hemispheric politics.

Notes

1. For further elaboration on the "democratic solidarity paradigm" see Bloomfield (1994); Acevedo and Grossman (1996); Cooper and Legler (2001, 2006).
2. This contrast provides one of the main themes in my co-authored recent book, *Intervention without Intervening?* (Cooper and Legler, 2006). On the intersection between norms and networks see Finnemore and Sikkink (1998); Sikkink (2002).
3. On the limits of US power over the OAS see Shaw (2003, 2004).
4. On the wider context see Cooper (2001).
5. For the importance of NGOs to forms of complex or networked multilateralism see O'Brien et al. (2000).
6. See also the Joint Resolution of the US Congress warning that "if the April 9, 2000, elections are not deemed by the international community to have been free and fair, the United States will modify its political and economic relations with Peru, including its support for international financial institution loans to Peru"; see Embassy of the United States of America in Lima, Peru (2000).
7. On the US role in the coup see DeYoung (2002); Hakim (2002); Kay (2002); Krugman (2002); Marquis (2002); Rosen (2002); Shifter (2002); Slevin (2002); Valenzuela (2002).
8. For a fuller analysis of this concept see Cooper, Higgott and Nossal (1991); see also Nye (2002).
9. For background see Ellner and Hellinger (2003); Sylvia and Danopoulos (2003). On the Venezuela-US relationship see Kelly and Romero (2002).
10. On the Friends of the Inter-American Democratic Charter see Carter Center (2005); Friends of the Inter-American Democratic Charter (2005).
11. See Thomas A. Shannon's statement to the Senate Foreign Relations Committee, 21 September 2005 (Shannon, 2005).

REFERENCES

Acevedo, Domingo E. and Claudio Grossman (1996) "The Organization of American States and the Protection of Democracy", in Tom Farer, ed., *Beyond Sovereignty: Collectively Defending Democracy in the Americas*, Baltimore, MD: Johns Hopkins University Press.

Agence France-Presse (2005a) "OAS to Consider Crisis Prevention in Latin American Democracies", Agence France-Presse, 5 June.

——— (2005b) "Alo Presidente Broadcast; Critical Time for Democracy in Americas", Agence France-Presse, 6 June.

Barclay, Eliza (2005) "OAS Rebuffs US Democracy Proposal", *United Press International*, 8 June.

BBC Monitoring (2005) "Venezuelan Foreign Minister Slams Sumate's Participation in OAS Meeting", BBC, 2 June.

Bloomfield, Richard (1994) "Making the Western Hemisphere Safe for Democracy? The OAS Defense-of-Democracy Regime", in Carl Kaysen, Robert A. Pastor and Laura W. Reed, eds, *Collective Responses to Regional Problems: The Case of Latin America and the Caribbean*, Cambridge, MA: American Academy of Arts and Sciences.

Bogdanich, Walt and Jenny Nordberg (2006) "Mixed U.S. Signals Helped Tilt Haiti Towards Chaos", *New York Times*, 29 January.

Brazil Report (2005) "Brazil and the US: Disagreement Over What Democracy Means", *Brazil Report*, 3 May.

Brinkley, Joel (2005a) "Latin American Nations Resist Plan to Monitor Democracy", *New York Times*, 6 June.

―――― (2005b) "US Proposal in the OAS Draws Fire as an Attack on Venezuela", *New York Times*, 22 May.

Cameron, Maxwell A. (2002) "Strengthening Checks and Balances: Democracy Defence and Promotion in the Americas", paper presented at Inter-American Democratic Charter Challenges and Opportunities Conference, Liu Institute for the Study of Global Issues, University of British Columbia, Vancouver, 12–13 November.

Carter Center (2005) "President Carter Delivers Keynote Speech to OAS Lecture Series of the Americas", 25 January, available at www.cartercenter.org/doc1995.htm.

Cevallos, Diego (2005) "Fox's String of Foreign Policy Woes Just Grows and Grows", *Inter Press Service*, 5 May.

CNN World Business (2005) "APEC Ups Trade Pressure on Europe", CNN World Business, 18 November.

Cooper, Andrew F. (2001) "The Quebec City 'Democracy Summit'", *Washington Quarterly* 24(2), pp. 159–171.

Cooper, Andrew F. and Thomas Legler (2001) "The OAS in Peru: A Model for the Future?", *Journal of Democracy* 12(4), pp. 123–136.

―――― (2006) *Intervention without Intervening? The OAS Defense and Promotion of Democracy in the Americas*, New York: Palgrave.

Cooper, Andrew F., Richard Higgott and Kim Richard Nossal (1991) "Bound to Follow? Leadership and Followership in the Gulf Conflict", *Political Science Quarterly* 46(3), pp. 391–410.

Cox, Robert (1992) "Multilateralism and World Order", *Review of International Studies* 18(2), pp. 161–180.

Daniel, Caroline (2005) "Bush Calls on Latin America to Promote Democracy", *Financial Times*, 7 June.

DeShazo, Peter (2004) "Moving Forward at the OAS", *Hemispheric Focus* 11, 1 November.

DeYoung, Karen (2002) "U.S. Seen as Weak Patron of Latin Democracy", *Washington Post*, 16 April.

Ellner, Steve and Daniel Hellinger, eds (2003) *Venezuelan Politics in the Chávez Era: Class, Polarization, and Conflict*, London: Lynne Rienner.

El Universal (2005a) "Mexican Opposition Parties Ask Foreign Affairs Minister to Withdraw OAS Leadership Bid", *El Universal*, 27 April.

——— (2005b) "Mexican Government Rejects US Proposal for Mechanisms to Protect Democracies", *El Universal*, 5 June.

Embassy of the United States of America in Lima, Peru (2000) "Statement on Introduced Bills and Joint Resolutions", US Senate, S.J. Res. 43, 28 March.

Financial Times (2000) "OAS Running Out of Money", *Financial Times*, 8 June.

Finnemore, Martha and Kathryn Sikkink (1998) "International Norm Dynamics and Political Change", *International Organization* 52(4), pp. 887–917.

Forero, Juan (2005) "Opposition to U.S. Makes Chávez a Hero to Many", *New York Times*, 1 June.

Friends of the Inter-American Democratic Charter (2005) "It's Taboo to Say Our Democracies Are Weak", *Miami Herald*, 2 May.

Gaviria, César (1998) "Address by the Secretary-General of the Organization of American States", presented at opening of Conference of the Americas, Washington, DC, 5 March, available at www.oas.org/csh/english/docspeech.asp.

Hakim, Peter (2002) "The World, Democracy, and U.S. Credibility", *New York Times*, 21 April, p. 39.

——— (2006) "Is Washington Losing Latin America?", *Foreign Affairs* (January/February).

Hester, Annette (2005) "The Eagle's Talons Loosen", *Globe and Mail*, 14 June.

Hilton, Isabel (2005) "Latin America Rises Up", *New Statesman*, 20 June, available at www.newstatesman.com/200506200004.

Jurnalo (2007) "Chávez Claims Victory Over US at OAS General Assembly", *Jurnalo*, 21 June.

Kay, Katty (2002) "Bush Team Met Chávez Coup Leaders", *The Times*, 17 April.

Kelly, Janet and Carlos A. Romero (2002) *The United States and Venezuela: Rethinking a Relationship*, New York: Routledge.

Krugman, Paul (2002) "Losing Latin America", *New York Times*, 16 April.

LaFranchi, Howard (2006) "UN Compromise Shows Limits of US Power", *Christian Science Monitor*, 3 November.

Latin American Weekly Report (2007) "Calderón's Honeymoon Ends", *Latin American Weekly Report*, 1 February.

Lobe, Jim (2005) "New Chief Takes Over at OAS and Gives Mixed Signals", *Inter Press Service*, 26 May.

Marquis, Christopher (2002) "Bush Officials Met with Venezuelans Who Ousted Leader", *New York Times*, 16 April.

McCoy, Jennifer (2001) "Comments on the Inter-American Democratic Charter", *Summits of the Americas Bulletin* 1(1), p. 3.

Noriega, Roger (2005) "Briefing by Assistant Secretary of State for Western Hemispheric Affairs to Thirtieth Special Session of the OAS on the occasion of the election of José Miguel Insulza to the office of OAS Secretary-General", Washington, DC, 2 May.

Nye, Joseph S. (1990) "Soft Power", *Foreign Policy* 80 (Fall), pp. 153–171.

——— (2002) *The Paradox of American Power: Why the World's Superpower Can't Go It Alone*, Oxford: Oxford University Press.

O'Brien, R., A. M. Goetz, J. A. Scholte and M. Williams (2000) *Contesting Global Governance*, Cambridge: Cambridge University Press.

OAS (1999a) "Weekly Report", Organization of American States, Washington, DC, 5 April.

———— (1999b) "Weekly Report", Organization of American States, Washington, DC, 12 April.

———— (1999c) "Work Plan of the Unit for the Promotion of Democracy (UPD)", Permanent Council of the OAS, Committee on Juridical and Political Affairs, Document OEA/Ser.G CP/CAJP-1436/98 rev. 2 corr. 1, OAS Department of Democratic and Political Affairs, Washington, DC, 4 February.

———— (2001a) "Inter-American Democratic Charter (2001)", Document OEA/Ser.P/AG/RES.1, XXVLLL-E/01, Organization of American States, Washington, DC, 11 September, available at www.oas.org/charter/docs/resolution1_en_p4.htm.

———— (2001b) "Quota Collection Report", OAS Department of Financial Services, Washington, DC, 30 September, available at www.oas.org.

Oppenheimer, Andrés (2007) "Some Success Predicted in U.S. Courting of Brazil", *Miami Herald*, 22 February.

Payne, Anthony (1996) "The United States and Its Enterprise of the Americas", in Andrew Gamble and Anthony Payne, eds, *Regionalism and World Order*, London: Routledge.

Rapoza, Kenneth (2005) "Brazil Resists Calls to Press OAS against Chávez", *Washington Times*, 10 May.

Reich, Otto (2005) "The Axis of Evil", *National Review*, 11 April.

Richter, Paul (2005) "Latin American Leaders Balk at US Plan", *Los Angeles Times*, 3 June.

Rohter, Larry (2005) "OAS to Pick Chile Socialist U.S. Opposed as Its Leader", *New York Times*, 30 April.

Rosen, Fred (2002) "Venezuela: Washington Suffers a Setback", *NACLA Report on the Americas* 35(6), available at http://global.factiva.com.proxy.lib.uwaterloo.ca/ha/default.aspx.

Sanger, David E. and Joel Brinkley (2005) "Bush Presses Latin American Free Trade Accord", *New York Times*, 7 June.

Shannon, Thomas A. (2005) Statement to the Senate Foreign Relations Committee, 21 September.

Shaw, Carolyn (2003) "Limits to Hegemonic Influence in the Organization of American States", *Latin American Politics and Society* 45(3), pp. 59–92.

———— (2004) *Cooperation, Conflict, and Consensus in the Organization of American States*, New York: Palgrave.

Shifter, Michael (2002) "Democracy in Venezuela, Unsettling as Ever", *Washington Post*, 21 April.

Sikkink, Kathryn (2002) "Restructuring World Politics: The Limits and Asymmetries of Soft Power", in S. Khagram, J. V. Riker and K. Sikkink, eds, *Restructuring World Politics: Transnational Social Movements, Networks, and Norms*, Minneapolis, MI: University of Minnesota Press.

Slevin, Peter (2002) "Chávez Provoked His Removal, U.S. Officials Say", *Washington Post*, 13 April.

Sylvia, Ronald D. and Constantine P. Danopoulos (2003) "The Chávez Phenom-enon: Political Change in Venezuela", *Third World Quarterly* 24(1), pp. 63–75.

Tesón, Fernando (1996) "Changing Perceptions of Domestic Jurisdiction and Intervention", in Tom Farer, ed., *Beyond Sovereignty: Collectively Defending Democracy in the Americas*, Baltimore, MD: Johns Hopkins University Press.

The Economist (2005) "The New Man at the Organization of American States", *The Economist*, 6 May.

Tobar, Héctor and Paul Richter (2005) "Leftist-backed Chilean Official Likely to Head OAS", *Los Angeles Times*, 30 April.

Valenzuela, Arturo (2002) "Bush's Betrayal of Democracy", *Washington Post*, 16 April.

Varela, Jose Luis (2005) "Latins Seduced, Jarred by China-led Asia", *China Post*, 16 November, available at www.chinapost.com.tw/business/detail.asp?ID=72036&GRP=E.

Weisbrot, Mark (2005) "Statement to OAS Meeting between Civil Society Organizations, the Secretary General, and Heads of Delegations", Washington, DC, 6 June.

9

Dealing with threats to democracy

Dexter S. Boniface

I want to start by pointing to something very important in the military develop-ments of April in Paraguay. Something novel, really new. The insurgents did not go for a traditional coup, that is, an undisguised overthrow of established authority in defiance of the Constitution. That was the traditional way. The in-surgents of April in Paraguay tried to inaugurate a new style, which I call "coup under the table." That is to say, a show of respect for existing laws and the Constitution while applying pressure or threats to remove the constitutional government through resignation. The leader of the insurgency did not aspire to the presidency, he only wanted it to go [to] the speaker of the Congress – the third in the constitutional order of succession. Thus, to all appearances, the Constitution and the rule of law were respected. The leader of the insurgency may have been seeking in this way to run the government from under the table. (Domingo Laíno, quoted in OAS, 1996: 8–9)

In October 2003 Bolivian President Gonzalo "Goni" Sánchez de Lozada reluctantly resigned after facing massive street protests. In an interview with the BBC days after his resignation, Goni blamed his fall from power on "a conspiracy, of sedition by armed groups, 'narco-syndicalist' groups, terrorist groups and cartels who created a confrontational situation, leav-ing me no way out but to resign" (BBC News, 2003). In April 2005 Ecua-dor's elected President Lucio Gutiérrez was removed from office by a controversial vote after he refused to step down in the face of escalating social protests. He was the third Ecuadorian president in eight years to be forced from office by street protests. In the midst of the crisis, he swore he would not resign, noting "I was elected for four years" (BBC

Which way Latin America? Hemispheric politics meets globalization, Cooper and Heine, eds, United Nations University Press, 2009, ISBN 978-92-808-1172-8

News, 2005a). From exile he later declared that he planned "to show there was a coup and that the president [successor Alfredo Palacio] is usurping power" (BBC News, 2005b). A month later, in June 2005, Goni's successor, Carlos Mesa, became the second Bolivian president in as many years to resign in the face of explosive protests.

Events in Ecuador and Bolivia were hardly unique in Latin America. In the past five years street mobs have helped to topple elected leaders in Argentina (December 2001), Venezuela (April 2002) and Haiti (February 2004) and rattled democratic governments in Belize, Mexico and Nicaragua, leading one observer to conclude that "In Latin America, coercive street protests rather than militaries now seem to be one of the biggest threats to democratically elected governments" (Hopgood, 2005). Indeed, although military coups have not completely receded as a potential threat to democracy in the region, it is clear that the challenges confronting democratic regimes are changing and that the destabilizing potential of street protests is a striking new phenomenon.

Of course, in assessing the consequences of Latin America's new civic activism for democracy, analysts reach widely different conclusions. Many regard the mobilization of historically marginalized groups as a positive advance for democracy that is helping to make Latin American politics more participatory and representative. Noted pollster Marta Lagos, for example, argues that "This is all a very healthy thing. People have an idea what real democracy is, and they know they don't have it quite yet. They want governments that represent them and they will go out to the streets to get that" (quoted in Harman, 2005). Yet critics of the new "people power" in Latin America regard the protestors as an unrepresentative (but vocal) minority who use mob tactics to undermine legitimately elected governments.[1]

To shed light on these recent developments, in this chapter I develop a two-part typology of democratic crises in Latin America, drawing a basic distinction between *endogenous* and *exogenous* threats to democratic regimes. In endogenous crises, the threat to democracy is internal to the regime, meaning it results from the undemocratic behaviour of constitutionally elected officials (generally those attempting to strengthen their power). In exogenous crises, the threat emanates from outside the regime – that is, from unelected persons, generally those whose interests are being challenged by the incumbent government's policies. Within this latter category of exogenous threats, I draw particular attention to the proliferation of a new form of "coup" – the under-the-table coup – in which violent pressure to remove an elected president through resignation is combined with nominal respect for the constitution and the rule of law.[2] Under-the-table coups occupy an ambiguous middle ground between traditional military coups, which involve the threat or use of violence, and constitutional impeachment processes, which involve respect for the rule of law. Because of their inherent ambiguity, such crises represent a particular obstacle for organizations dedicated to the protection and promotion of democracy in the region, above all the Organization of American States (OAS).

The chapter proceeds in three main sections. In the first, I inventory threats to democracy in Latin America since 1991 and present a two-part typology of democratic crises. In the second section, I review the underlying conditions, both economic and political-institutional, that appear to be at the root of recent democratic crises in Latin America. In the final section, I outline the types of measures international actors, particularly the OAS, might take to defend democracy against such threats.

The new instability in Latin America: A typology of recent democratic crises

Latin America has made impressive democratic gains over the past few decades, but the practice of channelling political conflicts through democratic institutions has yet to be fully institutionalized (Munck, 2006a). Thus, as new democracies have sprung up across the region, so too have new challenges.

Threats to democracy come in a variety of manifestations. In a recent survey, Jennifer McCoy (2006: 763) identifies nearly 50 different episodes of democratic crisis in Latin America over the 1990–2005 period.[3] In her analysis, McCoy distinguishes five distinct sources or origins of democratic crises: the military, incumbent leaders (i.e. presidents), different branches of government, armed non-state actors and unarmed non-state actors. McCoy (ibid.: 759) purposively differentiates the crises according to the actors that generate them, rather than by the nature of the threat itself, to underscore that "international actors respond differently not only to different types of democratic crisis, but also to different originators".

My analysis of democratic crises in Latin America proceeds in an analogous manner, but with a slightly different emphasis and increased attention to the strategies that actors employ. I argue that, at the most general level, one can distinguish recent democratic crises in Latin America by first drawing a basic distinction between endogenous and exogenous threats to democratic regimes. In the former, the threat to democracy is internal to the regime, meaning it results primarily from the undemocratic behaviour of elected officials; in the latter, the threat emanates primarily from unelected persons or those external to the regime.

Endogenous crises

Endogenous crises generally arise when incumbent presidents wish to accumulate political power at the expense of democratic accountability and the rule of law.[4] They do this in one of two ways. On the one hand, elected presidents and their allies may attempt to steal an election, thus undermining linkages of vertical accountability between citizens and their leaders – notable examples include presidential elections in the Dominican Republic in 1994 (under Joaquín Balaguer) and Peru in 2000 (under Alberto Fujimori) and the senate run-off elections in Haiti in 2000 (involving the Fanmi Lavalas party tightly associated with Jean-Bertrand Aristide). On the other hand, elected officials (generally presidents) might try to accumulate power at the expense of the other branches of government, thus undermining the checks and balances that ensure horizontal accountability in a democratic regime – examples include the *autogolpes* or "self-coups" in Peru in 1992 (under Alberto Fujimori) and Guatemala in 1993 (under Jorge Serrano) as well as instances of judicial meddling, such as court-stacking in Ecuador by President Gutiérrez in late 2004.[5] In some cases, furthermore, incumbents might steadily erode both vertical and horizontal accountability – Haiti under Aristide and Venezuela under Hugo Chávez arguably afford two examples. In short, a major – perhaps the greatest – threat to democracy in Latin America today emanates directly from those who are constitutionally elected to power.

What distinguishes these endogenous threats from one another above all is their relative severity. Sometimes, the threat elected officials pose to democracy is unambiguous, as in cases of rigged elections and *autogolpes*. As I elaborate later, the international community – in particular the OAS – has developed a reasonably robust (if imperfect) set of procedures for responding to the most serious endogenous threats to democratic rule. In other cases, however, the challenge to democracy can be less conspicuous, such as a questionable constitutional change or a minor electoral irregularity perpetrated by the ruling party (or parties). Examples of apparently less severe threats include the legislative removal of Ecuador's President Abdalá Bucaram by a dubious constitutional procedure in 1997, the usurpation of legislative prerogatives by the Venezuelan National Legislative Commission (the so-called Congresillo) in early 2000 and the series of questionable measures (often referred to as "the Pact") orchestrated by Daniel Ortega and Arnoldo Alemán in Nicaragua from 1999 to 2005. In such cases, one generally encounters a far more timid and problematic response by the international community. Developing effective mechanisms to deter elected leaders from subtly abusing their power is thus a critical challenge for the OAS.

Exogenous crises

An equally pernicious category of threats to democracy results from the illegal (or quasi-legal) actions of unelected officials. Historically speaking, of course, Latin America's militaries have been the most crucial un-elected actors to threaten constitutionally elected governments by means of coups d'état. Military coups have receded in recent years but have not yet disappeared, as the cases of Suriname (1990), Haiti (1991), Paraguay (1996) and Venezuela (2002) amply demonstrate.[6] Military officials (and other unelected actors) can use more discreet ways to threaten democracy, however, by pressuring and intimidating elected presidents while publicly demonstrating respect for the constitution – what Domingo Laíno labels a "coup under the table".

Here I must stress three critical points. First, the emergence of this new type of coup is not accidental. It is most surely a conscious effort by un-democratic actors to shield themselves from international criticism and potential sanction. As Mainwaring and Pérez-Liñán (2005: 49) astutely summarize:

> In some countries, impeachments (Brazil 1992, Venezuela 1993) and pseudo-constitutional forms of deposing presidents (Ecuador 1997) have become sub-stitutes for military coups. In the new inter-American system, the costs of overtly authoritarian rule have been prohibitively high. In contrast, the costs of alternative, even nondemocratic means of deposing presidents are low, pro-vided that the leaders of the effort to depose the president turn over power to someone else.

In other words, actors seeking to undermine democratic governments in the region are learning to adapt their strategies in the face of changing international norms supportive of democracy.[7] Second, as I suggested earlier, exogenous threats to democracy are not limited to the military but encompass a variety of unelected actors, including ordinary citizens – most significantly in the form of mass protests in the streets.[8] Third, all of this suggests the need to clarify both the actors involved and the strat-egies they employ (illegal, quasi-legal, legal) when analysing threats to democracy. As a first step in this direction, I propose a two-dimensional typology of exogenous democratic crises.

As figure 9.1 summarizes, in analysing the different manifestations that exogenous threats to democracy take, I make two key distinctions. First, the nature of such threats varies according to the primary actor or agent of change involved.[9] The threat may involve a massive social mobiliza-tion of ordinary citizens (as in recent crises in Argentina and Bolivia), a relatively narrow counter-élite with ties to the armed forces (as in recent

Agent of change

	Mass	Combination	Counter-élite

Illegal

Venezuela 2002   Haiti 1991
Haiti 2004   Paraguay 1996
Ecuador 2000   Paraguay 2000

Strategy of change

**Quasi-
legal**

Bolivia 2003

Ecuador 2005

Bolivia 2005

Argentina 2001

Legal

Figure 9.1 A typology of exogenous democratic crises
Source: Author's elaboration.

crises in Paraguay) or a combination of the two (as typified by Ecuador's
short-lived coup in January 2000, when the military and mass actors
joined forces to overthrow elected President Jamil Mahuad).[10]
   Second, the nature of exogenous threats varies according to the strategies actors employ. Some are patently illegal, such as the use (or credible threat) of force against an elected government – as in the cases of
Haiti (1991, 2004), Paraguay (1996, 2000), Venezuela (2002) and Ecuador (2000). Other strategies are legal or quasi-legal, such as combining
disruptive protests against the government with an emphasis on the constitutional chain of succession – well represented by the cases of Bolivia
(2003, 2005) and Ecuador (2005), and partially by Ecuador (2000) and
Haiti (2004).[11] These latter cases epitomize the challenge of the under-
the-table coup, when violent pressure to remove an elected president
through resignation is combined with nominal respect for the constitution
and the rule of law. Under-the-table coups represent a particular challenge for the OAS, which has been fairly consistent in denouncing traditional military coups. However, when the violent tactics of government
opponents are coupled with calls for a constitutional succession of power

(and ostensible respect for the rule of law), the OAS has found it far more difficult to react. Before turning to this topic, it is useful first to have a closer look at the crises themselves – in particular, their underlying causes.

Explanations for the new democratic instability

Why is Latin America experiencing continuing political instability today? A definitive answer is beyond the scope of this analysis, but I should begin by stressing two points. First, it is important to keep in mind that, as Munck (2006a: 11) notes, "threats to democracy have been largely contained" and "unambiguous violations of democracy have been rare and brief". Indeed, according to one recent assessment, Fujimori's *autogolpe* in Peru (1992) is the only case of a competitive regime breaking down into an authoritarian one during the third wave of democracy in Latin America (Mainwaring and Pérez-Liñán, 2005: 38). In other words, Latin America's current struggles generally involve momentary or partial deviations from democracy rather than permanent breakdowns into authoritarian rule.

Second, any attempt to evaluate the new political instability in Latin America must address the puzzle of why some countries have experienced repeated crises while others – Uruguay and Costa Rica, for instance – have enjoyed seemingly unqualified stability. In particular, a persuasive explanation for Latin America's new political instability would need to explain why democracy has been especially precarious in Haiti and the Andean region.

With these important observations in mind, I review four of the leading hypotheses for Latin America's recent political instability: poverty, inequality and neoliberal reform; presidentialism (and multipartism); the crisis of political representation; and weaknesses in the rule of law, including corruption.

Poverty, inequality and neoliberal reform

No discussion of democracy in Latin America is complete without reference to the region's underlying socioeconomic realities. Terry Lynn Karl (2000: 156) argues, for instance, that "excessive concentrations of wealth and poverty, in the context of a particularly volatile and speculative international economic environment, are a formula for political trouble". Latin America is, by most estimates, the most unequal region in the world (IADB, 1999). Moreover, in 2003 an estimated 43.9 per cent of the population of Latin America lived in poverty and 19.4 per cent in extreme poverty (UNDP, 2004). The neoliberal economic reforms of the 1980s and 1990s did little to ameliorate this disparity, and growth rates remain merely moderate (*The Economist*, 2006).

As stark as Latin America's economic realities are, however, they do not necessarily translate directly into political conflict. Recent evidence suggests that political institutions and attitudes mediate socioeconomic tensions in significant ways (Hagopian and Mainwaring, 2005). After all, poverty, inequality and relatively weak economic growth affect all of Latin America and provide, at best, a limited explanation for the instability of some countries versus others. Still, a few generalizations seem well sustained by recent experience.

First, though poverty levels are not necessarily correlated with regime stability, richer countries are more likely to enjoy "fuller democracy" as opposed to semi-democracy. This is arguably the case because "in the poor countries, non-democratic traditional elites are more powerful than in the middle income countries" (Mainwaring and Pérez-Liñán, 2005: 52). Second, evidence suggests that recent neoliberal reforms have indeed generated political instability. Hochstetler (2006: 406), for example, finds that South American presidents who followed neoliberal economic policies were far more likely to face calls for their resignation – and fall from power – than those who eschewed such policies. Governments that pursue neoliberal policies appear to be particularly vulnerable to instability when their policies fail to generate concrete gains (see Stokes, 2001: 122–153; Hagopian, 2005: 341–343).

In short, socioeconomic issues remain central to understanding the new political instability in Latin America, but determining how they interact with the broader political context in individual countries remains a central task for future research.

Presidentialism (and multipartism)

A broad research agenda has been dedicated to demonstrating the relative frailty of presidential versus parliamentary systems, particularly when the former intersect with multipartism in the legislature (see e.g. Linz and Valenzuela, 1994; Mainwaring and Shugart, 1997). In a recent contribution to the literature, Arturo Valenzuela (2004) argues that the rash of "interrupted presidents" (those who fail to finish their constitutional terms) in Latin America can be attributed, in part, to the fragility of presidential systems. He argues, in particular, that there is a serious gap between the high expectations Latin American citizens have of their presidents and the weak capacity executives actually enjoy – due to their lack of congressional support, often because of political fragmentation (multipartism) and weak party discipline in the legislature. The end result is often confrontation between the executive and legislative branches, gridlock and political crisis. Indeed, interbranch conflicts are a growing source of democratic crisis in the Americas.[12]

By itself, of course, presidentialism can hardly be blamed for the new political instability in Latin America, since practically every country in the region is presidential and yet some countries enjoy seeming tranquillity. Valenzuela (ibid.) observes, however, that the risks of presidentialism appear to be most salient in the case of minority presidents: of his sample of 14 interrupted presidents, 11 failed to obtain majority support in the first round of voting while 12 lacked majority support in the legislature. In a study of 10 South American countries, Hochstetler (2006: 408) finds confirmation of this argument, noting that "overall, presidents whose parties held a minority of congressional seats were more likely to be challenged by civilian actors and to fall".

This phenomenon, in turn, raises the question of why Latin America's political leaders so frequently enjoy such limited party support. In a general sense, the weak legislative support of Latin American presidents derives from two facts. First, in presidential systems the direct election of executives opens the way to political outsiders (including, most recently, neopopulists) who may have no political party background. Second, the use of proportional representation systems in the context of extreme societal fragmentation has given rise, in Latin America, to the highest levels of multipartism (and gridlock) in the developing world (IADB, 2000: 184–188). Historically speaking, moreover, multipartism has contributed to democratic regime collapse; a survey of Latin American regime changes in the second half of the twentieth century finds that multiparty systems "were more prone to breakdown than democracies with fewer than 3.0 effective parties" (Mainwaring and Pérez-Liñán, 2005: 35).

In short, attention to party systems (in the context of presidentialism) remains crucial to understanding political instability in Latin America, particularly endogenous crises that pit elected bodies against one another. Presidents with weak initial mandates and fragmented legislative support appear particularly vulnerable to political calamity.

The crisis of political representation

A third hypothesis traces Latin America's recent political instability to the long-term decay of traditional forms of intermediation among interest groups. In particular, this approach emphasizes the potentially destabilizing impact of the collapse of corporatism and, especially, the decline of established political parties (Domínguez, 1997; Hagopian, 1998, 2005; Roberts, 2002; Mainwaring, 2006). When traditional forms of interest mediation collapse, it is reasoned, citizens who lack institutional forms of representation (and face pressing issues of poverty and social exclusion) may take to the streets, seeking change outside the democratic institutional process (an exogenous threat). Conversely, they may vote for political outsiders with dubious democratic credentials to overhaul the system from within (an endogenous threat).

In his study of Venezuela's April 2002 "civil society coup", for example, Omar Encarnación (2002: 39) attributes the crisis to "the institutional decay and eventual collapse of the political system (especially political parties)" and to "the rise of an antiparty, antiestablishment leader ... whose commitment to democracy is at best suspect". In this context, Encarnación notes (ibid.: 38), "civil society, especially an invigorated one, can become a source of instability, disorder, and even violence".

Indeed, civil society does appear to be having a destabilizing impact in recent Latin American politics. Hochstetler (2006) notes that street protests were a factor in all nine cases of fallen presidents (i.e. those who resigned early) between 1978 and 2003, whereas presidential challenges that did not involve street protests failed. She concludes that "street protests by civil society actors, with or without parallel legislative action, appear to be the *poder moderador*, or moderating power, of the new civilian regimes" (ibid.: 403). While acknowledging the fragility of minority presidents in presidential systems, Hochstetler is critical of an overemphasis on purely institutional explanations of Latin America's recent instability; she calls instead for greater attention to be paid to state-society relations.

Weaknesses in the rule of law

Another hypothesis argues that much of Latin America's recent political instability can be explained by the weak rule of law that exists in the region, especially when coupled with the fragility of presidentialism. Cameron, Blanaru and Burns (2005) argue, for example, that presidentialism often offers weak incentives for opposing sides to cooperate when executive-legislative tensions develop; they also suggest that, where the rule of law is weak, there are strong incentives to use extra-constitutional procedures (quasi-legal impeachments, court-stacking, bribery to build coalitions) to resolve intergovernmental conflicts. In other words, the combination of presidentialism and weakness in the rule of law is a recipe for democratic crisis. Conversely, where the rule of law is strong, "the type of constitution [presidential or parliamentary] does not matter a great deal to political stability" (ibid.: 6).[13] Cameron, Blanaru and Burns argue that, rather than focusing on parliamentarism (an unrealistic goal in Latin America), democracy advocates should try to strengthen the rule of law.

As a corollary to looking at a state's propensity to uphold the law, many scholars draw attention to the damaging impacts of corruption on democratic stability. Hochstetler (2006: 406–408), for example, finds that presidents who faced credible allegations of corruption were far more likely also to face calls for their resignation and then to leave early than presidents who were not associated with such wrongdoing. Hagopian (2005: 350–353) cautions, however, that the links between corruption and democracy remain understudied, and that the impact of corruption may be mitigated by such factors as economic performance, the scale of corruption and public attitudes.

Summary

In this overview, I stop short of offering a definitive answer to the question of what ails contemporary Latin American democracies. Recent scholarship suggests that minority presidents, failed neoliberal policies, substantial corruption and street violence are significant warning signs of a mounting democratic crisis, particularly in countries where the rule of law is relatively weak. More rigorous analysis to parse out the causal significance of these and other explanations should help to inform possible policy solutions by those whose difficult task it is to protect and promote democracy in the region.

What can be done? Regional governance solutions in the Americas

What can regional governance institutions – the OAS in particular – do to promote the consolidation and deepening of democracy in Latin America? Here, I offer two brief and interrelated recommendations. First, the OAS and other regional actors should continue to develop long-term strategies to deal with the region's enduring structural problems – widespread poverty, staggering income inequality, fragile political institutions, pervasive corruption and weakness in the rule of law. Short of a radical shift in hemispheric priorities, however, it is difficult to see what a resource-poor institution such as the OAS can do to ameliorate these longstanding problems.

In practice, the OAS's main democracy-promotion arm, the Department for the Promotion of Democracy (DPD), has focused on a fairly narrow range of concerns, especially election monitoring. Within this more limited focus, one critical issue for the future is what international institutions such as the DPD can do to strengthen political party systems. In recognition of the need to be proactive, the OAS in 2001 spearheaded the formation of the Inter-American Forum on Political Parties to promote dialogue, exchange and cooperation among legislators. Thomas Carothers (2006: 219) cautions, however, that the effects of international party assistance "will be modest at best and unlikely in and of themselves to lead to any fundamental changes in the troubled state of the particular institutions with which they work". Indeed, it is difficult to see how multilateral institutions can ameliorate the severe challenges facing political party systems in the region's more troubled areas, like Haiti and the Andean region. In short, creative ideas for rejuvenating Latin America's political parties are desperately needed.

Turning away from these larger structural issues, a second set of recommendations concerns the more short-term issue of crisis response: how can the OAS respond more effectively to democratic crises? In answering this question, the first step is to acknowledge the diversity of the threats to democracy in the region and the particular challenges different types of threats pose to effective international intervention. In short, as the OAS and other concerned actors assess how to defend democracy, it is critical that they recognize the varied and evolving nature of the threats they face.

With regard to endogenous threats to democracy, or attempts by incumbents to undermine vertical and horizontal accountability, the OAS has developed a relatively dynamic set of procedures – ranging from diplomatic condemnation to the threat or imposition of sanctions – for responding to the most severe threats, such as *autogolpes* and unambiguous election frauds. Indeed, the *autogolpes* in Peru (1992) and Guatemala (1993) and glaring electoral problems in the Dominican Republic (1994), Peru (2000) and Haiti (2000) provoked significant international action on the part of the OAS and its most important member state, the United States.[14] In cases of seemingly less severe though no less significant threats, however, the OAS has been extremely reluctant to intercede. As Arceneaux and Pion-Berlin (2005: 122) skilfully summarize:

Democracies are sometimes altered in incremental, subtle, or insidious ways that once detected do not serve as effective rallying points for international outrage. Stacking a national election commission or high court with obsequious followers of the regime is unquestionably damaging to a democracy's integrity. But it can never measure up to the drama of a cancelled election or a closed judicial branch. Governments in Latin America have increasingly been able to get away with preserving the form of democratic institutions while debasing, sometimes gutting, their essence.

In short, an ongoing challenge for the OAS concerns its response to the less conspicuous threats that elected but illiberal presidents carry out, such as manipulating the courts and electoral bodies and other subtle abuses of power. Responding more effectively to such threats will require greater specificity in OAS protocols (as I discuss further below) and greater political will on the part of member states to use them.

The second step towards determining how the OAS can respond more effectively to democratic crises is to recognize the set of threats to democracy that originate from unelected actors – i.e. those exogenous to the regime. When these threats involve the use of force to unseat an elected government, as in the case of a classic military coup d'état, the OAS has been fairly consistent in its condemnation of the threat and defence of the elected government.[15] When the threats involve mass actors and employ legal or quasi-legal strategies to challenge a democratic government, however, the OAS's response has been more ambivalent. Indeed, the emergence of the under-the-table coup presents a particular challenge for the OAS.

From recent experience in Bolivia, Ecuador and elsewhere, a critical issue therefore concerns how the OAS should respond to the potential threat posed by unlawful street protestors who mobilize to remove an unpopular but constitutionally elected president. As McCoy (2006: 771) points out, the OAS recently has tended to support presidents who are besieged by street protests, but not to insist on their reinstatement if they are ousted as long as the chain of constitutional succession is maintained – even if their ousting involved questionable constitutional procedures. The problem with this response, however, is that street violence is a dangerous substitute for the process of constitutional impeachment. The international community thus risks encouraging further disruptions by granting legitimacy to the successors of such crises.

As intimated in the introduction, one of the difficulties the OAS confronts in dealing with the threat posed to elected leaders by street protests lies in determining whether (and at what point) such protests cross the line from being forms of legitimate protest to instances of unlawful coercion. On the one hand, the OAS must strenuously defend the right of citizens to assemble and protest peacefully – particularly perhaps in countries where citizens have historically lacked effective political representation. Furthermore, in cases where protests have been provoked by the autocratic actions of elected leaders, the OAS should stand firm in its defence of democracy against such endogenous threats. Yet it must also stand in defence of the rule of law and show no tolerance for unlawful protests and actions to remove presidents that violate the spirit of the constitution. How, then, might the OAS determine whether or not some form of intervention is warranted?

In his thoughtful analysis of the problem these new crises pose, O'Neill (2004) calls for a graduated approach to international intervention that would escalate from active diplomacy in the early stages of a democratic and civil crisis to "boots on the ground" (i.e. active military intervention) at the first sign of a political crisis turning violent. In a similar vein, McCoy (2006: 771) recommends that an "early warning system, along with clear criteria and tools for action" could assist the international community in developing a more proactive response to the destabilizing threat mass protests pose. Such a warning system could counter the long-standing criticism of the OAS that it fails to diffuse crises before they escalate and therefore performs a reactive or "firefighter" role (Acevedo and Grossman, 1996: 148). To date, however, the OAS has registered a collective resistance to such measures, most notably at the annual meeting of the General Assembly at Fort Lauderdale, Florida, in 2005, which soundly rejected a US-sponsored proposal to create a committee to monitor democracy in the region (Brinkley, 2005).

Nevertheless, inaction on the part of OAS member states need not preclude non-state actors from playing a critical role in the monitoring and defence of democracy. In fact, a substantial number of politicians, researchers, journalists and civil society organizations actively follow the region's democratic advances and setbacks, albeit in an uncoordinated manner. One of the difficult challenges, as Munck (2006b: 8–9) argues, is to find ways to bring politicians and researchers together in an institutionalized partnership. In recent years such initiatives have gained considerable momentum. For example, the UN Development Programme (UNDP) collaborated with leading scholars to develop its Electoral Democracy Index, a new dataset on Latin American democracy that could serve as a benchmark of a minimal definition of democracy (see UNDP, 2004). Future collaboration among scholars, non-governmental organizations (NGOs), the UNDP, the DPD and the Inter-American Commission on Human Rights could be extremely fruitful in developing mechanisms and criteria for monitoring threats to democracy in the hemisphere. A further challenge, however, lies in galvanizing the OAS into action when a clear threat to democracy has been identified.

Arguably, at the heart of many of these problems is that the OAS's main instrument for the defence of democracy, the Inter-American Democratic Charter (IADC), fails to specify precisely what constitutes a serious violation of democracy, making the determination a largely political judgement (Cameron, 2003: 112; Pastor, 2003: 20; McCoy, 2006: 769). In particular, it is not clear what qualifies, to use the IADC's rubric, as an "unconstitutional alteration of the constitutional regime". In practice, this lack of specificity frequently has led to inaction by the OAS, particularly as individual member states fear creating new precedents that could be used against their own (imperfectly democratic) state in the future. Among numerous proposals to rectify this problem is one from the Friends of the Inter-American Democratic Charter, an innovative NGO associated with the Carter Center and composed of former presidents and high-level officials from the Americas, which delineates a nine-point list of basic threats to democracy, encompassing a broad but still delimited set of core democratic rights (see McCoy, 2006: 770). Such an initiative could have a dramatic impact in clarifying (and perhaps deterring) democratic threats, but it remains to be seen what impact the "friends" will have on strengthening the OAS's resolve in the collective defence of democracy. On the positive side, the current secretary-general of the OAS, José Miguel Insulza, has stated he believes the charter should be more explicit in defining the conditions that constitute a basis for action in the defence of democracy (quoted in OAS, 2007).

A final consideration with regard to regional governance solutions for the defence of democracy concerns leverage. A critical weakness of the OAS, especially when compared with the European Union, is that, apart from prodding by the United States, it lacks substantial incentives to persuade member states to comply with democratic protocols. Thus a longer-term goal for strengthening the defence of democracy in Latin America should be to develop further linkages between democracy and development (especially trade), with the European Union serving as a potential model. Such an approach would call for rejuvenating the now moribund proposal for a Free Trade Area of the Americas and other initiatives aimed at hemispheric integration. Unfortunately, in light of the geopolitical impasse in which the region now finds itself, this may prove to be an elusive goal for some time into the future.

A final word

Scholars and practitioners have already contributed important insights into the economic and political-institutional conditions that undermine democratic stability in Latin America, but their dialogue on how best to protect and promote democracy in the region needs to continue. Successful collaboration among academics, NGOs and policy-makers could lead to innovative new ways of monitoring threats to democracy, possibly serving as an early-warning system for the OAS. The OAS, for its part, would benefit from more explicit criteria for determining when a democratic crisis is serious enough to warrant immediate international intervention. In today's tense geopolitical environment, galvanizing the OAS into action will not be an easy task. Thus, realizing the full potential of the

Democratic Charter, including developing more powerful tools for leverage, is a long-term political challenge.

Notes

1. Such a view is implicit in Encarnación's (2002) critique of the "civil society coup" in Venezuela. For a more explicit critique see *The Economist* (2005); *Miami Herald* (2005).
2. The term "under-the-table coup" derives from comments by Domingo Laíno, chairman of the Authentic Radical Liberal Party of Paraguay (see opening quotation), made at the Democratic Forum on the Institutional Crisis in Paraguay, sponsored by the OAS Unit for the Promotion of Democracy (now the Department for the Promotion of Democracy); see OAS (1996).
3. McCoy's is certainly the most exhaustive inventory of democratic crises in Latin America in the post–Cold War period. Other comprehensive attempts to catalogue recent democratic trends include Mainwaring, Brinks and Pérez-Liñán (2001); UNDP (2004); and several of the contributors to Legler, Lean and Boniface (2007).
4. Although rare, it is also possible for an endogenous threat to democracy to arise from the (undemocratic) actions of the legislature, as was the case in the Nicaraguan crisis of 2004–2005. Arguably, this was also the case in the congressional removal of Ecuadorian Presidents Abdalá Bucaram in 1997 and Lucio Gutiérrez in 2005; although, in the latter case, the key role played by mass actors in triggering Gutiérrez's removal leads me to classify it as an endogenous threat.
5. The political logic and consequences of *autogolpes* and other threats to horizontal accountability are ably analysed by Cameron (1998, 2003) and O'Donnell (1998).
6. These are the four cases involving traditional military force in the past 15 years that McCoy identifies. She defines traditional military force as "coups attempted by high-ranking military officers with support from the armed forces", as distinct from "coups attempted by lower ranking officers but put down by the high command" (McCoy, 2006: 759).
7. Similar arguments animate the literature on competitive electoral and semi-authoritarian regimes (see Levitsky and Way, 2002; Ottaway, 2003; Schedler, 2006).
8. Although beyond the scope of this chapter, an equally pernicious threat to democracy can arise from the actions of armed groups, such as organized crime, paramilitaries, gangs and revolutionary movements (see McCoy, 2006: 767). Armed groups represent a particular threat to democracy in Colombia.
9. My focus on actors and strategies owes much to a similar conceptual distinction made by Munck and Leff (1997) in their analysis of modes of transition.
10. Those in the political class (congress and the judiciary) also may join forces with unelected actors to undermine an elected president (in this case, the threat is exogenous to the president as opposed to the entire regime). This reality is reflected in the strategies that actors employ; the use of quasi-legal and legal strategies requires that unelected actors find allies in the political class.
11. The crisis in Argentina in late 2001, while initially involving violent protests in the streets, ultimately was resolved through legal-constitutional means (see e.g. Levitsky and Murillo, 2003).
12. In McCoy's (2006) survey of democratic crises, nearly one-third of all cases (16 of 49 country-years) and one-half of recent crises (1997–2005) involved some form of intra-governmental conflict.

13. The authors' study relies on World Bank governance data (see Kaufmann, Kraay and Mastruzzi, 2006) for measures of the rule of law and political stability. The World Bank study defines the rule of law as "the extent to which agents have confidence in and abide by the rules of society, and in particular the quality of contract enforcement, the police, and the courts, as well as the likelihood of crime and violence" (ibid.: 4).

14. The response by the OAS was certainly more vigorous with regard to the two *auto-golpes* than it was to the three failed elections. In the latter cases, the OAS stopped short of invoking its main legal mechanism for the defence of democracy (at the time, resolution 1080) and sent missions to mediate the crises rather than withdraw recognition of the governments. For further elaboration see Boniface (2007).

15. Controversy, however, surrounds two recent cases. First, in April 2002 the United States and its allies Colombia and El Salvador appeared, however briefly, to welcome the overthrow of Hugo Chávez before joining in the regional condemnation of the short-lived coup led by business magnate Pedro Carmona. Second, and more controversial still, the United States (as well as France and Canada) failed vigorously to defend Haiti's elected president, Jean-Bertrand Aristide, against an armed rebellion that openly rejected international mediation efforts; Aristide resigned from power on 29 February 2004, claiming he had been overthrown in a coup (CNN, 2004).

REFERENCES

Acevedo, Domingo E. and Claudio Grossman (1996) "The Organization of American States and the Protection of Democracy", in Tom Farer, ed., *Beyond Sovereignty: Collectively Defending Democracy in the Americas*, Baltimore, MD: Johns Hopkins University Press.

Arceneaux, Craig and David Pion-Berlin (2005) *Transforming Latin America: The International and Domestic Origins of Change*, Pittsburgh, PA: University of Pittsburgh Press.

BBC News (2003) "Bolivia's ex-President Blames Conspiracy", BBC, 21 October, available at http://news.bbc.co.uk/2/hi/americas/3210458.stm.

——— (2005a) "Ecuador Congress Sacks President", BBC, 20 April, available at http://news.bbc.co.uk/2/hi/americas/4466697.stm.

——— (2005b) "Ecuador ex-President Under Arrest", BBC, 15 October, available at http://news.bbc.co.uk/2/hi/americas/4341092.stm.

Boniface, Dexter S. (2007) "The OAS's Mixed Record", in Thomas Legler, Sharon F. Lean and Dexter S. Boniface, eds, *Promoting Democracy in the Americas*, Baltimore, MD: Johns Hopkins University Press.

Brinkley, Joel (2005) "Latin States Shun U.S. Plan to Watch Over Democracy", *New York Times*, 9 June.

Cameron, Maxwell A. (1998) "Self-Coups: Peru, Guatemala, and Russia", *Journal of Democracy* 9(1), pp. 125–139.

——— (2003) "Strengthening Checks and Balances: Democracy Defence and Promotion in the Americas", *Canadian Foreign Policy* 10(3), pp. 101–116.

Cameron, Maxwell A., Ana-Maria Blanaru and Lesley M. Burns (2005) "Presidentialism and the Rule of Law: The Andean Region in Comparative Perspective", working paper, Department of Political Science, University of British

Columbia, Vancouver, available at www.politics.ubc.ca/fileadmin/template/ main/images/departments/poli_sci/Faculty/cameron/Presidentialism_RuleofLaw.pdf.

Carothers, Thomas (2006) *Confronting the Weakest Link: Aiding Political Parties in New Democracies*, Washington, DC: Carnegie Endowment for International Peace.

CNN (2004) "Aristide Says U.S. Deposed Him in a 'Coup d'État'", CNN, 2 March.

Domínguez, Jorge I. (1997) "Latin America's Crisis of Representation", *Foreign Affairs* 76(1), pp. 100–113.

Encarnación, Omar G. (2002) "Venezuela's 'Civil Society Coup'", *World Policy Journal* 19(2), pp. 38–48.

Hagopian, Frances (1998) "Democracy and Political Representation in Latin America in the 1990s: Pause, Reorganization, or Decline?", in Felipe Agüero and Jeffrey Stark, eds, *Fault Lines of Democracy in Post-Transition Latin America*, Coral Gables, FL: North-South Center Press.

—— (2005) "Conclusions: Government Performance, Political Representation, and Public Perceptions of Contemporary Democracy in Latin America", in Frances Hagopian and Scott Mainwaring, eds, *The Third Wave of Democratization in Latin America: Advances and Setbacks*, New York: Cambridge University Press.

Hagopian, Frances and Scott Mainwaring, eds (2005) *The Third Wave of Democratization in Latin America: Advances and Setbacks*, New York: Cambridge University Press.

Harman, Danna (2005) "People Power Rattling Politics of Latin America", *Christian Science Monitor*, 29 April.

Hochstetler, Kathryn (2006) "Rethinking Presidentialism: Challenges and Presidential Falls in South America", *Comparative Politics* 38(4), pp. 401–418.

Hopgood, Mei-Ling (2005) "Street Protestors' Power Swells", *Miami Herald*, 28 June.

IADB (1999) *Economic and Social Progress in Latin America 1998–1999 Report: Facing Up to Inequality in Latin America*, Washington, DC: Inter-American Development Bank/Johns Hopkins University Press.

—— (2000) *Economic and Social Progress in Latin America 2000 Report: Development Beyond Economics*, Washington, DC: Inter-American Development Bank/Johns Hopkins University Press.

Karl, Terry Lynn (2000) "Economic Inequality and Democratic Instability", *Journal of Democracy* 11(1), pp. 149–156.

Kaufmann, Daniel, Aart Kraay and Massimo Mastruzzi (2006) "Governance Matters V: Aggregate and Individual Governance Indicators for 1996–2005", World Bank, Washington, DC, mimeo, available at http://siteresources. worldbank.org/INTWBIGOVANTCOR/Resources/1740479-1150402582357/ 2661829-1158008871017/gov_matters_5_no_annex.pdf.

Legler, Thomas, Sharon F. Lean and Dexter S. Boniface, eds (2007) *Promoting Democracy in the Americas*, Baltimore, MD: Johns Hopkins University Press.

Levitsky, Steven and Maria Victoria Murillo (2003) "Argentina Weathers the Storm", *Journal of Democracy* 14(4), pp. 152–166.

Levitsky, Steven and Lucan A. Way (2002) "The Rise of Competitive Authoritarianism", *Journal of Democracy* 13(2), pp. 51–65.

Linz, Juan and Arturo Valenzuela, eds (1994) *The Failure of Presidential Democracy*, Baltimore, MD: Johns Hopkins University Press.

Mainwaring, Scott (2006) "The Crisis of Representation in the Andes", *Journal of Democracy* 17(3), pp. 13–27.

Mainwaring, Scott and Aníbal Pérez-Liñán (2005) "Latin American Democratization since 1978: Democratic Transitions, Breakdowns, and Erosions", in Frances Hagopian and Scott Mainwaring, eds, *The Third Wave of Democratization in Latin America: Advances and Setbacks*, New York: Cambridge University Press.

Mainwaring, Scott and Matthew Sobert Shugart, eds (1997) *Presidentialism and Democracy in Latin America*, New York: Cambridge University Press.

Mainwaring, Scott, Daniel Brinks and Aníbal Pérez-Liñán (2001) "Classifying Political Regimes in Latin America, 1945–1999", *Studies in Comparative International Development* 36(1), pp. 37–65.

McCoy, Jennifer (2006) "International Response to Democratic Crisis in the Americas, 1990–2005", *Democratization* 13(5), pp. 756–775.

Miami Herald (2005) "Politics-by-Mob Claims Another Victim", *Miami Herald*, 22 April.

Munck, Gerardo (2006a) "Latin America: Old Problems, New Agenda", *Democracy at Large* 2(3), pp. 10–13.

——— (2006b) "Monitoring Democracy: Deepening an Emerging Consensus", mimeo, available at www-rcf.usc.edu/~munck/pdf/Munck%20Monitoring_Democracy%202006.pdf.

Munck, Gerardo and Carol Skalnik Leff (1997) "Modes of Transition and Democratization: South America and Eastern Europe in Comparative Perspective", *Comparative Politics* 29(3), pp. 343–362.

OAS (1996) "Democratic Forum: The 1996 Institutional Crisis in Paraguay", General Secretariat of the Organization of American States, Washington, DC.

——— (2007) "High-Level Panel Spotlights Role of Inter-American Democratic Charter in the Americas", press release, 24 May, available at www.oas.org/OASpage/press_releases/press_release.asp?sCodigo=E-135/07.

O'Donnell, Guillermo (1998) "Horizontal Accountability in New Democracies", *Journal of Democracy* 9(3), pp. 112–126.

O'Neill, Daniel P. (2004) "When to Intervene: The Haitian Dilemma", *SAIS Review* 24(2), pp. 163–174.

Ottaway, Marina (2003) *Democracy Challenged: The Rise of Semi-Authoritarianism*, Washington, DC: Carnegie Endowment for International Peace.

Pastor, Robert (2003) "A Community of Democracies in the Americas: Instilling Substance into a Wondrous Phrase", *Canadian Foreign Policy* 10(3), pp. 13–29.

Roberts, Kenneth (2002) "Party-Society Linkages and the Transformation of Political Representation in Latin America", *Canadian Journal of Latin American and Caribbean Studies* 27(53), pp. 9–34.

Schedler, Andreas, ed. (2006) *Electoral Authoritarianism: The Dynamics of Unfree Competition*, Boulder, CO: Lynne Rienner.

Stokes, Susan (2001) *Mandates and Democracy: Neoliberalism by Surprise in Latin America*, Cambridge: Cambridge University Press.

The Economist (2005) "Mob Rule, Not People Power", *The Economist*, 18 June.

—— (2006) "Improving on the Latin Rate of Growth", *The Economist*, 18 May.

UNDP (2004) *Democracy in Latin America: Toward a Citizens' Democracy,* New York: UN Development Programme.

Valenzuela, Arturo (2004) "Latin American Presidencies Interrupted", *Journal of Democracy* 15(4), pp. 5–19.

10

Monitoring elections

Sharon F. Lean

Globalization, understood as the intensification of political, social, economic and cultural interactions across borders, is perhaps the defining characteristic of our time, but it is not a uniform phenomenon. Political linkages develop at a different pace than economic ties, and the degree of connection varies in intensity across regions and countries, rural and urban settings. The Americas have experienced a period of heightened political interconnectedness over the past two decades, a phenomenon linked to the regional return to democracy. In the field of international law, scholars now defend the existence of a democratic entitlement, or what international relations specialists call a democracy regime (Fox, 2000; Franck, 1992: 147). While the worldwide reach of this regime is a matter of debate (see Donnelly, 1998: 18; Roth, 2000), a growing body of research suggests that the democratic entitlement is particularly strong in the Americas, reinforced through a series of agreements in regional and subregional organizations (Boniface, 2002; Muñoz and D'Leon, 1998; Schnably, 2000).

The Inter-American Democratic Charter, enacted by the member states of the Organization of American States (OAS) in 2001, represents the most ambitious attempt to date to legalize democracy norms in the Americas.[1] Its reach and efficacy are the subject of lively current academic debate (see e.g. Boniface, 2007; Cooper and Legler, 2006; Levitt, 2007). But legal instruments such as the charter are not the only referents that can help us understand regional political trends. In addition to legalization in the intergovernmental arena, many other practices constitute

Which way Latin America? Hemispheric politics meets globalization, Cooper and Heine, eds, United Nations University Press, 2009, ISBN 978-92-808-1172-8

the region's democratic commitment. Foremost among these is international election monitoring, or election observation.[2] The act of international election monitoring embodies the notion of political globalization. It entails the intensification of political relations across borders and a bending of conventional understandings of norms of state sovereignty and non-intervention. In the Americas, election observation has become both a fixture of regional politics and a matter of continued contention. As such, the politics of election monitoring illuminates broader regional debates on democracy and its international dimensions.

The third wave of democratization swept across the region, beginning with the election held in the Dominican Republic in 1978. Peru followed, holding a competitive election in 1980, and Argentina and Uruguay reinstituted elections after periods of authoritarian rule in 1983 and 1984, respectively. Since that time, all countries in the region with the exception of Cuba have embraced regular, competitive elections to select their leaders. Even Cubans now select representatives to their National Assembly by direct election, though they choose only among candidates from the Cuban Communist Party.

With the regional return to electoral politics, the Americas have accumulated a wealth of experience with international election monitoring, perhaps more than any other region of the world. Since the first OAS team observed the Costa Rican election of 1962, hundreds of international delegations involving thousands of election observers have watched over electoral processes in the region. Interestingly, decades after most Latin American nations began their "third-wave" transitions to democracy, the trend of international electoral supervision does not appear to be slowing. Has the region developed a distinctive and unique accord with regard to the legitimacy and desirability of election monitoring? What does the Americas' experience with election monitoring tell us about the reach and limits of a regional democracy regime? What lessons does this experience suggest about the future of international election monitoring, both in the region and in the world? To answer these questions, this chapter examines cross-national data on election monitoring in the region as well as case studies of recent experiences in Venezuela, Haiti and Mexico.

I take a transnational relations approach, which emphasizes the relevance of state, multilateral and non-state actors in generating political outcomes. Transnational relations can be defined as "regular interactions across national boundaries when at least one actor is a non-state agent or does not operate on behalf of a national government or an intergovernmental organization" (Risse-Kappan, 1995: 3). State, multilateral and non-state actors in the Americas are all deeply involved in the holding and supervising of elections in the region. State agencies such as the US

Agency for International Development and the Canadian International Development Agency underwrite international election-monitoring missions. The members of the European Union, separately and together, as well as many other states (notably Japan, Sweden and Norway) also provide political aid for elections and election observation. Intergovernmental organizations, most notably the OAS and the United Nations, conduct election observation missions of all sizes and also frequently provide technical assistance to election administration agencies. Alongside intergovernmental organizations, non-state actors, such as the Carter Center, the partisan institutes of the US National Endowment for Democracy (NED) – the National Democratic Institute for International Affairs (NDI) and the International Republican Institute (IRI) – and the many civic associations that organize domestic election-monitoring efforts are also prominent members of the transnational election-monitoring field. Because of the involvement of such a wide range of actors, each with different priorities, capabilities and resources, it is important to understand election monitoring as a form of transnational relations, rather than solely as the expression of the policy preferences of powerful states.

Institutionalizing election monitoring in the Americas

Have the Americas developed a unique accord with regard to the legitimacy and desirability of election monitoring? Answering this question requires examination of regional patterns. International election observation was first practised in the Americas when three delegates of the OAS watched the Costa Rican election of 4 February 1962. Between 1962 and 1972 the OAS sent 13 such diplomatic missions, after which it had a brief hiatus (Lean, 2007: 157). These early missions, however, were nothing like contemporary international monitoring efforts: in the words of Robert Pastor (1999: 127), early OAS missions served "less to monitor the electoral process than to show moral support for the incumbent".

Election observation in the Americas resumed in 1978, and by 1989 small groups of international observers had been present for 28 different Latin American elections. Organizations sending observers included not only the OAS but also a variety of non-governmental organizations (NGOs), such as the Washington Office on Latin America (WOLA), the International Human Rights Law Group (now Global Rights), the Latin American Studies Association, the NDI and the Carter Center (Lean, 2007: 157, 161).

After 1989 election monitoring expanded dramatically in frequency and scope, and became more tightly regulated. The Nicaraguan general election of 1990, the first in a sovereign state to be monitored by the

United Nations, was pivotal in extending the practice (Santa-Cruz, 2004). Since 1990 all countries in the region, with the exception of Cuba, have invited international observers to be present for elections on at least one occasion. In the 10-year period from 1996 to 2006, international monitors were present at nearly 80 per cent of elections in the region.[3] Of the 11 presidential elections held between December 2005 and December 2006 (involving 80 per cent of the region's electorate), nine were monitored by international observers.[4]

From the beginning there have been recognized norms for election monitoring – for example, virtually all international organizations that provide foreign monitors require an official diplomatic invitation from the state in question before they will agree to participate in elections. In the 1990s the legalization of election monitoring expanded, with many states introducing provisions in their respective electoral codes specifically authorizing international election monitors. The Mexican federal election code, for example, states that the Instituto Federal Electoral (IFE, or Federal Electoral Institute) must establish bases to receive international visitors (COFIPE, 1990). Other states have interpreted existing law to allow for election monitoring. In Nicaragua the Consejo Supremo Electoral (Supreme Electoral Council), under its authority to carry out scrutiny of the vote, has elaborated extensive regulations for electoral observation (Consejo Supremo Electoral, 2006). As with norms about invitations, these rules allow states to regulate the role of international observers, but they also give legal status and protection to observers and legitimize the regular practice of election observation. At a minimum, such rules signal the willingness of states to subscribe to regional norms of electoral democracy. A larger interpretation might claim that states are locking in the possibility of international oversight as a democratic guarantee.

International organizations have also engaged in self-regulation to increase the legitimacy of election observation; by the mid-1990s they were working together to elaborate and endorse criteria for international involvement and codes of conduct for observers (International IDEA, 1997, 2000). These efforts culminated in a UN Declaration of Principles for International Election Observation and Code of Conduct for International Election Observers, signed on 27 October 2005 by a wide range of parties, including many that are quite active in the Americas, such as the UN Secretariat, the OAS, the NDI, the IRI, the International Foundation for Electoral Systems (IFES), the Carter Center and the European Commission.

As well, election observation became not only more frequent and more regulated but also more technical. Qualitative surveys on the conduct of the polls at nationwide samples of polling sites and quick counts or parallel vote tabulations are now standardized elements of virtually every observation (Estok, Nevitte and Cowan, 2002). By the mid-1990s it was standard practice for election monitors to begin their assessments months in advance of the election. Monitoring also expanded from supervision of the conduct of the polls to include observation of conditions for free and fair competition prior to election day. NDI and domestic electoral observer groups in Mexico, Peru and elsewhere pioneered methods for monitoring the media for bias in quantity and quality of coverage in the pre-election period (Norris and Merloe, 2002). Domestic observer groups, such as Transparency in Peru, began to ask candidates from all major parties to sign civility pacts publicly committing to run a clean campaign. Most recently, groups such as the UN Development Programme (UNDP) and Civic Alliance in Mexico have begun to develop systematic assessment tools to detect vote buying and the improper use of social programmes to coerce voters. Their methods involve correlating statistics on poverty, social programmes and the distribution of public goods to identify high-risk areas, then conducting surveys and interviews with voters in those areas to detect problems (Alianza Cívica, 2006: 10–31). Governments and election administration agencies take these increasingly sophisticated assessments of election observers seriously. In Mexico, for example, following the 2006 election the IFE produced its own synthesis of international recommendations (Instituto Federal Electoral, 2006).

What do these patterns of expansion in the frequency, legalization and scope of international election monitoring show? First, in terms of frequency and legalization, although much of the literature on election monitoring focuses on the effect of international monitoring as a means of safeguarding democratic transitions, the Americas' example shows that monitoring has utility far beyond "first" or founding elections. Nicaragua, which holds simultaneous elections for its executive, legislature and the Central American Parliament, has invited international observers to all five general elections held since the overthrow of the Somoza dictatorship in 1979. Mexico, which holds presidential elections every six years and renews the lower chamber of the legislature in mid-term elections every three years, has allowed foreign visitors for all five national elections since 1994. Since the late 1980s Bolivia and Ecuador have each had six national electoral processes internationally monitored, while both Peru and Panama have had monitors present for seven national elections or referenda. For the Dominican Republic, El Salvador, Haiti, Paraguay and Venezuela, the number is even higher. Costa Rica, the longest-standing and most stable of Latin America's democracies, has regularly invited international election observers to provide third-party oversight of national elections since the 1960s. Election monitoring is, in fact, practised more intensively now than it was when the regional turn towards democracy first began. The region has embraced a hemispheric politics in which democratic consolidation, not just democratic transition, has a recognized transnational dimension.

Second, with respect to scope, the increasingly complex assessments made by election observers indicate aspirations to broaden the regional democracy regime. Monitors have embraced, and states have accepted, the use of techniques that allow observers to make statistically supported claims about the conduct of elections, confirm the accuracy of official results and assess broader conditions for fair competition. As these and new observation methods – such as ways to capture vote buying and the distribution of public goods and services for political gain – are incorporated into the regular repertoire of election observation, the exercise pushes beyond the terrain of purely procedural democracy into that of substantive democracy.

These patterns distinguish the Americas from other regions. Fawn (2006), for example, observes that, after experiences with election monitoring in founding elections, post-Soviet states began to show increasing resistance to international election observation, particularly missions organized by the Organization for Security and Cooperation in Europe. We see a similar trend in Africa, where Van Cranenburgh (2000: 31) cites regional disenchantment with observers because of their certification of domestically disputed "first" elections. Anglin (1998: 473) reports that, in second-generation African elections, "the practice of routinely relying on international monitoring became less consistent" due to "growing nationalist resentment at what some see as Western donor tutelage", and perhaps to a perception on the part of states that the need to signal their democratic credentials to the region and the world had lessened. While other regions have resisted the institutionalization and expansion of electoral observation, in the Americas it has become a fixture of hemispheric politics.

Election monitoring and the limits of the regional democracy regime

Santa-Cruz (2005a, 2005b) argues persuasively that, by changing state identities and interests, the emergence and normalization of election monitoring have transformed regional understandings of sovereignty in the Americas and helped to constitute the regional democracy regime. As a constitutive element of the regime, though, election monitoring also reveals some of its important limits. We can most easily understand the way in which international election monitoring embodies limits to the regional democracy regime through case studies. The remainder of the chapter thus discusses three cases that illustrate different ways in which the regional democracy regime is bounded: Venezuela's presidential recall referendum process from 2003 to 2004, and presidential elections in 2006 in both Haiti and Mexico.

Venezuela's presidential recall election of 2004

In August 2004 Venezuelan voters went to the polls to decide whether President Hugo Chávez should be recalled. Chávez, first elected in 1998, presided over a popular vote ratifying a new constitution in 1999. The new constitution set the terms for Chávez's "Bolivarian Revolution", which promised economic and political sovereignty, increased popular participation in politics and redistribution of the profits of Venezuela's vast oil reserves to benefit the poor. Not all sectors of Venezuelan society supported the Bolivarian Revolution, particularly Chávez's management of the economy and his moves to enhance the power of the executive.

In 2002 elements of the opposition and the armed forces staged a coup, successfully removing Chávez from office for three days before a wave of popular protest destabilized the coup government and swept Chávez back to his elected position. The political situation in Venezuela following the coup was polarized, the threat of violence omnipresent. Chávez and his supporters felt threatened by an opposition that had shown its willingness to use force, while opposition sympathizers feared retaliation by the reinstated government. Protest and counter-protest were frequent, and in early 2003 the opposition called a general strike that paralysed the Venezuelan economy.

The international community offered to mediate the crisis, and the Venezuelan government invited the OAS, the Carter Center and the UNDP to facilitate a dialogue designed to resolve the volatile political situation. Their multilateral mediation proved patient and innovative, and eventually enabled the divided Venezuelan élite to outline steps towards a peaceful political solution (Cooper and Legler, 2006; Legler, 2007). Under a provision of the 1999 constitution, the Venezuelan opposition began collecting signatures to petition for a presidential recall vote. Throughout the petition process, the OAS and the Carter Center mobilized international observer teams to provide third-party assurance to Venezuelans that the signatures were being gathered in a legitimate manner. After a number of opposition attempts to collect and submit a sufficient number of signatures (the Consejo Nacional Electoral, or National Electoral Council, repeatedly rejected the signed petitions based on questions regarding the validity of some signatures), the recall election was scheduled for 15 August 2004 (Carter Center, 2005: 29). International mediation helped to ensure that the recall vote would go forward by holding Chávez's administration to the provisions of the Bolivarian constitution and regulations developed by the National Electoral Council to govern the petition process.

International observers were not universally welcomed, however, and their actions were neither praised nor even respected by all parties. During the petition process Chávez repeatedly threatened to kick out the international observers, accusing them of violating Venezuelan sovereignty and being partial to the opposition (despite the fact that he had invited them). The opposition, similarly, perceived the observers as supportive of their cause and defended the legitimacy of international involvement so vociferously as to make it appear that the observers might indeed have a pro-opposition bias. The impression of observer bias was compounded by the fact that, in 2003 and 2004, the US-based NED had provided funding to a Venezuelan civil society group called Súmate that was actively involved in organizing the recall petition drive. The NED money had been earmarked to help Súmate "educate citizens on election law and to encourage and equip citizens with the tools to claim their right to free and fair elections" (National Endowment for Democracy, 2007). Relative to election spending and general election assistance, the sums in question were not large – the NED's 2004 allocation to Súmate amounted to US$31,150 – and the main actors monitoring the recall, the OAS and the Carter Center, whose operations were also funded in part by the US government, were not involved with Súmate. However, the fact that international assistance had been given to a partisan domestic group lent credibility to the Venezuelan government's claims of international bias.

When Chávez won the recall election by a wide margin, despite the hype about bias, the Carter Center and the OAS confirmed his victory, based on the reports of more than 100 international observers deployed throughout the country and on the statistical findings of an OAS parallel vote count. The opposition then accused the observers of incompetence by failing to detect the Chávez administration's supposed manipulation of the vote by rigging new electronic voting machines. Chávez, on this occasion, did not hesitate to reference the OAS and Carter Center findings, proclaiming that his win had been internationally validated.

The Venezuelan case exemplifies ongoing questions about the efficacy of international organizations in monitoring and mediating election processes. Given the fact that their neutrality was alternately questioned by government and the opposition, it is difficult to assert that international actors improved the democratic credentials of the recall referendum. Did the international presence guarantee the process? Possibly: the recall referendum might not have moved forward without steady international pressure and encouragement (see Legler, 2007). Did the international presence foster citizen confidence that the process had been fair, diffusing the political polarization that had characterized Venezuelan politics? Not significantly: as the act of election monitoring became politicized (a quality determined both by the actions of the international community and by political forces within the country), its value for the democratic process decreased.

Thus, even when international election observation is conducted by credible organizations and carried out with sensitivity and methodological sophistication, polarized political forces on the ground can manipulate the international presence to their own ends. The act of monitoring elections, whose value lies in the ability of third-party actors to provide neutral evaluation of adherence to accepted standards, is inescapably political. Similarly, the regional democracy regime cannot be constructed in a way that is politically neutral, a fact that has contributed to impasse in its development since the implementation of the Inter-American Democratic Charter.

The 2006 Haitian presidential election

On 7 February 2006, after four postponements, elections were held in Haiti to replace an interim government that had taken power as the result of a 2004 rebellion against President Jean-Bertrand Aristide.[5] René Préval, a candidate with ties to the ousted Aristide, was by far the front-runner in a field of more than 30 candidates.

The 2006 election was held in tense conditions under the supervision of a UN peacekeeping force. Canada and the Caribbean Community (CARICOM) organized a group called the International Mission for Monitoring Haitian Elections (IMMHE), which included observers from Japan, a number of francophone countries and the NGO IFES. In total, the IMMHE deployed 147 observers for the election; 20 had been posted around the country beginning six months prior to the election (IMMHE, 2006b). The European Union stationed 58 observers in Haiti for the election, including three members of the European Parliament (Union Européenne Mission d'Observation Electorale Haiti, 2006). International NGOs also played a role: the NDI trained 12,000 party poll watchers and 5,000 domestic election observers, while IFES sent 35 observers as part of the IMMHE team (Ingalls, 2006; NDI, 2007).

Election day proceeded relatively smoothly, to the surprise of many. The IMMHE (2006a) released a statement affirming that "Haitian voters turned out in massive numbers and the vote was carried out with no violence or intimidation, and no accusations of fraud". As the votes were tallied, however, it became clear that, while Préval had a substantial lead over his nearest competitor, he might not achieve the absolute majority required to avoid a second round. Moreover, as the vote count continued into the following days, serious problems began to emerge. The count included unusually high numbers of blank and null ballots (91,219 and 155,306, respectively – more than 11 per cent of votes cast), raising concerns of fraud. In addition, it was reported that approximately 190,000 votes from hundreds of polling stations could not be counted because of errors on the tally sheets or because the tally sheets from those polling stations had been destroyed, supposedly by anti-Préval gangs (Concannon, 2006). If counted, those votes might have sustained a first-round victory for Préval. Then, a week after the election, with official results pending, thousands of ballots, some blank and others marked for Préval, were found in the Trutier garbage dump north of the capital near Cité Soleil (Thompson, 2006). Préval addressed the nation, charging fraud. His supporters took to the streets, fearful that their votes would not be properly counted, and the situation devolved into renewed violence.

With just over 90 per cent of the vote counted and the above-mentioned problems pending resolution, Préval had obtained 48.7 per cent of the vote. His nearest opponent, Leslie Manigat, had just under 12 per cent (ibid.). The Haitian Conseil Electoral Provisoire (CEP, or Provisional Electoral Council) had a choice. It could try to resolve the anomalies, declare a run-off or try to agree on some other solution. The uncounted votes could be recaptured by tracking down the duplicate tally sheets that were given to political party representatives at each polling station. The null votes could be revised to try to ascertain voter intention. Either process would have taken weeks, however, and political unrest was mounting.

On 16 February 2007, after intense negotiations with the government and representatives of Préval's party and in the presence of international observers from the United Nations and the OAS, the CEP decided to distribute the blank votes proportionally among the candidates, which gave Préval just over 51 per cent of the vote, high enough to avoid a run-off. This solution obviated the need to resolve the problems of the erroneous and damaged tally sheets and the ballots recovered from the dump. It also provided quick affirmation of what would surely have been the eventual result either upon careful recounting or in a run-off, and brought the growing crisis to an end.

The Haitian case exemplifies the methodological limitations to election monitoring. Despite a massive effort by the international community, the vote was not properly protected; indeed, with implicit international agreement, the vote was not even fully counted. This case also shows the desirability of flexibility in electoral assessment (rather than total standardization or ever-stricter adherence to universal standards). International election observers supported the CEP's decision to distribute the blank votes, thereby circumventing Haiti's electoral law and achieving what Concannon (2006) describes as "the right outcome for the wrong reason". By endorsing such a solution, international observers contributed in their own way to stabilizing the political situation in Haiti, and the CEP and the incoming Préval administration were assured that the international community would not sanction them for their actions. For Haiti this was probably the correct thing to do; for the regional democracy regime, however, this case shows, as in Venezuela, the difficulty of maintaining neutrality – this time by choosing not to follow bureaucratic standards that would have required international observers to condemn the CEP's decision to circumvent election law, and perhaps to decertify the election.

The 2006 Mexican presidential election

On 2 July 2006 Mexicans went to the polls to elect a president and representatives to the legislature. The previous election, in July 2000, had ushered in a new era of Mexican politics with a win by Vicente Fox of the right-leaning Partido Acción Nacional (PAN, or National Action Party), the first by a candidate from a party other than the Partido Revolucionario Institucional (Revolutionary Institutional Party) in more than 70 years. In advance of the 2006 election it was evident that the presidential race would be extremely competitive. For months the candidate of the left-leaning Partido de la Revolución Democrática (PRD, or Party of the Democratic Revolution), Andrés Manuel López Obrador, led in voter intention polls, but beginning in May 2006 his lead narrowed.

The international community became involved early in the campaign, with groups including the NDI and WOLA conducting assessments of pre-electoral conditions and expressing concerns about the vicious campaign tactics that all sides employed. On election day numerous international observers – including 80 from the European Union, 25 organized by the US-based grassroots organization Global Exchange and 13 from the Canadian NGO Common Borders – were at the polls. In addition, the domestic election-monitoring organization Civic Alliance – one of the foremost in the region, with experience observing four federal elections and more than 50 state and local elections – conducted extensive pre-election studies of conditions for fair competition and on election day deployed 1,400 observers. The number of election-day observers was significantly smaller than in past elections, a fact that reflected both the smooth transition to a new government after the 2000 election and the credibility that the IFE had built up since 1994.

The polling process seemed to proceed smoothly, and in the early hours of the morning on the day after the election the EU delegation issued a preliminary declaration affirming that the vote had been conducted in conformity with international norms: "the presidential and parliamentary election of 2 July 2006 developed in a transparent and competitive atmosphere showing the Mexicans' firm commitment to the cause of strengthening and consolidating democracy" (Unión Europea Misión de Observación Electoral México 2006, 2006). As the vote was tallied, however, serious problems arose.

At 8 pm, when voting in Mexico's westernmost time zones ended, the IFE and the media (on orders from the IFE) did not announce the results of exit polls, as was the custom, but stated that the presidential race was too close to call. At 11 pm, when the next update was scheduled, the silence continued, raising the anxiety of citizens. Tension then rose still higher as both leading candidates began publicly to claim victory. By late in the evening on the following day, results posted by the IFE on the internet showed the PAN candidate, Felipe Calderón, in the lead by one percentage point with more than 98 per cent of the votes counted. Close examination of the results, however, revealed a serious error: 3 million votes supposedly included in that total were in fact missing (Aguayo Quezada, 2006: 2). Once this was corrected, Calderón's lead narrowed to 0.63 per cent. In subsequent days, newspapers reported that boxes of ballots and vote-tallying materials had been found in garbage dumps in Nezahualcóyotl, on the southern outskirts of Mexico City, and in the state of Veracruz (Avila Pérez, 2006).

The PRD contested the vote count in 30 per cent of the polling sites and later demanded a full recount, based on evidence of widespread fraud that was uneven at best (see Eisenstadt, 2007). Weeks passed, and the Tribunal Electoral del Poder Judicial de la Federación (TEPJF, or Electoral Tribunal of the Federal Judiciary) eventually ordered a recount of votes in polls in which there were "evident arithmetic errors" – about a third of the sites contested by the PRD (ibid.: 42). Following the recount, of 41.7 million total votes cast, Calderón received just 233,831 more than López Obrador, a margin of 0.58 per cent (Klesner, 2007: 11).

On 5 September 2006, a full two months after the election, the TEPJF declared Calderón the official winner, a resolution accepted by international observers. The domestic observer group, while it stopped short of declaring the election a failure, issued the following statement:

the closeness of the election, antecedents of electoral fraud in the collective memory ... the failures of the IFE ... and growing citizen indignation at irregularities on election day and in the district-level computation [of votes] combine to generate serious doubts about the presidential winner. Mexican society needs to have certainty about the results of the election. (Alianza Cívica, 2006)

López Obrador, however, refused to recognize the results. Throughout the dispute-resolution period his supporters staged a series of nationwide protests and shut down the centre of Mexico City with a massive, months-long encampment that began shortly after election day and lasted until Mexico's independence day, 15 September 2006, when the PRD held a parallel inauguration in the central plaza and declared López Obrador the legitimate winner. A year later López Obrador continued to maintain a website on the "Legitimate Government of Mexico" and a collective of civic associations made plans for a massive exercise in civil disobedience to be held in the capital on 15 September 2007, timed to compete with the traditional independence day address to be given by President Calderón (Méndez, 2007). This situation generated a gradual, ongoing crisis of governance.

The Mexican case resembles the Haitian, but with a twist. Despite many safeguards and an election administration agency widely regarded (at least until the 2006 débâcle) as among the most professional in the region, and despite the presence of international and domestic election observers and party representatives, the Mexican presidential election of 2006 ended in a contested outcome in which claims of fraud were not fully resolved. Unlike in Haiti, where electoral institutions are much more fragile, international observers deferred entirely to the TEPJF. Collectively, international observers represented a relatively small presence on election day, and they did not have information that could speak systematically on claims of fraud. Thus the international community, which had accompanied the electoral process throughout, did not participate in the dispute-resolution process after the election except to acknowledge the results once they were announced in September. A collective international call for a more thorough recount or a later audit of the votes might have influenced Mexican electoral institutions to take a closer look at the vote, which, in turn, might have raised citizens' confidence in the outcome of the election and averted the growing governance crisis. Given the political context, however, such an intervention would have been perceived as bias in favour of López Obrador. Instead, most international observers chose, not unreasonably, to respect the process outlined in the Mexican electoral code. The ultimate outcome, however, left considerable uncertainty about the democratic qualification of the 2006 election.

What can we learn?

Election monitoring continues to be an important means through which the Americas' democracy regime is constituted. It has become more frequent, more tightly regulated and more sophisticated. As much as election monitoring demonstrates strong regional democratic ambitions in these ways, however, it also exemplifies the limitations inherent in the regional democracy regime – particularly the inability of outside actors to guarantee electoral procedures fully in the highly competitive electoral atmosphere that marks Latin American politics today. Margins of victory in many elections are shockingly close, and the stakes are particularly high as the region finds itself at a political crossroads with the much-reported resurgence of the political left.[6] Because elections themselves are a critical political act, international election monitors find it hard to depoliticize their own role. It is difficult, and sometimes even undesirable, for observers to maintain the detached neutrality that is the linchpin of the monitoring exercise. Yet despite these challenges, the states of the region, along with NGOs and multilateral institutions, continue to see value in election observation, perhaps for lack of other regular, concerted opportunities collectively to encourage the protracted regional process of democratic consolidation.

Acknowledgements

This research was made possible by grant and fellowship support from the University of California Institute on Global Conflict and Cooperation, the Pacific Rim Research Program, the University of California Center on Mexico and the United States and the University Research Grant Program at Wayne State University.

Notes

1. For the text of this and other regional and subregional instruments on democracy see www.ohchr.org/english/law/compilation_democracy/americas.htm.
2. I use the terms "election monitoring" and "election observation" interchangeably in this chapter. Some analysts distinguish between monitoring as proactive and observation as passive activity, but I do not make these distinctions here.
3. These statistics come from a dataset compiled by the author from the primary documents of 14 international organizations about their election-monitoring activities in 24 Latin American and Caribbean states.

4. The 10 countries holding presidential elections between December 2005 and December 2006 were Bolivia, Brazil, Chile, Colombia, Costa Rica, Ecuador, Haiti, Mexico, Nicaragua and Peru. Only Brazil and Chile held elections without the presence of international monitors.
5. According to some sources, Aristide resigned; he later claimed he was forced out of office.
6. Calderón's razor-thin victory is not an isolated case. In Costa Rica, Oscar Arias won the 2006 election by an even tighter margin of 0.3 per cent; in Peru the eventual winner, Alán García, edged out the second runner-up in the first-round 2006 election by just 0.5 per cent.

REFERENCES

Aguayo Quezada, Sergio (2006) "Fraud in Mexico?", *Open Democracy*, 7 July, available at www.opendemocracy.net/democracy-protest/mexico_fraud_3716.jsp.
Alianza Cívica (2006) "Observación del Proceso Electoral Federal 2006", Alianza Cívica, July, available at www.alianzacivica.org.mx/pdfs/informeago.pdf.
Anglin, Douglas G. (1998) "International Election Monitoring: The African Experience", *African Affairs* 97(389), pp. 471–495.
Avila Pérez, Edgar (2006) "Encuentran actas electorales en basurero de Veracruz", *El Universal*, 5 July.
Boniface, Dexter S. (2002) "Is There a Democratic Norm in the Americas?", *Global Governance* 8, pp. 365–381.
——— (2007) "The OAS's Mixed Record", in T. Legler, S. F. Lean and D. S. Boniface, eds, *Promoting Democracy in the Americas*, Baltimore, MD: Johns Hopkins University Press.
Carter Center (2005) *Observing the Venezuelan Recall Referendum: Comprehensive Report*, Atlanta, GA: Carter Center Americas Program.
COFIPE (1990) "Cámara de Diputados del Congreso de la Unión, Estados Unidos Mexicanos", 15 August, revised 24 April 2006, Código Federal de Instituciones y Procedimientos Electorales, available at http://normateca.ife.org.mx/normanet/files_otros/COFIPE/cofipe.pdf.
Concannon, Brian Jr (2006) *Haiti's Election: Right Result for the Wrong Reason*, Silver City, NM: International Relations Center Americas Program.
Consejo Supremo Electoral (2006) "Reglamento de Observación Electoral: Elecciones 2006", Managua, Nicaragua, available at www.cse.gob.ni/documentos/observacion/reglamento_observacion.pdf.
Cooper, Andrew and Thomas Legler (2006) *Intervention without Intervening? The OAS Defense and Promotion of Democracy in the Americas*, New York: Palgrave.
Donnelly, Jack (1998) *International Human Rights*, Boulder, CO: Westview Press.
Eisenstadt, Todd (2007) "The Origins and Rationality of the 'Legal versus Legitimate' Dichotomy Invoked in Mexico's 2006 Post-Electoral Conflict", *PS: Political Science and Politics* (January), pp. 39–43.

Estok, Melissa, Neil Nevitte and Glenn Cowan (2002) *The Quick Count and Election Observation, An NDI Guide for Civic Organizations and Political Parties*, Washington, DC: National Democratic Institute for International Affairs.

Fawn, Rick (2006) "Battle Over the Box: International Election Observation Missions, Political Competition and Retrenchment in the Post-Soviet Space", *International Affairs* 82(6), pp. 1133–1153.

Fox, Gregory H. (2000) "The Right to Political Participation in International Law", in G. H. Fox and B. Roth, eds, *Democratic Governance and International Law*, New York: Cambridge University Press.

Franck, Thomas M. (1992) "The Emerging Right to Democratic Governance", *American Journal of International Law* 86(1), pp. 46–91.

IMMHE (2006a) "Declaration of Jean-Pierre Kingsley, Chair, on the Elections of February 7, 2006", International Mission for Monitoring Haitian Elections, available at www.mieeh-immhe.ca/media_feb0906_e.asp.

———— (2006b) "International Mission for Monitoring Haitian Elections Deploys Observers", available at www.mieeh-immhe.ca/media_feb0606_e.asp.

Ingalls, Laura (2006) "Haitians Brave Large Crowds, Delays to Vote", IFES, Washington, DC, available at www.ifes.org/features.html?title=Haitians%20Brave%20Large%20Crowds,%20Delays%20to%20Vote.

Instituto Federal Electoral (2006) "Informes presentados por Visitantes Extranjeros en el marco del Proceso Electoral Federal en Curso", IFE, Mexico City, available at www.ife.org.mx/portal/site/ife/menuitem.b9ee2c952b48c1f6eeae8860241000a0/.

International IDEA (1997) *Code of Conduct: Ethical and Professional Observation of Elections*, Stockholm: International IDEA.

———— (2000) *Guidelines for Determining Involvement in International Election Observation*, Stockholm: International IDEA.

Klesner, Joseph L. (2007) "The 2006 Mexican Election and Its Aftermath: Editor's Introduction", *PS: Political Science and Politics* (January), pp. 11–14.

Lean, Sharon F. (2007) "External Validation and Democratic Accountability", in T. Legler, S. F. Lean and D. S. Boniface, eds, *Promoting Democracy in the Americas*, Baltimore, MD: Johns Hopkins University Press.

Legler, Thomas (2007) "Venezuela, 2002–2004", in T. Legler, S. F. Lean and D. S. Boniface, eds, *Promoting Democracy in the Americas*, Baltimore, MD: Johns Hopkins University Press.

Levitt, Barry S. (2007) "Ecuador 2004–2005: Democratic Crisis Redux", in T. Legler, S. F. Lean and D. S. Boniface, eds, *Promoting Democracy in the Americas*, Baltimore, MD: Johns Hopkins University Press.

Méndez, Enrique (2007) "Convoca ONG al 'Grito de los Libres' el 15 de septiembre", *La Jornada*, 23 July.

Muñoz, Heraldo and Mary D'Leon (1998) "The Right to Democracy in the Americas", *Journal of Interamerican Studies and World Affairs* 40(1), pp. 1–18.

National Endowment for Democracy (2007) "Grants: 2005 Latin America and the Caribbean Program Descriptions", NED, Washington, DC, available at www.ned.org/grants/05programs/grants-lac05.html.

NDI (2007) "Latin America and the Caribbean: Haiti", National Democratic Institute for International Affairs, Washington, DC, available at www.ndi.org/worldwide/lac/haiti/haiti.asp.

Norris, Robert and Patrick Merloe (2002) *Media Monitoring to Promote Democratic Elections, An NDI Handbook for Citizen Organizations*, Washington, DC: National Democratic Institute for International Affairs.

Pastor, Robert A. (1999) "The Third Dimension of Accountability: The International Community in National Elections", in A. Schedler, L. Diamond and M. Plattner, eds, *The Self-Restraining State: Power and Accountability in New Democracies*, Boulder, CO: Lynne Rienner.

Risse-Kappan, Thomas (1995) "Bringing Transnational Relations Back In: Introduction", in T. Risse-Kappan, ed., *Bringing Transnational Relations Back In: Non-State Actors, Domestic Structures and International Institutions*, Cambridge: Cambridge University Press.

Roth, Brad R. (2000) "The Illegality of 'Pro-Democratic' Invasion Pacts", in G. Fox and B. Roth, eds, *Democratic Governance and International Law*, Cambridge: Cambridge University Press.

Santa-Cruz, Arturo (2004) "Redefining Sovereignty, Consolidating a Network: Monitoring the 1990 Nicaraguan Elections", *Revista de Ciencia Política* 24(1), pp. 189–208.

——— (2005a) "Constitutional Structures, Sovereignty, and the Emergence of Norms: The Case of International Election Monitoring", *International Organization* 59 (Summer), pp. 663–693.

——— (2005b) *International Election Monitoring, Sovereignty and the Western Hemisphere: The Emergence of an International Norm*, London: Routledge.

Schnably, Stephen (2000) "Constitutionalism and Democratic Government in the Inter-American System", in G. Fox and B. Roth, eds, *Democratic Governance and International Law*, Cambridge: Cambridge University Press.

Thompson, Ginger (2006) "A Deal Is Reached to Name a Victor in Haiti's Election", *New York Times*, 16 February.

Unión Europea Misión de Observación Electoral Mexico 2006 (2006) "Declaración Preliminar", Mexico City, 3 July, available at www.ife.org.mx/portal/site/ife/menuitem.b9ee2c952b48c1f6eeae8860241000a0/.

Union Européenne Mission d'Observation Electorale Haiti (2006) "Elections présidentielle et législatives, premier tour de scrutin du 7 février 2006, Déclaration Préliminaire", Port-au-Prince, available at http://ec.europa.eu/external_relations/human_rights/eu_election_ass_observ/haiti/declar_prelim_final_070206.pdf.

Van Cranenburgh, Oda (2000) "Democratization in Africa: The Role of Election Observation", in J. Abbink and G. Hessling, eds, *Election Observation and Democratization in Africa*, New York: St Martin's Press.

Part IV
Pivotal case studies

11

The Chávez effect

Thomas Legler

The foreign policy antics of Venezuelan President Hugo Chávez have appeared with considerable frequency and high visibility in the international media. His confrontational style has included referring to former US President George W. Bush as the devil, insulting the secretary-general of the Organization of American States (OAS), José Miguel Insulza, with one of the worst expletives in the Spanish language and labelling the Chilean Senate a bunch of fascists. Cultivating a "Robin Hood" image (with President Bush surely as the evil Sheriff of Nottingham), Chávez has delivered heating oil to poor communities in Brooklyn, Harlem and New Orleans. His foreign policy priorities have included constructing an anti-US alliance, shutting the United States out of Latin America, forging a regional integration arrangement called the Bolivarian Alternative for the Americas (ALBA)[1] and promoting the export of his "Bolivarian Revolution" (sometimes referred to as "socialism for the twenty-first century") with the help of ample oil export earnings. By June 2007, in pursuit of his foreign policy objectives, Chávez had made some 225 visits abroad and invested an estimated US$5.5 billion in his "petro-diplomacy" (Zerpa, 2007).

Does this flurry of Venezuelan foreign policy activism translate into an important impact on hemispheric politics in the Americas? What is the Chávez effect on the region? One of the challenges in answering this important question is overcoming US-centrism. Much of the existing focus in the literature is on the problematic Venezuelan-US bilateral relationship (Duarte Villa, 2004; Romero, 2004, 2006b; Shifter, 2007). Similarly,

Which way Latin America? Hemispheric politics meets globalization, Cooper and Heine, eds, United Nations University Press, 2009, ISBN 978-92-808-1172-8

often where regional dynamics are considered, Venezuela is incorporated in the analysis through the lens of US-Latin American relations (Hakim, 2006; Lowenthal, 2006; Roett, 2006; Shifter and Jawahar, 2006). The foreign relations of the United States with Venezuela and Latin America are certainly an integral, but not an all-defining, component of a broader understanding of hemispheric politics.

In this chapter I assess the Hugo Chávez effect on the Americas through a more holistic, hemisphere-centric perspective. I divide my analysis of hemispheric politics into three interconnected spheres: geopolitics, regional political economy and the realm of regional ideas and norms. On this basis, I argue that Chávez has indeed had a profound impact on the hemisphere, although not necessarily in forms that he intended or desired. We are presently witnessing a tectonic shift in hemispheric politics, in no small part thanks to the Chávez effect.

A revolutionary foreign policy?

Amid the novelty of the Chávez revolutionary project, it is easy to lose sight of important historical continuities in Venezuelan foreign policy (Duarte Villa, 2004; González Urrutia, 2006; Romero, 2006a). First, Chávez's international activism is nothing new in an important sense: Venezuelan governments have long promoted principled, activist foreign policy agendas. Going right back to the country's beginnings, independence hero Simón Bolivar first championed regional independence from Spain, and then Gran Colombia, the pan-American idea of a united South America. Following Venezuela's transition to democracy via the Pacto de Punto Fijo in 1958, President Rómulo Betancourt became a staunch advocate of representative democracy in the inter-American system, lending his name to a doctrine that called for the withdrawal of diplomatic recognition from any government that came to power by undemocratic means. In the 1980s Venezuela participated actively as a member of the Contadora Group in the effort to find a peaceful resolution to the Central American crises.

Second, three key features determining Venezuela's foreign relations and its identity on the international scene are oil, democracy and the bilateral relationship with the United States (Romero, 2006a: 98). Venezuela's impressive oil export earnings have propelled various episodes of internationalism. Together with oil, successive Venezuelan governments have also sought to export their country's brand of democracy: until 1998 representative democracy, and now participatory democracy under Chávez.[2] Finally, despite periodic flirtations with diversifying Venezuela's external ties, the country's commercial (oil), political and security relations with the United States have always assumed a determining role in its foreign policy.

Third, Venezuelan governments have invariably encountered a challenge in sustaining their principled, activist foreign policy agendas. Venezuelan presidents and political élites have long held regional-power ambitions and self-perceptions but with middle-power limitations. The limited size of Venezuela's economy, the ups and downs of its oil exports and recurring political problems on the home front have all made it difficult for Venezuela to promote continuity in its international activism. Until recently, the single-term limit for presidents was also an impediment.

Nevertheless, foreign policy under Chávez is a dramatic departure from that of his predecessors. A crucial beginning point is the replacement of the 1961 constitution and the enshrinement of the country's new foreign policy principles in articles 152 and 153 of the new 1999 "Bolivarian" constitution: independence, equality of states, self-determination, non-intervention, the pacific resolution of international conflicts, international cooperation, respect for human rights, solidarity with peoples in their struggle for emancipation, human well-being and Latin American and Caribbean integration (Gobierno Bolivariano de Venezuela, 1999).[3]

Of the three traditional fixtures of Venezuelan foreign policy, Chávez has transformed two. Once a staunch advocate of representative democracy, Venezuela has become a vocal opponent, pursuing instead a participatory alternative, while its traditional friendly and accommodative relations with the United States have been replaced by the politics of confrontation and a rabid anti-Americanism. Venezuela's foreign service has also felt elements of the country's social revolution. Mirroring Chávez's termination of the old Punto Fijo political system and his appropriation of the state bureaucracy and oil monopoly from incumbent *puntofijista* élites,[4] he has attacked the traditional corps of professional diplomats in the Ministry of External Relations and progressively replaced them with partisan recruits.[5] He is undertaking a process of the "ideologization" of the foreign service that offers revolutionary indoctrination as a staple of the training of new diplomats (González Urrutia, 2006: 165; Romero, 2006a: 102).[6]

Just as Venezuela's domestic social revolution has carried over into its diplomatic corps, Chávez's own neopopulist governing style has been projected into the country's foreign policy. Populism is a confrontational style of politics and discourse characterized by a strong anti-establishment bent, with an "us versus them" political dynamic that pits the underprivileged and exploited masses against their oppressors, the powerful élite establishment.[7] In classical populist discourse, the "us" was commonly referred to as "*el pueblo*" and "them" as "the oligarchy". While peppering his statements with classic terminology, Chávez has updated the discourse with his own contributions: *el pueblo* is also now referred to as "*el soberano*" or the "sovereign people". Government departments are also now called "ministries of the popular power". Another defining trait of populism is the charismatic leader who presents himself as one of the people and their champion against the unjust forces that hold them down.

While contemporary neopopulism in Venezuela often shares a common discourse with classical populism, it has its own distinct features. Neopopulism represents not just an attack on the oligarchy but on the entire "political class". Not only is the oligarchy perceived as rotten to the core, but so is the complete political system. Neopopulism aims to discredit existing political and social institutions, including political parties, unions and other civil society organizations. It is not just anti-establishment but anti-system. In tearing down or circumventing the existing political and social institutions of the Punto Fijo political system, the Chávez government has sought to establish direct, unmediated and highly visible links between the executive and the masses at the grass-roots level. Neopopulism's constituency is also different: it focuses not so much on the organized urban and rural poor but on the very poorest and previously least organized, such as urban slum dwellers and the landless rural poor.

Chávez's brand of neopopulism is divisive, polarizing, intolerant and anti-plural. Born of class, ethnic and racial conflict, it promotes continued conflict. The "us versus them"/people versus the oligarchy logic translates into citizens being forced to choose sides and declare their loyalty either for or against the populist leader and his movement, which can also feed perceptions of a zero-sum conflict where one side's gains are the other's losses.

No doubt a product of his own military training, Chávez has likened his run-ins with the opposition to "battles". In the 1859 Battle of Santa Inés, Federalists defeated the oligarchic Conservatives to win a civil war. In his struggle with the opposition, Chávez referred to the 2004 recall referendum as the "Second" Battle of Santa Inés – the battle analogy, with its clear victor and loser, evidently meant his intention to defeat the opposition, with no interest in national dialogue or reconciliation.

As an aggressive political style, neopopulism in Venezuela has systematically eroded any middle or autonomous ground in society, and with it pluralism. *Chavismo* has resulted in the systematic weakening of public spaces for dialogue and debate as well as channels of communication in society and politics, including the grassroots, the media and the legislature.

The neopopulist logic in Chávez's domestic agenda is also apparent in his foreign policy, where examples of his confrontational style abound.[8]

Chávez has cultivated friendly ties with international pariahs Saddam Hussein, Muammar al-Qaddafi and Mahmoud Ahmadinejad. He severely criticized the US invasion of Afghanistan and, as mentioned above, he has publicly insulted world leaders, including George W. Bush, Tony Blair, Vicente Fox and José Miguel Insulza.

In Venezuela's foreign relations, the "imperialist" United States plays the equivalent role of the oligarchy on the home front. Not surprisingly, under *chavismo* the United States and US multinational corporations become the allies of Venezuela's corrupt and self-serving oligarchy. On the international scale, Chávez is the champion not only of *el pueblo* in Venezuela but of all oppressed and downtrodden peoples in the Americas. Just as he brought down the Punto Fijo system domestically, Chávez seeks to emasculate the US-dominated inter-American system. Consistent with the domestic neopopulist logic, Chávez's international politics are intentionally conflict-oriented, in an attempt to oblige parties to choose sides. In the same way that Chávez portrays his conflicts with domestic opposition as battles, his national security strategy is anchored in the notion of "asymmetric war". On both home and foreign fronts, the Chávez government is preparing the country for what is perceived as an inevitable clash with the United States. Just as the politics of division along the *pueblo*–oligarchy divide work effectively as a mobilizing resource in a national context, so a distinctive tool of neopopulist foreign policy is "negative power": drawing on widespread anti-American sentiments to drive its international agenda successfully (Romero, 2006a).

The Chávez impact on geopolitics

Consistent with its foreign policy objectives, the Chávez government has contributed to pushing the Americas in an evolving multipolar direction. With impressive oil export earnings at its disposal, Venezuela has established itself as a rival pole of influence in the region. In energy cooperation alone, it currently disburses throughout the region assistance worth approximately US$1.6 billion, rivalling US foreign aid. Estimates vary regarding Venezuela's direct investment abroad in commercial credits, loans, debt purchases, donations, petroleum financing and stock purchases. However, a conservative estimate by Associated Press put Venezuela's petro-diplomacy expenditures abroad at an impressive US$5.5 billion (Zerpa, 2007).[9]

Venezuela cannot, however, take full credit for this trend. Simultaneously, the semblance of multipolarity in the region has been fed by other recent developments. For example, China has expanded its investment and commercial relations with Latin American and Caribbean countries dramatically in recent years. The European Union has also become an important trading partner in the region. Brazil, under Fernando Henrique Cardoso and now Luiz Inácio Lula da Silva, has asserted a stronger regional leadership role. The growing influence of these parties is owed in no small part to the US government's relative policy neglect towards the Americas as its attention has been distracted by wars in Iraq and on terrorism.

At the same time, Venezuela has managed to increase its autonomy and reduce its reliance on the United States. Its oil exports to China, for instance, increased dramatically during the 2004–2006 period from 12,300 to 150,000 barrels per day, with expectations of an additional increase to 500,000 barrels within five years (Shifter, 2007: 21), while China is increasing its capacity to refine Venezuela's heavy crude oil. Venezuela's state oil monopoly, PDVSA, has also been negotiating with India's Oil and Natural Gas Corporation to create a joint venture and construct a refinery in India for Venezuelan heavy crude. It is quite feasible that, in the not-too-distant future, given the rising demand by the dynamic economies of China and India and their enhanced capacity to refine lower-grade petroleum, Venezuela may no longer need to rely on the United States as a market for its oil exports (ibid.). Moreover, Venezuela now purchases arms from China, Russia, Brazil and Spain, rather than from the United States.

Despite a general downturn in US-Latin American relations and widespread anti-American and anti-Bush popular sentiments, however, Venezuela has met only mixed success in attempting to forge an anti-US regional alliance. Thus far, its advocacy of an alternative regional collective security arrangement without US participation has received little support. It counts on strong support from Cuba and, to a lesser extent, Bolivia and Ecuador, but most Latin American and Caribbean governments have chosen to avoid ideological extremes and a confrontation with the United States and to keep their options open (Romero, 2006a; Shifter, 2007). The Caribbean island states are illustrative. Although in June 2005 14 of them officially joined the Petrocaribe oil alliance, in which they enjoy access to generously subsidized Venezuelan oil, they have been reticent (with the exception of Cuba) to support Chávez's ALBA integration initiative. They also have not halted their ongoing collective pursuit of a more privileged trade and investment relationship with the United States (Burges, 2007; Sanders, 2007; Serbín, 2006).

Similarly, there is a myth held by many about Chávez's influence in the Caribbean, whereby he supposedly used the promise of subsidized oil to assemble a Caribbean voting bloc vote in favour of the successful candidacy of José Miguel Insulza, a Chilean, as secretary-general of the OAS against the US-backed Mexican candidate, Luis Ernesto Derbez. The truth, however, had more to do with the fact that Insulza and his supporters agreed to back a Caribbean Community (CARICOM) candidate, the Surinamese Albert R. Ramdin, as assistant secretary-general of the OAS.

Despite close cooperation with Venezuela on some issues, Brazil has also chosen to keep cordial bilateral links with Washington. In March 2007, ignoring Chávez's protests, Brazil signed a bilateral energy cooperation agreement with the United States for ethanol research and production. Uruguay, too – though an alleged staunch supporter of Chávez and having signed 78 cooperation agreements with Venezuela (Ríos, 2007) – negotiated a trade and investment agreement with the United States in early 2007 (Shifter, 2007: 23).

What the Chávez phenomenon and loose regional multipolarity have meant for many Latin American and Caribbean governments is the chance to diversify their external political and economic relations from a traditionally heavy or even exclusive reliance on bilateral ties with the United States. Given their age-old developmental obstacle of a persistent capital bottleneck, increasing economic activity by Venezuela, Brazil, China and the European Union has given these countries a welcome opportunity to pursue commercial and investment ties with a variety of different partners. Chávez has helped these countries to increase their autonomy, but not necessarily in the anti-US direction he would like.

In regional multilateral forums, Chávez has scored some important successes in his anti-US campaign. In the OAS – which has internalized the US–Venezuela conflict and found itself largely powerless to stop Chávez's provocative acts – he has sought to provoke tensions between the United States and Latin American and Caribbean member states. Chávez has also brought to a halt US-supported efforts to strengthen the Inter-American Democratic Charter (IADC) and the inter-American collective defence-of-democracy regime. At the OAS General Assembly in Fort Lauderdale, Florida, in June 2005 the Venezuelan government led the successful resistance to a US proposal to create an OAS mechanism for monitoring countries' compliance with the IADC (see Legler, 2007a). During the 2006 Peruvian electoral campaign, Chávez repeatedly intervened in that country's internal affairs to support presidential candidate Ollanta Humala and criticize his opponent, Alan García, harshly, without any significant response by the OAS secretary-general or Permanent Council. In Venezuela itself, the Chávez government and the Consejo Nacional Electoral (CNE, or National Electoral Council) did a masterful job of emasculating the OAS electoral observation mission to the December 2006 presidential election by forbidding it to invite observers with prior experience in Venezuelan electoral processes, strongly discouraging the invitation of Canadian and US observers and extending an invitation to the mission itself so late that it began its operations barely five weeks prior to election day. Then, in May 2007, Venezuela success-fully crafted an anti-terrorism declaration by the OAS Permanent Council aimed at the United States. The declaration was a thinly veiled allusion to an earlier controversy in which Venezuela accused the US government of harbouring a fugitive named Luis Posada Carriles who was wanted for acts of terrorism against Cuba.

Finally, apart from a single critical statement by Secretary-General Insulza concerning Chávez's refusal to renew the broadcast licence of the opposition media corporation RCTV in May 2007,[10] the OAS has failed to respond to what is arguably a serious case of authoritarian back-sliding.[11] In June 2007 US Secretary of State Condoleeza Rice made a personal appeal at the OAS General Assembly in Panama for the organization to send Secretary-General Insulza on a special mission to Venezuela to investigate the RCTV closure, but her appeal failed to galvanize action. The Venezuelan Foreign Minister Nicolás Maduro cleverly countered by insisting that the OAS investigate US human rights abuses at the military prison in Guantánamo Bay and along the US-Mexican border.

In addition to contributing to the current weak state of the OAS, Chávez has helped strengthen other multilateral forums where US membership is noticeably absent. In 2004 Venezuela enthusiastically supported Brazil and Peru in the creation of the 12-member South American Community of Nations (now called the Union of South American Nations, or UNASUR), which plans to combine the Andean Community of Nations and Mercosur in a single South American political coordination and economic integration scheme (see South American Community of Nations, 2004). UNASUR will have a permanent secretariat located in Quito, Ecuador. In April 2007 it sponsored the first South American Energy Summit at Isla Margarita, Venezuela, intentionally without US attendance. These groupings join various other existing "US-free" regional multilateral organizations, including the Rio Group and the Ibero-American Summits.

South American and hemispheric solidarity, nonetheless, has had its share of ups and downs as a result of Chávez's frequent run-ins with his neighbours. Indeed, the complexity of bilateral and multilateral relations in the hemisphere prevents any easy conclusion about the overall direction of hemispheric geopolitics. Venezuela's bilateral relationship with Brazil is a case in point. Although the two countries generally enjoy friendly relations, with a certain degree of ideological affinity between their two leaders, there has been tension as well as coincidence in their interests. The defeat of the Free Trade Area of the Americas and the construction of UNASUR are examples of cooperation between the two countries, while Venezuela's state oil monopoly PDVSA and Brazil's Petrobras have made a joint investment in the construction of the Abreu

Lima refinery in Pernambuco, Brazil. At the same time, however, the two countries' interests have clashed over the energy sector in Bolivia. Brazil also has little interest in Venezuela's ALBA scheme, and its initial reactions to Chávez's proposals for a South American development bank (Banco del Sur) and a South American OPEC-style cartel of gas-exporting countries have been lukewarm. The very real possibility exists that a mutually perceived regional-power rivalry will affect potential future cooperation between the two countries. Finally, Brazil's own vision of regional economic integration contrasts with that of Venezuela in foreseeing a continued crucial role for the business sector and private markets (Burges, 2007).

Tensions also exist between Chávez and a number of other Latin American and Caribbean countries. At the January 2004 Summit of the Americas in Monterrey, Mexico, Chávez offended the Chilean government with a public statement of support for Bolivian access to the sea. In April 2007 he again offended Chile by referring to its Senate as fascists after it had issued a statement critical of his closure of RCTV. Ecuador – which Chávez considers an important ally under its new President Rafael Correa – angered him by a recent decision to enter into an ethanol cooperation scheme with Brazil that is linked to the United States. Bilateral relations with Colombia have been tested by Venezuela's alleged support for anti-government guerrilla forces. Peru's relations with Venezuela have been strained by Chávez's sheltering of former security chief Vladimiro Montesinos in 2000 and 2001 and by his interference in Peru's 2006 presidential election in opposition to the eventual winner, García. In the Caribbean, both Barbados and Trinidad and Tobago opposed Venezuela's new Petrocaribe scheme, while Guyana was reluctant to rely too heavily on the scheme given its own ongoing border dispute with Venezuela. In sum, Chávez must contend with a sizeable number of problematic bilateral relationships in his efforts to advance his geopolitical agenda.

Finally, Chávez's aims at a global reach for Venezuelan influence have been stymied, at least momentarily. Although he has expanded markets for Venezuelan oil internationally and cultivated an anti-US international network of close ties outside the Americas with such countries as China, Iran, Russia, Belarus, Syria and Viet Nam, he failed in his 2006 bid to win a seat in the UN Security Council. In what was clearly an intentional confrontation with the United States, neither the US-supported candidate, Guatemala, nor Venezuela could garner adequate backing for the seat. Chávez hurt the Venezuelan cause with his offensive remarks at the United Nations against George W. Bush in September 2006, as well as his controversial support of Iran's nuclear programme. In the end, in November 2006 Latin American and Caribbean countries threw their support behind the compromise candidacy of Panama, a country more in the US camp (Gratius, 2006).

The Chávez impact on the regional political economy

In the domain of regional political economy, the Chávez government appears to have twin objectives: to redefine the terms of the insertion of Venezuela and the hemisphere (minus the United States and Canada) into the global capitalist economy, and to do so at the cost of the US government and US business interests. From a scan of Venezuela's foreign policy activism, it is advancing these dual goals on several fronts.

First, Chávez has promoted the increased retention by the producer countries of the global South of the rents from the commercial exploitation of natural resources. On the home front he has done this very effectively by a process of renewed nationalization of the energy sector, which has reduced multinational corporations to minority ownership in joint production arrangements called *empresas de capital mixtas* (mixed capital enterprises) (Romero, 2006a: 189) with the Venezuelan government, and increased their corporate taxes. On the international plane, Chávez has aggressively and successfully promoted a policy within the Organization of Petroleum Exporting Countries (OPEC) to increase international prices for oil. In September 2000 Venezuela hosted the Second Summit of Heads of State and Government of OPEC Member Countries, and pushed for greater unity, coordination and the revamping of OPEC (Valero, 2006). The disruption of Venezuelan oil production for 60 days during the opposition-organized general strike in December 2002 and January 2003 and widespread international perceptions of political instability in Venezuela during the 2002–2004 period played into Chávez's hands. His periodic radical pronouncements have also stirred nervous international markets: from less than US$10 a barrel in 1999, the world price for oil rose at one point to US$75 a barrel before settling into a highly profitable range of US$55–60 a barrel (Shifter, 2007: 17).

Second, Chávez has striven to defeat US-promoted integration schemes in the region. Venezuela was part of a successful effort involving Brazil, Argentina, Paraguay and Uruguay at the Summit of the Americas in Mar del Plata, Argentina, in November 2005 to bury the US-led Free Trade Area of the Americas (FTAA) initiative. Nonetheless, although the FTAA was defeated, the rest of the 34 member states present at the summit opted not to join the five dissenting countries, and the United States has successfully continued to sponsor trade and investment agreements in the Americas, including recently signed free trade deals with Peru and Colombia and a new trade and investment framework agreement with Uruguay. In 2004 the United States signed a free trade agreement with the Dominican Republic and Central American countries (CAFTA), and the Caribbean Basin Initiative continues to link CARICOM countries with the United States. Thus, although Chávez has thwarted some US hemispheric initiatives, a US-centric "spaghetti bowl" (Bhagwati, 1995) of bilateral and multilateral free trade agreements in the hemisphere persists.

Third, Chávez has sought to substitute US-led hemispheric integration with his own Bolivarian schemes. A prime objective has been regional energy integration, with an important human and social development component and a view to limiting US and Western ownership, investment and economic control, and reducing Venezuela's reliance on the US market (Morsbach, 2006). To date, Chávez's efforts have created three subregional, oil-based state enterprises under the overall rubric of PetroAmérica: Petrocaribe (the Caribbean), Petrosur (the Southern Cone) and Petro Andina (the Andean region). Through joint public enterprises, Venezuela is constructing new refineries in Brazil and Nicaragua, improving refining capacity in Argentina, Uruguay and Paraguay (*Latin American Weekly Report*, 2007b; Valero, 2006) and has additional petroleum-based agreements with Colombia and Ecuador. (It is noteworthy that, prior to the Chávez government, Venezuela exported little or no oil to its South American and Caribbean neighbours.) There has also been growing cooperation in natural gas. Colombia and Venezuela have a bilateral agreement to construct a gas pipeline that will eventually extend to Central America. Venezuela has also proposed the construction of a US$20 billion, 9,000-kilometre pan–South American gas pipeline that will connect it with Brazil, Bolivia and Argentina (Sánchez, 2007). Additionally, in April 2007 Chávez announced another new initiative: the creation of an OPEC-style South American gas producers' cartel, the Organización de Países Exportadores de Gas de Suramérica (OPEGAS SUR).

Nonetheless, energy-based integration has its down side. Chile, Peru and Mexico remain outside Chávez's energy schemes, while Brazil and Colombia are not enthusiastic about the proposal for a South American gas producers' cartel. Moreover, critics have cast doubts on the feasibility and environmental costs of Chávez's proposed South American pipeline, while Brazil continues to conduct technical studies on the initiative. Critics have also questioned the gas cartel, which might actually hurt South American consumers since so little gas is exported outside the region (*AFX International Focus*, 2007). In addition, Chávez's own formal hemispheric integration initiative, ALBA, has not garnered widespread regional support: thus far, only Bolivia, Cuba and Nicaragua have enthusiastically backed it, while several members of the Organization of Eastern Caribbean States – Antigua and Barbuda, Dominica and St Vincent and the Grenadines – signed memoranda of understanding with Venezuela in February 2007. Haiti's President René Préval and Ecuador's foreign minister attended the inaugural ALBA summit in Venezuela in April 2007 as observers; although, in a pragmatic move, Préval also subsequently paid a formal visit to President George W. Bush in Washington. Despite close cooperation with Chávez on other issues, Argentina's President Cristina Fernández de Kirchner has not yet given any clear indication that she wishes to join ALBA.

Finally, Chávez's Bolivarian regional integration has also recently pushed for a dramatic transformation of international finance away from US- and Western-dominated international financial institutions, with impressive success. Chávez began by repaying Venezuela's debts to both the International Monetary Fund (IMF) and the World Bank – in the latter case, in the amount of US$8 billion (Andean Group Report, 2007). In January 2006 the Venezuelan government purchased some US$2.5 billion in Argentine government bonds to help that country repay its US$9.5 billion debt to the IMF (Swann, 2007). Coincidentally, shortly beforehand the Brazilian government had announced that it was paying back its own US$15 billion debt to the IMF. Importantly, with these debt repayments the IMF lost its supervisory role in these countries' economic policy-making (*Latinnews Daily*, 2006). In April 2007 Chávez announced that Venezuela would withdraw completely from the IMF, the World Bank and the latter's International Center for Settlement of Investment Disputes. As a result, IMF lending to Latin America fell from 80 per cent of its global portfolio to just 1 per cent, or US$50 million, by early 2007 (Swann, 2007).

In place of – or at least in competition with – the IMF, the World Bank and the Inter-American Development Bank, in March 2007 Chávez announced the creation of a Banco del Sur (Bank of the South). The bank will have initial capital of US$7 billion and an underpinning commitment to social justice and regional integration. So far Argentina, Bolivia, Ecuador, Nicaragua and Paraguay have supported the initiative. After initial reluctance, Brazil also agreed to join (EIU Viewswire, 2007; Lapper, 2007). In June 2007 Chávez launched another financial institution, the ALBA Bank, for the four members of ALBA. If Banco del Sur and ALBA Bank do not replace existing international financial institutions in the region outright, they will certainly help democratize international finance in the region and provide debtors with alternative sources of funding in a context of increased competition for their business.

The Chávez impact on regional ideas and norms

Hugo Chávez has had varied effects in the realm of regional ideas and norms. His biggest ideas have had the least resonance in hemispheric politics. Apart perhaps from influence on Evo Morales's political project in Bolivia, he has not been able readily to export his Bolivarian Revolution.[12] The left in the Americas, despite its recent resurgence, is complex, heterogeneous, often divided and not always in accord with Chávez's own predilections (see Castañeda and Morales in this volume; Castañeda, 2006; Schamis, 2006). Looked at another way, despite a resurgence of anti-American sentiment across the region, much of the leftward trend is moderate, pragmatic and anti-radical. Indeed, in 2006 real or perceived linkages with Chávez proved costly liabilities for leftist candidates Ollanta Humala and Manuel López Obrador in presidential elections in Peru and Mexico, respectively. Chávez's proposal for an OAS Social Charter, with a focus on promoting participatory democracy and social justice to augment or even supersede the IADC, has made little real progress in negotiations.

Despite the extensive international media coverage that Chávez and his Bolivarian project receive, a September 2006 Gallup regional survey (Ríos, 2006) found that, among Latin Americans, Chávez fared little better in terms of his leadership approval rating (27 per cent) than did George W. Bush (26 per cent); furthermore, 30 per cent disapproved of Chávez's leadership, while 43 per cent disapproved of Bush's (ibid.). Similarly, renowned Latinobarómetro pollster Marta Lagos (2006: 95) found that 36 per cent of a survey of 20,000 Latin Americans did not even know who Chávez was, and of those who did know, only 41 per cent (or 26 per cent of the total) evaluated him positively. According to Lagos, more respondents in the survey approved of Bush's leadership (ibid.: 96–98).

Even though Chávez's main ideas have not taken hold, his project has unleashed substantial ideational and normative competition and tension. For instance, he has contributed strongly to the undermining of the regional hegemony of the twin public policy projects of the Washington Consensus and representative democracy. Although market-friendly policies persist throughout the region, Chávez has revived and demonstrated the viability of interventionist economic policies many thought long dead (and impossible to revive). The Venezuelan government has successfully nationalized most of the country's energy sector and, more recently, its electrical and telecommunications companies. Bolivia has followed suit in its energy sector.

The ideological extremes of the Washington Consensus economic policies and Chávez's "socialism for the twenty-first century", as well as the present polarization and confrontation between Washington and Caracas, have prompted other parties to propose a more moderate, pragmatic, less confrontational and social-democratic but more business-friendly third path. At the World Economic Forum on Latin America in Santiago, Chile, in April 2007, Presidents Lula of Brazil and Michelle Bachelet of Chile presented precisely such an alternative, which they have called the Santiago Consensus. Accordingly, we are now witnessing a very healthy three-way competition about ideas that will shape future regional economic policy preferences (see *Latin American Weekly Report*, 2007a).

Chávez has also consistently criticized the representative form of democracy promoted in the inter-American system. He has correctly drawn attention to the élitist, exclusionary nature of many contemporary democracies in the region and the persistence of poverty and inequality as impediments to political participation. He has also contributed an important innovation to democratic accountability practices in the form of the hemisphere's first constitutional recall referendum mechanism.

At the same time there is no shortage of domestic and international critics who accuse Chávez of authoritarian backsliding (see, for example, Corrales, 2006; Legler, 2007b; Shifter, 2006, 2007). Chávez and his loyal supporters, of course, claim they are engaged in a genuine experiment in participatory democracy. While Chávez's vertical accountability is quite solid, through a series of landslide presidential election and recall referendum victories dating back to 1998, he has eroded horizontal accountability in an alarming fashion. He has stacked the judiciary with loyalists, enjoys a 100 per cent majority in Congress and controls the CNE. Additionally, in January 2007 the Congress he controls passed a law authorizing him to rule by decree for the next 18 months. In May 2007, on the grounds of complicity in the April 2002 coup attempt against him, he closed down RCTV, one of two remaining opposition-owned media enterprises in the country, and appropriated its equipment. He also threatened legal sanctions against the surviving company, Globovisión. In June 2007 he successfully thwarted the US government's attempt to convince the OAS General Assembly in Panama to invoke the IADC to respond to his closure of RCTV.

In the context of strained US-Latin American relations, Chávez, playing on mounting Latin American distrust of US intentions, has effectively neutralized the once-promising OAS collective defence-of-democracy regime.[13] Although the current problematic state of regional geopolitics largely explains this current impasse in OAS democracy-promotion efforts, it has come at a cost. Chávez has helped resurrect a more traditional, absolute understanding of sovereignty at the expense of newer defence-of-democracy and human rights norms. Until recently it seemed as if sovereignty had been "democratically conditionalized" (Farer, 1996;

Van Klaveren, 2001): through such legal instruments as the Washington Protocol (1992), the Quebec Declaration (2001) and the IADC (2001), representative democracy had become a criterion of membership in the OAS and the inter-American system. The democratic conditionalizing of sovereignty was supposed to mean in practice that authoritarian or undemocratic national leaders could not hide behind the shield of sovereignty and that OAS member states held a collective obligation, as stated in article 1 of the IADC, to intervene to defend democracy.

Chávez has indeed successfully invoked sovereignty against attempts to organize pro-democracy intervention, with the endorsement of most Latin American and Caribbean member states. In part this has happened because of widespread suspicion that the United States was more interested in terminating Chávez's leadership than in defending democracy. No doubt the self-interest of member states has also played a role, to prevent the strengthening of interventionist prerogatives that one day could be turned on them. Also, although evidence is by no means clear, one would need to explore whether Venezuelan petro-diplomacy is helping to purchase increased member state pragmatism on the issue of enforcing compliance with the OAS Charter and the IADC. Theoretically, the decline of the OAS collective defence-of-democracy regime illustrates that regional democracy promotion and human rights norms are not unilinear in their evolution but are actually subject to reversal. In hemispheric affairs, the *de facto* erosion of democracy in Venezuela indicates that many governments are prepared to accept a return to earlier times, when regime type (democracy or authoritarianism) mattered little for international recognition.

It is fascinating that Chávez has not only brought sovereignty norms back into fashion; he has also helped reshape their meaning and added some clever innovations. Sovereignty, in Chávez's praxis, refers explicitly to self-determination, non-intervention and territorial inviolability *vis-à-vis* intervention by the United States or its perceived intergovernmental instruments, such as the IMF or the OAS. At the same time, Chávez has intervened repeatedly in the internal affairs of other states in the hemisphere – for example, by supporting electoral candidates in Bolivia in 2005 and Peru in 2006, and by distributing heating oil to poor people in the United States. The Chávez twist, however, is that these are not violations of sovereignty but legitimate examples of *solidarity* with oppressed peoples and their representatives. For the moment, he continues to get away with these forms of intervention/solidarity with seeming impunity.

Finally, Chávez has left an innovative mark on regional multilateralism and diplomacy. In terms of the former, the coincidence of interests between Venezuela and Brazil has helped promote a proliferation of new, viable forms of "US-free" subregional multilateralism – including the Union of South American Nations (UNASUR), ALBA, ALBA Bank, the South American Energy Summit and Banco del Sur – in addition to existing ones such as Mercosur and the Ibero-American Summits. With the support of ample energy resources (oil and natural gas) and large regional markets, these multilateral groupings may well prove their ability to function successfully without the United States.

Chávez has also given an important new impulse to complex multilateralism.[14] ALBA is becoming not only an intergovernmental grouping but also a transnational one. At the fifth ALBA summit in Barquisimeto, Venezuela, in May 2007, the member states established a new ALBA institutional architecture that includes a social movement council. In addition to the government representatives on hand, representatives from the Communist Parties of Chile and Cuba, the Salvadoran Frente Farabundo Martí para la Liberación Nacional, the Brazilian Landless Workers Movement and other social organizations were present. Civil society groups will participate in the elaboration of ALBA's charter of principles (Márquez, 2007).

Chávez has also shown himself a master of public diplomacy. In effect, his style of public diplomacy represents the "transnationalization" of neopopulism outside Venezuelan confines. He has extended the populist characteristic of direct, unmediated links between the populist leader and his mass following abroad. He has a habit while on foreign trips of making opportunistic, crowd-pleasing public appearances; in March 2007, for example, his appearance at a soccer stadium in Buenos Aires was timed to coincide with President George W. Bush's official Latin American tour. To extend his personal reach even further, Chávez created the public television station Telesur to broadcast sympathetic programming and his own show, "Aló Presidente", across Latin America.

Conclusion: The Chávez effect

Despite a strong tradition of activism in Venezuelan foreign policy, the Chávez government's ambitious international agenda surpasses all predecessors. As he was first elected in 1998, we have now had an ample period in which to gauge Chávez's effect on hemispheric politics. His impact, however, has not necessarily been according to plan. Thus far he has not managed to recast Latin America and the Caribbean in the image of Venezuela's Bolivarian, twenty-first-century socialism. His ALBA integration initiative has only three other adherents: Bolivia, Cuba and Nicaragua. Although popular and élite anti-American sentiments are at a historic high, he has been unable to forge a single, united South American bloc.

Nonetheless, the Chávez effect has been dramatic, contributing to a tectonic shift in the region's geopolitics, political economy, ideas and norms. After the US dominance of much of the Americas' policy agenda following the end of the Cold War, a multipolar system is emerging in the region. Alongside US power, it includes regional powers Venezuela, Brazil and Chile, as well as the growing influence of Canada and external powers such as China, the European Union and Spain. Although Chávez has sought to construct a more rigid anti-US alliance structure, with Venezuela, Cuba and Bolivia at its core, a looser South American alignment is emerging with Brazil and Chile at its centre. Other countries, such as Argentina and Uruguay, appear to oscillate in their alignments with the United States, Brazil and Venezuela.

The growing multipolarity of the Americas underpins increasing foreign policy autonomy, pragmatism and flexibility, rather than rigid geopolitical and ideological alignment (as Chávez might have wanted), while individual countries find themselves with increasing options in terms of trade, investment and finance. In terms of the economic policy repertoire, their options have expanded from the Washington Consensus to include the Santiago Consensus and Chávez's own brand of nationalist and statist policies.

Moreover, Brazilian and Venezuelan interests have coincided in underwriting an important trend towards "US-free" multilateralism. While Latin American countries continue to maintain their membership in hemispheric forums under US leadership, such as the OAS and the Summits of the Americas, there has been a proliferation of subregional forums that have intentionally excluded US membership: the Rio Group, the Ibero-American Summits, Mercosur, ALBA, UNASUR and the South American Energy Summits. As well, with Venezuelan petrodollars and large market size, these multilateral groupings are showing that the United States is not needed even for its financial backing. At the same time, after a brief revival in the 1990s the OAS and the inter-American system – which the United States traditionally has dominated – have been significantly weakened, particularly with respect to democracy promotion.

Chávez's anti-US foreign policy initiatives have also had the unintended consequence of broadening power politics in the hemisphere. The US–Venezuela confrontation is not the only one of note: Chávez's intensive regional activism and Venezuela's enhanced regional profile have inadvertently triggered a Venezuela–Brazil rivalry. Venezuela and Brazil now compete in terms of their respective integration projects, with Venezuela's more ideological and overtly political ALBA scheme confronting Brazil's more moderate, business-friendly approach. While both countries support UNASUR as an ambitious, US-free South American integration project, they are in competition to shape the form it will take. In the realm of ideas, Chávez's twenty-first-century socialism competes with Lula's and Bachelet's Santiago Consensus.

A dramatic trend in the region's political economy is the significant decline in the regional presence and influence of the IMF, which, together with the World Bank and the Inter-American Development Bank, is encountering increased competition from the Chávez-financed Banco del Sur and ALBA Bank. This is a very positive development for Latin American and Caribbean countries that seek international finance.

On a final, cautionary note, one must ask about the sustainability of Venezuelan foreign policy activism and the Chávez effect in the region. On the positive side, Venezuela has substantial oil wealth and the world's largest natural gas reserves with which to finance its president's ambitious international agenda. Moreover, Venezuela has barely begun to tap its vast energy resources. In addition, for the moment Chávez enjoys sizeable popular backing, and has just begun his most recent six-year presidential term.

On the worrisome side, Chávez's interventionist and redistributive economic policies might well be regarded as economic populism, which Dornbusch and Edwards (1991) have argued is unsustainable and eventually disastrous. The boom in the energy sector is showing possible signs of Dutch Disease. A decline in energy prices could have a negative impact on the economy as well. Politically, Chávez's confrontational style makes him plenty of enemies at home and abroad. Chávez was legitimately concerned when, in May 2007, the opposition-controlled media enterprise Globovisión hinted, through broadcasting on television the attempted assassination of Pope John Paul II, that this was the way to get rid of him.

In the end, one must recall that Venezuela's previous episodes of foreign policy activism proved unsustainable; the vulnerability of an ambitious middle power is precisely that problems on the home front and limits on its resources invariably divert its attention from the international arena. None of Chávez's predecessors, with the possible exception of Bolívar himself, ever had such a grand foreign policy. For what is still essentially a middle power, overstretch becomes a real possibility. Whatever happens, interesting times inevitably lie ahead for the Americas.

Notes

1. In Spanish, the Bolivarian Alternative for the *Americas* (my emphasis) appears in the singular: Alternativa Bolivariana para *la América* (my emphasis). *América* is understood as the entire region of the Americas, not just the United States.
2. For a look at Venezuela's democracy promotion prior to Chávez see María Teresa Romero (2000).

3. For a comparison of Venezuela's foreign policy provisions under the 1961 and 1999 constitutions see Romero, Romero and Da Silva (2003).
4. Space does not allow me to discuss Chávez's Bolivarian Revolution in detail. The best treatment of this subject is Ellner and Hellinger (2003). On the demise of the Punto Fijo political system see McCoy and Myers (2004).
5. Technically, the department is now called the Ministry of the Popular Power for External Relations.
6. I am grateful to Carlos A. Romero for this insight.
7. This discussion of neopopulism draws on Legler (2006).
8. Some scholars present a periodization of Chávez's foreign policy in which the initial phase was marked more by continuity with the past, such as pragmatism, openness to dialogue and the quest for non-confrontational solutions (Duarte Villa, 2004; González Urrutia, 2006). I would suggest, however, that there has been a growing anti-US confrontational logic to Venezuelan foreign policy since at least 2000, the year that Chávez undertook official visits to the US adversaries Libya and Iraq, and refused to allow the United States to conduct surveillance flights over its territory to combat drug trafficking. See Ellner (2000).
9. According to its own statistics, the Venezuelan government donates 1.4 per cent of its gross domestic product as official development assistance to Latin American and Caribbean countries (Valero, 2006).
10. The Inter-American Commission on Human Rights strongly criticized the Chávez government for the RCTV closure, but the secretary-general and Permanent Council of the OAS chose not to follow up by invoking the IADC. One of the frustrating aspects of the OAS is that, while the Commission enjoys organizational autonomy, its decisions and statements are not binding on the secretary-general or the Permanent Council.
11. Chávez's ability to undertake bold acts without any significant OAS response might also have to do with suggestions that Secretary-General Insulza is focused on his ambition to succeed Michelle Bachelet as president of Chile and is unwilling to adopt any strong measures that might alienate support for his candidacy.
12. Luis Vicente León Vivas, a director with the polling firm Datanálisis, indicated to me in an interview in Caracas in December 2006 that his firm's 17 November 2006 survey had found that the vast majority of Venezuelans, both *chavistas* and opposition, were opposed to twenty-first-century socialism. See also *The Economist* (2006); Toothaker (2006).
13. On the evolution of the inter-American collective defence-of-democracy regime see Boniface (2007); Cooper and Legler (2006); McCoy (2007).
14. On complex multilateralism see O'Brien et al. (2000). Cooper and Legler (2006) prefer "networked multilateralism".

REFERENCES

AFX International Focus (2007) "Chávez Wants South American 'Gas OPEC'", *AFX International Focus*, 2 March.

Andean Group Report (2007) "Venezuela Withdraws From the IMF and the World Bank", *Latin America Newsletters*, 10 May, London, available at www.latinnews.com.

Bhagwati, Jagdish (1995) "U.S. Trade Policy: The Infatuation with Free Trade Agreements", in Jagdish Bhagwati and Anne O. Krueger, eds, *The Dangerous Drift to Preferential Trade Agreements*, Washington, DC: AEI Press.

Boniface, Dexter S. (2007) "The OAS's Mixed Record", in Thomas Legler, Sharon F. Lean and Dexter S. Boniface, eds, *Promoting Democracy in the Americas*, Baltimore, MD: Johns Hopkins University Press.

Burges, Sean (2007) "Building a Global Southern Coalition: The Competing Approaches of Brazil's Lula and Venezuela's Chávez", *Third World Quarterly* 28(7), pp. 1343–1358.

Castañeda, Jorge G. (2006) "Latin America's Left Turn", *Foreign Affairs* 85(3), pp. 28–43.

Cooper, Andrew F. and Thomas Legler (2006) *Intervention without Intervening: The OAS Defense and Promotion of Democracy in the Americas*, New York: Palgrave.

Corrales, Javier (2006) "Hugo Boss", *Foreign Policy* 152(1), pp. 32–40.

Dornbusch, Rudiger and Sebastian Edwards, eds (1991) *The Macroeconomics of Populism in Latin America*, Chicago, IL: University of Chicago Press.

Duarte Villa, Rafael (2004) "Dos etapas en la política exterior frente a Estados Unidos en el período de Hugo Chávez", *Cuadernos del CENDES* 21(55), pp. 21–45.

EIU Viewswire (2007) "Latin American Finance: Is the Bank of the South Rhetoric or Reality?", EIU Viewswire, 27 March.

Ellner, Steve (2000) "Venezuela's Foreign Policy: Defiance South of the Border", *Z Magazine*, November, available at www.zmag.org/ZMag/articles/nov00ellner.htm.

Ellner, Steve and Daniel Hellinger, eds (2003) *Venezuelan Politics in the Chávez Era: Class, Polarization, and Conflict*, Boulder, CO: Lynne Rienner.

Farer, Tom, ed. (1996) *Beyond Sovereignty: Collectively Defending Democracy in the Americas*, Baltimore, MD: Johns Hopkins University Press.

Gobierno Bolivariano de Venezuela (1999) *Constitución de la República Bolivariana de Venezuela*, Caracas, available at www.constitucion.ve/.

González Urrutia, Edmundo (2006) "Las dos etapas de la política exterior de Chávez", *Nueva Sociedad* 205 (September–October), pp. 159–171.

Gratius, Susanne (2006) "Venezuela contra EE.UU: La lucha por el asiento Latinoamericano en el Consejo de Seguridad", *FRIDE Comentario* (November), available at www.fride.org/Publications/Publication.aspx?Item=1176.

Hakim, Peter (2006) "Is Washington Losing Latin America?", *Foreign Affairs* 85(1), pp. 39–53.

Lagos, Marta (2006) "A apearse de la fantasía: Hugo Chávez y los liderazgos en América Latina", *Nueva Sociedad* 205 (September–October), pp. 92–101.

Lapper, Richard (2007) "Washington Restive as Chavez Plans Pioneer Bank", *Financial Times*, 23 March.

Latin American Weekly Report (2007a) "ALBA versus Santiago Consensus: Same Aims, Different Approach", *Latin American Weekly Report*, 4 May.

——— (2007b) "Energy Summit Was Stage for Oblique Regional Leadership Contest", *Latin American Weekly Report*, 19 April.

Latinnews Daily (2006) "Argentina: IMF Debt Paid in Full", *Latinnews Daily*, 4 January.

Legler, Thomas (2006) "Bridging Divides, Breaking Impasses: Civil Society in the Promotion and Protection of Democracy in the Americas", Policy Paper 06-02, Canadian Foundation for the Americas (FOCAL), Ottawa.

——— (2007a) "The Inter-American Democratic Charter: Rhetoric versus Reality", in Gordon Mace, Jean-Philippe Thérien and Paul Haslam, eds, *Governing the Americas: Assessing Multilateral Institutions*, Boulder, CO: Lynne Rienner.

——— (2007b) "Venezuela 2002–2004: The Chávez Challenge", in Thomas Legler, Sharon F. Lean and Dexter S. Boniface, eds, *Promoting Democracy in the Americas*, Baltimore, MD: Johns Hopkins University Press.

Lowenthal, Abraham F. (2006) "From Regional Hegemony to Complex Bilateral Relations: The United States and Latin America in the Early Twenty-first Century", *Nueva Sociedad* 206 (November–December), pp. 63–77.

McCoy, Jennifer (2007) "Transnational Response to Democratic Response in the Americas, 1990–2005", in Thomas Legler, Sharon F. Lean and Dexter S. Boniface, eds, *Promoting Democracy in the Americas*, Baltimore, MD: Johns Hopkins University Press.

McCoy, Jennifer and David J. Myers, eds (2004) *The Unraveling of Representative Democracy in Venezuela*, Baltimore, MD: Johns Hopkins University Press.

Márquez, Humberto (2007) "Progressive Social and Political Movements Join the Governments of ALBA", *IPS Inter Press Service* (Latin America), 2 May.

Morsbach, Greg (2006) "Venezuela Basks in Oil Bonanza", BBC News, Caracas, 17 February.

O'Brien, Robert, Anne Marie Goetz, Jan Aart Scholte and Marc Williams (2000) *Contesting Global Governance: Multilateral Economic Institutions and Global Social Movements*, Cambridge: Cambridge University Press.

Ríos, Carlos (2007) "Signos de distanciamiento en Uruguay", *El Nacional*, 4 June, available at www.el-nacional.com.

Ríos, Jesús (2006) "Gauging the Chávez Effect", Gallup News Service, 29 September, available at www.gallup.com/poll/24814/Gauging-Chavez-Effect.aspx.

Roett, Riordan (2006) "United States-Latin American Relations: The Current State of Play", *Nueva Sociedad* 206 (November–December), 110–125.

Romero, Carlos A. (2004) "The United States and Venezuela: From a Special Relationship to Wary Neighbors", in Jennifer McCoy and David J. Myers, eds, *The Unraveling of Representative Democracy in Venezuela*, Baltimore, MD: Johns Hopkins University Press.

——— (2006a) *Jugando con el globo: La política exterior de Hugo Chávez*, Caracas: Ediciones B.

——— (2006b) "Venezuela y Estados Unidos: Una relación esquizofrénica?", *Nueva Sociedad* 206 (November–December), pp. 78–93.

Romero, Carlos A., María Teresa Romero and Elsa Cardozo de Da Silva (2003) "La política exterior en las constituciones de 1961 y 1999: Una visión comparada de sus principios, procedimientos y temas", *Revista Venezolana de Economía y Ciencias Sociales* 9(1), pp. 163–183.

Romero, María Teresa (2000) "Promoción de la democracia en la política exterior venezolana de los 90", paper presented at Conference of Latin American Studies Association, Miami, 18 March.

Sánchez, Fabiola (2007) "Gas Pipeline between Venezuela and Colombia to Be Finished in August", Associated Press Financial Wire, 16 April.

Sanders, Ronald (2007) "Expanding Its Sphere of Influence: Venezuela in the Caribbean", Caribbean-Britain Business Council Seminar Series 2007, Chatham House, London, 17 April.

Schamis, Héctor E. (2006) "Populism, Socialism, and Democratic Institutions", *Journal of Democracy* 17(4), pp. 20–34.

Serbin, Andrés (2006) "Cuando la limosna es grande: El Caribe, Chávez, y los límites de la diplomacia petrolera", *Nueva Sociedad* 205 (September–October), pp. 75–91.

Shifter, Michael (2006) "In Search of Hugo Chávez", *Foreign Affairs* 85(3), pp. 45–59.

——— (2007) *Hugo Chávez: A Test for U.S. Policy*, Washington, DC: Inter-American Dialogue, March.

Shifter, Michael and Vinay Jawahar (2006) "The Divided States of the Americas", *Current History* 105 (February), pp. 51–57.

South American Community of Nations (2004) *Declaración del Cusco sobre la Comunidad Sudamericana de Naciones*, III Cumbre Presidencial Sudamericana, Cusco, Peru, 8 December, available at www.comunidadandina.org/documentos/dec_int/cusco_sudamerica.htm.

Swann, Christopher (2007) "South America's New Piggy Bank; Chávez Uses His Country's Oil Wealth to Help Neighbors, Blunt U.S. Influence", *Toronto Star*, 1 March.

The Economist (2006) "Another Triumph for Hugo Chávez in Venezuela Probably Means More Concentration of Power", *The Economist*, 5 December.

Toothaker, Christopher (2006) "Chavez Says Re-election Win Shows Venezuela Backs Socialism", Associated Press, 5 December.

Valero, Jorge (2006) "La dimensión multilateral de la política exterior venezolana", speech given at Diplomatic Academy "Pedro Gual", Caracas, 8 November.

Van Klaveren, Alberto (2001) "Political Globalization and Latin America: Toward a New Sovereignty?", in Joseph S. Tulchin and Ralph H. Espach, eds, *Latin America in the New International System*, Boulder, CO: Lynne Rienner.

Zerpa, Fabiola (2007) "Los imanes de la política exterior de Venezuela", *El Nacional*, 4 June.

12

The impact of the 2006 Mexican elections

Arturo Santa-Cruz

Mexico's transition to democracy was long and anticlimactic – one could even say that it was boring. Formally initiated from above with the 1977 electoral reform during the days of the last "revolutionary" president, José López Portillo, it culminated 20 years later with the 1997 mid-term elections that saw the ruling party lose control of the chamber of deputies for the first time, under the watch of the uncharismatic technocrat Ernesto Zedillo, who had been elected president in 1994, the last president to come from the Partido Revolucionario Institucional (PRI, or Institutional Revolutionary Party). Thus, although three years later Vicente Fox of the Partido Acción Nacional (PAN, or National Action Party) ended the 71-year-long PRI regime, effectively inaugurating the *alternancia*, the emblematical sign of Mexico's successful transition, the political changes to come were bound to be minor. The challenges for the first PAN administration were not about bringing regime change, but simply to consolidate the country's still-blossoming democracy.

Then towards the end of the Fox administration, when Mexicans were supposed to be getting used to the boring democratic normality of a country with contested elections, separation of powers, checks and balances, an independent press and an autonomous electoral body – to name just a few features of the young Mexican democratic regime – the country went through an unexpected, and arguably also exciting, political upheaval. The 2006 electoral process thus seems to have made up for the uneventfulness of the 1997 transition to democracy.

Which way Latin America? Hemispheric politics meets globalization, Cooper and Heine, eds, United Nations University Press, 2009, ISBN 978-92-808-1172-8

Beyond the unusual sequence of events in the plot of the past three decades, the 2006 electoral crisis is of analytical interest because it enshrines both peculiar characteristics of the current Mexican political regime and wider trends taking place in Latin America. The former have to do with the background conditions that made the political crisis possible, such as pervasive social inequalities and the nature of Mexico's electoral institutions and main political parties, and the latter refer to the continent's apparent shift to the left in the past decade – precisely the period in which the nascent Mexican democracy was taking shape. The two sets of features are, of course, related, with the Latin American context influencing the Mexican case more than the other way around. What transpired in the 2006 electoral process, however, will have consequences both for the state of democracy in Mexico and for the country's hemispheric policy.

To consider these issues, I proceed as follows. In the first section I argue that Mexico's transition to democracy had taken place before Fox took office, with the *alternancia* as its most conspicuous event. In the second section I consider the implications of the *alternancia* for Mexico's foreign policy, and relate this issue to the 2006 presidential race. Thus, in section three, I ponder how the wider debates about the ascent of the left and the two kinds of left in Latin America, as well as the less-noticed issue of the two kinds of right in Mexico, evolved in light of the 2006 election. In the fourth section I look at the electoral race and the dispute over its legality. I conclude by considering what the implications of this event might be for both Mexico's democracy and its foreign policy.

A boring transition

Mexico's authoritarian regime was the longest in the twentieth century. It outlived that of any other Latin American country (and the totalitarian system of the Soviet Union, which, of course, was a different animal). Indeed, its resilience led Peruvian novelist Mario Vargas Llosa, in the aftermath of the Soviet Union's demise, to characterize it as the "perfect dictatorship". By that time, however, Mexico's transition to democracy was well under way. This process involved the gradual severing of the PRI's illegal ties to both the state and civil society, the creation of electoral institutions suitable for a multiparty system and, fundamentally, the gradual dismantling of what Mexican historian Lorenzo Meyer (1996: 23) has called the "anti-constitutional powers of the presidency". Among these prerogatives were the discretionary transfer of resources from the government to the PRI, control of the legislative and judicial powers, censorship of the media, control of governors and mayors and repression of political opponents.

The transition was formally initiated in the late 1970s (Becerra, Salazar and Woldenberg, 2000; Santa-Cruz, 2002). In 1977 the López Portillo administration (1976–1982) passed the aforementioned electoral reform, as well as other measures (such as an amnesty for political prisoners) that together formed what was referred to as the "political reform". The immediate objective of the new legislation was to widen the political spectrum, and in this it was successful. Thus in 1982 seven presidential contenders – as opposed to just one in 1976 – took part in the electoral process. But the recurring economic problems and internal political disputes that took place during the administration of Miguel de la Madrid (1982–1988) contributed to worsening the political environment, so that, a decade after the foundational electoral reform, new liberalizing measures in this realm needed to be taken.

These reforms notwithstanding, 1987 and 1988 saw the worst political crisis the "revolutionary regime" had experienced since its inception in the late 1920s. De la Madrid's choice to succeed him, Carlos Salinas, caused a split, led by Cuauhtémoc Cárdenas – the son of former President Lázaro Cárdenas (1934–1940) – within his party. Cárdenas then launched his own candidacy, supported by a coalition of formerly government-controlled parties, plus the successor of the Communist Party. Cárdenas came second in the 1988 election with a third of the votes – the highest ever for an opposition candidate – prompting a widespread feeling that the election had actually been stolen from him.

Thus, upon taking office, Salinas called for a "National Accord for the Enhancement of Our Democratic Life", which led to the 1990 electoral reform. The new electoral legislation again failed to normalize the political atmosphere. The PRI's recovery in the 1991 mid-term election had a detrimental effect on both sides of the government's opposition: on the one hand PAN, with which the government had negotiated the electoral reform, felt betrayed; on the other hand the Partido de la Revolución Democrática (PRD, or Party of the Democratic Revolution), whose establishment Cárdenas had spearheaded with the political forces that had supported his presidential bid, seemed to validate his claim that Salinas was not interested in bringing about a democratic transition. Thus, in 1992, Salinas offered to negotiate new electoral legislation, which was passed the following year.

Although the 1993 electoral amendment seemed to dissipate the political pressure, thus apparently guaranteeing that the new electoral legislation would be in effect for the following year's presidential contest, one unexpected event prevented it from having that effect: the 1 January

1994 Zapatista uprising in the southern state of Chiapas. This sole factor catapulted the need for the Salinas administration's third electoral reform, and within four months new electoral legislation was passed. Although the 1994 electoral reform contributed to the cleanest election Mexicans had seen up to that date, there was a widespread feeling that the electoral system was still lacking – indeed, the winner of the electoral contest himself later would recognize that the elections had been free but not fair.

Just as Salinas had done six years earlier, Zedillo called in his inaugural address for further amendments to the electoral law. The 1996 electoral law, under which the 2006 election took place, was thus the culmination of a process initiated in 1977. The most salient feature of the new legislation was the banishment of the government from the Instituto Federal Electoral (IFE, or Federal Electoral Institute). It was this reform that made it possible for electoral processes in Mexico really to be contested. As writer and historian Héctor Aguilar Camín commented, referring to the 1996 reform, "This perfect dictatorship has made one of the reforms which are going to lead it to lose power. It is a curious dictatorship" (quoted in Lemus, 1998: 46).

Indeed, the mid-term 1997 election completely changed Mexico's political landscape. For the first time the PRI no longer held an absolute majority in the lower house. Furthermore, the PRD's Cárdenas won Mexico City's first mayoral election. Thus, whereas in 1982 the PRI controlled 91 per cent of elected positions (including the presidency, seats in Congress, governorships, local congresses and mayoralties), in 1997 it controlled only 54 per cent (Begné Guerra, 1999). By this time the cornerstones of the Mexican authoritarian regime, the "anti-constitutional powers of the president", were history. Mexico's protracted transition to (formal) democracy thus took place three years before *alternancia*, the era of political alternation, was inaugurated.

That was why the outcome of the 2000 electoral process, although important for myriad reasons, was by and large unrelated to Mexico's transition to democracy – the 2000 electoral process simply confirmed the still-burgeoning political plurality. The victorious Vicente Fox achieved the highly symbolic feat of defeating the PRI with a plurality of the votes. Not surprisingly, for the second time the president did not have a majority in Congress.

As noted, the fact that Mexico's democratic transition was not brought about by the first non-PRI government does not mean that it was inconsequential – far from it. That the 2000–2006 administration was a party that had been in opposition no doubt had salutary consequences for the country's democratic consolidation process, but the reforms introduced during this period clearly were not the stuff of which democratic transitions are made. As Chappell Lawson (2007: 46) has put it, "As president, Fox presided over modest democratic deepening." Furthermore, the political skills a minority government needs to build the legislative majorities to pass its agenda were obviously lacking in the Fox administration. When it appealed to the electorate directly during the mid-term 2003 election with the motto "take the brake off change", the outcome was a failure: PAN ended up losing seats.

The Fox administration's most egregious political mistake, however, took place the following year, and had to do with the impeachment of the PRD main presidential hopeful: Andrés Manuel López Obrador. What started as a legal conflict over the expropriation of a piece of land carried out by López Obrador's predecessor in 2000 turned four years later into a full-blown political battle. The ostensible reason for the government's action was López Obrador's failure to heed the rulings of two judges on the expropriation issue. Thus, in 2004, the federal attorney general asked Congress to impeach the mayor of Mexico City – who happened to be the leading potential contender for the 2006 presidential election. The PRD and a wide spectrum of the population saw the attack as legalistic sleight of hand by the Fox administration to get rid of a formidable political opponent. Regardless of the legal merits of the case, prosecuting López Obrador was huge political blunder for Fox. In April 2005 PAN, in alliance with the PRI, voted to impeach López Obrador. After an intense political (more than legal) battle, the Fox administration dropped the case – and López Obrador ended up in a much stronger political position.

This background set the stage for the 2006 electoral process, one in which two political projects were taking shape.[1] The foreign dimension would also weigh in, both in the electoral contest and in the instantiation of the wider political trends taking shape in Latin America. The baseline of the partisan foreign policy debate was, no doubt, the Fox administration's performance on this matter; let us, therefore, briefly review it.

The *alternancia* and Mexico's foreign policy

On the foreign policy front, the changes brought about by the *alternancia* for the most part were minor, since, as in the domestic politics, the most substantial changes had taken place before the Fox administration was inaugurated. Indeed, changes in Mexico's diplomacy preceded the culmination of the country's democratic transition and were, by and large, unrelated to it. The main mutation in Mexico's foreign policy, a veritable about-face, took place in the early 1990s, when the Salinas administration decided to initiate negotiations leading towards the North American Free

Trade Agreement (NAFTA). As Humberto Garza Elizondo (1994: 536) has noted, "Few things changed more during Salinas' *sexenio* [six-year term] than foreign policy." The change, however, was not simply a fad: NAFTA became Mexico's "new grand strategy" (Mares, 1996: 36). Thus Zedillo continued his predecessor's policy of making the relationship with Mexico's northern neighbour the centre of its diplomatic activity; the Fox administration simply deepened this project.

To be sure, before Fox took office his foreign policy team had a well-articulated plan concerning Mexico's agenda towards its two NAFTA partners – fundamentally, the United States. The strategy was encapsulated in what came to be known as "NAFTA Plus": an improved NAFTA, inspired by the integration model that culminated in the European Union. Accordingly, the proposal included increased labour mobility and convergence funds for the less-developed areas – that is, fundamentally, for southern Mexico. Fox even visited Canada and the United States when he was still president-elect and put forward his proposal for deeper integration. Even though then Canadian Prime Minister Jean Chrétien and US President Bill Clinton gently rejected his suggestion, it was noteworthy that the future Mexican president was setting the trilateral agenda. The future of the relationship with the United States seemed to improve after the victory of George W. Bush in the disputed November 2000 elections. Thus, for instance, the first international trip of the new US president was to Mexico, in February 2001, and Fox was the first head of state to be received by Bush in the White House.

The "democratic bonus" of the *alternancia* was, of course a key token for Mexico in the dawn of this relationship. The Fox administration's democratic legitimacy was used to make the case for deepening NAFTA – specifically, in seeking both to obtain a sought-after agreement on migrant workers and to get rid of the anti-drug certification process in the US Congress. The strategy seemed to work, at least initially, but then came the terrorist attacks of 9/11 and their regrettable consequences not only for the United States but also for world politics – including the bilateral relationship. The honeymoon was thus short-lived – neither the deepening of NAFTA nor the agreement on migrant labour materialized.

On other fronts, however, the Fox administration fared better. The one other area in which the foreign policy team wanted to break with the PRI's foreign policy tradition was democracy and human rights. PAN's electoral platform, for example, asserted that "one of the running threads in the foreign policy of twenty-first-century Mexico should be the promotion and protection of human rights in Mexico and the world". The foreign policy programme presented shortly after the 2000 election maintained that the PRI had misinterpreted, or inappropriately implemented, the principle of non-intervention. Hence in the 2000–2006

National Development Plan, in which the policies of the incoming administration were spelled out in some detail, the first foreign policy goal was "to promote and strengthen democracy and human rights as the cornerstone of the new international system".

There was an explicit relationship between the domestic and the foreign realms. As Mexico's Foreign Minister Jorge G. Castañeda put it in June 2002, "The main point is the possibility that Mexican foreign policy might allow us to anchor the democratic change in our country." Hence, in his inaugural speech, Castañeda announced the opening of a human rights embassy and nominated a well-known human rights activist to head it. Although the original proposal did not materialize, as the Senate refused to confirm an ambassador whose diplomatic credentials were not going to be presented to any head of state, a deputy-office-level (undersecretary) bureau of human rights was established at the foreign ministry in Tlatelolco. Beyond the conceptual blunders in the creation of the new bureau and the mistakes the Fox administration might have committed in carrying out an active international human rights policy, the fact is that it showed consistency in this matter.

Furthermore, at the beginning of his administration Fox delivered an open, permanent invitation to the United Nations to send human rights reporters to Mexico, thereby sending a clear signal that the country was committed to respecting these fundamental prerogatives, both in its territory and abroad. Thus, for instance, the Fox administration declared before the UN Human Rights Commission that it considered human rights as universal and absolute, taking precedence over national sovereignty (Castañeda, 2006a). Evidence of the new impetus can be found not only in the official discourse but also in the response it and the government's actions elicited. Most significant in this respect is Mexico's election in 2006 to be one of the 47 members of the recently created UN Humans Rights Council and for the Mexican representative to be its first president. This was an explicit recognition of the Fox administration's policy, both domestic and foreign, on this matter (although, of course, this does not mean that human rights are yet fully respected in Mexico), an acknowledgement shared by leading non-governmental organizations, such as Human Rights Watch (Castañeda, 2006b).

In a similar vein, Mexico signed the September 2001 Democratic Charter of the Organization of American States. Furthermore, during the Fox administration Mexico played an active role in supporting representative democracy, as when it condemned – along with other Latin American countries and against the initial position of the United States – the failed coup against Hugo Chávez in 2002. Thus, even if the implications of the *alternancia* for Mexico's foreign policy seemed to have been rather modest, evincing more continuity than change, its more forthright discourse did have discernible effects on the 2006 electoral process, as I show in the next section.

The ascent of the left and Mexico's politics

Mexico's problems with leftist Latin American regimes, particularly those in Cuba and Venezuela, started early in the Fox administration. In large part this had to do, especially in the Cuban case, with the Fox administration's stand on democracy and human rights. Thus, for instance, in 2002 Mexico shifted its traditional position at the UN Human Rights Commission by voting for the first time in favour of a resolution condemning Cuba, a change that was bound to contaminate the whole bilateral relationship with the island. Moreover, Fox certainly did not excel at diplomacy, which made things worse. For instance, during the preparations for the UN Summit on Development in Monterrey in March 2002, in an effort to avoid the awkward situation of Bush and Castro running into each other, Fox naïvely suggested in a telephone conversation with Castro: "Have lunch (in Monterrey) and then you depart" (Petrich et al., 2002). Weeks later, after an ensuing quarrel, Castro made the conversation public, making Fox look both amateurish and subservient towards the United States.

With Venezuela, problems intensified in the context of the fourth Summit of the Americas, held in Mar del Plata, Argentina, in November 2005. Fox not only defended the US-backed Free Trade Area of the Americas but also cited Chávez for his contrary attitude. Chávez retorted by calling the Mexican president an "empire's puppet". The Fox administration demanded an apology, but Chávez, in his own folkloric way, warned Fox not to mess with him – or face the consequences (James, 2005). In May 2006 Chávez announced Venezuela was leaving the trade bloc his country had formed with Colombia and Mexico, known as the Group of Three. By that time not only had the continental debate on the rise of the left in Latin America started, but so had the preliminaries of the July 2006 presidential election in Mexico.

A series of electoral victories of left-leaning candidates in Latin America during the late 1990s and early 2000s prompted political commentators to notice that a "resurgent left" was replacing the Washington Consensus that had prevailed during the previous decade. The discourse on the rise of the left distinguished, first implicitly and then explicitly, between the "right" left and the "wrong" left. The former was represented by the governments of Michelle Bachelet in Chile, Luiz Inácio Lula da Silva in Brazil and Tabaré Vázquez in Uruguay. Theirs were market-friendly, moderate, modern and tolerant regimes – in short, they were social-democratic-like. The latter, in contrast, was represented, to different degrees, by the governments of Néstor Kirchner in Argentina, Evo Morales in Bolivia and Chávez in Venezuela. These governments were fiercely nationalist, fiscally irresponsible and led by charismatic leaders – they were, in a word, populist. As Jorge G. Castañeda (2006b: 32) wrote in an influential article on the matter, "Knowing where left-wing leaders and parties come from – in particular, which of the two strands of the left in Latin American history they are a part of – is critical to understanding who they are and where they are going."

In late 2005, in the milieu of the approaching presidential elections, the easiest political manoeuvre left for the incumbent PAN administration was to accuse (obliquely) López Obrador, the candidate of the "Coalition for the Good of All" – formed by the PRD and two other small parties – of being a populist. Although Fox was not running, he acted as if he saw the 2006 election as a plebiscite on his performance. Thus, in December 2005, he advised Mexicans "not to risk what we already have, and to be careful with our vote" (*Reforma*, 2005). Four months later, when López Obrador was well ahead in the polls, Fox declared: "We can continue advancing if we persevere in our effort, if we put aside easy promises and false illusions, the demagoguery and the populism" (McKinley, 2006a).

Similarly, as a political strategy, PAN candidate Felipe Calderón resorted to identifying López Obrador with populism in general and Chávez in particular. Thus, starting in March, Calderón's inner circle decided to run a US-style campaign – mud-slinging included (McKinley, 2006b). The bottom line of PAN's new tactic was to present López Obrador as "a danger to Mexico" and to depict him as, among other things, authoritarian, fiscally irresponsible, messianic and populist. More to the point, the PAN campaign associated López Obrador's image with that of Chávez, and suggested that relations with the United States would be endangered were he to become president (Klesner, 2007: 31). Taking advantage of a major blunder by López Obrador, when he compared Fox to a twittering tropical bird while commanding the president to shut up, Calderón's campaign ran TV ads featuring Chávez offending the Mexican president alongside López Obrador insulting Fox (McKinley, 2006a). The Venezuelan president intervened, complaining that his image was being used by the "right" in order to stop the advancement of the Mexican left. Calderón cleverly responded: "I am very happy that President Chávez supports López Obrador: the more he supports him, the more he weakens him" (*La Jornada*, 2006c).

More telling, though, was the opinion of independent scholars and intellectuals, many of them from the left, about the PRD's candidate. To be sure, their analysis was broader than a focus on López Obrador himself and framed in terms of the ascent of the left in Latin America, relating it to the real existing Mexican left. Although López Obrador was not the only leftist candidate in the 2006 electoral process, he was the most important one;[2] moreover, he faced no contender within his party for the presidential nomination. And in this respect, since the PRD had its origins in 1989 in an amalgam of dissident PRI members and communist activists, in which the former were hegemonic, the party was closer to the nationalist-*cum*-populist PRI than to a modern progressive organization (López Obrador himself was a former PRI official). Furthermore, also since its inception, the PRD had coalesced around two strong leaders: first, Cuauhtémoc Cárdenas, its "moral leader", twice presidential candidate and under whose protection López Obrador's leadership grew; second, López Obrador himself (Woldenberg, 2007). López Obrador then created a parallel structure, the "Citizens' Networks", run by people of his choosing (mostly former PRI officials), to further his control of the strategy of the overall electoral campaign (Alemán, 2006). It thus seemed that, as academic and former communist party member Roger Bartra put it (2006: 20), Mexico was "losing the possibility of counting with a modern and rational left".

The intellectuals' opinion most likely did not permeate beyond a fraction of the electorate, but Calderón's dirty war against López Obrador did. Thus, from March to May 2006, the distance between López Obrador and Calderón decreased steadily. Although slow to react at first, López Obrador responded with his own mud-slinging, recovering some of the advantage he had had at the beginning (*Mural*, 2006). In his attacks against Calderón, López Obrador portrayed him as a right-wing politician, as having been involved in a huge banking bail-out programme that had taken place during the Zedillo administration and as linked to an extreme-right organization called Yunque that had infiltrated PAN. Generally, though, López Obrador referred to Calderón as "the right's candidate" – significant because, in the same way that there was more than one kind of left in Mexico, there were also two kinds of right in the country: an archaic, conservative and religious right and a more modern, liberal and tolerant right. Interestingly, both rights were competing within PAN. And although Calderón represented the latter rather than the former (more on this below), his adversary could have accused him more consistently of belonging to the "wrong right" as a political strategy with potential benefits. Indeed, the extremist and religious right was in control of the party during the 2006 electoral process, and it was recognized that voters did not look favourably on the inclusion of religious ideas and interests in politics (see Bartra, 2006: 19; *Boletín*, 2003). This distinction, however, does not seem to have registered with the coalition's candidate: for López Obrador, Calderón simply represented the old conservative cause.

PAN is certainly heir to both the Conservative Party and the country's Catholic tradition (Paz [1985] 1987: 148–149). Since PAN's founding in 1939, it has contained both a secular and a religious current (Loaeza, 1999). Despite internal disagreements, the Conservative Party had strong doctrinary foundations that it resolutely refused to compromise; PAN thus became a testimonial party. That stance started to change in the early 1980s, however, as entrepreneurs, disgruntled with what they perceived to be communist or at least populist policies of the Echeverría and López Portillo administrations, started to join the party and then run as candidates, initially for Congress. The newcomers, called *neopanistas*, infused the party with new impetus and a much more confrontational position *vis-à-vis* the government.

Fox won both PAN's presidential nomination in 1999 and the following year's election practically as an external candidate. For a prominent member of the traditionalist wing, Fox's era represented "a kind of political amateurism which turned out to be very expensive both for PAN and for the country" (quoted in Delgado, 2006: 10). Indeed, it was under the Fox administration – and its attendant ascendancy over PAN – that Yunque was able to take control of the party. Interestingly, though, thanks in part to PAN's well-institutionalized political dynamics, the traditionalist wing, supporting Calderón, was able to win the presidential nomination in 2005, running against both the top echelons of the party's apparatus and Fox's explicit support of his dauphin, former Interior Minister Santiago Creel (Alemán, 2005). The split in the party was evident throughout the campaign, with the party's leadership at times ostensibly boycotting its own candidate (Fernández Menéndez, 2007: 14; Tello Díaz, 2007: 171). As a member of Calderón's inner circle saw it, the challenge for the candidate's faction was "to isolate the extremists within the PAN" (quoted in Delgado, 2006: 6). Interestingly, then, while both the PRD and PAN were led by their most radicalized wings, only in the latter was it eventually marginalized.

Having one kind of left (populist) and one kind of right (moderate) as the main political contenders had a clear effect on the foreign policy proposals at issue in the 2006 electoral process – and obviously for the government that would emerge from it. The differences between López Obrador and Calderón in this respect were indeed substantial. As was to be expected, López Obrador proposed a return to Mexico's "traditional" stand on foreign affairs, based on the principle of non-intervention (quoted in Glover, 2006). He also said his diplomacy would keep a low profile, since "that is not in agreement with Mexico's foreign policy tradition" (*La Jornada*, 2004). Indeed, López Obrador was not particularly interested in foreign affairs: for him, "the best foreign policy is domestic policy" (López Obrador, 2006).

Calderón, for his part, proposed a much more aggressive foreign policy. Critiquing López Obrador's foreign policy proposal, Calderón noted: "Those who think that foreign policy is a mere extension of domestic politics are mistaken" (Vega, 2006). Thus, for instance, he said his government would look for a non-permanent seat for Mexico in the UN Security Council during the 2009–2010 session. Calderón also stated that Mexico needed to "broaden and deepen" its relationship with its North American partners (*Crónica*, 2006). And, like the first PAN administration, Calderón promised to support democracy-promotion efforts in the hemisphere (Partido Acción Nacional, 2006). Although foreign policy was certainly not a major topic during the electoral campaign, the debate surrounding it served as a window into the deep differences between the main contenders, a window which served to prefigure the shape of things to come starting on 1 December 2006, when the new administration was to be inaugurated. Let us take a brief look at the evolution of the electoral process.

The exciting 2006 elections

By May 2006 López Obrador, having recovered from Calderón's negative campaign, arrived at election day with a very small lead over his rival, according to published polls (Tello Díaz, 2007: 60). In addition to Calderón's dirty war and López Obrador's response in kind, which caused the IFE to intervene, there were a few other incidents, such as President Fox's support of Calderón and the Mexico City administration's support of López Obrador, as well as TV ads paid for by a business group implicitly attacking López Obrador. When 2 July, election day, came, however, there were no major obstacles to holding a fair electoral process – indeed, early in the day the PRD's representative at the IFE noted that, thanks to the fair process, the electoral race was concluding on that date "with good results" (ibid.: 15).

The IFE had certainly done its job: it oversaw party finances, monitored news coverage, offered neutrality laws for public servants, invited foreign observers from more than 60 countries and trained citizens to serve as electoral officials. On election day more than 130,000 voting booths, staffed by more than 900,000 citizens, were installed (ibid.: 13). In addition, almost 400,000 party representatives were present at the polling places (IFE, 2007: 42). More than 41 million, or 58 per cent, of registered citizens voted. As Todd Eisenstadt has noted (2007: 39), the 2 July elections were a "'free and fair' contest organized by one of the world's more respected electoral institutions".[3]

The problems started when the president of the IFE's General Council, Luis Carlos Ugalde, scheduled to go on national TV to provide preliminary results, instead announced that "the estimated margins of statistical error [of the huge sample taken] do not allow us to clearly distinguish the political force that has obtained the largest percentage of the votes cast". A few minutes later López Obrador declared himself the winner by "at least 500,000 votes". Calderón, citing various exit polls and quick counts – none of which gave him a lead of less than two percentage points (that is, over 800,000 votes) – followed suit and asserted that he had won the elections (*La Jornada*, 2006a). By that time the IFE's online real-time vote census, Programa de Resultados Electorales Preliminares (PREP), gave Calderón a three-point lead, although, in three estimates based on a very large sample, this difference was reduced to only about half a point. Thus the tension on election night seemed far from the tranquillity expected of Mexico's democratic normality.

What had happened? To begin with, the election produced the worst result an electoral body can imagine: a very narrow victory for the incumbent party (Schedler, 2007: 88). By refusing to give preliminary results, Ugalde was simply following a previous accord among the parties; indeed, when he announced that the election was too close to call, he was simply reading a script based on one of four previously agreed-upon scenarios (Tello Díaz, 2007: 125). In any case, the PREP's results were not officially valid: these were to be produced by adding the results of the tally sheets of each electoral precinct in each of the 300 electoral districts starting on 5 July. Still, the final data produced by the PREP turned out to be almost perfect.

There had been one big blunder, however, on the IFE's part – or, more precisely, on Ugalde's part. When he went on national TV at 11 pm he failed to mention that, due to a previous agreement among the parties, the votes cast at polling places appearing in the PREP included tally sheets received "with inconsistencies in their filling out", that these cases had been placed in a separate file (the link to which was hard to find on the PREP website) and that the results from those sheets had not yet been computed. More than 2.5 million votes were contained in these tally sheets – and Ugalde did not bother to explain this to the audience watching him (ibid.: 163–164).[4]

Taking advantage of the IFE's gaffe, López Obrador announced, to great effect, that 3 million votes were missing. He knew that was not true. His campaign team had accessed those files 487 times during election night and knew the votes were not missing (ibid.: 163). As former IFE president José Woldenberg (2006) put it, "were it not a source of distrust, the claim that 3 million votes 'disappeared' would cause laughter". Furthermore, López Obrador's claim that he was ahead by at least 500,000 votes was also unsustainable. At 4 pm on election day one of his pollsters informed him that he was tied with Calderón (with 35 per cent of the votes each). Seven hours later, based on a quick count by his main pollster, López Obrador found out that he and Calderón were still tied (with 36 per cent each) and at 1 am he was notified that a quick count had him at 35.9 per cent, versus 37.2 per cent for the PAN candidate (Tello Díaz, 2007: 75, 160, 173).

On 5 July official results were to be produced by adding the tally sheets at the district level, but by that time López Obrador was already calling for either a total recount or the annulment of the electoral process. After first charging that cyber-fraud had taken place, he later asserted that the fraud had occurred "the old-fashioned way" (*El Universal*, 2006). The coalition then took its case to the Tribunal Electoral del Poder Judicial de la Federación (TEPJF, or Electoral Tribunal of the Federal Judiciary). At the recount that took place in the districts, 2,864 electoral packages were opened. This was a biased sample, as it was composed mostly of districts where Calderón had won and the coalition had challenged. In the end, however, all candidates lost votes, actually widening slightly the PAN candidate's lead over López Obrador. Then, on 5 August, the TEPJF ruled that a partial recount consisting of 11,839 electoral packages from 26 states was to take place. This again was a biased sample, as PAN had decided – in order not to stain the electoral process – not to contest the polling places where López Obrador had won.

As a way to exert political pressure over the TEPJF, the coalition's candidate had organized, starting on 3 August, a huge camp-out along one of Mexico City's main avenues, thus creating havoc with city traffic. It seemed that López Obrador did not place much faith in the partial recount. In an interview published on 20 August, eight days before the recount results were announced, he declared: "The most important changes in Mexico have never come about through conventional politics but rather from the streets ... Mexico needs a revolution" (Thomsonin, 2006). When the partial recount was finished, both López Obrador and Calderón lost votes: the former 73,254, the latter 83,357. Calderón thus saw his lead reduced minimally. Finally, on 5 September, the TEPJF issued its verdict on the electoral process. While noting that there had been some problems in the process, such as President Fox's constant interventions, it found no evidence of widespread electoral fraud, and therefore refused either to order a full recount or to annul the electoral process. In the end, Calderón won by 233,831 votes, or 0.58 per cent of the total – not far off the 0.64 per cent that the PREP had computed (TEPJF, 2006).

The camp-out ended on 15 September. The next day thousands of López Obrador's supporters, who had gathered in a "national democratic convention" in downtown Mexico City, proclaimed him the country's "legitimate president". He "took office" on 20 November and declared he was sending Mexico's institutions "to hell" (*La Jornada*, 2006b). López Obrador's strategy, however, did not end there. The aim was now to prevent the president-elect from taking his oath of office, as constitutionally mandated, before Congress. In the end the stratagem failed, and Calderón assumed the presidency in a tumultuous parliamentary session.

Final considerations

The outcome of Mexico's disputed 2006 elections no doubt will affect Latin American politics. The fact that a moderate, right-of-centre government is in power sends a clear signal to the continent. Early on in his administration, at a meeting in Davos, Switzerland, the Mexican president distanced himself from the alternative presented by Venezuela's Chávez, recasting the continental debate in terms of choosing not between right and left but between "the past and the future" – as he put it, "whether we are capable of moving forward in terms of markets and investment, or we go back to the old policies of the past, such as expropriation and nationalization" (*La Jornada*, 2007).

Interestingly, though, Calderón has also tempered his pro-US stand, emphasizing the importance of Mexico's ties with Latin America. Accordingly, his government has made some serious efforts to mend relations with both Cuba and Venezuela – even though the latter refused to recognize his government. Thus, even if the continental ideological confrontation persists, the Mexican side is weighing it from a more realist perspective. Calderón thus seems to be following a less idealistic diplomacy than his predecessor.

Ironically, Calderón's accession to power seems only to have increased the rivalries within PAN. Since the beginning of the new administration, former President Fox and several of his cabinet members have teamed with the party's president, Manuel Espino, to take on Chávez, thus interfering with Calderon's détente policy, and to try to retain the party's control in the next election.[5] So far, however, the president's team has come out victorious. At a recent meeting of PAN's National Council, it was able win a majority of seats for the forthcoming congress in which a new national leadership will be elected; it is now taken for granted that a member of Calderón's inner circle will become PAN's next president.

Within the PRD, on the other hand, analogous developments have not taken place. Although more modern and moderate currents within the party have re-emerged to contest López Obrador's hegemony, they still do not carry enough weight to move the party forward. Generally speaking, the PRD still holds its uncompromising positions. As Woldenberg (2007) put it, "with a consistency worthy of better causes, [in the PRD's] discourse the political battle seems like a confrontation between Saint George and the dragon". Thus, although an alarmingly high 38 per cent of the population do not believe the 2006 elections were clean, 65 per cent now approve of Calderón's performance (*Mural*, 2007: 4) and, not surprisingly, only 9 per cent of voters say they identify with the PRD (*Público*, 2007a).

Mexico's democratic institutions have survived a most difficult test – not only because it was a very close election, but also because the electoral edifice itself was questioned by one of the main contenders. One can therefore hope that the country's leaders will further strengthen the legitimacy of the democratic institutions that have been built over the past three decades. Furthermore, Calderón needs to take on the entrenched monopolies in order to send the signal that Mexico does not belong to a privileged élite. Such a progressive policy would not only alleviate the economic situation of millions of Mexicans but also increase the legitimacy of the current administration – and of the democratic regime. These potential steps notwithstanding, an effective social policy is imperative. As long as the gross inequality and poverty that exist in the country continue (the richest 10 per cent of Mexicans earn 24.6 times what the poorest 10 per cent earn; about half of the population lives in poverty), Mexico will be fertile soil for populist leaders to plough.

Notes

1. By March 2006 it had become clear that the PRI was not a real contender for the presidency.
2. Patricia Mercado of the Social Democrat and Peasant Alternative Party, who represented the "right" left, never carried more than 4 per cent of the votes in the polls.
3. Similarly, in their analyses of the 2006 electoral process, Aparicio (2006) and Estrada and Poiré (2007) conclude that there was no fraud.
4. The irregularities consisted mainly (92 per cent of the cases) of minor problems in entering votes, such as not indicating the number "0" where a small party had received no votes in the ballot box.
5. After Fox promised to ride his horse "to go south and defend" Venezuelans from Chávez's "authoritarian, demagogic and dictatorial" government, the business representative of the Venezuelan government in Mexico – Venezuela withdrew its ambassador during the Fox administration – even intervened to defend the Calderón administration (*El Universal*, 2007; *Público*, 2007b).

REFERENCES

Alemán, Ricardo (2005) "Itinerario Político: Creel ante el espejo", *El Universal*, 18 July.

———— (2006) "Itinerario político: López Obrador, muy lejos de Cárdenas y Juárez", *El Universal*, 18 June.

Aparicio, Javier (2006) "La evidencia de una elección confiable", *Nexos* 346, pp. 49–53.

Bartra, Roger (2006) "Fango sobre la democracia", *Letras Libres* (September), pp. 16–22.

Becerra, Ricardo, Pedro Salazar and José Woldenberg (2000) *La mecánica del cambio político en México: Elecciones, partidos y reformas*, Mexico City: Ediciones Cal y Arena.

Begné Guerra, Alberto (1999) "Y después de la transición?", *Nexos* 260, pp. 53–54.

Boletín (2003) "Rechaza la Sociedad Mexicana la intromisión de ministros de culto en asuntos políticos", UNAM-DGCS-644, 26 August.

Castañeda, Jorge G. (2006a) "Campeones acionales", *Reforma*, 17 May.

———— (2006b) "Latin America's Left Turn", *Foreign Affairs* 85(3), pp. 28–43, available at www.foreignaffairs.org/20060501faessay85302/jorge-g-castaneda/latin-america-s-left-turn.html.

Crónica (2006) "Cuatro candidatos coinciden en reforzar la relación diplomática con EU", *Crónica*, 4 June.

Delgado, Álvaro (2006) "O Calderón rompe con Fox y el Yunque o...", *Proceso*, 24 September.

El Universal (2006) "López Obrador ve fraude 'a la antigua', no cibernético", *El Universal*, 18 July.

———— (2007) "'Cabalgará' Fox contra Chávez", *El Universal*, 26 April.

Eisenstadt, Todd (2007) "The Origins and Rationality of the 'Legal versus Legitimate' Dichotomy Invoked in Mexico's 2006 Post-Electoral Conflict", *PS: Political Science and Politics* 40(1), pp. 39–44.

Estrada, Luis and Alejandro Poiré (2007) "The Mexican Standoff: Taught to Protest, Learning to Lose", *Journal of Democracy* 18(1), pp. 73–87.

Fernández Menéndez, Jorge (2007) *Calderón presidente: La lucha por el poder*, Mexico City: Grijalbo.

Garza Elizondo, H. (1994) "Los cambios de la política exterior de México: 1989–1994", *Foro Internacional* 34(4), pp. 534–544.

Glover, Amy (2006) "Águila o avestruz?", *Crónica*, 23 June.

IFE (2007) "Reporte final de los monitoreos de promocionales: Período del 19 de enero al 28 de junio de 2006", Instituto Federal Electoral, Mexico City, available at www.ife.org.mx/docs/Internet/IFE_Home/CENTRAL/Contenidos_Centrales/estaticos/Monitoreo/rep_final_monitoreos.pdf.

James, Ian (2005) "Venezuela's Chávez Tells Mexico's Fox: 'Don't Mess with Me'", *The Americas' Intelligence Wire*, 13 November.

Klesner, Joseph (2007) "The Mexican Elections: Manifestation of a Divided Society?", *PS: Political Science and Politics* 40(1), pp. 27–32.

La Jornada (2004) "Propone López Obrador apego a la no intervención", *La Jornada*, 5 May.

―――― (2006a) "El IFE, rebasado; aplaza el veredicto", *La Jornada*, 3 July.

―――― (2006b) "AMLO: Tendrá mi gobierno millones de representantes", *La Jornada*, 21 November.

―――― (2006c) "Debilita a AMLO apoyo de Chávez, dice Calderón", *La Jornada*, 23 March.

―――― (2007) "Calderón sufre acometida de Lula en Davos", *La Jornada*, 27 January.

Lawson, Chappell (2007) "How Did We Get Here? Mexican Democracy after the 2006 Elections", *PS: Political Science and Politics* 40(1), pp. 45–48.

Lemus, Silvia (1998) "De qué hablamos al hablar de transición?", *Nexos* 244, pp. 43–46.

Loaeza, Soledad (1999) *El Partido Acción Nacional, la larga marcha, 1939–1994: Oposición leal y partido de propuesta*, Mexico City: Fondo de Cultura Económica.

López Obrador, Andrés Manuel (2006) "50 compromisos: Respeto al derecho internacional", Mexico City, available at www.amlo.org.mx/50compromisos/36.php.

Mares, David R. (1996) "Strategic Interests in the U.S.-Mexican Relationship", in John Bailey and Sergio Aguayo Quezada, eds, *Strategy and Security in U.S.-Mexican Relations beyond the Cold War*, San Diego: University of California Press.

McKinley, James C. (2006a) "Feuding President and Mayor Eclipse Election Campaign", *New York Times*, 7 April.

―――― (2006b) "Election Crisis in Mexico as Top 2 Declare Victory", *New York Times*, 3 July.

Meyer, Lorenzo (1996) "La crisis del presidencialismo mexicano: Recuperación espectacular y recaída estructural, 1982–1996", *Foro Internacional* 36(1/2), pp. 11–30.

Mural (2006) "Encuesta Grupo Reforma: Elecciones 2006. Así llegan: Empate técnico y 12% de indecisos", *Mural*, 23 June.

―――― (2007) "Sube apoyo a Calderón", *Mural*, 1 June.

Partido Acción Nacional (2006) *Plataforma electoral 2006*, Mexico City: PAN, available at www.plataforma2006.pan.org.mx.

Paz, Octavio ([1985] 1987) "Hora cumplida (1929–1985)", in *El peregrino en su patria y presente fluido*, Mexico City: Fondo de Cultura Económica.

Petrich, Blanche, Rosa Elvira Vargas, Georgina Saldierna and J. M. Venegas (2002) "Orilló Fox a Castro a dejar la Cumbre; Bush llegó más tarde", *La Jornada*, 22 March.

Público (2007a) "Cada vez menos electores dicen que votarían por el PRD", *Público*, 4 June.

―――― (2007b) "Fox entorpece acercamiento con Venezuela: Gobierno mexicano", *Público*, 27 May.

Reforma (2005) "Pide Fox a paisanos voto cuidadoso", *Reforma*, 19 December.

Santa-Cruz, Arturo (2002) "From Transition to Consolidation: Mexico's Long Road to Democracy", *Revista de Ciencia Política* 22(1), pp. 90–111.

Schedler, Andreas (2007) "The Mexican Standoff: The Mobilization of Distrust", *Journal of Democracy* 18(1), pp. 88–102.

Tello Díaz, Carlos (2007) *2 de Julio: La crónica minuto a minuto del día más importante de nuestra historia contemporánea*, Mexico City: Planeta.

TEPJF (2006) "Dictamen relativo al cómputo final de la elección de presidente de los Estados Unidos Mexicanos: Declaración de validez de la elección y de presidente electo", Tribunal Electoral del Poder Judicial de la Federación, Mexico City, 5 September, available at www.trife.org.mx/documentos/computos2006/ReportePresidenteEUM.html.

Thomsonin, Adam (2006) "Mexico Poll Loser Vows Radical Fight 'On Street'", *Financial Times*, 21 August.

Vega, A. F. (2006) "Política exterior: En la frontera de lo imposible", *Excelsior*, 12 June.

Woldenberg, José (2006) "Cómo se recuentan los votos?", *Mural*, 6 July.

——— (2007) "Dieciocho años: Paradojas", *Reforma*, 10 May.

13

Quo vadis, Brazil?

Luiz Pedone

The election of Luiz Inácio Lula da Silva as president of Brazil in 2002 pointed towards significant economic, political and social change in Latin America's biggest country. Indeed, Lula's election is part of the most important political transformation that has taken place in Latin America since the transition from authoritarian regimes in the 1980s. New governments under Lula, Néstor Kirchner (Argentina, 2003), Tabaré Vázquez (Uruguay, 2004), Leonel Fernández (Dominican Republic, 2004), Evo Morales (Bolivia, 2005) and Michelle Bachelet (Chile, 2006) mark the rising of moderate-left parties to power and signal, in most of these countries, a movement away from the conservative, populist and neoliberal politics and policies of the 1990s. The trend, however, has not been uniform: the elections of Alan García (Peru, 2006) and Felipe Calderón (Mexico, 2006) represent victories for centrist or centre-right governments, while the elections of Daniel Ortega (Nicaragua) and Rafael Correa (Ecuador) and the re-election of Hugo Chávez (Venezuela) reaffirm the strength of the leftist outlook in the region.

Lula's presidency in Brazil is perhaps the most interesting one. He was elected in 2002 on his fourth attempt, on a palatable leftist platform. Nevertheless, in his first term he maintained all the economic stabilization mechanisms put in place by his predecessor, nominated banking executive Henrique Meirelles as his president of the central bank, the Banco Central do Brasil, and followed the most mainstream of economic policies. His leftist political platform dwindled substantially as pragmatism flourished. Yet despite corruption scandals that swirled around his closest

Which way Latin America? Hemispheric politics meets globalization, Cooper and Heine, eds, United Nations University Press, 2009, ISBN 978-92-808-1172-8

aides, the institution of programmes to help millions of Brazil's poor families – such as the Zero Hunger programme and later the Bolsa Família programme – gave him enough political clout to run for re-election.

It is through this innovative and pragmatic policy-making that Lula's government has nurtured public support for its agenda. Lula's adept governance has helped to foster the necessary atmosphere for implementing his policies. *Governance*, according to one definition, is "the ability of a government to exercise public policy" (Reinecke, 1998). Public policy, in turn, is enacted through legislative and judicial systems as a means of pursuing the public good. One of the things economic globalization did was to attain firm commitments on the part of governments "to regulate and supervise a variety of economic activities or to preserve what is the public's interest by providing public goods" (ibid.). One main aspect of governance, in practice, is the process by which authority is exercised in managing the economic and social resources of a country. Another is the capacity of government to design, formulate and implement policies (World Bank, 1992: 3b). Good governance is intrinsically related to government capacity: it is "central to creating and sustaining an environment which fosters strong equitable development, and it is an essential complement to sound economic policies" (ibid.: 1).

With this concept of good governance in mind, this chapter examines the Lula government's attempts to improve social conditions in Brazil by implementing innovative social and economic policies to redress inequalities and reduce poverty. Did these policies make a difference in Lula's successful re-election in 2006?

The Lula government comes to power

In October 2002, after the eight-year, two-term presidency of Fernando Henrique Cardoso, his health minister José Serra became the presidential candidate for the incumbent Partido da Social Democracia Brasileira (PSDB, or Brazilian Social Democracy Party). He stood no chance, however, against his opponent Lula, who was running for the fourth time as the candidate of the Partido dos Trabalhadores (PT, or Workers' Party). The unemployment and social impoverishment that resulted from the economic stabilization policies Cardoso had put in place were politically devastating for Serra's candidacy; further, since he could neither praise nor condemn his own party, his hands were tied. Lula, meanwhile, had cleverly crafted his electoral strategy to soften the ominous leftist-socialist ideology his party had used in previous elections.

Once in power, the Lula government offered up some surprises in its choice of people to fill certain ministerial positions. First and foremost was the nomination of Antonio Pallocci – a medical doctor, campaign co-ordinator and former mayor of the medium-sized city of Ribeirão Preto in the state of São Paulo – as minister of finance. Pallocci continued the firm application of extremely conservative monetary and fiscal policies, in order to keep inflation down and maintain the inflation targeting that had been established since the abrupt change in the central bank's board of directors at the beginning of 1999, after the devaluation of the real against the US dollar. Thus, even though the Lula government had been elected on a platform of "change", his predecessor's inflation policy remained untouched – indeed, inflation in Brazil continues to be held within the target band, according to the most recent data. The second important surprise was the nomination of Henrique Meirelles, former president of BankBoston International and a newly elected federal deputy of the PSDB in his home state of Goiás, as president of the central bank. His nomination was meant to offer guarantees to international financial institutions that Brazil would follow the rules, particularly after Argentina's default a few months before.

The economic climate facing the Lula government

After coming to power the Lula government faced several key economic difficulties. One was a low-growth economy. Since the 2001 energy crisis, Brazilian economic growth has gone in fits and starts. Indeed, until a relatively significant improvement in 2004, Brazil's economy grew at the lowest rate of any country in the region except Haiti, and the central bank projects the growth rate to remain relatively similar for the next few years, even with the development investment that the Lula government intends to make in the 2007–2010 period. Development policies also faced the challenge posed by the main objective of Brazil's economic policy: to keep inflation under control and produce a surplus (see fig. 13.1).

Then, after 2003, foreign direct investment diminished drastically in the absence of development drivers. Brazil discovered how vulnerable it was to changes in international trade and investment flows, particularly since its only sources of sustainable growth were its export-led industrial, mineral and agricultural commodities, which are particularly subject to international ups and downs. In recent years the Brazilian economy has been favoured by rising prices for commodities and increasing international trade, but an overvalued currency has led to the cancellation or reduction in scale of investment in numerous industrial projects. The country thus faces a development policy dilemma: should it have higher

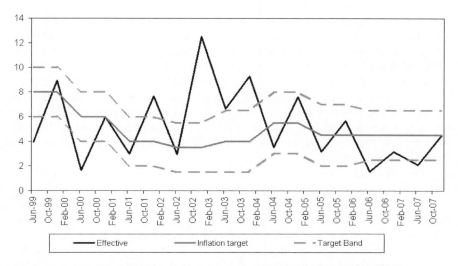

Figure 13.1 Brazilian Consumer Price Index, June 1999–December 2007
Source: Brazilian Institute of Geography and Statistics (2008); Central Bank of Brazil (2008).

state spending, with a higher tax burden and lower public sector invest-ment, or lower state spending with a lower tax burden and higher public sector investment? This is not a trivial dilemma to tackle. Not even Brazil's highly profitable energy companies can supply the investment capital that will be needed over the next few years (Castelar Pinheiro, 2005).

One important reason for the lack of investment is Brazil's low level of domestic savings. During the 1995–2002 privatization period a substantial amount – about US$30 billion – of foreign direct investment was injected into the Brazilian economy, much of it favouring the telecommunications and energy sectors. Now, however, large Brazilian companies are inves-ting abroad, especially in the energy, mining, steel and heavy construc-tion sectors, resulting in a net outflow of capital.

Brazil's high tax rates also continue to be a major impediment to attracting investment capital, according to the responses of senior managers in a 2005 World Bank Investment Climate Survey, in which Brazil received the highest percentage of investment firms reporting that the country's tax administration was a "severe" or "major" obstacle[1] (World Bank, 2005b). Compounding high taxes are a poor regulatory system, the lack of enforcement of contracts, high interest rates and a poorly trained labour force. By the same token, Brazil's tax burden of

36 per cent of gross domestic product (GDP) is totally out of line with international standards for developing countries (Oliveira and Giuberti, 2006) – approximately equal to that of countries such as Canada, the United Kingdom and Germany, with per capita GDPs 10 times greater than that of Brazil. Most Brazilian industrial federations and entrepreneurial associations condemn this heavy tax burden for its detrimental effect on the business climate. Moreover, inappropriate government expenditures provide more reason to criticize the tax burden, while Brazilian labour taxation induces the growth of a dual labour market, with a large informal sector.

Another impediment to the Brazilian economy is the "Brazil cost" – the name given to the bottlenecks caused by the poor physical infrastructure of roads and ports, shortages of energy and, perhaps most importantly, extensive and costly bureaucratic procedures, which are among the most onerous in the world (World Bank, 2005a).

One of Lula's election promises was to create 10 million jobs in the first four years of his government. The actual number, however, is well below that promised (see fig. 13.2). Furthermore, most gains have been in low-paid jobs, where previously informal agreements have been turned into formal contracts, such as those for maids and domestic workers. Meanwhile, during the period 1995–2005 the monthly real average income of labour force participants 10 years of age and older dropped (fig. 13.3). Moreover, average real income in Brazil's metropolitan regions also fell over the same period (IPEA, 2006: 12).

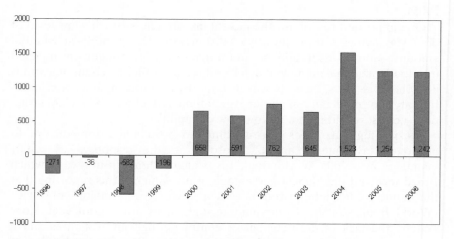

Figure 13.2 Formal employment: New jobs accrued per year (1,000)
Source: Ministério do Trabalho e Emprego (2008).

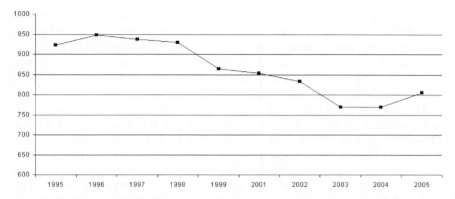

Figure 13.3 Real average income of all labour, ≥10 years of age, employed in the week of reference with income from labour, Brazil, 1995–2005
Note: Information for 2000 is unavailable.
Source: IBGE (2005: 41).

The Lula government's social policies

During its first term in office the Lula government implemented a number of social policies designed to help Brazil's poorest families. In this section, I provide a brief description and analysis of several of the more important of these programmes.

The Bolsa Família

One of the most important social policies implemented by the Lula government is the Bolsa Família (BF, or Family Scholarship) programme, the goal of which is to combat hunger and misery and promote the emancipation of the poorest families. Among its aims are to maintain school-age children in classrooms and to provide a full vaccination programme for children up to the age of six years old and pre- and post-natal care for pregnant women and nursing mothers. The programme is targeted at both poor families (those with per capita income between R$60 and R$120 per month) and the extremely poor (those who receive less than R$60 per month), who comprise roughly 40 per cent of the population, or some 75 million persons. Benefits range from R$15 to R$95 per month, depending on the family's per capita income and number of children. Between October 2003 and July 2006 the number of families receiving BF benefits increased from 1.2 million to 11.1 million, or more than 40 million persons. In 2006 the BF's budget was R$8.3 billion, a relatively small amount considering the valuable assistance the programme is rendering to Brazil's poorest families.

The BF's greatest relative impact has been in smaller municipalities and more poorly developed, primarily agricultural, areas, particularly in the north and northeastern regions. In this respect the programme represents an innovative social policy directed at cutting extreme poverty and improving governance by stabilizing the lives of large masses of impoverished Brazilians.

The northeastern municipality of Pedra Branca (Ceará state) is a typical example of a BF recipient. The town, which has about 40,000 inhabitants and is rated "low" on the Human Development Index (HDI), receives 43 per cent of its disposable income from the BF programme. BF transfers also account for 113 per cent of the municipality's public health budget and pay back 311 per cent of its contribution to the Tax on Circulation of Goods and 54 per cent of its share of the Fund of Municipal Participation. To communities such as Pedra Branca, one of the poorest in Brazil, the importance of the BF programme for improving school registration and the health of women and children is considerable. It has also had a definite influence in terms of lowering outmigration and even luring back some of those who left, thus reducing urban pressures in the southeastern and regional metropolitan areas.

Notwithstanding its importance for low-income communities, critics of the BF charge that it is not really an "exit door from poverty" but is more an assistance programme for the socially excluded, and that what is needed is not just to address social vulnerabilities but also to expand income and employment. The BF does indeed have some significant problems. One is that the programme has been politicized, transformed into a vote-getting instrument during the 2006 presidential campaign; indeed, Lula's passionate and emotional defence of the programme was detected in opinion polls as early as four months before the election took place.

Another problem is the lack of coordination among policies and programmes, and the failure to establish an information network for municipal, state and federal authorities. The programme's effectiveness could be improved by coordinating day care, school, professional training and micro-credit policies and programmes, as Mexico and Chile have done. Many political and administrative hurdles have also been put in place by competing interests at different levels of power – both licit and illicit, public and private – and the "vampires" that feed off this public assistance programme, contributing to corruption and the bad use of public funds.

Those in favour of the BF, however, argue that it permits families that are looking for future returns to keep their children in school, especially during the peak learning years up to age seven, and reduces the high cost of keeping children aged seven to 14 in school. Advocates also argue that the increased human capital in today's children will lead to better employment opportunities in the future and that the programme reduces inequality through the better distribution of education in society.

The BF programme might not be an "exit door from poverty", but is it enough to spur development? Is it merely a contemporary paternalistic programme of assistance to the poor that resembles policies implemented by Getúlio Vargas and in Argentina by Juan Perón in the 1950s, even though Lula claims that his government is the first to look out for Brazil's poor? Is the programme introducing oligarchic politics in the periphery of Brazil's large cities? Is Brazil facing a shift from the new syndicalism of the 1970s and 1980s to a new type of populism in the twenty-first century? These questions remain unanswered.

The Food Card

Soon after it came to power, the Lula government instituted the Cartão Alimentação (Food Card), the promise of which had been a major feature of its Zero Hunger programme announced during the election campaign. The programme attracted international attention since it followed the guidelines of the Food and Agriculture Organization Special Programme for Food Security and the World Bank food and nutritional policy recommendations – policies that are producing important results elsewhere. The Food Card was an emergency programme for those in a poor nutritional state receiving less then half the minimum annual salary of R$350 (roughly US$160). The programme was formulated by the Ministry for Food Security and for Combating Hunger and implemented through contracts with non-governmental organizations, municipalities, states and other federal institutions. The Food Card was later dropped in favour of a basket of programmes under the BF.

Higher education policy

Early in 2005 the Lula government instituted a new higher education policy, the Programa Universidade para Todos, or ProUni, to grant scholarships to low-income students to enable them to pursue an undergraduate degree in private higher education institutions, which in turn receive tax incentives. In its first year ProUni granted 112,000 scholarships to more than 1,000 private higher education schools. In addition, by 2010 it is expected that 10 new federal universities and 49 new campuses of existing institutions will be created to bring public and free higher education to the hinterland as a way of combating regional inequalities. The target is to have at least 30 per cent of youths between the ages of 18 and 24 in university, up from 12 per cent today.

Family agricultural policy

As another way to generate higher incomes in rural areas – and to absorb surplus labour and reduce outmigration from poor rural areas – the Lula government implemented the Programa Nacional de Fortalecimento da Agricultura Familiar (Pronaf, or National Programme for Strengthening Family Agriculture). The programme is aimed at small family farms, which account for a significant percentage of Brazil's production of numerous agricultural commodities (for example, 67 per cent of the nation-wide production of black beans, 97 per cent of tobacco, 84 per cent of cassava, 31 per cent of rice, 49 per cent of corn, 52 per cent of milk, 59 per cent of pigs, 40 per cent of chickens and eggs, 25 per cent of coffee and 32 per cent of soya). Pronaf organizes cooperatives to sell to industrial processing plants (modern agribusiness) in the states of Paraná and Santa Catarina in the south, and in poor areas in the southeast and northeast.

Evaluation of the results of the programme has found a small positive impact on the income and productivity of Pronaf beneficiaries except in the south, where family agriculture is better integrated with modern agribusiness. In the northeast it appears to work as a social assistance programme more than anything else. However, there are serious problems with the selection of recipients, and the effects on income and productivity are timid. Important modifications were made to the programme in 2003, but it is not yet possible to affirm whether they have improved its effectiveness or not.

Promoting the production and use of biodiesel fuel

In 2004 the Lula government established the Programa Nacional de Produção e Uso de Biodiesel (PNPB, or National Programme for the Production and Use of Biodiesel). Its purpose is to promote social inclusion and regional development through the generation of employment and income while reducing pollution and the emission of greenhouse gases from Brazil's buses and trucks. It also aims to guarantee competitive prices, quality and supply, and to produce biodiesel fuel from different oilseeds in different regions of the country.

Despite its environmental claims, however, the PNPB is more of a social assistance programme than an important energy policy, especially considering the modest targets that have been set for the programme (2 per cent of all diesel fuel sold to consumers in 2008, rising to only 5 per cent by 2013).

Declining income inequality in Brazil

Income inequality in Brazil's major metropolitan areas declined steadily between 2001 and 2006 (Paes de Barros et al., 2006: 10). However, the BF and other income transfer programmes introduced during both the Cardoso and the first Lula administrations (1995–2006) played only a small part – the BF, for example, represents only 0.5 per cent of national income. The greatest impact on reducing income inequality has come from the increase in salaries, retirement benefits and pensions for those below the minimum annual salary. Several factors in particular have helped to reduce income inequality:

• the reduction of unequal demographic distribution – that is, the number of adults is increasing in all income brackets
• income transfers through pensions and retirements paid by the social security system, the Benefício de Prestação Continuada (BPC, or Continuous Cash Benefits programme) and the BF programme
• an increase in non-labour income (which, however, represents less than one-quarter of total income)
• a dramatic increase in the number of self-employed with small amounts of capital
• better access to jobs, along with declining unemployment and increasing labour force participation
• declining education inequality among the employed and decreasing differences in labour income among workers with distinct levels of education.

Differences in labour income between state capitals and other average-sized cities in the country and between average-sized and smaller cities within the same state have also decreased. Discrimination, sadly, is still an important factor in the Brazilian labour market, with blacks receiving 30 per cent less pay in 2004 than whites with the same characteristics, while men earned 70 per cent more than women with the same observable characteristics.

In conclusion, there is a consistent trend of improvement in income distribution in Brazil, attributable both to labour market diversification and to the construction of social safety nets. Despite recent improvements, however, income inequality remains stubbornly high. For the past 30 years the richest 1 per cent of Brazilians have earned a little less than 20 per cent of total income while the poorest 50 per cent have earned around 12 per cent; more strikingly, the richest 10 per cent consistently get nearly half the total income while 90 per cent struggle for the other half. Moreover, notwithstanding the robust reliability of Brazilian data collection, between 5 and 7.5 per cent of national income remains unaccounted for. This represents income derived by Brazil's 20,000 or so richest families from undeclared interest earned in money markets, estimated to be worth between R$100 and R$150 billion per year. In short, to get in line with international patterns of income distribution for other medium-sized economic powers, Brazil would need to see a continuous decline in income inequality for the next 25 years at the rate observed since 2001.

If economic growth is the best way to reduce labour income inequality, policies need to be introduced to reduce wealth inequality as well. Such policies include:

• more stringent income and inheritance taxes
• equal opportunities for acquiring the education and training needed to qualify for higher-paying jobs
• improved access to the labour market to make productive use of capacities acquired
• reduced inequality in the treatment of gender and race in the labour market
• more efficient and progressive fiscal policy and spending
• stronger mechanisms to combat money laundering from illegal activities.

Such mechanisms are in common use in advanced industrialized countries that have gone through similar processes, but can they be implemented in Brazil as well?

The Lula government's re-election in 2006

Despite corruption charges brought against his closest ministers and friends from the Workers' Party and allied parties, Lula won his bid for re-election in the 2006 presidential election. Can his victory be attributed to the improvement in the distribution of labour income and to social assistance programmes, or simply to the choice of a weak candidate for president (Geraldo Alckmin) by the rival PSDB? In an attempt to answer this question, let us look at the results of the first round of the 2006 presidential election.

If we classify the 27 states of Brazil by their HDI from the highest (Distrito Federal) to the lowest (Maranhão), we see that Lula won 12 of the 13 states with the lowest HDI, while Alckmin won 10 of the 14 states with the highest HDI, sometimes with a substantial majority. One could argue from these results that the BF and other social programmes were important for Lula's victories in the lower-income states (see table 13.1). In this sense, the connection between income transfers and voting patterns sug-

Table 13.1 Minimum salary and pro-Lula vote in Brazil's 2006 presidential election, first round

Region	Families receiving BF payments (%)	Workers or social security recipients receiving minimum salary (%)	Pro-Lula vote (%)
Northeast	42.1–50.0 depending on state	46.0	56.1–80.0 depending on state
North	26.1–42.0	31.0	44.1–68.0
Southeast, South, Centre-West	10.0–26.0	18.0–23.0	20.0–44.0

Source: Bolsa Família; Instituto Brasileiro de Geografia e Estatística; Tribunal Superior Electoral.

gests low autonomous political behaviour on the part of voters – that is, as was the case during the Cardoso era, voters who receive more money in their pockets are more prone to vote for incumbent candidates.

The occurrence of a second-round run-off between Lula and Alckmin was a surprise to everyone, since Lula appeared to have gained victory in the first round. Nevertheless, the result of the second-round vote was decisive: Alckmin lost ground in 22 of the 27 states, irrespective of their HDI status, while Lula won by a wide margin in the vast majority of low-HDI states and even in such high-HDI states as Rio de Janeiro, Minas Gerais, Goiás and Espírito Santo – the crucial state of São Paulo gave Lula almost 48 per cent of the vote (see fig. 13.4).

So it was not only the BF and other social programmes that affected the electoral results. In Alckmin, Lula faced a weak opponent who failed to capitalize on the momentum of his first-round showing. More surprisingly, perhaps, Lula successfully managed to avoid having corruption charges stick to him. There was also a feeling among voters not to rock the boat.

Thus, the vote for Lula did not follow a rich/poor divide. Most of the middle class and a good part of the upper-middle class voted for him, despite seeing their incomes drop 46 per cent in the past six years. Did this give Lula a blank cheque to continue his policies?

One observation might be that, like Cardoso's 1994 election campaign, the 2006 Brazilian presidential election was a repeat of Clinton adviser James ("the Ragin' Cajun") Carville's maxim, "it's the economy, stupid". On the other hand, another Carville maxim, "change, not more of the same", which was true of Lula's success in 2002, was not even close to being true this time.

First round

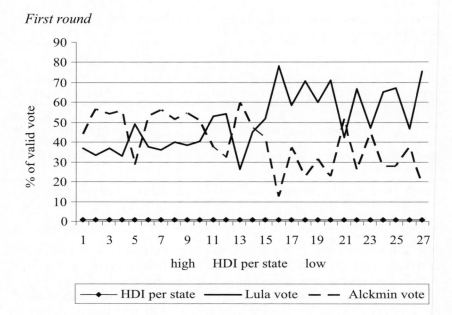

Second round

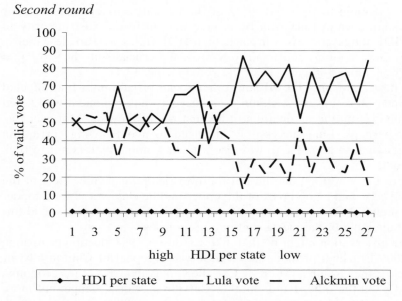

Figure 13.4 Lula versus Alckmin in the 2006 presidential election
Source: Constructed from UNDP and Tribunal Superior Electoral data.

Political questions for the Lula II government

What does it mean that Lula received 60 per cent of the vote in the second round of the 2006 Brazilian presidential election?

For the low-income worker, the Lula I government meant close to 6 million net new jobs and a 48 per cent increase in income for those earning between one and three times the minimum salary. For those getting no more than the minimum there were 2.2 million new jobs and a 124 per cent increase from 2003. The votes of the workers alone contributed a significant portion of Lula's overall total. Also, Lula now has the support of two-thirds of the elected or re-elected, and highly influential, state governors – even some, like Aécio Neves from Minas Gerais, from the Partido da Social Democracia Brasileira, a major opposition party.

What is Lula going to do with this political power? What kind of reforms will he push? Other presidents, too, have received a blank cheque: Fernando Collor de Mello (1990–1992) was going to kill inflation with one shot; instead he shot at middle- and upper-middle-class savings and salaries. Cardoso never mentioned a salary squeeze, bureaucratic anorexia, cutting down on university staff or privatization in either his first or second presidential campaigns. Unfortunately, the Lula II government is in a strong coalition with politicians connected to *fisiologismo*, oligarchic or patronage politics, and the likelihood of important changes on this old familiar ground is not great.

Another key issue is democratic governance. Computerized voting has largely solved difficulties surrounding vote counting and the actual act of voting, but a number of issues remain. These include the financing of political parties and electoral campaigns, the excessive number of political parties, the design of the electoral system and open or closed lists.

Corruption also remains so significant that not even a special government ministry to combat it is much more than a paper tiger. Fighting corruption requires the deep commitment of Congress, the executive and economic agents, which is far from being achieved in Brazil. On the contrary, the congressional budgetary process seems to nourish corruption: individual and state bench amendments are mainly "pork-barrel" projects.

Will Lula be able to curb the corruption that surrounds him? What will be the effect of the findings of congressional committees on cases already under investigation?

Economic questions for the Lula II government

How can the Lula II government establish a model for growth and development given the restrictions imposed by the inherited liberal model, vulnerability to external economic events, high public debt, low capacity for domestic saving, economies of scale and new competition coming from the industrialized South, mainly China and India?

Easing Brazil's serious structural and social bottlenecks in the areas of education, health, professional training, social security, crime prevention, transportation, energy and regulation will be crucial for sustaining the country's economic development in the years to come. On the macroeconomic front, Brazil's interest rates, though no longer as excessive as they once were, remain high, and the heavy tax burden is a major impediment to investment. But what are the chances of major economic reforms when the country needs tax, judicial and political revamping all at the same time?

Foreign policy under Lula

Under Foreign Relations Minister Celso Amorim – formerly Brazil's ambassador to the United Nations – and his Secretary-General Samuel Pinheiro Guimarães, the Lula government has returned to the tradition of an independent Brazilian foreign policy. As Andrew Hurrell (2008: 51) notes, after coming to power in early 2002 Lula's government worked to contrast its nationalist foreign policy against that of the preceding government, which was seen to be too accommodating to the liberalizing and globalizing agenda and not protective enough of Brazilian interests. Under this policy, Brazil is fostering strong alliances not only with the European Union and the United States but also with emerging economic and political powers such as China, India and South Africa.

In the case of the latter two countries, Brazil joined with them to establish the India-Brazil-South Africa (IBSA) dialogue forum (Devraj, 2004). At the time, the Brasilia Declaration[2] – which was the first official declaration of the trilateral group – demonstrated the three countries' willingness to work together to lobby for reforms to international institutions, specifically the United Nations, that will benefit developing countries (Flemes, 2007). That Brazil "has been the driving force" (Lechini, 2007) behind the alliance has demonstrated Lula's commitment, expressed in his inaugural address, to the belief that "the democratization of international relations, without hegemonies of any kind whatsoever, is as important for the future of Mankind as the consolidation and development of democracy within each state" (Lula da Silva, 2003).

As well as looking throughout the world for partners, in the words of Lula, Brazil's "special passion with Argentina" continues despite all past and existing problems. Mercosur (or Mercosul, in Portuguese), the customs union among Argentina, Brazil, Paraguay and Uruguay, recently expanded to include Venezuela as a full member and remains a priority. Is Mercosur a failure? Judged on the basis of 50 years of European integration through the establishment of stable norms and institutions, such as the various commissions, a parliament and a sole currency, Mercosur has not fulfilled its objectives. But where were we when Brazil and Argentina signed the Iguazú Declaration in 1985? At the time, some feared conflict between the two countries as both sought to develop nuclear technology and uranium enrichment in an old sentiment of struggle for hegemony in the region. In Mercosur's 15 years much has been done to harmonize policies, tariffs and rules, despite the macroeconomic difficulties. Most countries in the region must find models to resolve their social problems – most strikingly, acute poverty. If Mercosur succeeds in ending old conflicts and highlighting the reciprocal importance of the interchange of trade and investment, the chances of its becoming institutionalized will improve greatly.

The region is at a crossroads. Its societies are among the most fractured in the world, with great disparities between haves and have-nots, but it is also rich in natural resources. Some sectors of the regional economy contain firms that are leaders in world markets: in particular, in Brazil Petrobras is one of the world's largest energy companies and a leader in deep-sea oil exploration and production, Embraer is a strong competitor in the manufacture of aircraft for short- and medium-range air transportation and Companhia Vale do Rio Doce is a leading mining and industrial concern. Further, Argentina maintains a leading position in agricultural products, while environment concerns are giving more prominence to Brazilian ethanol.

Only with bold cooperation and communication among leaders in government, business and other interests will the region be able to face the trade and security challenges that lie ahead. Venezuela's rapid inclusion as a full member of Mercosur is a positive step, given that country's oil and natural gas resources and money to invest in the region, but it comes at the cost of potential political interference in the domestic affairs of other countries on the part of Hugo Chávez – witness his connections with Bolivia's Evo Morales, Peru's Ollanta Humala and Ecuador's Rafael Correa. Between the two regional leaders, Chávez and Lula, is there a duet in favour of energy cooperation or a struggle for regional leadership? The outlook for the future, given nationalist policies in the region, is at best uncertain.

Foreign policy questions for the Lula II government

Brazilian foreign policy, with Amorim and Guimaráes remaining at the helm, faces a number of diplomatic and international relations challenges.[3] One is concern about the state of democracy in Venezuela. Another is the fate of Mercosur, which, like a phoenix, keeps dying and coming back life. Given that Brazil's trade with South American countries is as important as its trade with the United States or the European Union, better coordination of policies is needed, along with a greater institutionalization of processes – such as a structural convergence fund and both a Mercosur parliament and a financial institution. Venezuela entered Mercosur with an energy cooperation and infrastructure investment agenda, but its international relations with Iran, the United States and the European Union and Chávez's political boldness raise scepticism about Venezuela's role. The potential addition of Chile might be a stabilizing factor for Mercosur; since its redemocratization in 1989–1990, however, Chile has been looking at Asia-Pacific links. Also, with the memory of Bolivia's nationalization of Petrobras's national gas interests still fresh, for the sake of regional energy security Lula will have to pay greater attention to his counterparts in Bolivia, Venezuela, Argentina and Chile.

Conclusion

The Brazilian case demonstrates the various factors influencing Latin American countries in the early twenty-first century. With his first election win in 2002, Luiz Inácio Lula da Silva seemed poised to bring about political, economic and social changes in Brazil. However, after running on a platform of change, Lula quickly moved towards a politics of pragmatism. The appointment of relatively surprising and conservative people to key positions – such as the minister of finance and Lula's nominee for the president of the central bank – demonstrated that Lula was happy to follow some of the policies of the Cardoso government in order to keep inflation down and promote prosperity in the country.

Lula's desire for pragmatism has not come at the detriment of socially progressive policies, however, as he has implemented various programmes to aid Brazil's poorest citizens. In doing so, he has maintained the support of the population and his ability to govern – and win re-election in 2006. That his social initiatives coincided with and contributed to a decline in income inequality in Brazil did not hurt his candidacy either. Yet, although the recent improvements in Brazil's situation have become a consistent trend, income inequality in the country remains persistently high – with a mere 10 per cent of the population enjoying half of the country's income while 90 per cent of the population share the rest. This fact demonstrates that Lula's second administration faces a variety of challenges; namely how he will use the political power that he has acquired, as well as whether or not his administration is willing and committed to ending the charges of corruption that are pointed at people in and around government.

While these problems are domestic, Lula must also keep a focus on Brazilian foreign policy. It is here that his government's progressive face can be seen most clearly. As Brazil continues to try to be regarded as a regional leader, it is also working with institutions such as IBSA and the G-20+ to become a voice for the global South at large. These commitments to reforming international institutions mean that Brazil is helping to bring Latin American issues to the minds of players in the global arena. However, with the growing roles and strength of other Latin American countries – such as Venezuela, Bolivia and Chile – Lula's administration must take note of its regional partners in order to mitigate instability in the region while also pushing for cooperation. The challenges facing Brazil and Lula in the upcoming years are many, and it will necessitate balancing pragmatism and progressiveness for the region's largest country to continue on its current path.

Notes

1. The other lowest-ranked countries were, in order, Ethiopia, Bangladesh, Kyrgyzstan, Guatemala, China and the Czech Republic.
2. For the full text of the Brasilia Declaration see www.ibsa-trilateral.org.
3. For more elaboration on Brazilian foreign policy see Gregory and de Almeida (2008).

REFERENCES

Brazilian Institute of Geography and Statistics (2008) *Statistical Database*, available at www.ibge.gov.br/.

Castelar Pinheiro, Armando (2005) "Accelerating and Sustaining Economic Growth in Brazil: A Microeconomic Agenda", paper presented at "Challenges for the Microeconomic Agenda", Brasilia, 13 December, available at www.cni.org.br/empauta/src/Apresentacao_castelar.pdf.

Central Bank of Brazil (2008) *Inflation Targeting in Brazil*, available at www.bcb.gov.br/pec/metas/InflationTargetingTable.pdf.

Devraj, Ranjit (2004) "India, Brazil, South Africa Ready to Lead Global South", Inter Press Service News Agency, 5 March.

Flemes, Daniel (2007) "Emerging Middle Powers' Soft Balancing Strategy: State and Perspectives of the IBSA Dialogue Forum", Working Paper No. 57, German Institute of Global and Area Studies, Hamburg.

Gregory, Denise and Paulo Roberto de Almeida (2008) "Brazil and the Heiligendamm Process", in Andrew F. Cooper and Agata Antkiewicz, eds, *Emerging*

Powers in Global Governance: Lessons from the Heiligendamm Process, Waterloo, ON: Wilfrid Laurier University Press.

Hurrell, Andrew (2008) "Lula's Brazil: A Rising Power, But Going Where?", *Current History* (February), pp. 51–57.

IBGE (2005) *Pesquisa Nacional por Amostra de Domicílios 1995/2005*, Brasilia: Instituto Brasileiro de Geografia e Estatística, Diretoria de Pesquisas, Coordenacão de Trabalho e Rendimento.

IPEA (Instituto de Pesquisa Econômica Aplicada) (2006) "Panorama Conjuntural", *Boletim de Conjuntura* 74 (September), pp. vii–xii.

Lechini, Gladys (2007) "Middle Powers: IBSA and the New South-South Cooperation", *NACLA Report on the Americas* (September/October), pp. 28–33.

Lula da Silva, Luiz Inácio (2003) "A New Course for Brazil", Address to Congress by President of the Federative Republic of Brazil on the Occasion of his Inauguration, 1 January, Brasilia, available at www.mre.gov.br/ingles/politica_externa/discursos/discurso_detalhe3.asp?ID_DISCURSO=2068.

Ministério do Trabalho e Emprego (Ministry of Labour and Employment) (2008) *Cadastro Geral de Empregados e Desempregados*, available at www.caged.gov.br/cagedweb/index.asp.

Oliveira, José Teófilo and Ana Carolina Giuberti (2006) *Tax Structure and Tax Burden in Brazil: 1980–2004*, Secretaria de Estado da Fazenda do Espírito Santo, available at www.sefaz.es.gov.br/publicacoes/arquivos/Taxation_in_Brazil.pdf.

Paes de Barros, Ricardo, Mirela de Carvalho, Samuel Franco and Rosane Mendonça (2006) "Uma Análise das Principais Causas da Queda Recente na Desigualdade de Renda Brasileira", IPEA Discussion Paper 1203, Instituto de Pesquisa Econômica Aplicada, Rio de Janeiro.

Reinecke, Wolfgang (1998) *Global Public Policy: Governing without Government?*, Washington, DC: Brookings Institution Press.

World Bank (1992) *Governance and Development*, Washington, DC: World Bank.

——— (2005a) *World Development Index*, Washington, DC: World Bank.

——— (2005b) *World Development Report 2005: A Better Investment Climate For Everyone*, Washington, DC: World Bank.

14

The Haitian imbroglio

Yasmine Shamsie

A number of countries in the Western hemisphere face profound development challenges, but Haiti stands alone. Not only is its economy in tatters but, for the second time in a decade, it sits at the centre of a full-blown multinational peacebuilding exercise.[1] On 29 February 2004 President Jean-Bertrand Aristide was forced into exile, leading to the establishment of the UN Stabilization Mission in Haiti, known by its French acronym MINUSTAH. Soon after, bilateral, multilateral and private development agencies arrived in Haiti pledging to support democratic development and post-conflict reconstruction.

Haiti's new President René Préval, elected in February 2006, set out his objectives for the country during his election campaign: enrol every child in school, create a functioning healthcare system, reform the judicial system and assist the peasantry (Mozingo, 2006: 3). Success on these fronts, however, will depend on the reactivation and development of the country's economy – a formidable task on its own, but particularly problematic given that, as Dani Rodrik (2001: 55) has observed, "Global integration has become, for all practical purposes, a substitute for a development strategy." This state of affairs poses serious challenges for small, dependent, post-conflict countries such as Haiti, which have few effective policy instruments for managing their relations with global markets. Moreover, they are often acutely dependent on external assistance, while donors are firmly committed to a neoliberal market-driven policy set. Finally, post-conflict states like Haiti must also grapple with externally driven state-building exercises, which further constrain the range of the possible.

Which way Latin America? Hemispheric politics meets globalization, Cooper and Heine, eds, United Nations University Press, 2009, ISBN 978-92-808-1172-8

This chapter examines two of Haiti's economic development strategies, both strongly endorsed by major donors: reinvigorating the country's export-processing zones, and harnessing the remittances of its large diaspora. I argue that neither strategy is likely to provide the foundations for a broad-based sustainable recovery that will benefit the majority of Haitians. Moreover, neglecting rural employment and development constitutes a weighty oversight that diminishes the prospects of establishing equitable growth.

The donor formula

It seems axiomatic, almost humdrum, to assert that globalization constrains states in pursuing their national policy goals. Equally evident is that it presents particularly formidable challenges to those states on the global periphery (Abrahamsen, 2000; Degnbol-Martinussen and Lauridsen, 2001; Halliday, 1987). And yet any discussion that explores the possibility of achieving social progress in a country of the global South today must begin with these observations. The problem is neatly captured by Caribbean scholars Anthony Payne and Paul Sutton (2001: 19–20):

> [States] now have to recognize the power not only of other states and inter-state organizations, on which international relations analysis has traditionally focused, but also of international capital, the banks and the foreign exchange markets, all of which constantly scrutinize what states are doing and have the means, by either bestowing or withdrawing their favour, to force them to adopt economic policies appropriate to capitalist interests.

In addition, it is widely acknowledged that the globalization of production, trade and finance is decidedly more injurious to weak states, or so-called fragile states,[2] that are already struggling to carry out their duties to their citizens.

It would be erroneous, however, to imply that globalization's constraints translate into hopelessness. Indeed, prominent development scholars have been exploring the problem of dwindling "policy space" and proposing alternative policies as well as theoretical approaches that could preserve and expand that space (see, for example, Gallagher, 2005). A recent comparative research study by Sandbrook et al. (2007) is noteworthy. In their examination of Costa Rica, Mauritius, Chile and the Indian state of Kerala, the authors convincingly demonstrate that "opportunities exist to achieve significant social progress in the periphery, despite a global economic order that favours the core industrial countries" (ibid.: 3). Still, these country case studies bear little resemblance to Haiti. Kerala and Mauritius (the closest in semblance to Haiti) exhibited features – astute leadership, a strong and capable state, particular historical conditions, which in the case of Mauritius included a powerful and cohesive bourgeoisie – that are absent in Haiti. Moreover, one could argue that, while each country exhibits a specific set of circumstances and historical trajectories that can prove to be a challenge, Haiti's "burdens of history" are particularly daunting (see Fatton, 2002, 2007).

Reflecting on the proper mix of policies to address unemployment, poverty, inequality and hunger is timely not only for Haitians but for Latin Americans in general. The failure of neoliberal-inspired Washington Consensus policies[3] to contribute to human betterment in the region has been well documented (Altimir, 2002; Londoño and Székely, 1997; O'Donnell, 1998; Portes and Hoffman, 2003; Teichman, 2001). While it is true that economic growth has occurred in certain sectors of individual countries, the populations most in need remain unaffected, if not worse off. Evelyn Huber and Fred Solt (2004: 156–158) show that while Latin America's more liberalized economies might have registered better economic growth statistics, "they suffered higher volatility, saw greater increases in inequality, and experienced higher levels of poverty". Further, Huber and Solt note that where higher levels of growth in the more liberalized economies did occur, there was no "trickle down", nor did growth relieve the higher levels of poverty in those more liberalized economies. A fresher assessment by a long-time observer of the region reaffirms these research findings:

> Economically, the region has been limping along for years. True, the past two years have brought mostly good news: foreign investment has started flowing in, trade has expanded at a strong pace, family remittances are surging, and inflation remains low. But few analysts are confident that the gains can be sustained. The region's economic improvement is mostly the result of a particularly benign global economy that has boosted Latin America's commodity exports and kept interest rates down, easing the burden of the region's high debt. (Hakim, 2006: 41)

Not surprisingly, the small, debt-distressed countries of the Caribbean have fared particularly poorly under the neoliberal policy set, with its accent on external openness. The options for these countries have narrowed significantly in the past decade, leading Payne and Sutton (2001) to suggest that "the development environment of the 1990s has been more forbidding than perhaps ever before". The authors follow this assertion with a dismal description of the region under neoliberalism:

endemically high employment, severe poverty amidst wealth and good living for some, social decay, growing amounts of crime and worrying levels of environmental deterioration. Within such a general context the pockets of prosperity that do exist do not generally extend to whole countries: they are based much more in certain sectors or districts set apart from, and increasingly guarded against (literally), the rest of Caribbean society. (Ibid.: 22)

This rather gloomy picture has triggered the emergence of various social movements across the region that have advocated for increased policy space. Notwithstanding these efforts, deviation from conventional economic thinking and associated prescriptions is extremely difficult (Sandbrook et al., 2007: 24–25). For Haiti, which depends on the international community for 60 per cent of its budget (Mulet, 2007), departing from donor formulas is impracticable.

The World Bank (2006a) has described Haiti's development pattern as "characterized by marked inequalities in access to productive assets and public services, which together with low growth, has resulted in widespread poverty". The International Monetary Fund (2007: 2) notes that more than 50 per cent of the country's population live below the US$1 a day poverty line and 76 per cent live below the US$2 a day poverty line. The UN Development Programme's 2006 *Human Development Report* (United Nations, 2006) ranks it 154th out of 177 countries based on achievements in life expectancy, educational attainment and adjusted real income. Moreover, the World Bank (2006b: iii) notes that the country "suffers from substantial inequality, with nearly half of the national income going to those in the richest 10 per cent of the population". Haiti's rural population and peasant farmers make up the largest segment of the poor and are the most destitute. The rural poor account for three-quarters of the country's poor, with only one-quarter having access to safe water and one in six to adequate sanitation (Erikson, 2004: 4). Currently, outside actors provide almost everything, from medical care to meals for school children to security in the streets. Given this extreme dependence, the policy space available to the Haitian government for crafting a national development strategy is limited.

Tony Addison (2005) argues that two major difficulties present themselves for post-conflict countries such as Haiti as they struggle to reconstruct and meet the welfare needs of their citizens. First, economic management can prove difficult given that the exports of post-conflict countries tend to be limited to a very small number of primary commodities; hence, "economic recovery can easily be derailed". Second, the protectionism employed by Western industrialized countries usually thwarts "trade-led agricultural growth", which is problematic given that "agriculture is a vital sector for post-conflict recovery and for the creation of peaceful livelihoods in general". While new aid modalities are attempting to address the first problem, the second difficulty is often overlooked. Addison (ibid.: 3) argues that, unless these obstacles are overcome, the best that can result from international efforts is a return to the pre-conflict state of things, "often resurrecting and exacerbating deep inequalities, and leaving countries weaker in their ability to achieve broad-based development".

The development model that foreign donors favour today in Haiti does not explicitly address these obstacles; rather, it is premised on a steadfast faith in export-led growth and the centrality of the private sector in the development process. Support for this approach stems from a continuing ideological adherence to neoliberal precepts combined with the belief that island economies are simply too small to consume the expanded production that growth implies (Dupuy, 1994). Accordingly, Western donors believe Haiti should exploit its two comparative advantages: the lowest-cost labour in the hemisphere and proximity and preferential access to the US market under the terms of the Haitian Hemispheric Opportunity through Partnership Encouragement Act (HOPE Act), a trade-enhancing provision of the Caribbean Basin Initiative.[4] Before the US Congress passed the Act in December 2006, apparel imports from Haiti qualified for duty-free treatment only if they were made from US or Haitian fabric. The HOPE Act allows duty-free treatment of apparel and automotive wire harnesses from Haiti if at least 50 per cent of their value derives from any combination of the United States, Haiti and partner countries of US free trade agreements or regional preference programmes. The quantity of apparel eligible for duty-free treatment under this provision is limited in the first year to the equivalent of 1 per cent of overall US apparel imports, expanding gradually over five years to reach 2 per cent in the fifth year. The HOPE Act also removes duties for three years from a limited quantity of woven apparel made from fabric produced anywhere in the world (Office of the US Trade Representative, 2006).

Hence, Haiti's development is seen as vitally dependent on re-energizing the country's export-assembly sector by capitalizing on the HOPE Act, the country's proximity to the US market and its low labour costs. Donors are also funding programmes to assist the Haitian private sector, viewed as the country's engine of growth, and to harness the financial resources and technological know-how of the Haitian diaspora. In sum, entrepreneurship, direct foreign investment and the Haitian diaspora are seen as key to encouraging higher growth rates of gross domestic product (GDP), increasing employment and creating a more diversified export economy (Haiti, 2004; Taylor, 2004; World Bank, 2006b).[5]

It is important to note that this strategy is similar to the plan donors endorsed a decade earlier. With the exception of the importance now attached to the migration and development nexus – the potential benefits of remittances from and exports to the diaspora – there appears to be little new for Haiti.

The absence of a strategic focus on the rural sector is noteworthy but not unanticipated. Historically, the Haitian government has placed little emphasis on the performance of smallholders and the area of food production for local consumption (Kumar, 2000). Moreover, agriculture has received little attention over the past two decades because of broader trends in development aid. Donors largely abandoned this sector because of perceived failures of earlier investments, a new interest in non-farm activities in rural livelihoods and the existence of fewer potential investments in agriculture due to the negative effects of agricultural liberalization policies. Hence, although the importance of agriculture is often acknowledged in countries such as Haiti, donors and governments have been supporting fewer and fewer investment programmes in this sector (Dorward et al., 2004: 612).

The revitalization of export-processing zones[6]

For almost three decades US manufacturers have been establishing operations in Central America and the Caribbean, where labour is abundant and cheap, in order to compete more effectively in global markets. As Portes and Itzigsohn (1997: 240) note, many Caribbean Basin nations have tried to link themselves to this corporate strategy by establishing export-processing zones (EPZs). Haiti is no exception.

The first generation of US firms, established during the dictatorship of François "Papa Doc" Duvalier (1957–1971), failed to spark development due in great part to a lack of infrastructure, local capital and basic services. Undaunted by these obstacles and encouraged by US President Ronald Reagan's 1982 Caribbean Basin Initiative, which promised duty-free access for specified items from designated countries of the Caribbean Basin, the regime of Jean-Claude "Baby Doc" Duvalier (1971–1986) expanded export manufacturing, with particular emphasis on the assembly industry (DeWind and Kinley, 1986; Dupuy, 2007: 48; Hooper, 1987). Incentives offered to attract US industries to the country were generous: tax holidays of 10 years, complete profit repatriation and a guaranteed non-unionized workforce. The result was a massive expansion of assembly operations, with exports from this sector growing at an average rate of 40 per cent a year during the 1970s (Deere and Antrobus, 1990: 175). By the early 1980s Haiti was second only to Mexico among the US subcontracting territories in the Western hemisphere, having attracted some 240 multinational corporations employing 60,000 workers (mostly women) (Thomas, 1988). In fact, in 1985, one year before Jean-Claude Duvalier's forced exile, Haiti was ninth in the world in the assembly of goods for US consumption, with this subsector generating more than half the country's industrial exports and earning one-quarter of its foreign exchange (McGowan, 1997).

The US government, Haiti's most important bilateral donor, vigorously supported this model along with the restructuring of the Haitian economy. For instance, Washington directed much of its aid to the country's infrastructure and technical-administrative apparatus, since these were viewed as crucial to the assembly sector's success. It should be noted *en passant* that establishing agro-processing industries constituted the other pillar of the export-based development strategy advanced by donors at that time (Dupuy, 1994; Robinson, 1996: 271). The US Agency for International Development employed a number of strategies to this end, including dumping massive amounts of rice on the Haitian market. By undercutting peasant producers, the agency tried to encourage a shift away from subsistence agriculture towards agricultural export production.

While export processing under Jean-Claude Duvalier's regime became the most dynamic sector of the economy, its effects were in the main disappointing. No backward or forward linkages to the Haitian economy were developed, and the industry's effects on Haiti's fiscal and debt situation, as well as on its balance of trade, were problematic (Shamsie, 2006). In part this was because export-processing industries generally earn less foreign exchange than do primary products, given the high import content of projects. Indeed, the data suggest that "even if exports of assembled goods increase significantly, this may not compensate for the loss of foreign exchange from traditional agricultural exports" (Deere and Antrobus, 1990: 180–181). Food prices also soared as rural workers from both the agricultural production and the food distribution sectors were lured to Port-au-Prince's manufacturing sector by the promise of better wages (Trouillot, 1990: 216). For example, women, the assembly industry's target labour force, were the mainstay of the country's marketing system for locally grown produce (Mintz, 1989). This urban-based strategy led to an increase in the price of local food and housing, with detrimental consequences for Haiti's poorest.

Inequality also increased during the years the model was employed, in great part because it favoured the economic development of Port-au-Prince (the urban sector) over the rest of the country (the rural sector): the gap between rich and poor widened as urbanization increased. The rapid spread of these urban-based industries served to reinforce an already worrisome economic polarization in the country. Trouillot (1990: 210) illustrates this tendency with developments in the electricity sector. He notes that while the production of electricity increased, only certain social sectors benefited, with Port-au-Prince and its surrounding boroughs consuming 93 per cent of the electricity produced in the country in 1979. The increased polarization was so obvious that, by the early 1980s, even the World Bank, a strong supporter of the assembly industry, suggested the model needed to be modified.

To be sure, corruption also played an important role in the failure of this development model. The expression *le siphonage*, or "siphoning off", has been used to describe the corrupt practices of the Duvalier regime. According to Michael Hooper (1995: 135–136), "In the four years before their flight, Jean-Claude Duvalier and his entourage stole much more than the country's annual national budget ... In addition to his salary, a US$2.4 million expense account and a US$2 million supplementary account, Jean-Claude Duvalier stole US$120.5 million and [his wife] US$94.6 million between 1981 and 1985." But even if one sets aside the effects of corruption, assembly manufacturing enterprises never became sufficiently developed to have a real impact on the overall economy or on Haitian society. Because these enterprises used "an accumulation model based on super-exploitation of labour (very low salaries, no social security, prohibition of bargaining rights etc.)", the trickle-down effect of the employment generated was minimal (Castor, 1994: 160).

Although EPZs have accomplished little in economic and social terms, they continue to appeal to bilateral and international aid agencies. The reasons are straightforward: they create jobs that countries like Haiti desperately need; they have allowed some countries – the so-called Asian tigers are often cited – to diversify their economies and achieve sustained growth; and, for Haiti at least, donors see very few other options. This argumentation may appear sound, but cautious scrutiny is warranted, for several reasons.

First, many of the trade policies that served the East Asian countries that successfully used EPZs are now largely proscribed by commitments made in bilateral or multilateral investment and trade agreements (Chang, 2002). Indeed, the benefits Haiti receives from trade-facilitating mechanisms like the HOPE Act are dwarfed by agreements produced during the Uruguay Round of trade talks: the Agreement on Trade-Related Aspects of Intellectual Property Rights, the General Agreement on Trade in Services and the Agreement on Trade-Related Investment Measures. These accords, in conjunction with continued protectionism by industrialized countries, make it exceedingly difficult for countries in the global South – let alone post-conflict states such as Haiti – to benefit from this export-led growth strategy (Degnbol-Martinussen and Engberg-Pedersen, 2003; Grinspun and Kreklewich, 1994; Rodrik, 2004; Sandbrook et al., 2007: 53; Stiglitz, 2002: 214). Robert Wade (2003: 621) offers an even harsher judgement, noting that together these agreements "make comprehensively illegal many of the industrial policy instruments" used by newly industrializing countries, locking in "the position of Western countries at the top of the world hierarchy of wealth". To be sure, the HOPE Act does provide some advantages, since it makes Haiti eligible for a few new trade benefits. However, as far as trade-facilitating mechanisms go, it is unexceptional; benefits are quite limited and come attached with a list of political and economic conditions.

Second, direct foreign investment, while certainly a valuable contribution to development efforts, will not be easy to attract given Haiti's profile. It is well known that investment is not evenly distributed among countries in the global South. Private capital tends to flow where opportunities for sizeable profits exist under predictable and stable conditions. Troubled countries like Haiti, that are beset by underdeveloped financial systems and economic infrastructure, social unrest and unevenly implemented economic policy, are barely magnets even for short-term investment in, for example, assembly manufacturing (Degnbol-Martinussen and Engberg-Pedersen, 2003: 72–73, 268–269).

Third, although the employment that EPZs generate makes them an attractive option, Haiti experts argue that priority should "be given to reversing the flow of migration from the rural hinterland to the urban ghettos by revitalizing the provinces economically and modernizing and energizing the agricultural sector" (Dupuy, 1997a: 98). If this EPZ strategy leads to an increase in inequality between urban and rural Haitians, as it did in the past, it will be problematic. Hence, it seems essential to challenge the model's urban bias, with the objective of ensuring that the employment that EPZs generate directly affects the rural areas, where the poorest Haitians live and work.

Scholars have pointed to Taiwan's development experience as a source of important lessons for agrarian societies undergoing change (see, for example, Griffin, 1989; North and Cameron, 2000). Taiwan achieved impressive and rapid agricultural and industrial growth, while improving the distribution of income, by employing a "rural-friendly" industrial strategy. As North and Cameron (ibid.: 1754) note:

decentralized rural industrialization was favored and played a critical role in expanding off-farm employment and farm family incomes. By 1971, over 50% of labor-intensive industries such as food processing, textiles, and light agricultural machinery production were located in rural areas; by 1976, that proportion had increased to 64% ... The promotion of labor-intensive rural industry, along with public works, played a critical role in generating employment, in narrowing the income gap between urban and rural families, and in stimulating the growth of domestic demand. The massive rural to urban migration and re-sultant growth of shantytowns typical of most other developing countries were avoided.

The point of this digression about Taiwan is not to suggest that Haiti could follow the pattern of the Asian tigers. Clearly, Haiti does not ex-hibit the traits that Taiwan did prior to its economic development, and the Haitian state is too weak to undertake the critical and highly inter-ventionist role the Taiwanese state assumed. Still, there is a key lesson here for countries that cannot escape the narrow focus on free markets and globalization but need to address rural poverty in a timely way: if at all possible, situate EPZs in rural areas.

"Wire-transferring" development?

While scholars are still debating whether, and to what degree, remittances can contribute to development, aid donors have already accorded these transfers a prominent place on their development and reconstruction agendas. In fact, "leveraging remittances" has been referred to as the newest "development fad" (Davis, 2006). The statistical argument for this new focus is both appealing and convincing. The Caribbean's dias-pora community is one of the largest in the world in proportion to its population. While Mexico and Central America export more migrants in absolute terms, a recent World Bank study notes that "the small Caribbean islands clearly dominate the migration charts when we look at migration flows in relation to each country's population" (Fajnzylber and López, 2007: 10). The region received about US$5.7 billion in remit-tances in 2002 and, as Keith Nurse (2004: 5) points out, "remittances have emerged as the fastest growing and most stable source of capital flow and foreign exchange in the last decade", outstripping both foreign direct investment and official development assistance. To many, these statistics are grounds enough for immediate consideration on the devel-opment front. Still, the linkages between migration and social and eco-nomic development are not clear.

In the past, the term "remittance" was used to refer almost exclusively to money sent by migrants to family members in the country of origin. Today, however, the notion has been broadened to include "collective remittances" and "non-financial remittances". The former refers to the pooling of funds from diaspora associations, often called Hometown As-sociations, which are then used to invest in community projects in the country of origin. Non-financial remittances include skills, knowledge, new social practices and business opportunities (Dade, 2006). Luin

Goldring (2003: 3) adds that "although investment capital is not strictly speaking a remittance, the presence of government programs designed to attract such funds from successful migrants points to the utility of identifying entrepreneurial or investment remittances as a kind of remittance or pseudo-remittance". Similarly, the notion of political remittances, or "changes in political identities, demands and practices associated with migration", has become a subject of interest to development scholars (see Fitzgerald, 2000; Smith, 1998).

The increased importance of these collective and non-financial remittances, according to Dade (2006: 87), is "a direct result of the impact of accelerated globalization on migration". The significance of these funds and the recently renewed interest in the migration and development nexus are also due to the dramatic increase in the amount of money sent back to migrant-producing countries (Goldring, 2003: 1). In 1990 Latin America and the Caribbean received US$6 billion in remittances; by 2004 remittances totalled US$41 billion (World Bank, 2006c: 11). It is also, according to Goldring (2003: 3), a response to the political and economic contexts within which "remittances circulate today, most notably the ascendance of a development discourse and policies that privilege markets and private investment or private-public partnerships to replace state investment. This, in turn, has drawn attention to various non-state actors, such as migrant organizations, and the goals they want to accomplish through remittances."

In Haiti's case, donors focus on the diaspora because of its size and the substantial remittances it supplies. In 2002 remittances were at least six times greater than the sum of development financing from the United States, France, Canada, the Inter-American Development Bank, the World Bank, the European Union and the United Nations – in short, the remittances Haiti receives often exceed the contributions of all international actors combined (Council on Hemispheric Affairs, 2006), an amount that, in 2006, was more than US$1.65 billion (Inter-American Development Bank, 2007).[7] Moreover, since these funds are not in the form of loans, "they impose no future financial obligations on the government of Haiti" (Dade, 2006: 90).[8] The economic importance of these funds is underlined by the fact that, in 2004, remittances represented 52.7 per cent of Haiti's GDP (Fajnzylber and López, 2007; Nurse, 2004).

Also worth noting, when considering the development impact of these transfers, is that close to half of the Haitian families that receive remittances earn less than US$500 a year, and these funds are most often used for basic expenses. Still, it appears that some families are able to save or invest a portion, and these savings are often directed towards investing in small businesses, building or improving homes and educating their children.[9] For instance, the Inter-American Development Bank

(2007: slide 32) estimates that, in 2006, remittance recipients spent more than US$350 million on so-called economic development investments (see also ECLAC, 1998: 9).

If these funds were pooled they might constitute a formidable and powerful economic force, though the economic development potential of remittances from the diaspora remains uncertain (Fagen and Bump, 2005; Goldring, 2003; Orozco et al., 2005; Waller Meyers, 2000). On the positive side, remittances can keep countries afloat, particularly during crisis periods; they also constitute an important source of income for many lower-income households (Itzigsohn, 1995),[10] particularly in communities where large concentrations of recipients reside. As Nurse (2004: 5) notes, "In many respects remittances are filling the gaps that the state and development agencies have been unable to plug." This has certainly been the case for Haiti, although, as the World Bank notes, "the potential poverty and inequality reduction of remittances is, in most cases, quite modest" (Fajnzylber and López, 2007: xii–xiii).

Thus Haiti's national poverty and inequality statistics remain unchanged, despite an ever-larger influx of outside funds. Clearly, remittances have not led to sustained growth and development. In part this is because recipients use remittances mostly to meet basic subsistence needs or for conspicuous consumption, neither of which contributes to growth or development. Even the Inter-American Development Bank study (2007), which is hopeful in tone, reveals that only a small fraction of the money sent back to Haiti has been invested in urban or rural enterprises that produce employment. Moreover, given the high import content in the consumption pattern of countries like Haiti, research has shown that "the impact on the balance of payments can be negative" (ECLAC, 1998). Remittances in kind in the form of conspicuous consumption goods have also been tagged as problematic, since they often create an imitative demand for these goods by others in society (ibid.).

In any case, it is difficult for Haiti (or any country, for that matter) to direct remittances towards national development goals. Although the Haitian government plans to create investment vehicles for Haitians abroad in order to fund projects and industries, it is unclear whether these will bear fruit. The government of El Salvador, for instance, matches collective remittances in order to encourage investment from its diaspora, but "efforts have fallen well far short of the need" (Davis, 2006) – and El Salvador provides a far more investment-friendly environment than does Haiti. According to Thomas-Hope (2002: 14, 19), remittances are an unlikely resource for national development since their flows are not received in amounts, or a time frame, that is predictable. As such, they cannot "provide a solid basis for investment planning by the national bank and development planning for the country".

Studies have also shown that skills acquired abroad are not necessarily relevant in local labour markets, and that remittances have polarized incomes and land-holding (see, for example, Goldring, 2003). Moreover, the migration flows that bring much-needed remittances are not without costs to Haitian families and to Haiti itself. As Martin (2006: 1) notes, "The emigration of foreign professionals and the tendency of foreign students to remain abroad ... raise brain drain fears whose impacts on development are unresolved." In the case of Haiti, the World Bank notes that "more than 80 per cent of people born in Haiti who have college degrees live abroad, mostly in the United States" (Fajnzylber and López, 2007: 11). This might be positive on the remittance front, but it has grave implications for the long-term development of the country.

To be sure, Haiti would benefit if these migrants took their skills and experience home – their presence could certainly boost productivity. It would be difficult, however, to entice this skilled stratum of society to return, despite the support of donor countries for policy initiatives aimed at such a goal. In sum, the mixed impact of migration flows on Haiti suggests remittances should be viewed, as one observer has noted, as a "band-aid on fundamental development problems" rather than as a pillar of the country's development strategy (Yang, quoted in Davis, 2006).

Conclusion

In this chapter I have examined two of Haiti's economic development strategies: attracting export-processing firms and harnessing the economic potential of the Haitian diaspora, both of which make a firm bow to the neoliberal view of development.

Attracting export-processing firms is an old idea that is being given a new *élan*. While the ability of this model to generate employment makes it attractive, scepticism is warranted given that this trade-led approach has been unsuccessful in the past (see Dupuy, 1989, 1994). Although EPZs have produced jobs, they have failed to spark development and have intensified inequalities. Fortunately, neoliberalism's stranglehold on development policy does not entirely prevent Haiti from tweaking such an approach this time around. A decentralized rural industrialization plan that situates labour-intensive EPZs in different parts of the country (as was the case in Taiwan) rather than around the capital, Port-au-Prince, could help foster a much-needed rural-urban balance. Still, it is timely to recall the US General Accounting Office's assessment of the Caribbean Basin Initiative – the trade-enhancing initiative that encouraged export processing two decades ago – which it credits with fostering trade and investment opportunities, although these have "not been sufficient to generate broadly based economic growth, alleviate debt servicing problems, or create lasting employment" (quoted in Deere and Antrobus, 1990: 182).

As for harnessing the diaspora, Goldring (2003) is correct in associating interest in doing so with prevailing political and economic ideas. Specifically, migrant organizations and remittances fit nicely with a development discourse that privileges markets, private investment and public-private partnerships. In the end, migration offers Haiti both advantages and disadvantages, but the potential of these flows is best summarized by the World Bank's pithy assessment: "neither 'manna from heaven,' nor a substitute for sound development policies" (Fajnzylber and López, 2007: 59). The point to stress is that remittances, while valuable, are unlikely to boost employment and economic development in a significant way, which highlights the need for a measured position on the development potential of such transfers.

Given that a combination of EPZs and collective and individual remittances is unlikely to drive poverty reduction and development, it seems fitting to reconsider a place for agriculture in Haiti's sustainable development plans. An important body of research has argued convincingly for support to the country's agricultural sector, the rural poor and rural income-generating activities (DeWind and David, 1988; Dorward et al., 2004; Dupuy, 1997b; Fatton, 2002; Laraque, 1987; Maguire, 1984; Trouillot, 1994). Indeed, Dorward et al. (2004: 619) show "the importance of smallholder agriculture development (with institutional support for labour-demanding technical change) in driving growth in poor rural areas". Moreover, given the introduction of pro-poor policy regimes of late, it seems appropriate to focus on employment-intensive agricultural and rural growth, since it is on this sector that the bulk of Haiti's poor still depend for their livelihood. In short, donors should reconsider their retreat from the rural world. The fact that, for the first time in 25 years, the World Bank's annual *World Development Report* (World Bank, 2007) is dedicated to agriculture suggests this recommendation is neither romantic nor impractical.

Robert Wade (2003: 630) has correctly described the prescribed route to economic development for countries in the global South as "liberalization and unmediated integration into the world economy, supplemented by domestic institutional reforms to make deep integration viable". This market-driven approach to national development leaves little room for countries in the global South to manoeuvre. While all states must contend with limits on national decision-making, these countries face a number of other problems that make development tricky: trade and balance-of-payments deficits, shortages of productive capital, the absence of a modern industrial bourgeoisie or a highly trained professional and technical labour force, high unemployment and an often unstable security situation (see Degnbol-Martinussen and Lauridsen, 2001; Rampersad, 2000). In its search for a glimmer of hope in the development murk, Haiti's strategies of re-establishing EPZs and developing stronger links with its diaspora fall within the narrow parameters of the possible. Yet the fact that both strategies have observable limitations serves as a reminder of the difficulties facing small, dependent, post-conflict states that are attempting to develop in the current landscape of global politics.

Notes

1. The first peacebuilding exercise was between 1994 (when President Aristide was returned to power after three years of military rule) and 1998–2000 (when many donors suspended their aid due to election irregularities).
2. The term "fragile state" first appears in Christopher Clapham's (1996) work on Africa. It was later picked up and developed by the UK Department for International Development in its report on conflict and development (DFID, 2005).
3. The neoliberal approach stresses integration into the international economy, allowing countries to determine and build on their natural comparative advantage, which in turn leads to the highest sustainable rate of growth. The role of government is limited to providing "a stable macro-economy with clear rules of the game, a fully open economy, and essential public goods like human capital and infrastructure. This approach is backed by industrialized countries and the Bretton Woods institutions and is enshrined in [the World Trade Organization] rules" (Lall, 2005: 33).
4. The HOPE Act is a diluted version of an earlier bill drafted in 2004 known as the Haiti Economic Recovery Opportunity, or HERO, Act. This legislation would have allowed all Haitian-made apparel to enter the US market duty free, regardless of the origin of the cloth.
5. In 2004 the US undersecretary of the treasury noted that central to US reconstruction and development efforts were the Haitian private sector and the diaspora (Taylor, 2004).
6. This section draws on Shamsie (2006).
7. Approximately US$1.17 billion of the total sent came from the United States, which has large diaspora communities in Miami, Boston and New York. Other sources of remittances were Canada (about US$230 million in 2006), France (US$130 million) and the Dominican Republic and the Bahamas (around US$33 million each). Lesser sums were sent from Martinique, Guyana and Spain (see *Caribbean Current*, 2007).
8. Of interest as well is that just over 1 million Haitians receive remittances about 10 times a year, with an average amount of US$150 per time.
9. It is worth noting, however, that while remittances tend to increase a family's investment in education and health, this seems to be true only for households in the middle to upper segments of the income distribution, with Mexico being an exception (Fajnzylber and López, 2007: 11).
10. For recent research on the effect of remittances on poverty see Acosta et al. (2006); Adams and Page (2005); Page and Plaza (2005).

REFERENCES

Abrahamsen, R. (2000) *Disciplining Democracy: Development Discourse and Good Governance in Africa*, London: Zed Books.

Acosta, P., P. Calderon, P. Fajnzylber and H. López (2006) *What Is the Impact of International Remittances on Poverty and Inequality in Latin America?*, Washington, DC: World Bank.

Adams, R. and J. Page (2005) "Do International Migration and Remittances Reduce Poverty in Developing Countries?", *World Development* 33(10), pp. 1645–1669.

Addison, T. (2005) "Post-conflict Recovery: Does the Global Economy Work for Peace?", WIDER Discussion Paper 2005/05, UNU-World Institute for Development Economics Research, Helsinki.

Altimir, O. (2002) "Distributive Tensions under the New Economic Order", paper presented at conference on Social and Economic Impacts of Liberalization and Globalization: Effects on Labour Markets and Income Distribution, Toronto, 19–20 April.

Caribbean Current (2007) "Remittances to Haiti Topped $1.65 Billion in 2006", *Caribbean Current*, 8 March, available at www.caribbeancurrent.com/easterncaribbean/story_id_003.html.

Castor, S. (1994) "Democracy and Society in Haiti: Structures of Domination and Resistance to Change", in S. Jonas and E. McCaughan, eds, *Latin America Faces the Twentieth Century*, Boulder, CO: Westview Press.

Chang, H.-J. (2002) *Kicking Away the Ladder: Development Strategy in Historical Perspective*, London: Anthem Press.

Clapham, C. (1996) *Africa and the International System: The Politics of State Survival*, Cambridge: Cambridge University Press.

Council on Hemispheric Affairs (2006) "Canada's Aid to Haiti: Commendable or Making Amends for a Discredited Anti Aristide Strategy?", COHA Report 06.04, Washington, DC, available at www.coha.org/NEW_PRESS_RELEASES/New_Press_Releases_2006/COHA%20Report/COHA_Report_06.04_Canada_Haiti.htm.

Dade, C. (2006) "The Role of the Private Sector and the Diaspora in Rebuilding Haiti", in Y. Shamsie and A. S. Thompson, eds, *Haiti: Hope for a Fragile State*, Waterloo, ON: Wilfrid Laurier University Press/Centre for International Governance Innovation.

Davis, B. (2006) "Migrants' Money Is Imperfect Cure for Poor Nations", *Wall Street Journal*, 1 November.

Deere, C. D. and P. Antrobus, eds (1990) *In the Shadow of the Sun: Caribbean Development Alternatives and U.S. Policy*, Boulder, CO: Westview Press.

Degnbol-Martinussen, J. and P. Engberg-Pedersen (2003) *Aid: Understanding International Development Cooperation*, London: Zed Books.

Degnbol-Martinussen, J. and L. S. Lauridsen (2001) "Changing Global and Regional Conditions for Development in the Third World", Occasional Paper 21, Roskilde University, Roskilde.

DeWind, J. and K. David (1988) *Aiding Migration: The Impact of International Development Assistance on Haiti*, Boulder, CO: Westview Press.

DeWind, J. and D. Kinley III (1986) *Aiding Migrations: The Impact of International Development Assistance on Haiti*, New York: Columbia University, Center for the Social Sciences.

DFID (2005) *Fighting Poverty to Build a Safer World: A Strategy for Security and Development*, London: Department for International Development.

Dorward, A., S. Fan, J. Kydd, H. Lofgren, J. Morrison, C. Poulton, N. Rao, L. Smith, H. Tchale, S. Thorat, I. Urey and P. Wobst (2004) "Institutions and Policies for Pro-Poor Agricultural Growth", *Development Policy Review* 22(6), pp. 611–622, available at http://ssrn.com/abstract=614134.

Dupuy, A. (1989) *Haiti in the World Economy: Class, Race, and Underdevelopment since 1700*, Boulder, CO: Westview Press.

───── (1994) "Free Trade and Underdevelopment in Haiti: The World Bank/USAID Agenda for Social Change in the Post-Duvalier Era", in H. Watson, ed., *The Caribbean in the Global Economy*, Boulder, CO: Lynne Rienner.

───── (1997a) *Haiti in the New World Order: The Limits of the Democratic Revolution*, Boulder, CO: Westview Press.

───── (1997b) "Peasant Poverty in Haiti", *Latin American Research Review* 24(3): 259–271.

───── (2007) *The Prophet and Power: Jean-Bertrand Aristide, the International Community, and Haiti*, Lanham, MD: Rowman & Littlefield.

ECLAC (1998) *The Contribution of Remittances to Social and Economic Development in the Caribbean*, Port-of-Spain: UN Economic Commission for Latin America and the Caribbean.

Erikson, D. (2004) *Haiti: Challenges in Poverty Reduction*, Washington, DC: Inter-American Dialogue.

Fagen, P. and M. Bump (2005) "Remittances from Neighbors: Trends in Intra-regional Remittance Flows", in *Beyond Small Change: Making Migrants' Remittances Count*, Washington, DC: Inter-American Development Bank.

Fajnzylber, P. and J. H. López (2007) *Close to Home: The Development Impact of Remittances in Latin America*, Washington, DC: World Bank.

Fatton, R. J. (2002) *Haiti's Predatory Republic: The Unending Transition to Democracy*, Boulder, CO: Lynne Rienner.

───── (2007) *The Roots of Haitian Despotism*, Boulder, CO: Lynne Rienner.

Fitzgerald, D. (2000) *Negotiating Extra-territorial Citizenship: Mexican Migration and the Transnational Politics of Community*, La Jolla, CA: University of California, San Diego, Center for Comparative Immigration Studies.

Gallagher, K. (2005) "Globalization and the Nation State: Reasserting Policy Autonomy for Development", in K. Gallagher, ed., *Putting Development First: The Importance of Policy Space in the WTO and International Financial Institutions*, London: Zed Books.

Goldring, L. (2003) *Re-thinking Remittances: Social and Political Dimensions of Individual and Collective Remittances*, Toronto: Centre for Research on Latin America and the Caribbean.

Griffin, K. (1989) *Alternative Strategies for Economic Development*, New York: St Martin's Press.

Grinspun, R. and R. Kreklewich (1994) "Consolidating Neoliberal Reform: 'Free Trade' as a Conditioning Framework", *Studies in Political Economy* 43, pp. 33–61.

Haiti (2004) *Interim Cooperation Framework, 2004–2006: Summary Report*, Port-au-Prince: Haiti Cadre de Cooperation Interimaire (Haiti Interim Cooperation Framework), available at http://haiticci.undg.org/index.cfm?Module=ActiveWeb&Page=WebPage&s=introduction.

Hakim, P. (2006) "Is Washington Losing Latin America?", *Foreign Affairs* 85(1), pp. 39–53.

Halliday, F. (1987) "State and Society in International Relations", *Millennium* 16(2), pp. 215–229.

Hooper, M. (1987) "Model Underdevelopment", *NACLA Report on the Americas* 21(3), pp. 32–39.

——— (1995) "Model Underdevelopment", in NACLA, ed., *Haiti: Dangerous Crossroads*, Boston, MA: South End Press.

Huber, E. and F. Solt (2004) "Successes and Failures of Neoliberalism", *Latin American Research Review* 39(3), pp. 150–164.

Inter-American Development Bank (2007) *Haiti Remittance Survey*, PowerPoint presentation, Inter-American Development Bank, Washington, DC, 7 March, available at www.iadb.org/news/docs/HaitiSurvey.pps.

International Monetary Fund (2007) "Haiti: Interim Poverty Reduction Strategy Paper", Joint Staff Advisory Note 07/3, IMF, Washington, DC.

Itzigsohn, J. (1995) "Migrant Remittances, Labor Markets, and Household Strategies: A Comparative Analysis of Low-income Household Strategies in the Caribbean Basin", *Social Forces* 74(2), pp. 633–655.

Kumar, C. (2000) "Peacebuilding in Haiti", in E. Cousens and C. Kumar, eds, *Peacebuilding as Politics*, Boulder, CO: Lynne Rienner.

Lall, S. (2005) "Rethinking Industrial Strategy: The Role of the State in the Face of Globalization", in K. Gallagher, ed., *Putting Development First: The Importance of Policy Space in the WTO and International Financial Institutions*, London: Zed Books.

Laraque, F. (1987) *Défi à la pauvreté*, Montreal: Éditions du CIDICHA.

Londoño, J. L. and M. Székely (1997) *Persistent Poverty and Excess Inequality: Latin America, 1970–1995*, Washington, DC: Inter-American Development Bank.

Maguire, R. (1984) "Strategy for Rural Development in Haiti: Formation, Organization, Implementation", in C. Foster and A. Valdman, eds, *Haiti – Today and Tomorrow: An Interdisciplinary Study*, Lanham, MD: University Press of America.

Martin, P. (2006) "The Trade, Migration, and Development Nexus", paper presented to conference on Migration, Trade, and Development, Federal Reserve Bank of Dallas, 6 October.

McGowan, L. (1997) *Democracy Undermined, Economic Justice Denied: Structural Adjustment and the Aid Juggernaut in Haiti*, Washington, DC: Development Gap.

Mintz, S. (1989) *Caribbean Transformations*, Baltimore, MD: Johns Hopkins University Press.

Mozingo, J. (2006) "Préval's Return to the Ballot Shakes Haitian Establishment", *Miami Herald*, 31 January.

Mulet, E. (2007) Speech presented to "Roundtable with Ambassador Edmund Mulet", Center for International and Strategic Studies, Washington, DC, 27 January.

North, L. and J. D. Cameron (2000) "Grassroots-based Rural Development Strategies: Ecuador in Comparative Perspective", *World Development* 28(10), pp. 1751–1766.

Nurse, K. (2004) *Diaspora, Migration and Development in the Caribbean*, Ottawa: Canadian Foundation for the Americas.

O'Donnell, G. (1998) "Poverty and Inequality in Latin America: Some Reflections", in V. Tokman and G. O'Donnell, eds, *Poverty and Inequality in Latin America*, Notre Dame, IN: University of Notre Dame Press.

Office of the US Trade Representative (2006) "U.S. Trade Representative Schwab Welcomes Bipartisan Senate Vote Approving Key Trade Legislation", Washington, DC, available at www.ustr.gov/Document_Library/Press_Releases/ 2006/December/US_Trade_Representative_Schwab_Welcomes_Bipartisan_ Senate_Vote_Approving_Key_Trade_Legislation.html.

Orozco, M., L. Lowell, M. Bump and R. Fedewa (2005) *Transnational Engagement, Remittances, and Their Relationship to Development in Latin America and the Caribbean*, Washington, DC: Georgetown University, Institute for the Study of International Migration.

Page, J. and S. Plaza (2005) *Migration, Remittances, and Development: A Review of Global Evidence*, Washington, DC: World Bank.

Payne, A. and P. Sutton (2001) *Charting Caribbean Development*. Gainesville, FL: University Press of Florida.

Portes, A. and K. Hoffman (2003) "Latin American Class Structures: Their Composition and Change during the Neoliberal Era", *Latin American Research Review* 38(1), pp. 41–77.

Portes, A. and J. Itzigsohn (1997) "Coping with Change: The Politics and Economics of Urban Poverty", in A. Portes, C. Dore-Cabral and P. Landolt, eds, *The Urban Caribbean: Transition to the New Global Economy*, Baltimore, MD: Johns Hopkins University Press.

Rampersad, F. B. (2000) "Coping with Globalization: A Suggested Policy Package for Small Countries", *Annals of the American Academy of Political and Social Science* 570, pp. 115–125.

Robinson, W. (1996) *Promoting Polyarchy: Globalization, U.S. Intervention, and Hegemony*, Cambridge: Cambridge University Press.

Rodrik, D. (2001) "Trading in Illusions", *Foreign Policy* (March–April), pp. 54–63.

——— (2004) "Industrial Policy for the Twenty-First Century", Cambridge, MA: Harvard University, John F. Kennedy School of Government, available at http://ksghome.harvard.edu/~drodrik/UNIDOSep.pdf.

Sandbrook, R., M. Edelman, P. Heller and J. Teichman (2007) *Social Democracy in the Global Periphery: Origins, Challenges, Prospects*, Cambridge: Cambridge University Press.

Shamsie, Y. (2006) "The Economic Dimension of Peacebuilding in Haiti: Drawing on the Past to Reflect on the Present", in Y. Shamsie and A. Thompson, eds, *Haiti: Hope for a Fragile State*, Waterloo, ON: Wilfrid Laurier University Press/Centre for International Governance Innovation.

Smith, R. (1998) "Transnational Localities: Community, Technology and the Politics of Membership within the Context of Mexico and U.S. Migration", *Comparative Urban and Community Research* 6, pp. 196–238.

Stiglitz, J. (2002) *Globalization and Its Discontents*, New York: W. W. Norton.

Taylor, J. B. (2004) "Remarks on Haiti's Economic Reconstruction", presented at Jean-Jacques Dessaline Community Center, Miami, 23 August, available at http://usinfo.state.gov/articles/washfile-english/2004/08/20040823150228GLnesnoM8.291262e-02.body.

Teichman, J. (2001) "Latin America in the Era of Globalization: Inequality, Poverty and Questionable Democracies", Working Paper 2001-2, University of Toronto, Centre for International Studies, Toronto.

Thomas, C. (1988) *The Poor and the Powerless: Economic Policy and Change in the Caribbean*, New York: Monthly Review Press.

Thomas-Hope, E. (2002) "Skilled Labour Migration from Developing Countries: Study on the Caribbean Region", International Migration Papers 50, International Labour Office, Geneva.

Trouillot, M.-R. (1990) *Haiti: State against Nation: The Origins and Legacies of Duvalierism*, New York: Monthly Review Press.

——— (1994) "Haiti's Nightmare and the Lessons of History", in NACLA, ed., *Haiti: Dangerous Crossroads*, Boston, MA: South End Press.

United Nations (2006) *Human Development Report 2006: Beyond Scarcity: Power, Poverty and the Global Water Crisis*, New York: UN Development Programme, available at http://hdr.undp.org/en/media/HDR06-complete.pdf.

Wade, R. H. (2003) "What Strategies Are Viable for Developing Countries Today? The World Trade Organization and the Shrinking of 'Development Space'", *Review of International Political Economy* 10(4), pp. 621–644.

Waller Meyers, D. (2000) "Remesas de América Latina: Revisión de la literatura", *Comercio Exterior* 50(4), pp. 275–283.

World Bank (2006a) *Haiti: Overview*, Washington, DC: World Bank, available at http://siteresources.worldbank.org/CDFINTRANET/Overview/21021963/Haiti08-11-06.doc.

——— (2006b) *Haiti: Options and Opportunities for Inclusive Growth*, Country Economic Memorandum, Washington, DC: World Bank.

——— (2006c) *The Little Data Book 2006*, Washington, DC: World Bank.

——— (2007) *World Development Report 2008: Agriculture for Development*, Washington, DC: World Bank.

Part V

Afterword

15

Strong winds of change: New politics and new connections

Andrew F. Cooper and Jorge Heine

Latin America can be viewed robustly but incompletely through a familiar set of frameworks. One dominant image is of a region going left ideologically in a comprehensive fashion. Another is the return of personalistic forms of leadership, symbolized by Hugo Chávez. Both are connected to what are taken to be profound shifts in the economic and diplomatic context within the region. Support for the tenets of the neoliberal orthodoxy established in the aftermath of the Cold War has eroded considerably. And, as a recent report put it, "if there was an era of U.S. hegemony in the region, it is over" (Council on Foreign Relations, 2008: 5).

Yet anxiety about US coercive power – whether it is acting alone or through proxies – remains implanted in the collective mentality of the region. In episodes where there appears to be some reassertion of this muscle, Latin American countries have been quick to react and reject US intervention. One sign of this collective mentality shone through the attempted coup in 2002 against President Chávez. Another appeared more recently during the cross-border intervention of Colombia into Ecuador in pursuit of FARC (Revolutionary Armed Forces of Colombia). In both cases the Rio Group, a regional forum excluding the United States, was used as the preferred diplomatic instrument.

In the latter case, the fact that the Rio Group helped to diminish the tensions between Colombia and Ecuador illustrates the changing situation in Latin America. The legitimacy of regional institutions underscores the weakening influence of the United States – with governments no

Which way Latin America? Hemispheric politics meets globalization, Cooper and Heine, eds, United Nations University Press, 2009, ISBN 978-92-808-1172-8

longer looking to it first as an arbiter in regional disagreements.[1] After the Rio Group Summit on 7 March 2008 (Bi, 2008), this sentiment was raised by the Dominican Republic's Foreign Minister Carlos Morales Troncoso as he praised the ability of the Rio Group to reach a resolution over the conflict, saying "we have to remember that the Rio Group is the only political forum that we Latin Americans have, [and] without the influence of anybody we have come to an agreement and resolved this big problem" (quoted in Sugget, 2008).

In light of the changing landscape in Latin America we must reassess the orthodox boundaries that we hold in regards to our understanding of both Latin American politics and its society. As well, it is important to test these notions against where the region stands in regards to the international environment. The three chapters that comprise the first part of this volume help to establish the new challenges facing the region and call into question classical assumptions.

Up to a point, the classic images of Latin America presented here have some accuracy. However, when accepted as a package without nuanced analysis, they border on caricature. This collection locates the region as being in an in-between state. Latin America still exhibits not only a well-entrenched regional profile in international relations but a set of distinctive nationalist characteristics. Often this has been revealed through the promotion of state sovereignty with a strong aversion to external interference, the pre-eminence of "presidentialism", a disproportionately sized military, hybrid religiosity, a protest culture with a robust civil society or even the various expressions of cultural creativity and the sporting industry (Munck, 2006). The subtle mixture of these characteristics, with a blend of collective and individual cultures, gives Latin America its unique flavour.

For all the continuity, though, the dynamics of change are still compelling. Anxiety about the United States as an overbearing disciplinarian is still well entrenched. It just comes out in different forms, and is increasingly jumbled up with images of the United States as being both aggressive and disengaged. Mistrust of US motivations, with its specific set of priorities and interests, has spread into a wide number of alternative domains in the post-9/11 world. The emphasis on border security at all costs is viewed as having serious implications for the region, through the tightening of visa/travel restrictions. And the invasion of Iraq is not only taken to damage US international credibility – especially with the controversies swirling around Guantánamo and Abu Ghraib – but has distracted the United States away from the Americas.

This distraction has been exemplified by the relative silence of the 2008 presidential candidates in regard to Latin America. Aside from the differ-

ences that John McCain and Barack Obama showed regarding Cuba – with McCain supporting a continuation of current US relations and Obama suggesting moderate reforms, including meeting with Cuban President Raul Castro – neither candidate expressed serious or detailed positions regarding the region (Charles, 2008). Further, State Department official Charles Shapiro has recently suggested that the new US administration will make only modest, nuanced changes to relations with Latin America (quoted in Green, 2008). This continues a trend noted by Peter Hakim (2006) where "after 9/11, Washington effectively lost interest in Latin America", and relations between the country and the region have now deteriorated to their lowest point since the Cold War.

With the weakening of ties and interests in the US administration, Latin America is given further impetus to look towards new arrangements with global actors. Moreover, the wave of discontent in the aftermath of the failed neoliberal experiment and the breakdown of the Washington Consensus has not brought with it calls for new forms of economic discipline or other manifestations of a conservative political backlash. While concerned about many issues – including the manner by which the United States has managed relations with Latin America – the élite within the region retain an optimistic spirit about the future (Contreras, 2007). As this collection has shown, this future is marked by a dynamic intersection of regional politics and global interaction. Another sign that Latin America is willing to bend its old habits comes out in gender politics. If Chávez harkens back to the image of the Latin American military strongman, the region has shown a confidence in its willingness to embrace a new wave of female leaders. Having lagged behind other regions, the impressive victories of Michelle Bachelet in Chile and Cristina Fernández de Kirchner in Argentina have revealed that Latin America is now prepared to move out ahead. As a contributor to this book, Michael Shifter, has commented elsewhere (quoted in Barrionuevo, 2007), the rise of female heads of state in Latin America is the result of "the breakdown of traditional political structures" and has been demonstrated by the inclusion of previous outsiders – in this case women – in the political process. These former outsiders now have the means to affect the direction of the countries in the region.

What this collection demonstrates just as strikingly is that these domestic ingredients must be seen as being enmeshed with a different array of global forces. As alluded to above, the political economy of Latin America is increasingly and intensely a globalized political economy, not just via connections with the United States and the former metropolitan centres in Europe. In the latter case these connections look to be ready to grow further, as the relative resilience of Latin American economies during the late-2008 global economic downturn led some observers to claim that the region offers a "favourable climate for European investment" as well as an opportunity for the European Union and the region to "take greater advantage of the growing consensus on issues that face both regions" (Mendizábal and Edwards, 2008). Latin America's character, then, and location in the world can be described as both multipolar and multi-actor. Statism remains at the core of policy-making, with some considerable powers over regulation and the setting of rules. But in a good many ways governments have retreated – not only in terms of legitimacy but in terms of resources and responsibilities. This decentralization promises improved efficiency of both the economy and democracy by creating a public sector that is better able to respond to the needs of the citizenry; however, in Latin America decentralization has yet to meet the ideals it is purported to create (Remmer and Wibbels, 2000).

The most concrete indication of the influence of this new multicentric world is in the partnerships and competition that the Asian drivers – both China and India – provide for Latin America. Markedly different in diplomatic style and material conditions than the United States and Europe, these big, globally oriented rising states must be considered in any analysis. One image in relation to the impact of these new actors sees a heightened sense of vulnerability. Another views this impact as one allowing novel opportunities. Either way, these emerging global powerhouses are having a marked impact on Latin America. While China offers the opportunity for Latin American countries to export resources, it also must be taken into account how a country's competitive position with third parties is affected by China's rise; furthermore, the amount of interaction with China varies dramatically between the countries of the region (Jenkins, Dussel Peters and Moreira, 2007).

Partly due to the desire to become globally active, Latin American countries – particularly Brazil – have begun to play a larger role in international institutions. As a leader and entrepreneur of the G-20+, and as one of the most frequent complainants at the WTO's dispute settlement system, Brazil has exercised increasing amounts of clout in these institutions (Shaffer, Sanchez and Rosenberg, 2008). Further, as a member of the India-Brazil-South Africa forum (IBSA), Brazil looks to use its influence as a regional leader in Latin America to play a greater role in foreign policy instruments (Flemes, 2007). While atypical of the level of influence wielded by Latin American countries, Brazil looks poised to put regional issues on the tables of international institutions.

All of this signals the demands for change in our understanding of Latin American politics and society. Hanging on to well-entrenched but misleading conceptualizations about the political dynamics in the region is no longer an option. The standard images of ideological polarization, personalism, populism and strategic marginality are attractive as much for their clarity as anything else. Yet the significant changes that we are witnessing in the region in the course of this decade point us in a very different direction.

What we have, rather, is a region that is pulling away from ideological strait-jackets as it tries to contend as best it can with globalization. In terms of domestic politics and policies, it has pulled away from the "one-size-fits-all", cookie-cutter approach of "opening, deregulating, privatizing" of the Washington Consensus, while preserving the elements of fiscal prudence embodied in it. In many ways this is what the policies of "new left" governments like those of Presidents Cardoso and Lula in Brazil, Lagos and Bachelet in Chile and Vásquez in Uruguay have done. That these policies have prevailed mostly in the Southern Cone countries should not be surprising; they reflect a different level of social and economic development from those of the Andean nations, as well as a different type of state apparatus from that extant in the rest of Latin America. Interestingly, however, it is precisely these countries (though, admittedly, more Brazil and Chile than Uruguay) that have been most assertive in engaging the rest of the world: Brazil with a truly global perspective and an ambitious foreign policy agenda focused on the global South, and Chile with a somewhat narrower approach largely driven by economic priorities – but both with a sophisticated understanding of the imperatives of globalization. Not surprisingly, Brazil and Chile, with their highly dynamic economies, are considered to be among the best and most reliable international partners, in both the North and the South.

A somewhat different picture emerges in the Andean region, the broad arc that goes from Venezuela, Colombia and Ecuador all the way down the Pacific coast to Peru and then into Bolivia. The much more radical process of political change that is taking place in countries like Bolivia, Ecuador and Venezuela is often described as "populist". Yet this rather facile labelling exercise fails to come to terms with the deep crisis that has affected the Andean region over the past 30 years or so, largely because of difficulties in adapting to a changing international environment, i.e. globalization. Andean countries have been mostly unable to find a suitable niche for their exports, except their most prized one – illegal drugs. Bolivia and Ecuador have been the poorest and hardest hit, despite their valiant efforts at economic reform and to apply the Washington Consensus to the letter and beyond. Ecuador even went so far as to adopt the US dollar as its national currency in 2000, with the predictable inflationary effect.

The growth of resource nationalism in these countries springs from this economic lag, while the "refoundational" new constitutional charters (from 1998 to 2008 five new constitutions saw the light in the Andean region) arise from the long tradition of weak "stateness" in the Andes, highly unsuited to the new demands of the international environment, as well as from the need to incorporate into the polity vast segments of the hitherto-excluded sectors of the Amerindian population, something especially acute in Bolivia and Ecuador.

The authors of the chapters in this collection deliver not only in their attention to nuance but in their ability to make these more shaded conclusions as comprehensible as possible. Amid very detailed discussions, the basic debates essential to the region are opened up. The task of pushing against the orthodox boundaries in terms of our understanding of Latin American politics and society – and the location of the region in the larger international political economy (IPE) environment – is facilitated by the three penetrating works that constitute the introductory section of the book. Meanwhile, the second section of the collection brings out the centrality of a globalized political economy for Latin America. As a complement, the third section turns to concentrate on the institutional fabric that allows – or hinders – collective activity in the region. By including a number of country-specific case studies, the final section of the book brings the analysis away from the regional and global levels to return to the national one.

Throughout the four sections the location and potential relocation of the region within the global political economy are given pride of place. However, the impact of personal and collective diplomacy, normative questions pertaining to democracy promotion and governance more widely constructed are not neglected. The search for regional big-picture overviews is balanced by the inclusion of the key country-specific case studies. As in any edited collection there are gaps, above all those pertaining to national/geographic representation in the book. But within the defined space of the undertaking, this book combines ambition in scope with intense but more manageable snapshots in order to comprehend what is happening in a region riveted by change.

Note

1. For more information on the Río Group Summit declaration see Bi (2008).

REFERENCES

Barrionuevo, Alexei (2007) "Political Tango, Women in Lead", *New York Times*, 4 November.

Bi, Mingxin (2008) "Summit Ends with Declaration, Accepts Apologies from Colombia", *China View*, 8 March, available at http://news.xinhuanet.com/english/2008-03/08/content_7744676.htm.

Charles, Jacqueline (2008) "Our Neighbors, the Caribbean and Latin America", *Miami Herald*, 25 July.

Contreras, Joseph (2007) "The Upbeat Upperclass: An Exclusive Poll Shows Latin Power Players Buoyant on Their Future, Despite Simmering Unrest. Will It Last?", *Newsweek*, 15 January.

Council on Foreign Relations (2008) "U.S.-Latin America Relations: A New Direction for a New Reality", Independent Task Force Report No. 60, Council on Foreign Relations, New York.

Flemes, Daniel (2007) "Emerging Middle Powers' Soft Balancing Strategy: State and Perspectives of the IBSA Dialogue Forum", Working Paper No. 57, German Institute of Global and Area Studies, Hamburg.

Green, Eric (2008) "Next US President Unlikely to Alter US Latin America Policy", US State Department, 21 August, available at www.america.gov.

Hakim, Peter (2006) "Is Washington Losing Latin America?", *Foreign Affairs* (January/February), pp. 39–53, available at www.foreignaffairs.org/20060101faessay85105/peter-hakim/is-washington-losing-latin-america.html.

Jenkins, Rhys, Enrique Dussel Peters and Mauricio Mesquita Moreira (2007) "The Impact of China on Latin America and the Caribbean", *World Development* 36(2), pp. 235–253.

Mendizábal, Enrique and Guy Edwards (2008) "Relations between Europe and Latin America and the Caribbean: The Partnership Phase", *Overseas Development Institute: Opinion* (September), pp. 107–108.

Munck, Ronaldo (2006) *Contemporary Latin America*, 2nd edn, Basingstoke: Palgrave.

Remmer, Karen and Erik Wibbels (2000) "The Political Economy of Decentralization in Latin America", *APSA-CP Newsletter* 11(1), pp. 28–31.

Shaffer, Gregory C., Michelle Ratton Sanchez and Barbara Rosenberg (2008) "The Trials of Winning at the WTO: What Lies Behind Brazil's Success", *Cornell International Law Journal* 41(2), Minnesota Legal Studies Research Paper No. 49, available at http://ssrn.com/abstract=1137905.

Suggett, James (2008) "Venezuela and Ecuador Resolve Differences with Colombia at Regional Summit", VenezuelanAnalysis.com, 8 March, available at www.venezuelananalysis.com/print/3255.

FURTHER READING

Seligson, Mitchell A. (2007) "The Democracy Barometers: The Rise of Populism and the Left in Latin America", *Journal of Democracy* 18(3), pp. 81–95.

Index